Praise for *Achieving Class A Business Excellence: An Executive's Perspective*

From day one, the three overarching principles of The Oliver Wight Companies have been:

- advocate only the proven processes, often the latest, but leave the untested theories for academia to debate.
- consult only with companies truly committed to succeed in transforming their business to be the best it can be.
- only coach the company's people, through knowledge transfer, so that they, not us, can lead and make the changes.

Many years and thousands of companies later, these principles still differentiate our associates.

This book continues this successful formula. The authors have created people you'll recognize, dealing with problems that confront all companies. It may be entertaining to read about their struggles; the greater value, however, is to grasp how they changed from an out-of-control operation to an effective team capable of achieving ambitious company goals.

Accomplishing this dramatic journey of change is demystified; no longer a reactive hit or miss effort. What is presented to you as foresight comes from the collective experiences of the authors and their colleagues, 20/20 hindsight, in helping companies avoid the pitfalls and focusing them on the prerequisites in order to make smart decisions and timely progress. To ensure the many events are done in the proper sequence, even a road map is included!

Armed with helpful advice always makes a tough task easier, yet implementing company-wide change remains a major challenge. Staying on course is vital—the tenacity of the leaders will be frequently tested.

Although this representative company and its characters are "figments of the authors' imagination," take good notes as the lessons are real.

—Walt Goddard
Chair Emeritus, Oliver Wight International

"An excellent book! The issues identified here are the kind that can keep business executives awake at night; however, with identified critical tasks and a proven path, the resultant change can be both transformational and sustainable. This book clearly articulates the manner in which this type of change takes place and a method for achieving that change."

—Jason Thorne
Director, ABeam Consulting USA

"Multi-national operating companies, global brand proliferation, outsourced design and manufacturing, and mass-customization capabilities, enabled by multi-language/multi-currency enterprise-scale information systems . . . this is the arena in which senior management is innovating and competing, irrespective of industry or geography.

Achieving Class A Business Excellence articulates a contemporary, pragmatic, and comprehensive example for business model innovation. Leaders who equip their senior management team with these catalytic mechanisms, and oversee the deployment and execution, will transform companies and cultures."

—Jim Denney,
President, CAP, Inc.

ACHIEVING CLASS A

BUSINESS EXCELLENCE

OLIVER WIGHT

ACHIEVING CLASS A
BUSINESS EXCELLENCE
An Executive's Perspective

DENNIS GROVES
KEVIN HERBERT
JIM CORRELL

WILEY

John Wiley & Sons, Inc.

For general information on our other products and services or for technical support,
please contact our Customer Care Department within the United States at (800)
762-2974, outside the United States at (317) 572-3993 or fax (317) 572-4002.

Wiley also publishes its books in a variety of electronic formats. Some content that
appears in print may not be available in electronic books. For more information about
Wiley products, visit our web site at www.wiley.com.

Library of Congress Cataloguing-in-Publication Data:
Groves, Dennis, 1942-
    Achieving class A business excellence : an executive's perspective / Dennis Groves,
Kevin Herbert, James Correll.
        p.   cm.
    Includes bibliographical references and index.
    ISBN 978-0-470-26034-0 (cloth : acid-free paper)
        1. Management.   2. Strategic planning.   3. Leadership.   I. Herbert, Kevin
(Kevin P.)   II. Correll, James G.   III. Title.
HD31.G7645   2008
658.4'09—dc22
                                                                    2008012266

Printed in the United States of America.

10 9 8 7 6 5 4 3 2 1

This book is dedicated to William Doug Burns, a valued Oliver Wight Principal colleague and friend, who died far too prematurely. He supported us in the early days of writing this book with the same extraordinary technical expertise and commitment he provided to all his clients. We'll remember you always, Doug.

Contents

Prologue

Service Industries

We begin with an explanation for readers who have a service industry background. Although this book relates a story about a manufacturing company, the principles, processes, and cultural aspects apply equally to the service sector. Our work with service companies, including financial institutions, law enforcement, driving license bureaus, even local government, shows that very little tailoring of the *Class A Business Excellence Checklist* content is needed, and is mostly confined to the details in the chapter dealing with managing internal supply. Even there, tailoring may be a question of changing the terminology to words that are more familiar in service industries. The major concepts of product, demand, and supply are universally acceptable. So we encourage you to read the book and to mentally align the manufacturing terminology to service terminology where necessary.

Introduction

Six months into his new job, Greg is desperate. The list of problems he faces might signal the end of his career as president of the Cosmetics Products division of Amalgamated Consumer Products Corporation, Inc.

Imagine coming to work and facing these conditions day after day:

- Revenue and profit falling short of commitment
- Dreadful customer service, resulting in sales managers spending more time apologizing to customers than in building the customer base
- New products introduced late, and then not meeting share, revenue, and profit expectations
- Inventories expanding outside the walls of the warehouses, while orders are shorted, and expired and obsolete products are scrapped
- Functional managers who are operating as silo managers, and are at each others' throats
- Marketing campaigns repeatedly beaten by the competition

Whether you are a senior executive or a mid-level manager with aspirations to reach the senior management ranks, you can empathize with Greg. Without robust, integrated management processes, disasters like these are all too common.

We hope you have avoided the simultaneous convergence of all these conditions. Greg has not been that lucky. He has to deal with all of them.

In this book, you'll look over Greg's shoulder as he confronts and overcomes these conditions. You'll watch him make some traditional, expedient, and very counterproductive decisions as the pressure to improve business results increases. You'll watch as he learns to think differently about his company's business processes and their impact on the entire supply chain. He will learn how to integrate those business processes to meet the needs of his customers while simultaneously improving service to his suppliers, employees, and shareholders. No software or any other magic bullet or quick fix can deliver the turnaround that Greg needs. Instead, Greg learns that excellent business results depend on a system of well-designed and fully integrated business processes operated and managed by knowledgeable and committed people. Greg's journey will change the way he manages Cosmetics Products and will change the way every employee operates within that business. The journey from near failure to becoming the "best of the best" is long. There are no easy solutions to the problems Greg is dealing with. You may be tempted to stop reading when you come to a potential solution for your latest nagging problem. We encourage you to resist that temptation and keep reading to get a vision of what is possible.

Amalgamated Consumer Products Corporation and the characters in this book are figments of the authors' imaginations. But the people, the businesses, the situations, the challenges, the conversations, the conflicts, and the outcomes are based on our experiences, the success of our remarkable clients, and the collective knowledge of our esteemed colleagues in The Oliver Wight Companies. We hope you benefit from Greg's journey and, like Greg, develop a new, comprehensive way to think about and improve your company's business results.

OPPORTUNITY

*Be careful what you complain about; it just might
become your responsibility.*

"I want you to be the new President of Cosmetics Products."

Susan Barnett, Chairman and Chief Executive Officer of Amalgamated Consumer Products Corporation, had been eagerly looking forward to her 10:00 A.M. meeting with Greg Sanders. She had worked with Greg about 10 years earlier at Hillcliff Cosmetics, which owned a number of popular brands. She had held him in high regard then and had followed his career ever since. They still ran into each other at various management forums where they shared their career experiences during breaks. While at Hillcliff, Susan occasionally had dined with Greg and his wife Penny in their home. Susan and Penny had a natural rapport. Now Susan planned to offer Greg the position of President of Amalgamated's Cosmetics Products division and hoped he would consider the offer too good to refuse.

Despite the unusually blustery and gray March Monday morning in Atlanta, Greg arrived for his meeting on time. They chatted first about family, friends, former colleagues, and general economic conditions. "I appreciate your continuing interest, friendship, and support over the past 15 years. I can't tell you how much I enjoyed the time we worked together; I learned a lot from you, Susan. But I was really surprised by your call last week. Fortunately, I'm vacationing at home, so it was easy to make the trip downtown."

"I'm glad you could make it. Now, let's get down to business. I know I was a bit vague on the phone last week, and I appreciate your patience. At the time, I wasn't at liberty to tell you very much about why I asked you to visit.

Now I am, and I want to come right to the point. As you know, we have a new Cosmetics Products division that didn't exist three years ago. I need to give you a little of its history first. Cosmetics Products is a small but viable division that we created through the acquisition of four companies and several additional spin-off brands. Product Categories acquired for the Cosmetics Products portfolio include Hair, Lips, Eyes, Face, Body, all for women; and Shaving, Grooming, Cleansing for men. We also have an Accessories category. Along with new brands, Amalgamated acquired the human and capital resources of the smaller companies. As often is the case, none of the individual companies used the same business language, procedures, or tools.

"After rationalizing the disparate manufacturing and distribution sites, Cosmetics Products has ended up with plants and distribution centers in Atlanta and Dallas, and additional distribution centers in Los Angeles and Lititz, Pennsylvania. In these cities, Cosmetics Products uses space in distribution centers already operated by Amalgamated's other divisions.

"Cosmetics Products represents $200M in sales; it's actually our smallest business unit, but it's the Amalgamated business with the greatest potential growth. The current President, Stu Tillman, is about to retire, and I want you, Greg, to be the new President."

After sitting in stunned silence for what felt like an eternity, Greg looked at Susan. "I see you've not lost your sense of timing or directness, but you just threw me a real curve. I'm not even sure how to react. I actually thought we'd be talking about improving the working relationship between your company and mine. You know that we've been complaining about Cosmetics Products' poor customer service for the past two years. I'm not exaggerating when I tell you that you've delivered less than half our orders complete and on time since we started buying from you.

"My very first boss must have been prophetic. He told me to be careful what I complained about, because it might just become my responsibility to fix it some day! Okay, I know you'd prefer a simple yes or no answer, but I have a million questions. How much time can you spend with me today?"

"I've cleared my agenda through lunch, Greg, and I would like you and Penny to join my staff for dinner tonight if you can manage it. Sorry for the short notice, but it would be good for both of you to meet some of the characters you might be working with. Greg, I'll be happy to answer all of the million questions you have, but first let me put all my cards on the table. I'm offering you the smallest operating division, granted, but it's also the hope for the future for Amalgamated. And, to be very clear, it's in a real mess. I created the division. For that reason alone, setting aside for the moment the business imperative, I want it to be successful. I know you've met Stu Tillman, the current division President, during our recent meeting with key customers. Stu has done a great job of pulling together the semblance of a unified division. More than once he's told me he feels as though he's herding cats, but he has built an operating division, and we're in business. Although his folks don't know it yet, he's very close to retirement and fully supportive of your becoming the new President. Quite frankly, the business isn't doing nearly as well as I'd hoped; the division's in serious trouble. As much as I like and respect Stu, I think this change at the top will do us a world of good. But before I get into the details, I want to influence your decision even more."

Susan handed Greg a document approved by the Chairman of the Board detailing the proposed salary and benefits package for the new President. He studied the details at length and again sat silently for a moment. "Susan, I'm a sales and marketing guy, and take pride in never being speechless. Twice in the past half-hour you've left me speechless. This is far more than generous; I'd say it's astounding. It's well beyond my current salary and benefits package. Are you telling me that I get the ego satisfaction of having the title of President and all this, too?" Susan smiled.

"Okay, you've successfully influenced my decision, but the size of the offer leads me to believe that you either have some very big plans or some huge problems! Mother regularly told me that there's no such thing as a free lunch."

Over the next two hours, Susan described Amalgamated's structure, products, operating and financial results, strategic direction, key people, and key initiatives. She discussed her excitement about creating the Cosmetics Products division and her more recent disappointment in its operating results and contribution to the company.

"Look, I've said it several times already, but I want to reinforce it again. Stu did me a great favor in stepping out of his comfort zone in Personal Products to take the reins of this new business. He has extensive experience in marketing and is greatly respected there, but he has never really learned how to manage this business. He seems out of his element in trying to provide guidance to the supply side. Costs continue to rise; you know very well that our customer service track record is about the worst in the industry; profits are eroding quickly; our warehouses are bursting at the seams; and the only consistent aspect of our new product introductions is that they're unpredictable, and full of unwanted surprises.

"I need the person at the top to be a true business leader, to pay attention to and orchestrate all parts of the business. In his role as President of Personal Products, Stu knew enough about the industry to be successful, and he had an experienced leadership team and organization running pretty much on automatic. However his knowledge didn't translate to the Cosmetics Products business where we're facing different problems."

Greg interrupted, "Let me get this clear in my own mind. In addition to the sales and marketing responsibilities, you'd also hold me accountable for the performance of product development, finance, supply, and distribution operations? You know my background is sales and marketing, and, as with Stu, I know very little about the supply and the technical sides of the business. That feels like a real leap for me. On top of that, you've told me the business is 'in a real mess,' to use your words. I now understand the size of the compensation package a little better. Guess Mom was right after all. There really is no free lunch! Seriously, why do you think I'm the person for you, given the scope of what you want the new President to accomplish?"

Susan paused, and then she continued, "I've heard from others over at Blackstone that your management and problem-solving abilities are still alive and well. The skills and energy you bring to the table are exactly what we need to get this new business moving." She leaned forward and spoke in a measured voice, "I know you can succeed in this role. I need you to succeed in this role and will do everything possible to support you. I'm offering you complete control of the business." She leaned back in her chair and continued, "Clearly, what we are currently doing is moving us in the wrong direction. Do what you need to; go where you need to in order to learn; even change the staff, products, and services if you believe it will help. Just stay within your budget, which I think you'll find to be very generous. In fact, let me go a step beyond that. If you have any specific funding needs that would take you beyond your budget, come to me and I'll see what we can do. Bottom line, I view Cosmetics Products as my creation, and I need it to be successful. The Board sees Cosmetics Products as the key to Amalgamated's future, and they also need it to be successful . . . but soon. We all have complete confidence in your ability to make it happen."

Greg thought for a moment before responding. "This looks to be an incredible challenge, and I'm confident I can meet your expectations . . . if I accept the offer.

"The idea of a group dinner tonight is a good one. It'll be great to meet your staff, especially in a casual setting. That makes it easier to learn about the situation and the people behind the positions.

"Speaking of your staff, I'd appreciate your observations about the players, their roles, and how they operate with the business unit Presidents and Senior Vice Presidents. I'd also like your perspective on the Board of Directors and what they expect of you and the senior management staff."

Susan went on to describe how Amalgamated was organized.

She gave Greg an organization chart [Figure 1.1] and a thumbnail sketch of the people on the Board and on her staff. Amalgamated's Board was made up predominately of people outside the company, with Jim Richards III (grandson of the founder, James R Richards) as the Chairman Emeritus. The Board gave her and her Executive Committee plenty of room, but paid close attention to strategic plans, company image, shareholder and employee relations, government relations, product performance, and profitability. Susan told Greg that the Board was extremely supportive of branching out into the cosmetics industry, but was clear about its expectations for profitability and growth. Lately, she explained, Board members had been asking some unusually probing and uncomfortable questions about the future of Cosmetics Products and about the missed expectations. There was no question about their still being supportive, but they were looking for a return on their investment and were becoming impatient.

Organization Chart

Amalgamated Consumer Products Corporation, Inc.
Founder: James R. Richards   Established: July 1, 1936
Corporate Offices in Atlanta, GA.

Sales : $1.7B

Operating Divisions:

Personal Products	$700M
Home Products	$500M
Food Products	$300M
Cosmetics Products	$200M

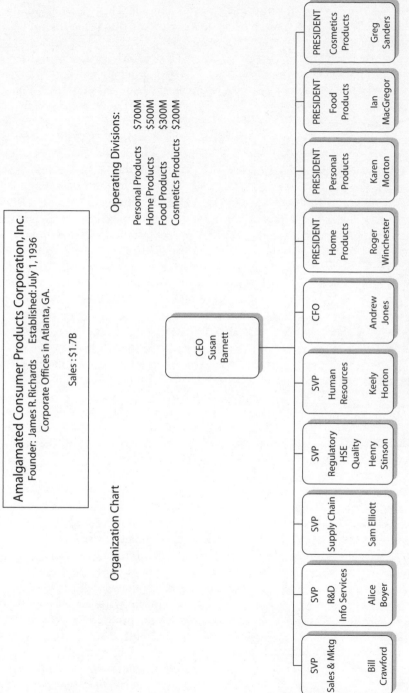

CEO Susan Barnett

SVP Sales & Mktg	SVP R&D Info Services	SVP Supply Chain	SVP Regulatory HSE Quality	SVP Human Resources	CFO	PRESIDENT Home Products	PRESIDENT Personal Products	PRESIDENT Food Products	PRESIDENT Cosmetics Products
Bill Crawford	Alice Boyer	Sam Elliott	Henry Stinson	Keely Horton	Andrew Jones	Roger Winchester	Karen Morton	Ian MacGregor	Greg Sanders

Figure 1.1   Corporate Organization Chart

In terms of her Executive Committee, Susan explained that the Senior Vice Presidents (SVPs) gave her guidance and support, and also provided guidance and support to operating division functional leaders. One of their primary functions was to ensure uniformity across all operating businesses. Her organization was much like a matrix in which, for example, a business unit's Human Resources (HR) Vice President reports directly to the business unit President, but also has a dotted-line relationship to Senior VP of Human Resources, Keely Horton.

"On the one hand, Greg, you'd provide direction to your VPs and call all the shots for Cosmetics Products. You'd conduct the performance reviews and make salary and career decisions for your staff. On the other hand, I'd expect the Senior VPs to be a resource for you and your staff. I look to them to deploy strategic priorities uniformly, develop and deploy common key performance indicators across all businesses, calibrate salaries, and make sure Amalgamated is taking advantage of leading-edge thinking. That's the role of the Senior VP's, but they know that Karen Morton runs Personal Products, Roger Winchester runs Home Products, Ian MacGregor runs Food Products and, hopefully, Greg Sanders runs Cosmetics Products."

"That sort of structure worked pretty well for us at Hillcliff, Susan. But remember all the major turf issues that erupted when a manager got caught between his or her line VP and the staff VP? Any of those problems here?"

"I think we're well past the start-up problems that surfaced when we implemented this structure three years ago, Greg. At first I saw many of the same problems that we saw at Hillcliff, but we solved them quickly. The new roles and responsibilities took some getting used to. But now I think you'll find the Senior VPs to be very supportive of this way of operating as well as of change in general, providing there's a compelling business case for making a change. Don't let your VPs blame the Senior VPs for getting in the way of change. If they do, just sit down with the appropriate Senior VP and explain what Cosmetics Products wants to do and why. I'll get involved if I need to, but that should be a pretty rare event. In fact, that's an excellent topic to discuss with the Senior VPs at dinner tonight. Test their openness to change; ask them what changes they've made recently. Ask them what types of change in Cosmetics Products they'd want to know about in advance. I think you'll be very pleased; I know I am. It may be that Stu spent too much time trying to reconcile detailed differences in the ways his people did things in their old companies prior to acquisition. In fact, even now you might be hard pressed to identify the 'Amalgamated way' of doing things among his staff. Each acquisition company brought its own way of working. Some procedures were better than the Amalgamated way, others worse, but there's still little consistency. People tend to rely on what they already know and resist anything that's 'not invented here.' All that is well and good, but in the Cosmetics Products division it seems almost pathological. It's as if we've lost sight of the fact we are supposed to be saving the ship, not rearranging the deck chairs.

"Let me remind you that one of the reasons you have the offer in front of you is because of your success at looking at businesses differently and improving results. Every one of the Senior VPs has heard that from me. They've seen the evidence from your career themselves and are eagerly looking forward to the energy and improvement you will bring. After all, part of their compensation is based on growth and profitability, so you'll definitely find them supportive of changes that help the bottom line!"

"Sounds excellent, Susan. I'll be testing your perceptions this evening, but it sounds as if you have a first-rate group of executives. Now, let's turn to the people a bit closer to my potential new home. I'd value your thoughts about the performance of the Cosmetics Products division and the people who make up the senior staff. What keeps you awake at night when you think about that business? What are the problems you'll expect me to attack and solve, again, if I accept the offer? By the way, if I don't accept the offer, you can count on me to keep all the information you are sharing in absolute confidence."

"I appreciate that, Greg, and never have had any concern about your keeping all of this in confidence. Let's turn to the hard stuff closer to home, as you put it. I won't put these in any order of priority except for the first one. It's the one you've already experienced, and it's the one that could conceivably sink us. Customer service is completely unacceptable. We receive complaints about incomplete orders and missed delivery dates on about 40 percent of our shipments."

"You're absolutely right about the need to solve the customer service problem. I can tell you first-hand, Susan, that your delivery performance on shipments to Blackstone isn't even as good as 60 percent. My purchasing folks tell me that at least half the orders have been incomplete or past due. If you add billing errors to your measure of 'on time and complete,' your performance is well below 50 percent, and it's driving our Blackstone Accounts Payable, Merchandising, and Purchasing people crazy. What are your folks telling you about the root cause of the problem?"

"It really depends on the situation and whom you ask, Greg. If you ask Kari Crawford, the VP of Sales and Marketing, it's that Manufacturing is unreliable and inflexible. Ask Tony Caruso, VP of Manufacturing, and you'll hear that the production planners change the schedule so much that Manufacturing's most frequent activity is executing unplanned and lengthy product changeovers. If you ask David Simpson, the VP Supply Chain, you'll get the answer that Sales can't anticipate what the customers want and never saw an order they didn't take even when we don't have the product to ship. The external sourcing team will tell you that the suppliers are doing everything they can, but Manufacturing is changing the schedule so fast they can't keep up. We did a supplier survey recently: the overwhelming response was that they have trouble meeting our needs because we don't know what we need from one day to the next! And I haven't even touched on new product introductions, quality issues, or the billing problem you mentioned. You want more, Greg?"

"Susan, I think that's plenty to think about for now! And I believe you just introduced me to some of the cats that Stu has been trying to herd. Tell me, are these problems unique to Cosmetics Products, or do you also see them in the other businesses?"

"I would have to say they are present, but certainly not to the extent that we see them in Cosmetics Products. I suspect that's because we built the other businesses more slowly, and from the ground up, so we had a chance to learn at a reasonable pace. Cosmetics Products came together quickly—some would say too quickly. Everyone followed his or her own way of operating to take orders and get product out the door quickly. The Senior VPs have done their best to bring some order out of the chaos, but there's only so much they can do while also serving the other businesses.

"You now know a little more about the customer service challenge. As I said, it's the problem that concerns me the most. We might have the best products in the world at half the cost of our competitors, but if we can't get the right product in the right quantity and quality to the right place at the right time, we won't have a need for any products at all. Any thoughts about what I've told you, Greg?"

"I couldn't agree with you more about the priority of the customer service problem. I've talked about that issue directly with Stu; complained on any number of occasions. Interestingly, your service to Blackstone actually improved for a week or two each time we spoke; and just as quickly reverted to an unacceptable level. From what you said, it sounds as though people are spending more time blaming each other than looking for and eliminating the cause of the problem. There just seems to be a total lack of integration among the players. A bit of strong leadership with clear priorities would go a long way to fix this one, Susan, although I certainly don't want to oversimplify the situation or take a cheap shot at Stu. I could bring a strong customer focus perspective, provide some horror stories to motivate the troops, and set some compelling priorities for the leadership team. That's always helped solve service problems whenever I've faced them in the past, and it should help here at Amalgamated."

"We really could benefit from the first-person customer perspective you bring, Greg. And your other comments reinforce my observation that you're a decisive leader."

"Tell me more about the inventory situation, Susan. I'm a bit confused. You said Manufacturing complains about all the unanticipated product changeovers they are forced into, but you also said that your warehouses are overflowing. What's going on there?"

"It depends on who you ask, Greg."

"Wait a minute, Susan; am I detecting a pattern here? Does anyone agree on anything in that business?"

"I always knew you were a fast learner. That's one of the reasons why I invited you here. Let me tell you a bit about what I've learned. I'm not necessarily saying that it makes sense, but it appears there are several reasons for the excess inventory. When a manufacturing operation shuts down for an unexpected changeover, all the materials the plant needed to make the originally scheduled product are either in the plant already or are en route. Worse than that, the materials needed to make the product added to the schedule at the last minute probably aren't in the plant and must be expedited by Purchasing. Net result, too much inventory of materials we don't need, premium prices for the materials we didn't know we needed and, in all likelihood, delayed shipments to the customers. I've talked with enough planners to know they feel personal responsibility if plants run out of materials. Because they don't trust the schedule, they try to guess what they might need and keep an ample supply of those materials just in case they might be needed. Need I say that they rarely guess accurately?

"The same is true for finished product. Distribution planners don't believe the sales forecast. Woe betide the planner who runs out of finished product and causes an order to be shorted. So they tend to guess for themselves what will sell, and keep extra just in case. I know, Greg, I know. How can we have a dismal customer service record when we have extra inventory? Simple. We have plenty of finished products in inventory, but they are the wrong products in the wrong warehouses. We repackage overbuilt displays into open stock shipping containers and redistribute some of the product, but those are expensive rework options. Further, too much of our finished product in the warehouses goes beyond the expiration date, and has to be destroyed. Oh, and then there's my all-time favorite. Sales tells me that we've actually cut some orders because we didn't have product when the truck arrived, but learned later that it was a matter of the warehouse people just not being able to find it. Why? You guessed it; because the warehouse was overcrowded. Then add the issue of frequent delays in quality assurance releases and you build yet another layer of 'just-in-case' raw material and finished product to fit into the warehouses.

"I believe my analysis is accurate, but I haven't had the time to jump into the details and try to get to the root cause. And Stu, I'm afraid, doesn't have the technical depth required to ask the right questions. There is a good deal more that I could tell you, but at this point I'd want to make sure I answer your questions and hear any thoughts you might have about getting inventory under control."

"The common theme that keeps coming up for me, Susan, is the absence of clear priorities and information. Don't hold me to this yet, but it seems as if everyone is trying to do what's best. It seems as though they just need clearer direction that their first priority is customer service. Close behind that is reducing inventory. Improving these results would do wonders in kick-starting their creativity, and it should get them moving together along the right path. I'm a firm believer that necessity is the mother of invention. The President of the business has to define the 'necessity' part as well as the consequences if the 'invention' part doesn't show up quickly. I think they need to apply some of our old Hillcliff continuous improvement thinking; get to the root causes of your problems and eliminate them for good. Your products, by and large, are pretty simple. Getting inventory down shouldn't be that difficult, Susan. Don't take this as a commitment by any means, but I'm getting excited as I think about what could be done in this area. As I'm sure you're well aware, your inventory is tying up a good deal of cash that would help the bottom line and appease the Board.

"Your comments, Susan, lead me to believe you need a stronger hand on the tiller, so to speak. But, like you, I don't want to sell Stu short. I've heard about his outstanding marketing reputation. That makes me want to know more about the players on his staff. Do they have the necessary horsepower to get the job done, or do you have some of them in place because of acquisition contractual agreements?"

"To be sure, there are contractual agreements defining how we assimilate people and manage salaries, benefits, and the like, Greg, but that doesn't tie our hands. We can staff the organization in any way that allows us to run the business and achieve our goals. Too much is at stake to do otherwise. If we need to move some people or even remove some people, I have the complete backing of the Board to make the moves and pay the contractual penalties. That should be another indicator to you of the support you'll receive in turning around this business. Overall, I think you'll find some good people on your staff. Here's a copy of Cosmetics Products' organization chart [Figure 1.2]. Greg smiled as he saw his name as President!

"Sara Miles, your VP Finance, and David Simpson, the VP Supply Chain, are long-time Amalgamated folks and are top-notch performers. You'll find them responsive and real team players. They should be your first source when you need straight information. Sara is probably our best Business Unit Finance VP, and David has a clear grasp of 'supply chain' with a capital S. He gets it and encourages his people to embrace the concept of the supply chain spanning all the way from the customer's customer to the supplier's supplier. If we had everyone operating with his mindset, we'd probably have fewer customer service problems.

"Your other VPs are from recent acquisitions. They're all good people and work hard. Their skills vary, as you might expect, in relationship to the sophistication of their former companies. Being senior managers, they all have pretty clear ideas of how things ought to be done, but those ideas match how things worked in their old companies. Collectively, they don't all agree on much of anything. Blending and teaming the resources was only one of many priorities as we completed the acquisition process, moved people and capital resources, tried to learn about our new products and customers, and so on. It makes my head spin just thinking back over all the crises during that period. The good news is that it's all behind us. Now we can focus on building a world-class team and business.

"Kari Crawford, VP of Sales and Marketing is creative and energetic. I think she is still a bit reluctant to rely on her own ideas since she operates in the

Organization Chart

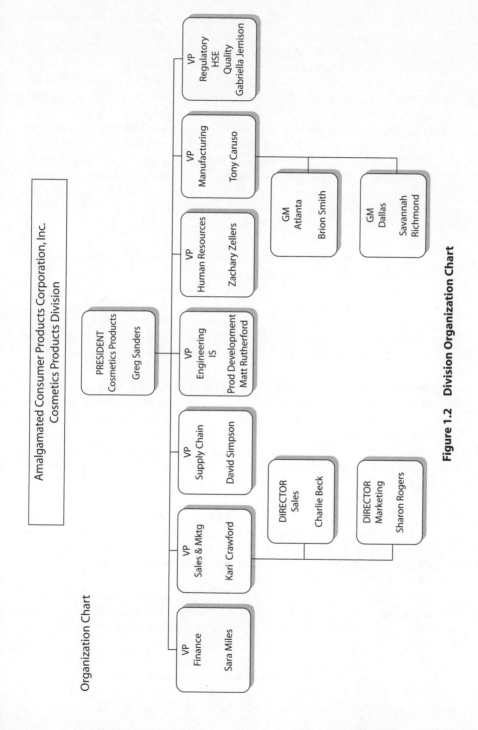

Figure 1.2   Division Organization Chart

shadow of Stu. Freeing her of that constraint should allow her to create new marketing plans and get her field salesforce on that same page with her.

"Matt Rutherford has a great deal of Product Development experience and is a first-rate Development Engineer. On the downside, sometimes he's obsessive about the details and misses the big picture. Our last product launch was a mess; we missed the launch date after a heavy advertising campaign. Development was buried in the details and wasn't providing a good enough picture of potential delays, so I hear. Worse, they were reluctant to share some problems they thought were major issues with the leadership team until it was too late. Turns out that the big problems they kept working on really weren't big deals to the Sales and Marketing folks. As a result, it seems we missed the launch for no good reason. Notice the common theme: even though Kari and Matt are senior managers, they're young and still tentative. They still see themselves as outsiders and frankly, it's hurting their performance and the company's, as well.

"You have a gem in Zachary Zellers, your HR VP. He worked very well with Keely Horton in creating and selling the transition packages for early retirement, education, and outplacement following the acquisitions. Keely couldn't say enough good things about Zach. Same is true for Gabriella Jemison, your VP of Regulatory, Health, Safety, Environment (HSE), and Quality. She knows what she is talking about and always presents a compelling case for her positions and recommendations. She knows when it makes sense to take a prudent risk."

Over lunch, they continued their discussion. "Last, but not least, is Tony Caruso, your VP Manufacturing. Tony has spent his whole career in manufacturing organizations. It's hard to believe, but he's been in the automobile industry, steel, electronics, food, and now cosmetics. I've probably even missed a few of his former career landing points. He's a hard-nosed, traditional, toe-the-line kind of a manufacturing guy. Don't get me wrong, he's a doer; he can make things happen. But you might find him a bit inflexible. Frankly, he tends to drive Kari over the edge from time to time. You know the standard conflict between Sales/Marketing and Manufacturing: 'We want what we want when we want it' versus 'you'll get what we've got when we've got it!' Now that may be an exaggeration, but you get the drift. I don't want to disappoint you; you'll find the old Sales versus Manufacturing conflict is here in Cosmetics Products in all its glory."

"Well, I guess the good news is that it won't be the first time I've had to deal with that, and it probably won't be the last. I know I'll have a chance to meet with your staff tonight, but what about meeting my potential, I repeat potential, leadership team before I give you my decision?"

"Good question. I anticipated that you'd want to meet them, so I arranged a visit for Wednesday of this week. I hope that day works for you. They all will be in town and have you penciled in for a visit that day. As far as they know, you will be here as a customer to learn what they are doing to improve customer service for Blackstone. I guess that's both true and useful no matter if you remain with Blackstone or join us, isn't it? Stu will be your host for the day, but will find reasons to give you plenty of one-to-one time with individuals or with the team. Just tell him what you need during the day."

"Thanks for setting that up for me. Wednesday will work just fine. I suppose you'll be looking for an answer from me soon. How about by the end of the day on Thursday? If the answer is yes, I'll need a couple more weeks to wrap things up at Blackstone so that I don't leave them in a bad spot. I expect they won't be too happy if I leave, unless I commit to taking care of your customer service problems once and for all!"

"Thursday afternoon is just fine, Greg. Let me know if you need an extra day or two. I really do need an answer by noon Monday, either way."

"You've asked good questions today, Greg. We can continue tonight, but I would rather you spend the time at dinner pumping others for their perspectives on the opportunities and challenges you might face with Cosmetics Products. Besides, I have a lot of catching up to do with Penny! You can also call me tomorrow for any clarifications about what we discussed today or what you hear tonight. Same goes for any questions you might have after meeting with the Cosmetics Products leaders on Wednesday. Any other questions for now?"

"No. I just need some time this afternoon to sort out what you've told me and to organize my thoughts for tonight. This is a wonderful opportunity. I can't thank you enough for thinking of me as the person you want to lead Cosmetics Products. See you at the restaurant later."

Penny was already dressed and ready when Greg arrived at home. While he freshened up and dressed for dinner, Penny listened to Greg recount his meeting with Susan. "It's an exciting offer. I would have complete control of the business and would work for a CEO I've admired since those days at Hillcliff. I won't even tell you about the salary and benefits package yet, except to say that if you tried to guess, you wouldn't come close. I want you to be unbiased; tell me what you think about the people you meet tonight and your assessment of the overall feeling in the room."

"I'll be glad to give you my opinion, Greg, but I won't make the decision for you. You know I'll support whatever decision you make. But tell me, what is it about this opportunity that gets you excited?"

"Frankly, there are several things. I'd finally get a chance to be President of a business that just happens to be getting the greatest degree of scrutiny from the corporate Executive Committee and the Board. Cosmetics Products is expected to grow, so I can expect support for any reasonable direction I want to take it. As I said, I already have the support of the CEO and enjoy working with her. And if the business grows as planned, I should have an opportunity to take on even greater responsibility in the company."

"I sense some hesitation in your voice. What's causing that?"

"There is no question that Amalgamated and Susan are eager for me to accept their offer. It's a hard one to refuse, but it's not without serious challenges. The scope of the job is broader than I've ever tackled. I'd be accountable for the performance of the entire business, all functions. I've never been accountable for areas such as manufacturing, product development, logistics, and the others. So I'd have lots of homework until I learn what a President needs to know about strategic planning, finance, product development, supply and distribution, and then get those areas under control. For that reason alone, it can't be just my decision. I like spending evenings and weekends with you and the boys. That could change, at least for a while.

"The business is not meeting performance expectations; I sense Susan is under enormous pressure, and you know that only flows downhill. The Board is looking for a quick turnaround. From what Susan told me about my prospective staff, and what I could read between the lines, the leadership team is not focused or aligned on a common agenda. They're still, at least to a degree, holding on to how things were done in their companies before they were acquired by Amalgamated."

"Doesn't sound to me like anything you can't handle, Greg. You've always been able to turn challenges into résumé fodder! Some of those problems sound familiar to me. You've solved them for other companies in the past; no reason you can't solve them for Cosmetics Products."

"Part of my concern is that all of this happened so quickly. I had information overload today, and I still have a bunch of questions to ask tonight. Well, I'm ready. Let's be off!"

The private dining room in the nearby restaurant was perfect. During the social hour, there was plenty of room and time for Greg and Penny to circulate and get to know a little about each member of Susan's staff. As the discussions turned more to business details and the expectations that the Senior Vice Presidents had of Greg, Penny excused herself so that she and Susan could catch up on events since their Hillcliff days. "You realize that besides just wanting to see you again, Penny, I asked Greg to bring you along so I could influence you as well!"

"I do appreciate the invitation, Susan. It was very kind of you. But I reminded Greg as we were getting ready this evening that this has to be his decision. It sounds like a huge opportunity, and, according to what he's told me already, a real challenge. I know from my days as a managing partner in the investment industry, running a business is a big job. Having the top spot can be exhilarating and, at the same time, draining. I have all the confidence in the world in Greg; I know he'll make the right decision.

"I've really enjoyed meeting your senior managers. Looks as if they're already digging deeply into business details with Greg. I know that'll make him comfortable and probably influence his decision as much as your meeting today and the agenda you have planned on Wednesday."

The rest of the evening was filled with animated discussions covering a mix of topics. On the drive home, Penny asked Greg if he were any closer to making his decision. "Yes and no. Yes, if the decision were just about working with that group of people. Did you notice how the room was full of energy all evening? They clearly enjoy working and just being around each other. I noticed the same thing with Susan's team at Hillcliff: she's a great motivator and a leader who gives everyone the respect and credit they deserve. Most of all they trust her. No, because I still need to meet the Cosmetics Products leadership team and try to get more information about the mess the business seems to be in. This evening's dinner could have helped me say no, but it did just the opposite. The decision now depends on how Wednesday goes."

"I agree. We met a great group of people tonight. They were gracious and welcoming. And you know how I feel about Susan. She's done an amazing job of balancing her career and family. But regarding the offer, I certainly saw no storm warnings. Ball's still in your court, Greg."

Wednesday's visit progressed without a hitch. Stu met Greg in the lobby and spent the first hour with him. Always gregarious and a good listener, Stu made Greg feel at ease immediately. Stu also allayed Greg's initial concerns about whether he was really retiring or being eased out of the company. Stu was eagerly anticipating retirement and talked at some length about an around-the-world cruise he and his wife had been planning for the past five years.

"Just want to be clear, Greg, the staff doesn't know about my retirement date. They know I've been planning for retirement, just not the specific date. So your visit here today is about our customer service issues. Everyone knows the day's schedule and that I have a meeting with Susan for most of the day. I'll be with you for a group session in which we'll explain our current approach to improving our service reliability for Blackstone. Then you have some time individually with each member of the leadership team. Here's a copy of the schedule and topics they have prepared. Your last session is with David Simpson, the Supply Chain VP. He will wrap up the day and see you out. If you want to talk about anything you hear today, please give me a call tonight. I'll be home all evening."

"Thanks very much, Stu. You've been very kind, and I appreciate your hospitality. I've always enjoyed working with you on customer service issues."

"What a way to begin a retirement! I'm envious of your cruise. I'd like to hear about the trip when you return."

"That's a deal, as long as you don't mind looking at a few thousand photos! Let's go into the conference room; the folks should be coming in about now."

Despite having to restrain himself and keep his questions focused on the Blackstone customer service issue, Greg learned what he needed to know during that day. He began to get a better feel about the people on the Cosmetics Products leadership team and about the challenges ahead of him if he were to accept the job. There were plenty of those storm warnings Penny was looking for during Monday night's dinner. But Greg didn't hear anything that seemed beyond his ability to positively influence and resolve.

Penny greeted Greg as he entered the kitchen Wednesday evening, "What's the verdict; yes or no? Tell me about your day."

Greg recounted his meeting with Stu, and Stu's retirement plans. He summarized the meeting with the entire team and the sessions with the individuals on the team. "You know, I couldn't ask all the questions I wanted to ask, but I confirmed much of what Susan told me. The people are working hard and long hours; they care about the business; they are proud of their functional organizations, but still seem to exhibit loyalty to their preacquisition companies. Each of the functional leaders has a clear strategy and supporting plans for solving the customer service problems. But I didn't get a sense of there being a coordinated plan that they were all supporting. Some of those functional plans seemed to be at odds with others. It was pretty subtle, but I got a clear sense of internal finger-pointing. Perhaps I'm being a bit over-critical, and it really isn't all that bad. I have to admit that I just didn't have the time or the freedom to explore deeply enough to see how all the functional plans fit together.

"We were interrupted with phone calls and crises in many of the meetings. That tells me they do too much firefighting—not a surprise given their track record of customer service with Blackstone. I suppose I could characterize the business as being in a state of mild chaos. Perhaps it's beyond mild. A little chaos is fun, but not as much as I observed today."

"So your decision is no?"

"I want to sleep on it tonight, but if you are still supportive in the morning, I think the answer will be yes. Of course I also need to figure out how to break the news to Marty at Blackstone. He's been a great boss and will be disappointed but hopefully not too surprised. By the way, before I give Susan my decision tomorrow morning, I'll tell you about that salary and benefits package."

First thing Thursday morning Greg called Susan with his decision. "Good to hear from you, Greg. I hope you're calling with a positive response to my offer!"

"Susan, you certainly haven't lost any of your powers of persuasion. I talked with Marty first thing this morning. He didn't like the idea of my leaving, but since I am coming to Amalgamated, he felt a lot better about it. In fact he gave me an assignment to solve the customer service problems. He seems really happy that I've been offered an opportunity such as this. As it turns out, we have three people pretty well prepared to step into my shoes at Blackstone. Marty will decide today who it will be, and I'll be joining Amalgamated on April 1."

"I can't tell you how pleased I am, Greg! Please thank Penny for helping you see the light! Really, that's the best news I've had in a long, long time. I'll have a courier bring over some information later today to help you get a running start. In the meantime, let me know if there is anything I can do to help with the transition.

"I'll give the good news to the Board members and to my executive committee today. I'll give Marty a call, and if the timing is right with him, we'll make an internal announcement and send out a press release on Monday morning.

"Come directly to my office on April 1. We'll take care of all the administrative and legal details then. I'll have my staff members bring you up to date during the rest of that day, and start the transition with Stu on April 2. I'll let you and Stu reach agreement on his official retirement date. Whatever date between April 2 and June 1 that gives you enough time with him and still gives him enough time to prepare for his cruise will be fine with me. Is it reasonable to ask you to spend half a day with me on May 1 to go over your thoughts and initial plans based on what you've learned?"

"The dates sound great, Susan. And thanks for the flexibility on the overlap with Stu. I want to make certain I get enough information from him so that I don't let anything fall through the cracks, especially in my support of the leadership team. But I'll do that as efficiently as possible so that we don't waste money on two Presidents or confuse the staff about which President is in charge.

"May 1 also sounds good. That should give me plenty of time to get a strategy and some plans in place. By then we should have taken quite a few steps forward. Thanks, again, Susan for the great opportunity. I may be checking in with you before then, but for sure, I'll see you April 1."

FACT-FINDING—GREG MEETS HIS TEAM

Status quo is the Latin term for the mess we are in now.

That tells me we are rewarding effort rather than results.

The time between Greg's acceptance of Susan's offer and his first day with Amalgamated flew by. Greg had to wrap up his responsibilities and train his replacement at Blackstone while absorbing the background information that Susan sent to his home. The more he read, the more excited he became about this opportunity. Blackstone's President was disappointed about the loss of his Executive Vice President, but knew it was a good opportunity for Greg and was confident that Greg would improve customer service from Blackstone's worst performing supplier. They parted on friendly terms and agreed to stay in touch.

Greg's first day at Amalgamated was uneventful. The administrative and legal details were taken care of efficiently, allowing him to spend most of the day reconnecting with Susan and each member of her staff. They all gave him satisfactory answers to the questions he had developed from the material sent to his home. He was eager and well prepared for the first day with his new leadership team.

Stu Tillman, Cosmetics Products President, welcomed Greg on April 2 as warmly as he had in early March. They tentatively agreed on a target date of June 1 for completion of the transition and Stu's retirement. "I have a lot of confidence in this company and will be holding onto a good deal of stock and options. Your job is to make some money for this company and to support my comfortable retirement! Just know that I'll continue to do anything I can to help you be successful, Greg.

"My weekly meeting begins in 10 minutes. We refer to ourselves as the 'Leadership Team,' although I suspect others might have a different name for us. Let me pull a few things together and we'll get started. By the way, the team has been pretty excited about your arrival since Susan made the announcement. They suspected something was up during your last visit, but didn't say anything to me until the announcement made it official. They're a little feisty at times, but I think you'll like working with this group. Here's a tentative schedule of one-to-one meetings that will carry you through the first week. Feel free to rearrange it. We just wanted to get you off to a running start and enable the VPs to block an appropriate amount of time for you in their schedules." Stu settled back in his chair.

"I know you've met Cynthia Roberts, your Executive Assistant; she's commandeered a conference room for your temporary office. You'll have plenty of room to spread out until you're ready to move in here and tell me either to move into the temporary office or, better yet, go play some golf. Cynthia knows practically as much as I do about the business and is far more efficient! She'll take care of anything you need in the way of supplies, equipment, travel arrangements, meeting schedules and routine corporate reports and requirements. Just let her know what you need."

The Leadership Team meeting began promptly. Stu led off with the introductions. He also announced his tentative retirement date of June 1. The people assembled assured Stu that he would not get away without an appropriate dinner and "roast." They agreed on a date for that event, and moved on to welcome Greg to the team.

Sara Miles, VP Finance, made the first remarks. "Even as important as customer service is to Blackstone and to you personally, Greg, I have to tell you that every one of us thought your visit a month ago was a bit unusual. We sensed something was up just by the way you acted. It felt to us that you were chomping at the bit to ask us some tough questions, but you'd always pull back, shift position in your chair, and look uncomfortable. Now that you can ask as many questions as you wish, and as much as we're going to miss Stu, we want to welcome you to the Cosmetics Products team."

The rest of the team echoed Sara's comments and made Greg feel at home. The meeting reinforced Greg's confidence that he had made the right decision. "And I thought I was being very cool when I was here last month. Guess I should never try being a spy, should I?" They appreciated his humor.

"Very perceptive!" responded Tony Caruso, VP Manufacturing, prompting a collective chuckle from the group.

Greg continued, "But you were all right on target about how difficult it was for me to control my questions. The longer I spent with you that day, the more excited I became about the business and about working with you. I have a lot to learn about the company, and I count on you to get me up to speed. I know we have some serious problems, and that you're all completely dedicated to making this a successful business. As we meet over the next few weeks, it's important that you are absolutely honest with me about the state of the business.

Don't sugarcoat anything. Don't pull any punches. Over the next month, and even after I take the reins from Stu, be straight with me. If you think I am not doing my job or am making a poor decision, tell me. I'll either be able to persuade you that I am doing the right thing, or you'll be able to give me the information I need to change my position. Either way, Cosmetics Products wins. On an ongoing basis, I want the facts and your recommendations about what we need to do to get the business on the right track. Thanks to you and Stu, Amalgamated is now in the Cosmetics Products business. That was an enormously successful accomplishment for which all of you should be proud. There aren't many times in a career when you have the opportunity to start a new business. Now, our collective task is to take the division to the next level of success. I have every confidence we can make that happen." Greg looked around the room to make sure he had their attention, and then continued.

"I see that the tentative schedule of one-to-one meetings begins with Matt, right after this meeting. I'm looking forward to talking with you, Matt, about the new products we're working on. I'd also like to learn a little more about your Information Services (IS) group, things like the Information Technology (IT) infrastructure, capacity, the Enterprise Resource Planning (ERP) system, and future developments.

"In the meantime, I want all of you to be clear that my door is always open. The better we are at sharing information openly and in a timely manner, the better we will do as a company."

There was a good deal of positive energy and chatter in the room as the meeting broke up two hours later. Greg felt good about the first encounter with his staff and was thankful that the waiting was over. After a short break, Matt knocked on Greg's open door and entered the temporary office.

Greg Meets Matt Rutherford

They first discussed their backgrounds, families, and interests outside work, and then Greg asked Matt to describe his organization, the new products and services pipeline, and the development process. Matt explained how the development team was assembled from the four acquired businesses and formed into teams that specialized in their major product categories. "Currently these are, as you may already know, for women: Hair, Lips, Eyes, Face, and Body; and for men, Shaving and Grooming; and finally Accessories—the things we offer to promote our own products. These are mostly outsourced, but to our requirements. Of course, the Personal Products division augments the total Amalgamated offerings. We have an impressive array of products for a relatively new company, Greg. There are well over 500 stock-keeping units (SKUs) for which we provide technical product, process, and packaging engineering support as well. We have a great team. They are well qualified, and some are well-known outside Amalgamated. We encourage our people to publish in various journals to enhance their reputation as well as ours. We all take a good deal of pride in how well we develop our engineers and scientists, and how well we can design products from the standpoint of speed, quality, and cost. In just the past year, we launched four new product lines and about 30 new SKUs." Greg wanted more information.

"That's impressive, Matt. You have every reason to be proud of your development team. But I understand there have been problems with product launches, especially with the last launch. I hear we missed the launch date, our salespeople went through some pain and suffering at the hands our customers, and we have yet to meet our sales objectives. As critical as customer service is under normal conditions, it's even more critical to have new products available on their launch dates after we've positioned and promoted them. What happened, and what have we learned?" Matt was eager to respond to Greg.

"You went right to a 'hot button' for me, Greg. We did take a good deal of heat over that last launch, but Development certainly wasn't alone when it comes to blame."

Greg interjected, "Not to interrupt your thoughts, Matt, but I want to be clear about something. I am not interested in blame. Companies seem to excel at developing a culture of blame. I really want to know how well we learn from our mistakes. That's critical to improving our performance. A Chinese philosopher once said something like, 'Failure is essential to growth,' and I go along with that, if, in fact, we learn from our experiences." Matt smiled.

"I'm glad you said that, Greg. It will make answering your question easier for me. We develop lots of products and do it well when we have stable performance targets to design against. Any number of times, my team accomplishes borderline miracles in getting the products ready for Manufacturing, but on the last one we simply ran out of time. Marketing has a well-known track record; just ask any of my product engineers and you'll hear how Marketing changes the design requirements right up to the last minute. There is no specific point in the development when the design is frozen and protected from further change. Let me tell you that even building contractors have that time fence when changes can't be made without big premium charges. My wife and I learned that when we built our house." With a resigned look, Matt continued.

"So Marketing feels free to change the design at the last minute and expects us to jump through hoops to get all the testing done to ensure our products are marketable and safe. That was the case with the last launch, but that particular product had more changes than normal, and some that came later than we had ever experienced. After we do get our products into the marketplace, we often go through a series of design improvements, but these requested changes, according to Marketing, had to happen prior to launch. My team is excellent, but this time we just couldn't pull off another miracle. When we finally had to say we couldn't meet the launch date, Marketing complained that the last few changes they asked for were minor, really not important enough to the consumer to delay the launch! It took me several days to get that product team off the ceiling, and they're still angry."

Greg looked puzzled, "Isn't there some kind of protocol for developing and commercializing new products, Matt? Don't we have an operating procedure that says what should be done and when? Don't we have a filter for determining what projects to pursue? And for when the design template should be frozen, as well as development milestones, and Stages and Gates?" Greg asked these questions in a way that caused Matt to become a little defensive.

"There is a development protocol, Greg, and it's a good one. But you have to understand something about this place. You did ask us to be open, didn't you?"

"Sure did, Matt. I want to know facts and opinions from everyone about how we can make this business successful," Greg replied.

"Good. In that case, you need to understand that, except for the regulatory procedures we have in place, documented procedures—whether on a piece of paper or in a computer file—don't necessarily mean much in this division. It is very difficult to get Marketing, Sales, and Manufacturing to follow the product launch protocol. We are so focused on meeting the needs of every single customer and in getting every last consumer unit sale, that we completely ignore the protocol, make last-minute changes on the fly, confuse everyone, and end up hurting the customer expecting our new products. This is, when you think about it, somewhat like a fashion business at heart. Product launches are textbook cases of chaos. We've never seen a milestone or deadline that we couldn't ignore, except for the start of shipments date. As a result, we end up working overtime and weekends even to make some pretty simple packaging graphics changes. We've even been known to make changes after Tony has started production. Let me tell you that he can be a pretty unpleasant fellow when he has to repackage product he produced earlier with weekend overtime crews!" Matt paused before continuing.

"Don't get me wrong, Greg. When our products get into the consumers' hands, they meet all our founder's values of 'high quality products that meet or exceed consumer expectations at affordable prices, representing great value.' It's just that we don't accomplish those values with anything resembling effectiveness or efficiency. You can see that in our declining margins." Greg looked a little surprised.

"The current operating mode sounds very expensive to me. Why haven't you been able to get people to follow the protocol?" he asked.

"I don't intend to point fingers, Greg, but I have done everything possible to get people to follow the protocol, including begging. Part of the problem is the priorities Stu sets. He has the reputation here of being a marketing genius and everyone knows how he built the Personal Products division. He's been in the company his entire career; his family and the Richards family have been good friends since he was very young. You have to remember that he built Personal Products into the biggest division in the company. He was one of the first in the entire industry to recognize the importance of marketing anti-aging products to baby boomers. As a company we owe him a lot. Frankly, however, Stu doesn't know much about how product engineering and development fit with supply. He always takes Marketing's recommendations when making decisions, probably because that's where he grew up, and that's what he knows. If Marketing says a product change will sell more of the product, and we say making that change at this point in time will jeopardize the launch, Stu tells us we are a creative bunch and should be able to figure it out. Satisfying Marketing's interpretation of the market research data is always the top priority. But last time, it backfired on us." Matt took a sip of his coffee and continued.

"The Manufacturing side of the business also contributes to the problem. We hand off the design to them; then we learn they want some additional changes to make the product easier to manufacture, or they want some additional process equipment bells and whistles added. Same effect. We usually get them done, but it isn't a pretty thing to watch."

Greg thought he knew what was coming next, but he asked his question anyway. "Thanks for being straight with me on your observations. What you've described must take a heavy toll on morale in your group and on your budget, Matt." Matt smiled knowingly.

"A toll on morale? Definitely. On budget? It used to be that way, but over time, I've learned to plan for additional people, time, and money to deal with the last-minute changes. You asked me what we've learned from the last launch. Collectively, I would say not much. We aren't doing anything different today as a company. It is pretty much status quo, which is, as President Reagan once defined it, 'the Latin term for the mess we're in now.' We tend to move from one launch crisis to the next, and each launch seems to have a shorter lead time than the last because the previous product took longer than expected. A nasty spiral. As a product development group, we've learned to anticipate last-minute changes by—and I am really going to regret saying this down the road— inflating the development budget and lead time. We've also learned (again and again I might add) that following the protocol would be helpful, but we have just about given up on that one. One exception, of course, is that we follow our internal product development portions of the protocol rigorously until the last-minute changes hit us and it all turns to . . . well, let's say it turns into chaos." Matt leaned back in his chair, but Greg wasn't finished yet.

"If I posed the same question to the others, how would they respond?"

Matt waited a moment, as if thinking about it, then replied, "I expect you would hear much the same from everyone about our chaotic product development and launch process. People actually seem to enjoy the adrenaline high, and then the celebration of victory when we finally ship the first case of product, regardless of the date. I also expect you'll hear that the product engineering team is the crux of the problem; that we are uncooperative, too rigid, always preaching about the importance of following the protocol, always pushing back on last-minute design changes, not understanding Marketing needs or Manufacturing limitations. If you learn anything different from that, I'd be surprised and would like to know about it, Greg."

Over the next hour, Greg dug into the new products and initiatives portfolio and schedules. He also had Matt go over the key players on his team with a focus on individual and collective strengths and plans for improvement.

Since they intended to work through the lunch hour, Greg asked Cynthia to have lunch delivered to his office.

As the lunch tray arrived, Greg asked Matt for a synopsis of the Information Services staff and their plans. Specifically, since Matt was also responsible for the Information Services group, Greg wanted to know more about the current effectiveness of the ERP business system. Matt became more relaxed with the change of topic.

"I have to tell you, Greg, the ERP implementation and start-up in 1999 was an exciting time at Amalgamated. We spent a lot of resources and money to protect ourselves from the possible Y2K threat. We actually eliminated dozens of high-maintenance, independent legacy systems. In IS, the ERP system runs successfully. But that's the end of the good news. The users still don't like it and ignore it whenever possible. They have never spent time learning how to configure the new system to work best for Amalgamated. As a result, they don't understand it, and think of it as a pain. Except for Finance, which can now see detailed and aggregate views within and across Divisions like never before. That would be great, but the data in the system needs a lot of massaging to make any sense out of it. One day, it's all going to catch up with us, and then we'll have to reimplement, but we'll do it properly next time.

"So today, our people spend less time using the system than they do complaining about how the system is set up and how they don't trust what it recommends. Whenever there is a problem, all I hear about is how the system makes them work harder and causes them to make bad decisions. In reality, I think they believe they have to work harder because the system forces some discipline in how they do their work, and they don't like that. But in IT terms, we are operating on the new system, and we are providing an up-time availability of well above 99 percent. I expect you know that's an enviable benchmark in the industry, Greg."

When they finished their meeting, Greg wrote up a summary of their discussion:

April 2

Matt Rutherford, VP Engineering, IS, Product Development

1. Young, talented, and energetic VP. Has lots of potential. Calls it like he sees it; doesn't mince words. Seems to have problems working across functional boundaries. Should his group be responding more effectively to operational complaints from both Marketing and Manufacturing? Are the priorities clear?

   Action: Review the product development protocol.

   (Continued)

(Continued)

2. Product Development team is talented and committed. Something doesn't make sense about how they work with Marketing and Manufacturing. Seems like a lot of rework and firefighting. If they are all that talented, why aren't launches smoother?

3. Lots of products are in development and also in the portfolio. Not sure of product priorities or how they fit into any coherent growth strategy.

   Action: Check this with Kari Crawford and Sara Miles. Are all products necessary and profitable? Are we developing products for the sake of developing products? With all those new products, why isn't the business growing?

4. Why was IT unable to convince people to use the ERP system to exploit its capabilities? Why don't people use the system?

   Action: Ask Tony Caruso and David Simpson.

Greg Meets Kari Crawford

After finishing his notes, Greg met with Kari Crawford, his Sales and Marketing VP. After asking Kari about her background and interests, and answering her questions about his, Greg followed up on his notes from the morning's session about the product launch process and the last-minute product design changes.

"Look, Greg, Marketing is often between a rock and a hard place in this business. Our success, and our compensation, depends on our getting new products and promotions to our customers' shelves. It is all about volume and share for us; those are both driven, in large part, by the number of new product launches and promotions, and the related advertising. By the way—I'll show you all the details later—our pipeline of products and promotions is full over the next year. We've met every marketing target over the past two years regarding number of products launched. Some time, I would welcome your perspective about our direction and how well our initiative plan lines up with the business strategy." But Kari didn't wait for a response.

"Now, I'll agree totally that Matt is right on one point. We often give him design changes at the last minute, but we also know that his development time line is padded with extra time and money. He may not have told you that. He has some great development engineers, although they tend to whine from time to time. Look, sometimes the marketplace forces us to challenge their creative capacity at the last minute. Before we put a product into the trade, we want to make sure it's the best design in terms of consumer needs. We take full advantage of all the information we gather from test market trials; sometimes that information comes in very late. Launches tax the entire organization, so we want to get the product and packaging right before we pay the slotting allowance and put it on the shelves. We don't want to launch and then second-guess ourselves about not making those changes that would have made the difference between a success and failure, especially when we had the data in hand before launch. If Product Engineering has a problem with some of our last-minute requests, it's up to them to raise a flag. It can't be up to us to anticipate what they might or might not be able to accomplish. I mean, they've managed most of it somehow and have pulled off some big changes at the last minute. So I often wonder how much is just griping for the sake of griping."

Greg jumped in. "Later I would like to see how all those new products fit into our strategy, Kari, and how we determine if a product or SKU is carrying its weight in terms of profitability. Before we go there, however, you said you were often 'between a rock and a hard place' in driving volume and share. I think you just described product development as the rock. What's the hard place?" Greg guessed what would be coming next, but Kari needed to get a point across first.

"Before I answer that question, I want to pick up on your comment about profitability. I'm not the right person to answer that question. Stu wants me to focus on growing volume and share. I am responsible to meet my budget, but I don't get involved in discussions about profitability of any particular SKU. Those decisions are between Stu and Sara.

"Going back to the question about the hard place—that would be manufacturing. If we are going to be successful, we actually have to get the new products into the trade and be responsive to our customers. If we get an unexpected order from, say, Value Market, we need to be able to fill it. We can't tell them, 'Thanks, but you have to give us three weeks notice.' That's especially true when we have positioned new products for customer promotional support in newspapers or flyers. If we delay one of those, there is a high risk that they may fill their shelves with our competitors' products and say 'sayonara' to any of our products that they carry. But if we do take the order, all we hear from Manufacturing is how we don't know how to do our job, and how we don't understand the complexities of supplying products. Give me a break! They tend to forget that the only reason they are here is to meet the needs of our customers." Suddenly, Kari was on a roll.

"We give them forecasts that are as good as they can be in this industry. In our business, as in any fashion-related business, I'm not yet convinced anyone can forecast customer preferences well, but we do our best. And our customers aren't interested in our supply problems when they place an order. They just want product for their shelves. All we hear is how we don't know what we are doing and that Manufacturing could do a better job of forecasting the business. Oh, would I ever like to take them up on that challenge! I do know one thing. Tony Caruso doesn't pay much attention to our forecasts. He runs his business based on what he thinks he'll have to ship. I can't get the details from him, but I'm fairly certain that he is sitting on more capacity than he wants us to know about. It's the only way I can figure out how he complains as much as he does about emergency orders, and then plays the hero with last-minute manufacturing miracles. 'You want the product, put it in the forecast!' What a pain. Wish I had a buck for every time I've heard him say that. His inflexibility and dramatics have cost us some business in the past and will cost us more in the future. He just has to understand that the only reason his organization exists is to make what we sell." Greg wondered if Kari would ever surface to breathe as she continued.

"Interestingly, my Sales and Marketing team gets rewarded, in part, for customer service, while Tony's gets rewarded for production efficiency and asset utilization. We are constantly getting penalized for missing our customer service targets because Tony hasn't made the products for us to ship, while Manufacturing always gets its bonus. That makes no sense to me at all while I can't ship products. Yet Manufacturing meets its efficiency and utilization targets; their warehouses are full; and we have major customer service problems. Nothing personal about this; I just need Tony to be a team player. Hopefully, you can help him understand the importance of filling customer orders. I've about given up; might as well talk to one of his machines. I will give him credit for one thing. He certainly knows his plant operations, but he is about the most inflexible person I have ever met!" Now Kari caught her breath, and slowed a little.

"Wow, I apologize for that outburst, Greg."

Greg smiled, "That's okay. There's no longer any question in my mind about how passionate you are about marketing and customer service, Kari. I like to know that people are passionate about their work, but one of my jobs is to keep that passion and emotion constructively focused. I'll need your help with that, especially in your organization's relationships with Product Engineering and Manufacturing. Now tell me about the two sides of your own organization, Kari. How effectively do your Marketing and Sales Directors work with each other?" Greg asked. Kari became the consummate professional again.

"Charlie Beck is my Director of Sales, and Sharon Rogers is Director of Marketing. Let's start with Sales. Charlie is a sharp guy, very outgoing and opinionated as well. Says what's on his mind. I worked with him for several years prior to our being acquired by Amalgamated. He coaches the Sales team well and is about as good as anyone I've seen in maintaining positive relationships with our customers. He is probably the main reason we didn't lose some of our key accounts during the last product launch. You can imagine how difficult that was with our history of customer service and launch problems. Through no fault of his own, he has to spend too much time apologizing to existing customers, and too little time developing new customers and markets." Greg looked puzzled.

"When I look at the sales figures I notice that we're selling more than the forecasted volumes of existing products, especially some of our low margin products, and are falling short with almost every high-margin product introduced in the past 18 months. What's causing this pattern, Kari? Aren't we focusing on the new products to build the business?"

"Of course we are, but part of that pattern is due to the launch problems we've been discussing, Greg. In addition, I have to admit we also have our own internal marketing and sales issues. I don't know if you've had a chance to look at the compensation system yet, but you might want to take a close look at the incentive program factors. The Sales team is rewarded for meeting their sales dollar volume objectives by quarter. Charlie takes a great deal of pride in meeting his quotas. It is one of the primary ways he keeps his Field Sales force motivated and happy. Given the problems getting new products out and on the shelves, and the time it takes Field Sales to convince customers that we'll be better with the next product launch than we've been in previous launches, he goes along with his folks in pushing the older products. We know those products come out of Manufacturing more reliably, with fewer quality problems, and cause fewer customer service failures. Frankly, they take less sales time to get an order and are easier to sell in high volumes. Another problem is that Charlie just doesn't get excited about many of our new products. On top of that, he isn't often in agreement with the array of promotional items and events that our Marketing team comes up with. He and Sharon Rogers, my Marketing Director, in fact don't see eye-to-eye on many issues." Greg thought about that for a moment, and then commented.

"From what you've told me so far, Kari, I'm surprised our customer service and overall volume results, not to mention profitability, aren't worse than they are. You are playing referee too much. How does Sharon view Charlie and his Sales team?" Kari opened up to Greg.

"We've been hammering away at teamwork since we created the Division. Their relationship is better than it used to be, but they still have some trust issues. Each of them filled Sales and Marketing VP roles in acquired companies and didn't feel too good about losing their titles when they came into Cosmetics Products. And they each believe they know how to do each other's jobs better then they are being done. Charlie is quick to complain that the products aren't exciting, the advertising lacks creativity, the packaging graphics don't command attention on the shelf, and the promotions don't offer the customer or consumer enough of an incentive to increase trial usage.

"Sharon will counter that her advertising meets all recall objectives, that the product and package designs are based on solid market research, and that the products could be sold if the Sales team just would do its job and stop second-guessing Marketing. Between the two of them, they waste too much time arguing about the forecast. Charlie thinks Sharon is too optimistic so that she can justify new products and get more marketing money from the company. Sharon thinks Charlie keeps the expectations low so that his folks can exceed their quotas and maximize bonus. I guess this contributes to Tony's operating with his own forecast in Manufacturing. Sharon believes that Sales is the fundamental reason we have such a poor performance in selling in new products and promotions." Greg tried to look sympathetic.

"Sounds like you, too, are between a rock and a hard place, Kari. I can help with the manufacturing issues, but you're going to have to get your own shop in order. Sharon and Charlie need to work together, or we might have to find replacements for them. They are no longer working for their old competing companies, but it sounds as if they think they are. They are now on the same team and had better start acting that way. I'll make sure they get that message loud and clear from me whenever I have a chance to meet them. In the meantime, let me know if there is anything specific you would like me to say or do. I'll help any way I can, but I'm counting on you to get this one under control and to get it done quickly." Kari looked Greg in the eye.

"I'll do my best, Greg." Greg smiled at this brief retort.

"I know you will. Overall, Kari, how do you feel about the level of spending being authorized for launching new products and for promotions, especially sampling and other trial increase initiatives? Could that be part of the volume shortfall in the business?" Kari started off again.

"It certainly could be, Greg. You asked me about profitability earlier, and I told you that Sara and Stu keep those cards face down on the table. It's also true with our advertising budget requests. I forward pretty detailed funding requests with a ton of justification from our brand managers when we launch and when we plan other initiatives. I have yet to be fully funded. I am sure Sara does a good job and has a lot of responsibility, especially since we are under the Board's microscope. My gut says, however, we are saving pennies and losing dollars. I can't get at the balance sheet, so I can't prove that, but I know advertising builds a business. Just look at the size of advertising budgets for some of our key competitors. As a percentage of sales, their spending makes ours look puny. So does their return on their advertising investment."

Greg finished out the day by reviewing the schedule of new product launches and promotions. He satisfied himself that, for the most part, they tied in nicely with the current Cosmetics Products strategy. He could see Stu's fingerprints on the marketing plan and recognized that he was effectively developing Kari's skills and insights into the world of marketing. Leadership skills were a different story. He would have to coach her heavily on those.

Before Kari left, Greg had one more request. "Over the next couple weeks if you can make the arrangements, Kari, I would like to go with you to our top five to ten customers to learn more about how they view Cosmetics Products and our key competitors. I certainly don't question your assessment about how we are performing in the marketplace. I just want to meet them and get their assessment firsthand. I also want to give them a chance to meet me and vent some of their frustration at the new guy on the block. I think it will reassure them that we care about them. At the same time, it will give me a chance to really understand what they need from us. Just work directly with Cynthia to get the visits on my calendar." Kari relaxed and happily replied.

"Sure will, Greg. I think that's a great idea."

Greg jotted down a few thoughts and follow-up items:

April 2

Kari Crawford, VP Sales and Marketing

1. Kari seems to have a good handle on marketing strategies; a good array of new products and promotions.

2. Needs a new perspective and approach to resolve the interface conflicts she is facing.

   Action: Arrange for some leadership and conflict resolution training for her.

3. Missing predicted volumes in general, but especially on launches and promotions. Is market research data causing us to develop the wrong products or is the problem with Sales? Customer service problems in general could also be the problem.

   Action: Visit a few key customers and get their perspective.

4. What's going on with Manufacturing?

   Action: Ask Tony for his assessment of his working relationship with the Sales, Marketing, and Finance organizations.

That evening Greg shared the day's highlights with Penny. "I think I underestimated the problems. The bad news is that there are more of them and they are deeper than I anticipated, especially within the leadership team. There's good news, though. I think some clear direction, expectations, and priorities will get the group to start acting like a team. I'm hearing the problems loud and clear, and am already developing the plan I need to present to Susan at the end of the month. So far so good!"

Greg Meets Sara Miles

A meeting with Sara Miles, his VP of Finance, launched Greg's schedule the next morning. "Volume and revenue are down, compared with last year's same quarter and year-to-date results, by 10 percent; we reduced our profit commitment three times over the past 18 months; margin is down by about 20 percent and costs continue to climb. Other than that, the financial outlook doesn't look all that bright, Greg."

Greg thought, "Someone from Finance with a sense of humor," as Sara continued.

She was getting right to the heart of Cosmetics Products' problems at 7:00 A.M. on Wednesday. "Things were rocky at the beginning when we were trying to get the business off the ground, but we all expected that. As we got our feet on the ground and sales kicked in, we began launching some new products and revenues grew steadily to $200M. In retrospect, the business should have been growing faster, given the energy being expended, the number of launches, and the deals being offered to our key customers to help offset the impact of our start-up problems. I suppose all of us were in a bit of denial about that. Over the past year, however, we would have been happy if we continued to see that kind of growth. This is really the first time we have seen a dip in the results, and I'm not certain we have a really good handle on the cause beyond our customers' screaming about poor service." Greg interjected a question.

"What part of the downturn do you attribute to the service problem, Sara?" Sara was ready for that question.

"I'll show you the details a bit later when we go through the financials, but if our service level matched the average of our competitors, we would be getting profit on the orders we can't fill, we would have some increase in share and volume from those customers who now buy from more reliable suppliers, and our Sales staff could spend more of their time selling new business. Obviously, we are spending lots of money on entertainment at trade shows to help the Sales group mollify our customers until things get better. All of that would help create volume and profit. It would be a bit of a guess to predict how much that revenue and profit would be, but I can guarantee you that we would not be under the Board's microscope. I estimate that our growth in volume and profit would be the envy of the company. Instead, we are the goats." Greg smiled wryly.

"Tell me about the cost side of the equation. I noticed in the material Susan sent me that our price and cost variances are very high. What's going on?" Sara got serious.

"We pay suppliers for a lot of special handling. We send them a purchase order inside their lead time, or we change the order after they have already received it. Our suppliers gladly meet our requests, but for a significant premium. I keep hearing that it's just the nature of the cosmetics products industry, but I don't buy it. It's a similar story for the cost of production. We spend lots of time setting standards for the year, but no one seems to pay much attention to them. Tony knows a lot about supply operations, but his budgets are always fat. We wrestle with the numbers for months and agree on the final standards, but then Manufacturing goes off and marches to its own drummer. They haven't been held accountable for the variances, so they just keep expediting, incurring premium rates for airfreight, working high levels of overtime, and overspending in general." Greg changed subjects.

"You know the other divisions pretty well, Sara. What do you see different in Cosmetics Products? Are we using different policies, incentives, pricing structures, or anything else that we could change to make a difference?" Sara thought for a few moments before replying.

"On the surface, we have the same basic policies, procedures, and even software that everyone else uses. What seems different here is a total lack of alignment. Everyone is working hard and delivering good results in their own areas. But when you roll it all up, the business results just don't cut it. Maybe Stu has been too close to retirement, but I don't see him keeping the leadership team very well focused, pushing us, or holding the team accountable, I mean really accountable, for improving our business results. Lots of people are running at the maximum level of bonus and stock options even though our overall results continue to decline. That tells me we are rewarding effort rather than results. I can tell you from personal experience that it is not fun or motivating when we have to go to Susan and explain that we have to reduce our profit commitment. I think because of Stu's great record with the Personal Products division, his long service, and his personal relationship with Jim Richards, the Board cut him some significant slack. I also think it is good for Stu that he is retiring because that slack is quickly disappearing. Just my personal opinion, but that's not very good news for you Greg." He looked thoughtful for a moment.

"Thanks for your opinions, Sara. You've given me a lot to think about. Let me change subjects for a minute. We have a large portfolio of products for such a new business. How do we know that all of them are profitable? Do we have some products that should be harvested? Are we adding costs to the business unnecessarily by keeping some of our smaller brands on life support? Are we kidding ourselves about expected volumes for new and existing products? After all, we are under the forecast volume on nearly every new product." Sara got into gear again.

"Forecasting is a problem for us. It's a real headache for Finance, especially when we have to reduce our commitment to the company. I know the game. Marketing tends to aim high to get more advertising support money, and Sales shoots low to maximize incentives. As a result, our Finance group spends countless hours doing our own financial forecasting.

"To make profit matters worse, we spend heavily on marketing promotions and advertising, but I'm not convinced we are getting value for the money spent. For our kinds of products, I think we spend far too much on celebrities to make TV ads." Her eyes sparkled with intensity.

"We have a large array of products, but that's part of our strategy for growing the business. Sales couldn't get enough products and promotions when we started the business. Their objective was to be a full-service supplier for their customers; eliminating a single SKU is not even in their thinking. As service problems got worse, and they were repeatedly burned on launch product availability, they began to back off the new products and sell the products they knew they could get. Short-term financial impact is that we don't recover development costs, and scrap out-of-date product; long-term result, we keep pushing products that are in their decline. Promoting old, low-margin products reduces our revenue and profit even further. We are not sophisticated enough to use Activity Based Costing, but if we were, I'm confident that we would find many of our older and smaller SKUs are being subsidized by the others. Granted, a small number of the products may be needed by Sales to get into certain accounts, but they certainly aren't carrying their weight. We do a pretty good job reporting overall financial results, but we really can't get the data we need to do a good job supporting decisions on which SKUs and products to discontinue." Greg was becoming impatient and a bit angry.

"You mean, Sara, that we've spent well over $10M on IT infrastructure and that ERP system and can't get the data we need? Why not?" Sara read his anger and replied.

"Oh, I think we've spent far beyond $10M. The trouble is the users resist using the system. They have a whole bundle of excuses. Fundamentally, the data and transaction integrity is poor. Some of my counterparts in other companies tell me that budgeting in their companies is easier and closing the books is like a non-event. That's not been the case for us. I hear lots of complaints about what the system won't do for people, but not many good words about it. I know that it takes us quite a bit of time each month to reconcile the system reports with our financial spreadsheets. I hear the same thing goes on in Purchasing and Manufacturing." Sara watched as Greg's frustration got the better of him.

"Why don't we just tell people to use the darn system? I don't handle it well when people make excuses for not doing their jobs. We spent a lot of money on the ERP software and counted on a good rate of return. Let's just tell them to use the system!" With a degree of calm that surprised her, Sara provided some coaching to Greg.

"I'm not so sure that's a good idea, Greg. If people relied totally on the system for decision making, our results would probably get a lot worse real fast. Let me give you some examples. We audit warehouse inventory counts every month. The data in the system has the wrong inventory numbers about half the time. Variances are huge. The system never gives us good data about the amount of materials used or the cost of those materials. And that's only the beginning."

Greg and Sara spent the rest of the morning going through financial details and projections. The gap between commitment to the company and actual results was large and growing. Sara told Greg that the line organization was hoping to close the gap in the third and fourth quarters. Given the recent track record, Greg was convinced that closing the gap would require more than hope; it would require a significant course change.

He added to his notes from the previous day:

April 3

Sara Miles, VP Finance

1. Sara is talented, just as Susan promised. Knows the financials inside and out. Has a good perspective on how Cosmetics Products' results affect Amalgamated's results.

2. Too many products. Some "stars" must be subsidizing many other products.

   Action: Discuss further with Sara how we can reflect more realistic costs by product line and SKU without a complete shift to Activity Based Costing if that's too big a change to undertake now.

3. More confirmation that the users aren't using our ERP system.

   Action: Talk with Alice Boyer Sr. VP of R&D and Information Systems. What's her perspective?

4. Need a plan quickly to close the financial gaps; first order of priority at the next leadership team meeting.

   Action: Get a plan in place and moving before the May 1 meeting with Susan.

5. Very impressive member of the team. Good development candidate.

   Action: Determine how to support Sara's development. Agree with Susan that she has the potential to move to the next level of responsibility based on what I've seen so far.

Greg Meets David Simpson

Greg began his afternoon meeting over lunch with David Simpson, VP Supply Chain. David explained his education and work experience. After college, where he majored in logistics, he worked for smaller companies in the areas of planning and distribution, and then joined Amalgamated 12 years ago as Logistics Manager in the Personal Products division. He was promoted to Vice President when he was assigned to the Cosmetics Products division. While they finished lunch, David described the Cosmetics Products' supply chain from the consumers through their customers, the four distribution centers, two plants, some contract manufacturers, and on into the supplier base, down to second tier for key suppliers. It was a description and analysis that was far more comprehensive than Greg had heard from anyone in any other company.

When they settled back into Greg's office after lunch, he started off by asking, "With the level of understanding you have about our supply chain and how it works, why are we struggling so much to meet our objectives?" David was wary in his reply.

"What I explained is the ideal structure and how it should work, not how it does work. In our company, there are some major barriers to closing that substantial gap. For one thing, our customers aren't very happy with us. You were on that side of the table just last week, so that shouldn't be a surprise to you. Based on conversations I've had with suppliers, customers, and our order fulfillment people, I could describe our customer service like this. If you place an order with us, chances are very good that you will receive the wrong products or the wrong quantities or it will show up late. If you happen to get the right product in the right quantity at the requested time, it is purely by chance. If you are one of our suppliers and we place an order with you, chances are very good that we placed the order with less than the lead time we agreed to, we will change the quantity before you ship it to us, or we will cancel the order and ask for something else. Our external sourcing team members are specialists in reordering and expediting, and that's not what we need them to do. We need them to develop better ways to work with suppliers and figure out how to drive waste out of the supply chain. Instead, we seem to foster adversarial relationships, much like we do with our customers. As a result, our supply chain is in a constant state of change and is pretty badly broken." Greg looked more than a little annoyed.

"Look, David, you have responsibility for distribution, planning, and purchasing. Shouldn't you be able to get some of this under control? Seems to me that if you make enough of the products and put them in the warehouses, then Field Sales can sell what it needs to and the customer service problems go away. That's true also, isn't it, for raw and packaging materials? Just keep enough so that Tony can make what he needs to make. I haven't talked with him yet, but I understand he is always complaining about running out of materials and having to change over to another product. Just make sure you have enough of everything and he won't have that excuse!" David responded in kind.

"Greg, you just described perfectly how our supply chain is working today. That is essentially what we are doing, and you can see the results. We try to guess what everyone will need and end up with high costs, bulging warehouses, and shrinking volumes, share, and profit. Are you saying you want me to do more of that?" The tension in the room began to build, and Greg did nothing to alleviate it.

"Perhaps you aren't yet at the critical mass of finished products and materials required to get the business under control. We have no choice on this one, David. It has to be your top priority! Do you have another approach?" But David was in no mood to compromise on his principles.

"Do you realize that one of the things you just asked me to do is to begin forecasting sales? In other words, decide what Field Sales is going to sell and make sure I have plenty of it on hand in the warehouses. You already have Kari's group doing forecasting; my group should be planning a schedule to deliver against those forecasts, not second-guessing Kari's forecast. Fact is, we are already doing some forecasting. The only thing that drives Sales is its quarterly forecast, and that is in total dollars. Kari's forecasters take whatever information they can get from Sales and try to predict what will be sold by SKU, but they aren't very good at it. In my opinion, those forecasts are guesses at best. We start with Kari's forecasts and add some of our own intelligence based on shipment history to decide what to schedule. Let me give you an example, Greg. We know that Sales traditionally underforecasts some products so they can oversell and meet their quotas. On new products, we schedule what the product team wants for the launch and pipeline fill. We don't want to run out of a new product, but we also know Sales will not meet those targets. Bottom line, we have to second-guess the forecasts, but shouldn't be in the forecasting business at all. We are simply not close enough to the customer." David was getting agitated and tried to calm down as he continued.

"On the manufacturing side, we give Tony manufacturing schedules and arrange for materials to be on hand to support those schedules. We even keep some extra materials on hand to allow for last-minute changes. My master schedulers in the plants spend a good deal of time making sure we have enough materials and capacity to support the schedules, but then Tony's group gets in the act. They take phone calls from the field, respond to requests from product development and marketing and forget to tell the schedulers about maintenance needs and line trials requested by Product Development. By the time we send a schedule to the floor, it's obsolete and the calls begin to come in about the need to expedite materials from suppliers to run something that's not even on the schedule. At month end, we never know what Tony might be running. He overrides the schedule to run products that run with high efficiency so that he meets his overhead absorption, efficiency, and utilization targets for bonus calculation. Before you ask me, the answer is yes; we have talked about these issues in the Leadership Team, but functional objectives always seem to override business objectives."

David eased back in his chair while Greg at last sensed the tension and tried to be less aggressive. "Thanks for your candor, David. Like everyone else so far, you have given me a lot to think about. I like your explanation about how a supply chain ought to work. It seems to me it's a good theory, but I don't see how it could work like that in our kind of business. Things are always changing between us, our customers, suppliers, and even competitors. What's clear to me is that we have to get enough of the right product out in the distribution centers so that the customers can have whatever they want whenever they want it. I'm counting on you to help make that happen. Furthermore, it has to happen soon." David grasped the olive branch, but knew that the branch came with some significant thorns. He sensed that Greg needed more coaching about supply chain operation.

"You can count on me to do everything I can to make the business successful. And I must tell you that my supply chain description is not just theory. It works. I'm sure some of our competitors hurting us today have their supply chains fine-tuned. We'll probably have to take some well-orchestrated emergency steps to get out of the hole, but we're going to have to figure out how to overhaul our supply chain mechanics if we are to have any sustainable improvements."

Greg decided to explore his concerns from previous interviews about the use of the business system. "You didn't mention the ERP system, David. Shouldn't that have taken care of most of the problems you've described? Don't your people know how to use the system?" David was quickly back on the defensive.

"That's another misconception, Greg. The ERP system does not solve problems; it's just a tool. My folks spent countless hours in training on how to create schedules, launch purchase orders, update bills of material, release products for shipment, check inventories, and create item masters and routings for capacity planning. They are all fully qualified and know how to use the system."

Greg posed an "innocent" question. "So they are using the system effectively to run the business, but still getting poor results?" But his annoyance broke through again. David snapped back at Greg's sarcasm.

"I sure hope you are not getting too angry with me for being candid, Greg, but you are wrong on two accounts. First, my staff is not getting poor results, although the business is. They are working harder than any group I've led. My staff is getting good results; they are producing schedules based in large part on the forecasts we get from Sales; they are giving schedules to Manufacturing to support those forecasts; and they are arranging for materials and capacity needed to produce those schedules.

"Second, they are using the system, but not to run the business. The system was configured in a way that makes scheduling and materials requirements planning extremely cumbersome. Coupled with the poor data and transaction accuracy, the recommendations that come out of the system are so erroneous that if the planners made decisions based on those recommendations, our business results would be far worse than they are now. So they use the system to store data, but they really run the business with the spreadsheets they have always been using."

Greg could see he was not being constructive, so he sought out safer territory. "Thanks for providing straight answers. It may seem like it, but I'm not getting angry with you. I am simply beginning to realize that the problems we face are far deeper than I ever imagined. I guess that comes out as frustration and anger as I learn more. Don't take it personally, David. You are doing exactly what I asked for when we met as a team on Tuesday. Susan told me you had a great grasp of how a supply chain should work, and she was right. Where did the knowledge come from?"

David relaxed, knowing this was neutral ground.

"My degree program began to introduce me to the concepts and theory, but I didn't have an opportunity to work in industry as part of a co-op program or during the summers. As I began my career, it quickly became clear that I needed additional education. I managed to get into some Effective Management courses where I learned about planning, top to bottom, from some very experienced people."

"What is this Effective Management group? I've not heard of them," Greg interrupted.

"Effective Management, Inc. is a global education and consulting company. They have an excellent reputation for helping companies improve their business processes resulting in bottom line improvements.

"As an aside, I managed to get myself invited to their Proven Path Club Business Excellence seminar, with topics presented by their own experts, and with case studies presented by people from industry. I'm sure I could get you an invitation to come with me to the next meeting in five weeks. You would learn more about how other companies are approaching their business issues, and especially the importance of good customer service." Greg now took control, and in a calmer mood continued. But he'd need to keep himself in better control in the future.

"Thanks for the invitation. I just might take you up on it once I get settled here. For now, I think I need every available moment to help formulate a plan to turn around our results. I'm glad you're on our team. I think you can provide some fresh ideas about how to get the results we need from our supply chain. Let's spend the rest of the afternoon looking at the details of planning, the production capability of our supply chain, and what's out in the distribution centers."

As David left the office, Greg compiled his notes from the meeting:

April 3

David Simpson, VP Supply Chain

1. Interesting grasp of the supply chain; has ideas that sound good, but seems like too much theory that will take too much time to implement and get results.

   Action: See which of the concepts could be implemented now and deliver quick results.

2. David has responsibility for what gets made and when. Why can't he either determine the business needs better, or get his message about the supply chain planning needs across to Kari and Tony?

   Action: Coach him on the importance of customer service and how to work better with others on the leadership team.

(Continued)

(*Continued*)

3. Supports his planning group as doing excellent work, just like every other VP I have interviewed this week. How can each leader feel good about their people and their results while our business results are in free fall?

   Action: Establish some clear business objectives for the Leadership Team.

4. He may have a point about the value of sharing customer service perspectives, but there is too much to work on here to get involved just now.

   Action: Defer David's invitation to an Effective Management Proven Path Club Business Excellence seminar.

5. Appears that everyone is avoiding using the ERP system. Explains why we have not seen the benefits to date.

   Action: Make it clear to everyone that I expect everyone to use the system starting now.

"You may be overreacting a bit, Greg." Stu finished up a brief conversation with Greg as they headed for the parking lot at 6:30 PM. "You have good people in place and they are working hard. I've pressed them a good deal on the recent decline in results and they each have made a compelling case about the business turning around soon. I know you are eager to show improvement to Susan and the Board, but be careful you don't push your people too hard. We are probably just one invention away in Development. A product breakthrough and a brilliant marketing campaign is what did it for us in Personal Products. It will happen here, too. Just be patient. I'll tell Susan the same thing so she doesn't crowd you too much or too early. Have a good evening, Greg, and give my best to Penny."

Greg reviewed the day with Penny over dinner. He was still convinced that clear priorities and direction from the top were required. A breakthrough invention would be nice, but he couldn't wait for a miracle like the one that propelled Personal Products.

Greg's meeting agenda on Thursday would include discussions with Zachary Zellers, VP Human Resources; and Gabriella Jemison, VP Regulatory, Health, Safety, and Environment, (HSE), and Quality. He expected no surprises in these interviews. Susan had prepared Greg well for what he would hear.

Greg Meets Zachary Zellers

Zachary was bright and had done a great job through the period of acquisition and downsizing. He explained to Greg his functional responsibilities and how he organized his HR plans to meet the expectations of Keely Horton, Senior VP.

The company had done an excellent job of keeping in touch with and anticipating the needs of its workforce. As a result, they enjoyed a good working relationship between managers and their people; the staff was well educated and trained; and there had never been a need for a union to represent the employees. They also discussed at length the compensation and reward systems. Of specific interest to Greg was the incentive portion of compensation.

That led to Greg's follow-up note from the session:

April 4

Zachary Zellers, VP Human Resources

1. Zach operates and acts like a long-term Amalgamated executive. Can't tell he is from an acquisition. Respects the capabilities of the Sr. VP and works well with her. Seems to be a pro at HR.

   Action: Find out more about why others haven't made the transition to Amalgamated equally well.

2. Incentives are in place for most managers, both options and cash for senior managers. Appear to be very functionally oriented, and most managers are running near the maximum allowed in the plan.

   Action: Work with HR to modify the incentive program to put more weight on overall business results and less on functional results.

3. Corporate HR and Board Compensation Committee closely control compensation plans.

   Action: Discuss with Keely Horton and Susan how to get approval of the modified plan.

Greg Meets Gabriella Jemison

Gabriella was energetic and every bit as knowledgeable about regulatory and environmental requirements as had been described by Susan. She explained how her Quality Assurance and Laboratory operations were organized and how she was working to reduce unnecessary costs. "We will take no unnecessary risks. I can assure you of that, Greg. And I'll make both you and your Senior VP, Henry Stinson, aware of any changes before they happen."

It was already late in the afternoon when Greg completed the review with Gabriella. He finished the day reviewing marketing plans, then completed his notes from the meeting with Gabriella.

April 4

Gabriella Jemison, VP Regulatory, Health/Safety/Environment, and Quality

1. Gabriella is fully on board as a Cosmetics Products executive. No hint she was from an acquisition.

   Action: Same as with Zachary Zellers on why her transition seems more complete than others. Perhaps they have a stronger focus on the customer and less on protecting their turf.

2. Gets very excited about quality, environmental, and regulatory issues. Works well and knows how to take advantage of her experience and the legal skills of Henry Stinson.

Greg Meets Tony Caruso

Greg arrived at the office Friday at 6:30 A.M. to prepare for his last VP interview, this one with Tony Caruso, VP Manufacturing. He reviewed his notes from the meetings with the other VPs to help him recall the specific issues he intended to follow up with Tony. But he first asked Tony about the plant managers.

"Brion Smith and Savannah Richmond are excellent General Managers, Greg. We did a good job of assessing the resources we had available after acquisition and put the very best of the lot in charge of our two plant sites. Their results in the face of some pretty tough challenges are as good as anyone could expect."

"Here we go again," thought Greg, "Another group doing superb work while the business is going down in flames."

"I have to be straight with you, Tony. Over the past few days, I've heard more than a couple of concerns raised about Manufacturing. I'd like to hear your perspective about some of the conflicts." Tony leaned forward in his chair.

"Doesn't surprise me even a little bit that people were taking shots at us. We are a big, visible target and take some stands for the good of the business that ruffle feathers from time to time. Give me some examples of what you heard and I'll give you my perspective." So Greg dove in.

"Let's start with Sales and Marketing. Why don't you describe the working relationship between your organization and Kari's?" Tony knew this was coming, so he'd mentally prepared what he wanted to say, and wanted to be diplomatic with his response.

"I'll be the first to admit they have a really tough job. They have to figure out what people want, and then design the products that people will buy. We can debate all day about how well they do that job. Sales doesn't move the new products we build for launches. By the way, those products keep changing up to the last minute, and even later than that sometimes. Can you believe that we have actually had to stop production of new products, scrap or salvage the materials and start all over with a new package, or a new fragrance, or a new color? I don't know whether that's just poor market insight, or indecision. When you sit in an ivory tower, with no concept of what it takes to actually make products, it's real easy to say 'Stop production, make that change, but don't delay start of shipments!' All marketing people should have to spend at least a couple years in Manufacturing to get a grasp of reality. But even with all those changes, if Sales can't move what we make, I question how well we are designing new products and promotions for that matter." Tony looked up, as if for empathy before continuing.

"We build those products, often on overtime because Development gets the specifications to us late, then the products sit in the warehouse. Know what happens next? I get a call from Stu or from Finance asking why I have so much of that product in inventory. Now while I'm building those new products that aren't going to sell, and struggling through the start-up learning curve, Sales decides to promote some other product. Guess who they don't tell about it? Manufacturing, of course. Know what happens next? I get a call from Stu or from Sales asking why I ran them out of that product." Tony was running out of diplomacy fast as he continued.

"Sales is supposed to be accountable for forecasting, according to everything I read. I think they must be using a random number generator for that task because the forecast never resembles what we are asked to ship. If we ran to their forecast or to what's on the planners' schedule, I would probably be the first person to be fired. We wouldn't have half as good a customer service record as we have now. I am certain Kari and David told you that we ignore their forecasts and the master schedules, and run what we want. If they said that, they are only partly right. We always start our batch scheduling process with those forecasts and master schedules, but then we apply some of our historical perspective and Manufacturing intuition. It's a good thing that we do. We've saved the company a ton of money. Even at that, there's not a day that goes by that we don't get at least one phone call from the Field asking for product to cover an emergency order. I could understand if that happened only occasionally but, for example, how can Sales get an order from a brand-new customer and be surprised by it? Someone out there had to have an idea that order was coming before it showed up as an emergency. They need to start talking with us earlier. I can even show you examples of orders placed by customers two weeks earlier but that didn't print out in the shipping office until the day we were supposed to ship them. Where have those orders been for two weeks? The shop floor schedulers have been doing their best to fill all those orders, but I'm about to put an end to that." Greg reacted immediately with a sharp edge to his voice.

"Why would you do that, Tony? Turn away those orders and we lose volume, customer service gets even worse, and costs go up. Sounds like you are being a bit inflexible to me." Tony knew this wasn't going well.

"You've got it exactly backward, boss. It's way too expensive to do business that way. Those emergency orders cause unscheduled product changes. Changing from one product to another is no small task. We've been working to reduce the time required, but it can still take more than a shift for some of those changeovers. During the time we are changing from one product to the next, we make nothing. When that happens, customer service gets worse, not better; volume goes down, not up; and costs go up, not down." But Greg wasn't giving up yet.

"If you follow the schedule and put enough of the right product in inventory, couldn't you avoid those extra changeovers altogether?" Tony was now exasperated, and it showed.

"Sure, but tell that to the forecasters and to the planners. I would love to simply produce to the master schedule. It would make my job easier. But between constantly changing forecasts, production schedules, and emergency orders, that's impossible! My job is to optimize the use of your supply capacity and resources. That forces us to do our own forecasting, decide what's best to run, and to say 'no' on occasion to Sales, Marketing, and Planning." But Greg hadn't finished either.

"Tell me about how our current incentives might influence what you produce at the end of the month. I understand that Manufacturing might produce product that isn't on the schedule or even needed while we are cutting orders for other products. Any truth to that?" Tony decided not to back down, knowing far more about manufacturing than Greg.

"Sounds like some other groups are whining about our ability to maximize the bonus part of our compensation! It's not quite like they say it is. We never produce product that we don't need. We might produce it earlier than absolutely needed, however. The forecasts and schedules change so much that we don't put much faith in them, as I've already said. One of my responsibilities is to help my folks maximize their compensation within the policy and rules set up by HR. If, at the end of the month, we have been battered by unplanned changeovers or other problems, and other conditions are right, we will look forward in the schedule, and pull in some product that we know will be needed to run in the future anyway. If that helps the bonus picture, it is a win-win change. If the forecasts get better and the schedules stabilize, we'll run to schedule, and let the bonus chips fall where they may. Until then, I have to call the shots in terms of what we run." Before Greg could get a word in edgewise, Tony forged ahead!

"And there's another side to this story, Greg. We do have too much inventory. We are soon going to have to look for more warehouse space unless Sales begins selling the product that we already have. Have you asked Kari about that? We make an attempt to run what they want, especially with new product launches and promotions. We can show you a history of low-balling the forecasts on our big, open stock products, but invariably the new products sit in warehouses until we have to repackage it, sell it as distressed goods, or scrap it. When we were making that stuff, we could have been making product that Sales actually intended to sell. Now, that's a problem far worse than running product a little early so that I can reward my Manufacturing folks. Has Stu or anyone else told Sales to stop selling what's easy to sell and to sell the products we already have?

I don't think so. That's one way you could solve some of the problems in this division and make a name for yourself, Greg." Greg realized Tony was on a roll, and was digging a very deep hole for himself, so he let him continue.

"And then there is also the requirement to meet the overhead absorption goal. If we miss that one, we get hammered financially right in our wallets. From my standpoint, that's an old and useless financial measure that doesn't help the business. If sales are off, we shouldn't be running more products to put in the warehouses. But if we stop running, we are penalized by Finance, and then Sales uses us as the excuse for not having enough of the right products. While I'm talking about Finance, they give us standards that are totally unrealistic. You can see that in the variances each month. As a result, any finance report will show Manufacturing to be doing poorly while my measures show good perform-ance results. I don't know what they do with the budget numbers we send up, but it's pretty clear they don't need to know much about manufacturing to count beans." Greg knew it was time exercise his authority in this conversation.

"Just to be clear, Tony, I'm not interested in making a name for myself, but I am interested in delivering the business results Susan and the Board are expecting. That will take all of us working together. It also means that you will have to figure out how to resolve the differences you have with most of your peers." Tony now knew he'd gone too far.

"I thought you wanted facts and opinions, Greg. That's what I just gave you. Perhaps I shouldn't have been so open." Greg felt like throwing him out, but tried to complete the conversation on his own terms.

"Not at all, Tony. Being open and direct with each other is the only way we will turn the results around. But we can't just be direct; we need to resolve some of the issues that face us, and that means working better as a team. I expect you and the rest of us to do a better job of that. If we have disagree-ments, I expect them to be worked out quickly and creatively. If we can't work them out together, I'll make the decisions. Any decision is better than the internal disagreements I see here in Cosmetics Products." Greg changed tack.

"One last topic, Tony. Give me your impression of how the ERP system is working. I understand we started up without some of the major problems other companies have seen, but we aren't getting the results predicted. What do you think?" Tony had calmed himself down by now and was eager to reply.

"All my people are trained to use the system, but other than keeping track of inventory, my folks say it makes their jobs harder. Today they have to load data into the system, and still have to put data into their spreadsheets. They use those spreadsheets to run the business." Now on safer ground, or so he thought, Greg continued.

"That's what I expected to hear, Tony. A number of people have told me a similar story. I have one other request. I would like to meet Brion Smith and Savannah Richmond and tour their plants with you in the next couple weeks. Can you arrange that for me?" With relief that the interview was coming to and end, Tony replied.

"Sure can. The plant people will be happy to see you and show you what they are doing. I'll check their schedules and work out the details with Cynthia. Let you know tomorrow."

After Tony left the office, Greg spent a few minutes sitting in his desk chair and looking out over the lawn and into the woods beyond the building as he decompressed and organized his thoughts. He then turned to his notes to record highlights from the last of the interviews with members of his leadership team.

April 5

Tony Caruso, VP Manufacturing

1. No question that Tony is a manufacturing pro, but appears to be difficult to work with. No one outside his organization seems to do anything that satisfies him.

   Action: Observe further on plant visits to see if his attitude has spread to other plants, in which case he will delay progress.

2. Quick to point out problems in other areas, but didn't take responsibility for own shortcomings, for example, late requests for process design changes that Matt mentioned.

3. Bit of a wild card; likes freedom to decide how to run his shop.

   Action: Find out how much of this was condoned and/or encouraged by Stu?

4. First impressions tell me Tony is far too manufacturing numbers myopic in his views and decisions.

   Action: High Priority—develop a succession plan if he cannot become the team player we need running Manufacturing.

Greg reviewed all his notes before closing the office and heading for home late Friday afternoon. Over the weekend he tried to clear his mind while attending his youngest son's soccer game, and then going out for dinner and a late movie with Penny. It didn't work. He kept refining the action plan in his mind. He awoke on Saturday and Sunday mornings at 5:00 A.M. with his mind racing. Each morning he decided to get up and try to put an action plan on paper in his home office. During the following two weeks, Greg continued his learning process in meetings with other key people in the organization, including his peers who led the other Amalgamated divisions. He also completed the plant and customer visits arranged by Kari and Tony.

On April 14, he asked his leadership team to clear their morning calendars for an April 22nd meeting with him. The agenda was to include a summary and analysis of what he had learned about the business and the organization, and to present a clear set of priorities for moving the business forward.

3

GREG'S DIRECTIVES

The "enemy" is outside the walls of our buildings, but any outside observer who has heard what I've heard would believe that the enemy is inside. That must end now.

The Leadership Team gathered early on the morning of April 22 and talked quietly in twos or threes until Greg entered the conference room. He invited the team to take their seats.

"I want you to know how much I appreciate your clearing schedules to allow us to meet this morning. I also want you to know just how much I appreciate all the information you've been sharing to help get me up to speed quickly. You've done everything I've asked, and you couldn't have given me a better introduction to the company. Thanks especially to you, Kari, and to you, Tony, for arranging visits to our key customers and our plants. Those were beneficial trips and really helped me understand how the business is working today.

"As you know, Susan and the Board are expecting great things from us. They expect us to turn the business around quickly. I would like to take it a step further. My vision is that within 10 years, Cosmetics Products will be the largest, most profitable operating division in Amalgamated Consumer Products and one of the top five largest producers of cosmetics products in North America."

That statement brought the leadership team upright and to the edges of their chairs. Glances were exchanged among Greg's Leadership Team before there was a consensus of nods and smiles. It was a clearly stated vision and was already energizing the team. It was also, by definition, a breakthrough vision since no one in the room had any idea how they could make it happen.

They all tacitly agreed, however, that it was a vision worthy of a strong leader and just might get the organization moving.

"I sense as I look around the room that you can buy into that vision. That is very important because it will take enormous effort and will require each of us to change the way we do our work. Further, it won't happen overnight or be driven by wishful thinking. It will take more hard work than you can imagine. I will understand if any individual wants to opt out. If you do, let me know by tomorrow morning and I'll work with you to make the transition out of the business more than fair to you. If you are in, I want you to let me know that, too. I won't put you on the spot now; let's do that one-to-one later today or first thing in the morning.

"What I'll share with you today are some specific directives and marching orders that will get us started as we work together to clarify our strategy and action steps. My overall assessment, based on my three weeks here, is that the Amalgamated strategy is excellent. The Cosmetics Products strategy is supportive and pretty close to what it needs to be, but lacks clarity. It needs some work and a more precise statement of the future to better match the environment we're in. Our execution of the strategy we do have has been something less than poor. That's why I am going to state my expectations today.

"Just so you know, I discussed this yesterday at great length with Stu. He is in fundamental agreement, but thinks I am being a bit too aggressive. He continues to believe we should be patient, push for a product breakthrough, and then marshal all the 'marketing brilliance' we can pull together to propel the division into a leadership position. As you might have guessed by now, I am not that patient; nor is Susan; nor is the Board. We either turn the business around very soon, or Amalgamated might be back to three divisions again. That will not happen on my watch!

"On May 1, I will share this information and direction with Susan. I expect that by then we will have taken many of these steps and will be delivering some early positive results. If you have any concerns about the directives I lay out, or believe I have misinterpreted any information you shared with me, let me know before I go to Susan. Otherwise, I'll expect complete alignment and support from each of you. The 'enemy' is outside the walls of our buildings, but any outside observer who has heard what I've heard would believe that the enemy is inside. That must end now. Any questions before I begin?"

No one voiced any questions or concerns, but the tension in the room was plainly evident. To date, no one had heard Greg speak so directly or seriously. He seemed to be a different person.

"First I want to say right up front that each of you, and every individual that works for us for that matter, is a part of Amalgamated Consumer Products Corporation's Cosmetics Products division. Our old companies no longer exist. We are members of the same team and must start behaving like we are. That means we adopt some common procedures and stop comparing how we do things here with how we used to do them in our old companies.

"Next, you were open with me. Now I want you to be open with each other. If one of you has a problem with what someone is doing or how someone is performing, I want you to talk with that person and decide together what to do about it. If you can't resolve the difference, let me know and I will help facilitate resolution. We must stop wasting time and energy with internal conflicts that only drain energy.

"Now let me turn to some operational expectations I have. It is no secret that our results are unacceptable. I wish all of you could have been with Kari and me when we visited our customers. They told us pointedly that we are unreliable suppliers. They and their customers like the quality and value of our products, but they all told us that we are costing them money when our shelf space or display pegs are empty. I might add that those empty spaces are also costing us money and are delighting our competitors. From this point on, I want a daily report of any orders shorted or shipped late. Every one; every day. I expect that report to include an analysis of the cause and the action steps being taken to eliminate the problem.

"Beginning right now, we will operate from the position that all customer orders are sacred. We will no longer tolerate not having the product to ship when we get an order. To that end, beginning next week we will meet every Friday afternoon at three to reach agreement on the following week's volume forecast and quarterly volume forecast, and to look at our performance against volume and profit commitments for the month and quarter to date. If we are behind, I expect a plan to catch up, and I want recommendations on how to keep from getting in that position again. Kari and Sara, I would like you to lead those meetings. By the way, Kari, I would like your Sales and Marketing directors, Charlie and Sharon, to participate in those meetings every week, even if it's by conference call."

Zachary offered a suggestion. "Greg, I recommend that we have those meetings on Thursday afternoons. I don't mind staying here until well after six during the week and normally do, but I like to get an early start on the weekend. I know that's true for several of us on the team. Anything magic about Friday?"

"When we meet, Zach, I want us to have all the information possible to predict the upcoming week and assess what happened in the current week. But you may have a good idea. Our biggest customer has similar meetings every Saturday morning. Given their history of growth and the fact that they are the largest company in the free world, they may be on to something. Would anyone prefer Saturday morning over Friday afternoon?" The meeting time remained as scheduled, Friday at 3 P.M.

Tony spoke up, "Could I ask a clarifying question, Greg?"

"Of course you may, Tony."

"What do we do when one of the Field Sales people places an order for a product that exceeds the entire inventory that we have in the distribution system?"

"That's an issue that you and Kari need to discuss and resolve. If you need my help after you've talked, let me know. Just remember, we will operate as though customer orders are sacred. We don't cut product from orders and let the customer find out about it when the truck arrives at their dock. This is especially critical in the first three months of a product launch. Let me be perfectly clear. There is just no acceptable excuse for cutting a customer order during the first three months of a launch." Everyone shifted uncomfortably in their chairs.

"Closely associated with that is how we utilize our supply organization's assets. On paper we have plenty of manufacturing capacity, but based on what I observed in the plants, we are spending too much unplanned time changing from one product to another. A couple of key performance measures that I will look at monthly include our efficiency and our utilization of those assets. In other words, the percentage of the hours in the week the production assets are actually running, and how close they are coming to producing ideal output during those operating hours.

"By running more steadily and better, I expect that we can build the inventory we need to improve customer service. I know our warehouses are bulging at the seams, but I think the problem is that we have underestimated the amount of inventory it takes to provide good customer service in this industry. Building more inventory will increase costs, but costs are not our most pressing problem today. We simply have to eliminate customer service problems in a hurry to buy the time we need to work on costs. I'll make sure Susan knows our direction and that our first priority is customer service. I know Susan well enough to know that she will be totally supportive.

"Tony, I expect you to keep me informed of our performance and let me know what you are doing if we are headed in the wrong direction on those measures, or, for that matter, if we are running at maximum capacity and still can't keep up with shipments.

"Kari, there's a piece of this measure that's up to Sales. I want a plan on my desk a week from today that shows how we are going to start selling some of the product that is still in the warehouse from older product launches and promotions. We need to do a better job of selling what we already have while Tony gets caught up on the products that have a low inventory level. I would also like to know just how much of our total inventory falls into that category. David, I'd like you to help gather that information for Kari. It's great that Field Sales can oversell forecast on the products that are easy to sell. I want to see them begin to oversell forecast across the board!"

Tony started to object to that directive, but stopped just as quickly as he started when Greg continued without pause.

"Additionally, Kari, I want you to rein in the entertainment spending your Sales team is doing. That shouldn't be a problem since we will be improving the customer service results. The money saved can go directly to fund your marketing plans. And I want the marketing campaigns to be more effective in building the business.

"Let me go back to new product launches for a minute. We will not delay the product launch dates in the future. We will begin following the formal launch protocol today. If there is any probability that an issue will delay a launch, I want to know about it immediately. I also want a recommendation about what to do to resolve the issue. Matt, I'll look to you for that. If, for some reason, there is no way to overcome the issue, I will make the delay decision. I fully expect that I will never have to make that decision.

"Finally, two other points about cost control. Until we get the business growing again, and with the exception of routine purchases of materials required to make our products, I want to make any purchase decision over $50,000. David, I'll expect you to ensure that those purchases of raw and packaging materials are reasonable and absolutely required to run the business. I also want each of you to personally approve any other expenditure over $5,000 requested by people in your organizations.

"One other thought, Kari. If you would like me to go over these points with Charlie and Sharon, I would be happy to do that. Same offer is in place for you, Tony, with Savannah and Brion. Just let me know. Other than that, any questions?"

Greg answered a few minor clarifying questions, but was surprised that the normally vocal group was so silent. He offered them the use of the conference room for the rest of the morning and excused himself. Greg suggested they use the time to begin working on plans to carry out the new directives.

After Greg left the room, they all agreed that they had just entered a new era. Stu had never been so direct or intense with them as Greg was in this meeting. There was no question that the baton had been passed. With that transition came the weight of accountability they had not felt in quite the same way before. The vision of being Amalgamated's largest division and a key player in the industry was galvanizing to the team. They talked together for the next two hours about how they could make that happen, but each of them had unspoken reservations about their collective ability to pull it off.

On May 1, having had no one opt out and no significant input from his team, and having made no changes to the directives he set out just a week before, Greg met with Susan as she had requested. He reviewed the current operating results, marketing and sales initiatives, new product plans, and the results from his visits with key customers. Greg was particularly optimistic about the launch of "Quiet Nights," a new aromatherapy formulation that had a remarkable ability to provide consumers a restful night's sleep despite their level of daily stress. Perhaps it would be that breakthrough product Stu had been counting on. Greg explained to Susan, however, that he was not counting on any particular product to deliver a quick turnaround. He reviewed with her the meeting with his Cosmetics Products Leadership Team. He covered each directive, his rationale, and the expected results. Greg made a compelling presentation and assured Susan that these action steps had worked for him in the past, although he had never been in a position that required taking all of them simultaneously; and he hoped to start delivering business results within the next three months.

Susan asked some probing strategy questions. From his answers, it was obvious to Susan that Greg was confident about his plan. She certainly hoped it would deliver the results she needed. She especially liked the plan for a weekly meeting in which the leadership team would agree on the monthly and quarterly plans to close any gaps.

Greg finished his presentation by reviewing his assessment of the Cosmetics Products Leadership Team, the development plans he had in mind for each individual, and his concerns about some of them, including Tony's apparent inflexibility. Susan was impressed.

"You've done a magnificent job of quickly getting your arms around Cosmetics Products, as I knew you would. It sounds like the plan you shared should stabilize the business and get it growing again. My next request of you is to do a deeper review of the overall business strategy. I would like your thoughts about the current mix of products, services, and channels, what additional lines we might add and what potential consumer needs we should be addressing. I still believe, as you do, that Cosmetics Products will be the biggest and most profitable division. Nothing would make the Board and me happier. I'll get an hour on the Board's agenda in July so that we can present our updated strategy and plans for Cosmetics Products."

It had been a tough month of travel, meetings, and long hours, but Greg was pleased with his accomplishments during his first month as President. He had taken the reins and was obviously in control. Stu suggested that he and Greg switch offices and that he spend very little time in the office. Stu wanted the Leadership Team to see that he was no longer running the show. "I'll be on call for you, Greg, either at home or on the golf course. Don't think twice about picking up the phone and calling me about anything at any time." What Stu did not say was that he had some serious reservations about the radical changes Greg was making. He did not want to be seen as responsible for the fallout he suspected was coming. He had told Greg to be patient, but that was not in Greg's make up. Greg quickly agreed to Stu's offer since he, too, wanted to be seen by the staff as the clear leader of the business.

The transfer of Presidents was completed a month early. The stage had been set. Greg was confident it was now only a matter of time, hard work, and follow-up with his staff until the results improved.

4

BREAKDOWN

*If you think you know all the answers, chances are you may
not even understand the questions.*

A breakthrough may first require a complete breakdown.

I push them, and results get worse.

After lunch on the first Monday in July, two months after Greg's meeting
with Susan, business results were looking no better as Greg prepared for his
Leadership Team's monthly planning meeting. In fact, results continued to
trend downward across the board. Profits were still declining. Costs were still
increasing. Despite building larger inventories, as Greg had requested, the
supply organization didn't yet seem to have enough inventory, or the right mix
of inventory, to deliver improved customer service results. On the bright side,
Manufacturing was delivering improved numbers. Utilization and efficiency
numbers had risen markedly, but so had the expense for both inbound and
outbound premium freight. This didn't make sense to Greg. "How can inventory increase and shop floor utilization improve, but customer service get
worse all at the same time?" he thought to himself.

His new weekly meetings were taking place every Friday so that Greg's
team could agree on the forecast and make plans to close any gaps between the
latest prediction and their firm volume and profit commitments. These meetings had been getting longer and less productive over the past eight weeks.
From beginning to end, the meetings consisted of arguments over what the
forecast numbers should be. Greg usually made the final call. One thing was
certain. Their ability to forecast the business was poor at best. Perhaps Kari

was right when she told Greg back in April that it might be nearly impossible to forecast this business. He was glad he had decided to build finished product inventory, but frustrated that the increase had not yet delivered the customer service improvement he had promised Susan.

Following the detailed results review that began every monthly planning meeting, Greg addressed his team. "It looks like almost all the results are headed in the wrong direction. Even most of the function-specific results are dropping, and that hasn't happened in the past, at least that I know of. Next week I'll be meeting with Susan to give her an update on our progress. I'm not looking forward to that meeting. As you have just seen, there is little good news to share beyond improved operating utilization and efficiencies on the shop floor. Good work, Tony! Beyond that, I am hard pressed to come up with enough good news to satisfy either Susan or me. You all look at the same results. See any good news that I'm missing?" David broke the silence.

"I hate to be the person to pour cold water on the only improved result that you highlighted, but that improvement just might be part of the problem." Greg was puzzled.

"I'm not following you at all, David. How does Tony's running better cause us to have worse results?" David decided to lead Greg rather than tell him.

"Let me ask Tony to clarify something for us, Greg. Tony, can you tell us what you've done to increase your utilization and operating efficiencies?" Tony smiled and replied.

"Easy one to answer, David. Our direction from Greg was to get better utilization and to build inventories. We accomplished both with one simple change. We now run longer cycles. When we change from product to product we stretch out the run as long as we can. That operating strategy puts more of each product in the warehouse and allows us to avoid running that product again for a much longer period. As a result, we have reduced product changeovers, built inventory, and improved our operating results, including unit cost and overhead absorption. It's really quite simple."

Kari jumped into the discussion, "Why don't you actually try running what we forecast or what we're selling for a change? We have over a year's forward coverage on some of our products while we're almost out on others. Still making maximum bonus, aren't you Tony?" Tony rose to the attack.

"You could actually try selling product that we have, Kari. We have over a year's coverage because your people sell what's easy to move. Have them sell what's in the warehouse for a change!"

"That's enough from both of you," Greg admonished. "Let's keep the dialogue constructive and return to where we were, David. Tony seems to be doing exactly what I asked him to do. How does that hurt our results?" David could see that Greg still didn't get it. Time to open the can of worms.

"Over the past two months it hasn't hurt us as much as I expect it will in the third quarter. Since May, it's true that our overall inventory level has been increasing in the distribution network. But if you look closely, the number of SKUs below safety stock has also been growing. Tony is running as long as he possibly can on each product, but when we get an unexpected surge of orders on one of those SKUs below safety stock, he has to expedite the changeover. That often takes overtime personnel, requires the planners to rework the schedule, frequently necessitates using airfreight to get the materials to make the short product, and sometimes even requires shipping the finished product by air. I know that cost control is our number two objective for now; that's not my concern. My concern is that the number of SKUs below safety stock is growing rapidly and will require even more frequent emergency production changes and expediting in the near future. Eventually the long cycle time strategy might do the trick, if we live to tell the story; but in the interim, I think we are going to see even worse customer service results." Tony wasn't going to let that go.

"Seems to me like we're right back to where we were two months ago; blame Manufacturing. Look, I agreed to build inventory and improve operating up-time. I've delivered on both the objectives that are in my control. I can't help it if Sales oversells the forecast and causes a product shortage. Everyone here knows what we are producing today, and also knows what our schedule is for the next couple weeks. That's the product that will be available and that's the product Field Sales should push until the total inventory of all products is increased, as Greg requested. I have a good manufacturing organization, and we are building inventory fast, but we can't build the inventory of all products overnight! We are still reacting to too many product shortages, but I make the call not to change over to that short product if I think the long-term cost will outweigh the customer service benefit. I have to agree that I've noticed an increasing number of emergency product outages in the past month. But don't look at Manufacturing. What other organization is meeting Greg's objectives? I think we'd better look at a couple other areas besides Manufacturing, although Manufacturing is an easy target. I know a couple of those shortages were caused by product essentially disappearing from the distribution centers (DCs). If the ERP system stock record says inventory is on hand, it had better be on hand. That's another area we in Manufacturing don't control. David, that's your responsibility, not mine. And another area outside my control is the usefulness of the forecast. We all agreed to meet weekly to improve the forecast, but all you people do is argue about the numbers. Frankly, that meeting is a waste of my time. I haven't seen any improvement. Kari, that's your responsibility, not mine. There is no need to take more of the group's time on this disagreement. David and I will discuss this whole issue outside this meeting." Greg took command again.

"Okay, Tony, for now, but in a week I would like to see a plan you and David put together to grow inventory and at the same time reduce the number of SKUs below safety stock. Agreed?"

"Sure, boss."

"Speaking of forecasting, Tony says he has seen no improvement in our ability to forecast the business. Has anyone else noticed an improvement?"

Sara replied, "We see an improvement in cost forecasting because of the reduced variances from Manufacturing's longer run cycles; and run rates are now closer to standard. Additionally, spending has dropped pretty dramatically since you began signing all purchase orders over $50,000. Over the past month, however, we saw variances climbing again. The last discussion about an increasing number of emergency product changes explains that for me. We are still doing our financial forecasts the same way as before." Sara Miles continued. "We start with Kari's sales forecast and our cost standards, but then apply our experience and best-guess to improve the forecasted shipment numbers. Can't say we have made any significant progress."

Greg learned over the next half hour that sales forecasting was no better than before despite the weekly meetings. Each function was still developing its own forecast of future demand based on functional experience and was making its operating plans accordingly. It seemed that despite his clear direction two months ago, every person on his staff was still operating from a functional basis; there was no sign of the team he had envisioned.

"Kari, talk to us about the marketplace. Any signs of improving news on volume or service out there that I can share with Susan next week?" Kari wasn't pleased about being the bearer of bad news, but knew she would be.

"Wish I could give you some good news, but I can't. Our performance on the two new products we just launched, including our big hope, 'Quiet Nights,' was no better than any launch in the past couple of years. The objective of following the launch protocol more strictly may pay dividends eventually. But with these last two launches, we had a hard time even getting the attention of our customers. They just don't trust us to deliver on our promises any more. For those customers who did take the new products, we didn't make them believers. It wouldn't do much good to talk more about this problem here. It would waste everyone's time. Matt and I have set up a postmortem for those launches for next week. We'll let you know what we learned and what we will do differently in the future." Kari continued.

"As you requested, we have been examining the customer order failures and reviewing each one with you. What's frustrating to me is that there seems to be a new cause every time. We haven't spotted a quick fix so far, but hopefully we'll see a pattern soon and take action to improve the results. At this point, though, our service level is getting worse. What I just heard from David about the increasing number of SKUs below safety stock is unacceptable and depressing. We can't handle many more months like this. And we may be in for a battle on a new front, too. Charlie Beck heard from his people in the field that some of our key competitors are talking price reductions. We believe their strategy is to capitalize on our service problems and take away our shelf space."

Sara Miles jumped into the discussion. "If we try to match their price reductions, our financials quickly become unacceptable. There is little chance we could build enough volume to offset the hit we would take. It would be your decision, Greg, but I just can't support any kind of price war." This was worse than Greg expected, or believed possible.

"All right, folks. We'll look at the plan David and Tony pull together to build inventory and reduce the number of SKUs below safety stock. I don't think we can afford to wait for a week; better bring me what you have in two days, David. Also, if we have to continue shorting orders for a while, let's make sure it's not with our top 20 customers. Kari, give me your recommendation on whether we should go on allocation with some of our products. If we do, we'll try to keep it low key. We don't want to start a feeding frenzy among our customers or the competition. Do what you have to with smaller customers, including talking with them frequently, but continue to involve me in any decision to short our best accounts. In the meantime, get your salespeople serious about selling the products that we have in inventory. Work with Zachary and propose a change in the incentive package for our Field Sales people if necessary. I want them beating the forecast regularly. If they can't figure out which products to push and which to avoid from an inventory standpoint, have them call David." Greg's direction continued.

"In terms of product launch problems, get the new products out on time and flawlessly, Matt. I don't want to hear any more excuses for delays or service problems with new products or promotions. We have to change our image in the trade."

The meeting broke up at 6:00 PM, and Greg had nothing positive to add to his agenda for the upcoming meeting with Susan. He went through his e-mail, returned calls from a stack of phone messages, and took another look at the draft agenda for Susan's meeting. He arrived home after 7:30 P.M.

"Sorry I'm late again, Penny. Another long day." Penny couldn't hide her irritation.

"You know, I'm really getting worried about you, and so are the boys. Talk to me about what's going on. It certainly won't make you sleep less or feel worse!"

Greg apologized for his behavior and self-inflicted isolation during the past few months. After dinner, Greg and Penny went into the study to talk. Greg shared what had been going on since he took over as President.

"The directives you gave your staff seem pretty straightforward to me, although some of them are very controlling and un-Greg like. Why haven't people been following them?" Greg responded quietly and with a good deal of introspection.

"It seems to me that they have been trying, but the outcomes don't look much like what I envisioned or what I've experienced in the past when I've taken similar actions. I push them, and results get worse. Inventory goes up, but customer service gets worse. Manufacturing starts to run more efficiently, but costs keep climbing. I bring the leadership team together more frequently and talk more openly with them, but the relationships get worse and people start closing down. The outcomes of the actions are exactly 180 degrees from what I expected. It is completely baffling. I can't tell you how often people want to take a problem 'off line,' as they call it, rather than working it out together so we all can learn from the discussion. Between you and me, and I would never admit this to anyone else, I am beginning to wonder if I'm in over my head. I have never faced this many difficult business conditions at the same time, and I've never before had all the functions reporting directly to me. I take an action in one place, and something goes wrong in some other place. It seems there are interdependencies that keep things hopelessly tangled no matter what I do. I'm really getting concerned about my ability to do this job."

"I can tell that you're under enormous stress. Just a thought, Greg. Isn't there someone at work or in your network of peers who you can confide in and ask for ideas or a fresh perspective? Who is the most solid person on your staff? Can that person help?" Greg brightened up a little.

"Actually, there are a couple of pretty solid people. Sara knows finance and gives me a straight analysis of the financials when we are exploring ideas and options. David has a great command of how a supply chain should work. He is probably the most levelheaded and knowledgeable of my VPs. I think he has tremendous potential."

Penny cautioned Greg. "That's great, but I expect you can't share your innermost thoughts with either of those two since they report to you. How about among your peers?" Greg paused for a moment.

"I hadn't thought much about that, but I have a pretty good relationship with Roger Winchester, who runs Home Products. He is an old pro at being a business unit President, and I always enjoy talking with him. Doesn't seem real aggressive, but his results are good. I'm sure he's been through some rough times and would be willing to give me some advice." Penny encouraged him, "That's a great idea." Greg sounded a bit more cheerful.

"Here's what I think I want to do. First, I want to make sure people know I am still serious about the directives I put in place. I continue to believe they will help even though we haven't seen improved results yet. I'll go back over them at the next staff meeting just to make certain no one thinks I've backed off. Second, I'm not going to let people take issues 'off line.' We are a team, and we have to start listening and supporting each other. I know we can solve some of the problems if everyone will just get their cards on the table and agree to talk through them. I also need to look for some additional talent. I think we're going to need it. Specifically, I no longer think that Tony can stay with us. He seems to bring out the worst in everyone and is probably the single chief cause of poor team morale. It's time to make a move. I'll have to talk this one over with Susan first, though. I'm sure there is a big buyout that the Board will have to approve. Last, but not least, I'll call and make an appointment to see Roger as soon as I get the situation with Tony resolved. That should do it for now." Penny smiled.

"Sounds like the old Greg to me. Feel better?"

"I have a plan of sorts, thanks to you, and that always makes me feel better."

Greg began the next day early, as usual, but with a renewed sense of energy. He picked up the phone and called Susan, knowing that she would be at her desk already reviewing today's edition of the *Wall Street Journal*. She answered the phone on the first ring and greeted Greg. "How's it going with your game plan, Greg? Any signs of progress yet?"

"I really wish I could give you a bundle of good news, Susan, but I can't, at least not yet. I'll be clear with you when we have our regular meeting on the first of August, but for now I'll just say that our efforts to date haven't produced any significant improvements. I am not going to blow smoke or sugarcoat things. I think you already know that about me."

"Sure do, Greg. We don't have time for political games, and I know you don't like them any more than I. What can I do for you this morning?" Greg continued.

"I want to take you up on your offer about making a change in the organization. I expect this move will prompt some questions, but it's time to take action. You told me that Tony was a pro at his job and that I might find him a bit inflexible. You were right on both counts, as usual. He knows manufacturing and how to keep his people aligned and happy. Give him a manufacturing measure or objective, and he'll figure out a way to meet the target. Unfortunately, he does it in a way that allows him to look good while the company suffers. You were far too kind when you said he is inflexible. He sets the universal standard for inflexibility. Nothing he or his organization does is ever wrong. Whatever goes wrong is the fault of Sales, Product Development, Purchasing, or someone else, including me. Worse than that, he is a divisive member of the leadership team. When he is confronted about having large inventories of some of his products while an increasing number of products are below a safe inventory level, he is likely to report that he is doing his job well, his team is making the maximum bonus, and the fault lies in the Sales organization's not doing its job. He is absolutely draining the energy out of my team. Unless you tell me to back off, I am going to meet with him next Friday and tell him that it is his last day with us. I know there's probably a sizable buyout package that he's entitled to, but I think it will be worth the expense. Do I have your support?"

Without hesitation, Susan replied, "Of course you do, Greg, although I am a more than a bit surprised. Have you given him any warning that this might come to pass if he didn't change his ways?"

"Tony and I have had lots of talks since I arrived. And we had a pretty formal review of his performance about a month ago. He didn't like it; thought I was crowding his ability to run Manufacturing and siding too much with Sales and Marketing. He got a bit out of line, but I told him I could understand his frustration with the lack of positive business results. That can take a toll on anyone's psyche. I did make it clear, however, that I was not happy with his apparent resistance to my direction, his functional bias, or his overall ability to be a team player. I also told him that I was holding him personally accountable for becoming a good team player and doing a better job of meeting our customer service objectives. I followed up with a letter to him stating the particular performance patterns I wanted him to change. Since then, I haven't seen any difference or any noticeable effort to improve. All his actions continue to be about defending Manufacturing. Others on the team have already run out of patience with him." Susan sounded genuinely surprised.

"I had no idea he was that dysfunctional on the team. Stu never even mentioned that his behavior was causing problems. I do have one question, though. Isn't this a bit precipitous? Wouldn't you like to keep Tony around for a few weeks to train his replacement?" Greg was ready for that question.

"Absolutely not. I am afraid he would only poison his replacement's attitude and create hard feelings within the Leadership Team and in Manufacturing. The only reason I am delaying the move until next week is to give myself time to work with HR, and for you to take care of anything you might have to clear with your staff or the Board. I think the best strategy, by far, is to move ahead quickly, pay any package we are obligated to pay and get on with the business. I'll make certain we also offer him the package we offered others in terms of tuition and outplacement support. He'll be plenty upset; I want to help him save face if I can. No sense in creating a mortal enemy in the industry."

"Okay," said Susan, "but I have another question, Greg. Who will replace Tony? Will you have to go outside the company, or do you have someone within Amalgamated in mind? Going outside could add months to the process of replacing him. Either way, what will you do until someone else is in place and up to speed?"

"Well," said Greg, "I've been thinking about this possibility for several weeks. I have a solution that minimizes the transition time and reduces our budget at the same time. Both plant managers are solid people and manufacturing professionals. They know how to keep plants running, but they need more effective direction. I wouldn't call them change agents, but they will follow a strong leader. We've already seen that with Tony's leadership. We just need to give them better quality leadership. Temporarily, I'll have both plant managers report directly to me, but I intend to add Tony's manufacturing responsibilities to David's role."

Susan hesitated for a moment; then she asked, "Won't that be a stretch for David?"

"Perhaps for a while, but I believe he has plenty of capacity to take it on. The resulting organization design will match your Senior VP structure with Sam Elliott handling Manufacturing as a part of his Supply Chain role; it's a model that fully integrates all aspects of supplying goods and services. Sam will be a good role model and coach for David. As it is, David gets frustrated when his planners produce a schedule and Manufacturing essentially ignores it. Now David will have all the resources at his disposal to make sure that his schedules are actually executed. He has a great grasp of his current Supply Chain responsibilities and a good planning staff, so he should have the time to focus on his new responsibilities. After watching him for a few months, I agree with you that he has great potential and a much-needed grasp of how a supply chain should work. I think he'll do a fantastic job. Additionally, this approach is minimally disruptive to the organization and, as I mentioned earlier, reduces the budget as well."

"Okay, Greg. It's your call. You have my support. I'll review it with the Compensation Committee of the Board, but since they already gave me the green light to make any changes I thought appropriate, you can safely assume you have the green light to move ahead."

"Thanks, Susan. I'll talk with Tony next Friday after I work through the HR details with Keely Horton and touch base with Legal on any details we need to be aware of."

"Let's hope this helps, Greg. I've been watching the customer service results and inventory level. We aren't making the progress you promised with the plan you laid out to me three months ago, and we badly need that progress. Let's talk further about that on the first. In the meantime, good luck in your meeting with Tony."

Just after lunch on the following Friday, Greg asked Tony to come to his office. Greg told Tony that he had observed no effort on Tony's part to change his behavior or performance despite repeated coaching and for that reason, this would be Tony's last day with Cosmetics Products and Amalgamated. "Tony, you are an old pro at manufacturing. You are probably one of the best in the business at taking care of your people and meeting your functional objectives. I'll tell anyone that. But the world is changing, and you seem incapable of changing along with it. That makes you something of a dinosaur. We need someone in your role who can work better with peers and be better focused on the needs of our customers. I think I have been more than clear with everyone, especially you, about the changes we need to make. Your approach to building overall inventory and improving efficiency and utilization was good for Manufacturing, but not good enough for the company. I see the number of SKUs with low inventory climbing rapidly. The situation today looks to me like an impending train wreck. You knew what I was after, but you seem to refuse to meet my clearly stated objectives. I am concerned that if we don't make an immediate and substantial change, we will have even worse customer service performance. Finally, I keep seeing examples of your inflexibility despite our efforts to improve teamwork. Bottom line, although I don't like to say this, there is no longer room for you in the company." Tony was shocked and angry.

"This is pure BS, Greg. I can't believe you are doing this to a loyal and committed employee. You have to see that I am the only person on your staff meeting performance goals and preventing that train wreck you are predicting! You have a bunch of lightweights on your staff, but I guess you just can't see it. Trust me. With me gone, you'll find out sooner than you think. You know, about a year ago I was led to believe that I would be the one to replace Stu, but Susan passed right over me to get to you. They made a big mistake in hiring you, and now you do this to me. Unbelievable. Let me give you a prediction. You're about to see the roof cave in on you."

"I would like to believe that isn't a threat of some kind, Tony."

"Not a threat at all; it's just a statement of fact. I've seen it happen before, and you're going to see it happen soon. You'll be sitting right in the middle of the fallout."

"I really don't think so, but I'll just have to take that risk, Tony. I am sorry to have to take this step, but I want to treat you well as we part ways. I'll give you the opportunity to resign. If you don't want to do that, I'll still not share the details with anyone beyond those who absolutely need to know, and that does not include the Leadership Team. Here is a summary of the separation package including the compensation that was negotiated as part of the acquisition of your old company along with the value of the accumulated vacation and benefits to which you are entitled. You'll receive all of that. Additionally, you are welcome to take advantage of outplacement services and the other options that have been offered to those who have been terminated because of the downsizing. You can get further details from Keely about the package." Tony responded dismissively.

"Well, thanks at least for meeting your obligations on the compensation package. You can tell people whatever you want; I really don't care one way or the other. Beyond the compensation that I've earned, I don't want or need any handouts from either you or the company. I'll just be happy to leave quickly and go to a company that knows something about Manufacturing. I'll have another job long before you know just how much trouble you're in here. Between you and me, although I doubt you want my opinion today any more than you have in the past, I think you're in way over your head, Son. I'll pack up my office and be out of here in less than thirty minutes. I know the drill. I'll stop by Keely's office, sign the paperwork that I'm certain is already on her desk, and then check out through Security. I won't even talk with the Plant Managers. I'll let you do that and try to explain your decision to them. Good luck with that one. Unless you want to say anything else, I'm leaving. Good luck; you and this business are going to need it."

Greg waited an hour after that confrontation. He then called Roger Winchester, President of the Home Products division, explaining some of the issues he was facing in Cosmetics Products in the hope of getting some advice. "Of course, Greg. I'd be happy to talk with you about those issues. Not sure how much help I'll be, but I am always willing to listen." They made arrangements to meet on Monday morning when both had a two-hour schedule opening. "I can't and won't tell you what to do, Greg, but I can share with you how I thought through and dealt with some similar situations when I first took over this business. It can feel more than a little lonely at the top. I've asked peers for advice myself on occasion. Actually, never did get any easy solutions to my problems now that I think of it, but I always find that just being able to talk through problems with a receptive listener makes all the difference. I'll do whatever I can to help."

Greg was excited about the opportunity to open up and learn from Roger. As he was making notes at his desk in preparation for that meeting, Cynthia informed him Kari would like to meet with him as soon as possible.

"What now?" Greg thought. "I don't think I am up to the task of hearing about another disgruntled customer or about how Manufacturing failed to run to the forecast. Kari should be handling these situations without needing my intervention. Probably still a bit unsure of herself and her leadership abilities." Greg told Kari he was available to talk with her now for an hour, but had to leave the office by 6:30 that evening. The meeting took far longer.

"Greg, I am afraid I have some bad news for you. As you know, I have been totally frustrated by our customer service performance and by our inability to get Manufacturing's attention. This situation has been draining my energy, and someone on the Leadership Team has been driving me crazy. I just can't work with him any longer. I know you have been trying to make a difference. I really like your growth vision, but I just don't see any possibility of getting there from where we are today.

"A month ago, a company approached me with an offer to take their Sales and Marketing VP role. I want to assure you that it is not a competitor. In fact the company is not even in the consumer goods industry. At first, the only thing about the offer that interested me was that it would be a chance to get away from Tony, but the more I talked with that company and thought about the job, the better it sounded. It really is a wonderful opportunity that I can't pass up. I intend to start with them in two weeks to give you time to fill in behind me." Now it was Greg's turn to be stunned!

"Kari, this is terrible news for me personally and for Cosmetics Products. You've been an important part of this team. I know I've given you some pretty tough coaching from time to time, but that's because all the Division Presidents know you have great potential. It's no surprise that you've been upset with our customer results and with Tony. I want you to know that as of today Tony is no longer a part of this company. In fact, he's probably gone already. Does that make a difference in your decision?"

"It probably would have a month ago, Greg. In fact, had Tony been gone when the other company called, I wouldn't even have agreed to talk with them. But at this point, I've made my decision. I know it's a similar role, but the company is larger and has a much bigger and more effective sales and marketing capability. I'm surprised and flattered that they offered me the position. As I said, I just can't pass it up."

Greg and Kari talked into the early evening, but Greg was unable to persuade Kari to change her mind. In one day, Greg had lost two vice presidents. The loss of Tony would help the company; the loss of Kari was attributable, at least in part, to Greg's failure to take action sooner on his instincts about Tony. Now, his results were still unacceptable, and he was seriously understaffed in his senior management ranks. Greg knew that many people in the organization admired Tony and Kari and could be influenced to follow them to their new companies. More potential black clouds on the horizon.

Penny again served as a much-needed listener and sounding board for Greg throughout the weekend. Greg knew the needed changes were now underway.

Except for the unexpected loss of Kari, the changes were the ones he had personally framed. There was no question in his mind that teamwork and results would improve with Tony out of the picture.

On Saturday afternoon, Greg finished compiling his questions for Roger Winchester and the notes he would use on Monday morning to explain to his team why Tony had suddenly disappeared. Before that team meeting, he would inform David of his new, added responsibilities and then call the two plant managers to explain the situation.

David was pleased that Greg and Amalgamated senior management supported adding Manufacturing to his functional responsibilities. He had spent some time in a plant assignment early in his career and saw this change as an opportunity for personal growth. His response and enthusiasm buoyed Greg's spirits. Already the level of teamwork was improving. David decided to call the plant managers in each of the plants as soon as Greg made the announcement and make arrangements to visit the plants to learn more about the production processes, the people, and their current challenges.

The leadership team was uneasy about the loss of Tony. True to his promise, Greg chose his words carefully about Tony's departure. Nevertheless, the unspoken consensus of the team was that Greg fired Tony. No one was shocked by the sudden move, but it instantly highlighted the consequences of poor performance.

The team was more shocked when Kari announced her intention to leave the company. They expressed their disappointment and then turned to Greg to ask how the two roles were to be filled. He explained David's new and expanded role, which pleased everyone on the team. David was viewed by everyone as smart, a solid performer, and a good team player. No one doubted that their cross-functional relationships with Manufacturing would improve dramatically. Greg explained that Kari's replacement would be announced later. In reality, Greg had informed Susan about Kari's decision, but had yet to determine how he would replace her. There was no question in his mind, however, that he needed to move quickly.

The two hours Greg spent with Roger later on Monday went by quickly. Greg surprised himself in how openly he shared his challenges in the new job and even how he was questioning his ability to succeed in the role from time to time. Roger admitted he had been there himself. "Look, Greg, if you think you know all the answers, chances are you may not even understand the questions. All of us have voices in our heads. You just have to figure out when to tune them out, or they'll drive you nuts. You also have to be honest with yourself about your strengths and weaknesses. If you are, it's easy to find the kind of people you need to have around you. Based on what you told me about the personnel change you made, seems to me you are already moving in the right direction. But I don't think you've righted the ship yet by a long shot. You are beginning to learn what it takes to run all aspects of a business, but don't be surprised if you haven't hit bottom yet. Sounds like the problems are deeply entrenched in Cosmetics Products. I know you're looking for a breakthrough, but people still seem to be holding onto what's worked for them in the past. A breakthrough may first require a complete breakdown to get everyone's attention and make them realize just how much they have to change. I don't have the answers for you, Greg, but I can tell you that to get dramatically better results, you are going to have to make some pretty dramatic changes in your people's behaviors and in your business culture and processes. I have a couple ideas that might help, but let me think through what you've told me today and get back to you."

"I can't tell you how much I appreciate your listening and coaching, Roger. Although I haven't known you very long, I count you as a good friend and now mentor. I really do hope you are wrong about our not having hit bottom yet. I don't think we could survive one of those breakdowns you described. Feels like I've already been on the bottom a number of times since taking this job."

Roger agreed to keep an open door for Greg. He appreciated Greg's position and welcomed the opportunity to help a colleague. Sometimes, he thought, it's just nice to be asked for advice. He knew Greg would listen to what he had to say.

As Greg headed back to his office to get ready for his remaining afternoon commitments, he was confident Cosmetics Products would make the progress needed and avoid that breakdown Roger warned him about. That confidence was shattered shortly after he reached his desk.

"Greg, there's a Martin Bennett on the phone for you. Isn't he the President and CEO of Blackstone?"

"Sure is, Cynthia. Marty is also my old boss and now valued customer as well. Wonder what he's up to. I'll take the call. Make sure I don't get interrupted while I'm on the phone."

"How are Penny and the boys, Greg? It's been quite a while since I've seen them." Marty and Greg shared some small talk for a few minutes. Then Marty turned to the reason for his call. "Greg, I wanted to be the one to tell you personally about this before you hear it from anyone else. You know as well as anyone that customer service from Amalgamated's Cosmetics Products division has always been poor. Lately, it's gotten even worse. I've been hoping beyond hope that you could fix the problem. I'm not sure what you're facing over there, but I know it must be dreadful or you'd have it under control by now. We've held out as long as possible, Greg. We're losing revenue and profit because of the empty shelf space that should be filled with your products. Your competitors have been all over us to give them your space, but until now we have been resisting that move. Despite the loyalty we have for you, this is still a for-profit venture and we just can't delay the decision any longer. As of today, we are canceling all orders with you. We'll sell out your remaining stock and give away your space. I know this has to be a real blow, but I also know you're smart enough to have seen it coming. This move can't be a complete surprise. When you're in a position to provide reliable customer service, come and see me. I know you'll get there at some point. If at that point you can convince me, I mean make a solid business case, I'll make certain we start doing business with you again. I really am sorry, Greg. Good luck with the business, and give my best to the family."

Greg was stunned, but he thanked Marty for the personal call and promised he would be back in the game soon, although that nagging concern about being in over his head flooded his thought patterns again. Greg immediately phoned Kari to see if she had heard anything or had suspected Blackstone would make this move. She assured him that she had no advanced warning. On the other hand, she had heard other rumblings in the past few days from some of her sales managers. They were hearing a stronger level of complaints, bordering on ultimatums, from customers. Blackstone's decision suddenly felt like an early warning of more bad news to come. For Greg, Roger had been prophetic. This has to be the breakdown; the event that would free everyone from thinking they could tweak their current business and make it successful. What was it Roger had said about knowing all the answers? In his past jobs, everyone always looked to Greg to have those answers. This time he didn't have them. As Roger had put it, he didn't even understand the questions except for the first one: how would he break the bad new to Susan?

Amalgamated had hired Greg to fix these Cosmetics Products problems, but they had only gotten worse since he took over from Stu. Greg knew he was accountable. His job was to fix customer service and deliver a quick business turnaround; to this point he had been unable to do it. He finally admitted to himself that he simply did not know what to do next. "How," he questioned himself, "could you have gotten this far, have been so successful and not know what to do next, Greg?"

As supportive as Susan had been, Greg knew her patience was running out. He knew she was displeased by his inability to reverse the business trends and would be even more displeased about the loss of a key customer. He knew she was under intense pressure from the Board, which expected their investment in Cosmetics Products to begin paying big dividends soon.

Greg didn't like how he was feeling; he didn't like the self-doubt, what was happening to his normally positive outlook, or what was happening to his relationship with his wife and sons. He couldn't go back in time six months and return to Blackstone; and it was clear that if he didn't get control of this business, he might not be able to go forward six months with Cosmetics Products.

What he already knew about business wasn't helping either him or the business. Greg knew that he was missing something; he knew that he needed help and needed it soon. Roger warned him that a breakdown might be coming, but didn't tell him what to expect after it occurred. Greg knew that he was about to find out.

LISTENING . . .

What I already know ... seems to be getting in my way.

No matter the problem, someone, somewhere, has solved it before.

If you do what you've always done, you'll get what you've always gotten.

Greg informed Susan immediately about Blackstone Drugs' decision to discontinue selling Cosmetics Products' brands. She was obviously unhappy about this turn of events and also about the rumors of other accounts that might follow Blackstone's lead. But she was not entirely surprised. She had observed the downward trend long before Greg's arrival and suspected Cosmetics Products could not avoid the loss of some key customers. On a more positive note, she confirmed that Blackstone's decision about Cosmetics Products would not affect its relationship with Amalgamated's other divisions. Although deeply concerned about the future of Cosmetics Products, Susan knew the current events were the result of conditions that had developed during Stu's watch, not just since Greg's arrival. She still had confidence in Greg's abilities, but knew from the tone of his phone call that he was not feeling good about his own performance. She and Greg agreed to meet the following day to plan the next steps.

As the meeting began the following morning, Greg bypassed pleasantries and got right to the point. "I would understand completely if you asked me to step down as President of Cosmetics Products, Susan. In fact I've contemplated resigning so that you could bring in someone else."

"Get those thoughts out of your head right now, Greg. I hired you because I have confidence in you. You accepted the job knowing full well that there were deep problems in the business. You didn't cause Blackstone to stop doing business with Cosmetics Products. Problems like these aren't created overnight, and they certainly aren't corrected overnight. First things first, however. I spoke with Roger Winchester after you told me of Kari's decision to leave the company. He told me about your talking with him and asking for his perspective and advice. Greg, that's a sign of a real leader, and it's one of the reasons I hired you. But the reason I called Roger was to talk about someone on his staff, a Regional Sales Manager by the name of Alexandra Templeton. We've been planning to promote her for some time. This looks to me like the perfect opportunity. I'm personally concerned that if we pass up this chance to move her in behind Kari, we might lose her also. I want you to talk with her, but the decision is yours. If you see a good fit, we could move her quickly. Roger does a great job with succession planning and has her replacement ready to step in. Alex already knows your channels. She knows many of your key customers in her region, and in most of the other regions as well since we've been moving her around over the past couple years."

"That sounds really promising, Susan. I have a lot of faith in Roger's judgment as well as in yours. If you and Roger say Alexandra is good, I have no reason to doubt that. I did have a great session with Roger the other day, and I expect to tap his knowledge a good deal more in the future. I'll talk with Alexandra today or tomorrow. She could save us lots of time in filling the job and in getting up to speed. I expect my Sales and Marketing Directors will be fine with the move also. I've talked with both of them recently, and neither one anticipates a promotion."

"Just let me know what you decide, Greg, and we'll either make the announcement or come up with 'Plan B.' Now, let's get down to your development! I've been investing heavily in your education; what have you been learning?"

"I'm glad . . . no, I should say that I'm thankful, Susan, that you consider the last few months an investment in me. I've never worked harder, but I haven't thought of it as education. Put in that context, however, I've learned a lot. I've learned there are apparent cross-functional interdependencies in the business that I don't understand. To be perfectly honest, until recently I had no idea that those interdependencies even exist.

"I've learned that what I already know about running a business from, essentially, a Sales and Marketing perspective seems to be getting in my way in coming up with new approaches to solving my problems. I keep trying variations of what's worked for me in the past, but it's not working here. I know that I can't just tweak our current business model and get the results we need. And I also know that I don't have the answers to the problems or a clear vision of what the new business model should be. Roger was on target when he told me that if I thought I had all the answers, I probably didn't even understand the questions. I still don't have the answers, but I am beginning to get a sense of the questions. In short, I think I am beginning to know what I don't know." Susan smiled.

"One of many reasons I hired you, Greg, is because you have an ability to look at problems differently and to apply what you learn. Based on what you just told me, I think I just got a phenomenal return on my investment in your education. You are one of the smartest guys I know. To hear you admit that you don't know the answers, or even the right questions, makes you even smarter than I thought. Many people in your shoes would try to bluff their way through this situation or use brute force to improve results. That approach can work for a while, but it won't provide any sustained results. People burn out and create no lasting effect. In fact, the changes made with that approach usually result in even bigger problems. I sense that you were headed down that road for a while with the decisions you were making, but now I see you looking for a better way. Learning that gives you a master's degree in corporate leadership in my book. In your search for that better way, you'll earn yourself a doctorate." Greg began to relax a little.

"You're giving me far too much credit for not knowing what to do next! We're still facing a potential business disaster. I still believe that some of the moves we've made to date will pay dividends, but nothing close to what we need."

"You're wrong about my giving you too much credit, Greg," said Susan. "You should know by now that I don't give credit unless it's earned. My assessment is that you are now becoming free of your business history and are eager to learn. You might not realize how important that is on our journey, but I do. As far as business results go, you've taken some crucial steps. You'll have David managing the entire supply chain and working far better with the others on your leadership team. With Tony out of the picture, I expect that you'll have a much stronger and far more creative team. If you do bring in Alexandra, she'll provide some new perspectives as well. On reflection, I think you had a bunch of people who had painted themselves into corners and could no longer be objective or open in their relationships with each other. You've radically altered that dynamic. While you've freed yourself from your own history, you've also freed your Leadership Team from its history as well. Don't forget, too, that you upped the ante for everyone on that team by firing Tony. You gave each of them a personal reason to become more effective.

"I'd suggest that you now give them some room to learn how to work together and to run the business for you while you work on developing a new vision and direction for Cosmetics Products. You've been pressing them pretty hard. Now would be a good time to back off a bit and take a fresh look at the problems and at the business. I've learned that no matter the problem, someone, somewhere, has solved it before. Talking with Roger was a good move. I would also recommend looking for new ideas outside the company. Make some contacts with other business leaders, even people outside our industry. See what they are dealing with and how they think about their businesses. Their products might look different, but somehow I suspect their problems just might be similar to ours." Susan paused, and then continued.

"Ease up on yourself, Greg. You still have my complete confidence. Let me know your plans in a week or so for gathering those new perspectives but relax tonight and don't lose sight of your number one priority. Spend the evening with Penny, not with your problems!" Greg did just that.

The next morning Greg dropped in on Roger to learn more about Alexandra Templeton. Her record was impressive and Roger's assessment nothing short of glowing. Greg knew that Alexandra would be in the office that day and made arrangements to meet with her before lunch. Alexandra arrived at Greg's office promptly at the scheduled meeting time.

Greg learned that she was a personal friend of Kari, knew some of Cosmetics Products' war stories, and knew about Sales and Marketing's poor relationship with Manufacturing. He grilled her on her sales and marketing knowledge and experience and was impressed, especially with the examples she shared of getting results through effective cross-functional supply chain teams. He could already envision a great fit with the others on his team, and decided she was the right person for the job. He spoke first with Roger, and could see no reason for delaying her promotion.

"You've made a great choice, Greg. I hate to lose Alexandra, but it's right for her and it's absolutely right for Cosmetics Products. Kari was strong in that role. Her departure represents a great loss for the company, but your business hasn't been growing. Kari and her Marketing and Sales teams failed in their responsibility of building that business, so perhaps the change isn't all bad news. I think Alexandra has at least as much potential as Kari, and probably more. You'll find that she'll settle in quickly and work well with her peers even though she is a new VP. She's good at collaborating and in coming up with win-win solutions.

"Let's call Susan and tell her of our decision. Then we'll call Alexandra and give her the good news. I think we should make the formal announcement tomorrow. We can make this a very quick move, but, if you agree, I'd like to keep her in Home Products for a week. Her replacement reports directly to her and is ready to take over, but I think he'll be more comfortable if we give them a week to make the transition." Greg made a mental note to have Cynthia update his organization chart to reflect the loss of Tony and Kari, and the addition of Alexandra to his staff [Figure 5.1].

As Greg was about to leave, Roger motioned for him to stay. "I have another idea for you, Greg." Roger said. "It's the idea I had when we last talked, but I wanted to check my notes and think more about it. A couple years ago, my Supply Chain VP invited me to an Effective Management, Inc. Business Excellence seminar. He wanted both of us to learn a little more about integrating business processes and about principles and best practices involved in managing supply chains. This particular seminar included some guest speakers who had worked with Effective Management and who had made the transition to what is called 'Capable Planning and Control.' That's a key step toward achieving Effective Management's 'Class A Business Excellence' certification.

Greg interrupted, "Class A? I've never heard of it." Roger responded.

"I'm still learning more of the details myself, Greg, but it's the zenith of business performance achieved by running a business with excellence at all

Organization Chart — Rev 2

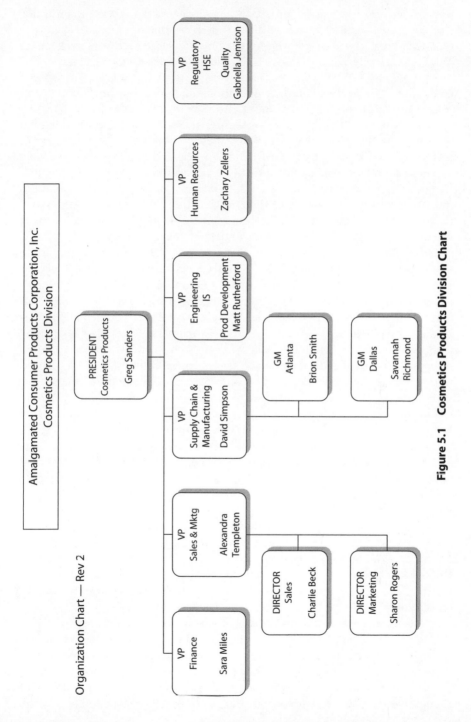

Figure 5.1 Cosmetics Products Division Chart

levels and in all functions. It means you meet some very rigorous performance standards and consistently achieve at least upper quartile business results in your industry. When you achieve this level of performance, Effective Management's recognition is called Class A Business Excellence certification.

"A better question might be, 'just what is business excellence?'" Roger continued. "There are published definitions and models from lots of companies and academics. Many of them look convincing, but most of them shy away from being definitive. They're theoretical, and depend a good deal on interpretation by the reader. But as an executive I need to know what excellent performance looks like, and I need to recognize the areas where Home Products falls short against best practices. If I can understand both of those things, I'll have a pretty good idea what to do next. Effective Management has put some flesh on the bones of their model, some understandable descriptions, based on their personal experience of best practice applications in a whole range of companies. They accumulated this information into what is called their *Class A Checklist for Business Excellence*. They've published credible Checklists since back in the 1970s. As the performance high bar gets raised over the years, they regularly update their Checklist with tougher standards and expectations. The latest Checklist provides a worthwhile challenge. When you meet those standards and expectations, you become a truly business excellent company and consistently operate in the upper quartile of your industry at a minimum. That's what they call Class A. I'll give you an example. One of the tougher performance expectations that got my attention was 99.5 percent customer service. How's that for a minimum customer service target?"

"Absolutely beyond comprehension, and also unattainable! I could never keep enough inventory to do that." said Greg without hesitation.

"That was my exact reaction too, until I thought more about it. Let's not talk about how to do that yet, but let me challenge your thinking. What customer service level do you think is needed for Cosmetics Products to succeed?"

"Well, Roger, given where we are today, I'd say 95 percent on time in full would be spectacular!"

"Okay then, how many orders a day do you handle, Greg?"

"About two to three hundred as I remember."

"So at 95 percent customer service performance, you would fail to meet the expectations of 10 to 15 customers each day. You would fail to meet the expectations of one out of every 20 customers. Is that what you mean by spectacular?"

"Not when you say it that way! I should have recognized that."

"Don't feel alone, Greg. Most managers and executives talk about 95 percent as good performance. But it's only relatively 'good' performance if your competition is delivering 85 percent of its orders in full and on time.

"Guess you can add me to the list of 'most managers'! A few minutes ago I thought 95 percent was spectacular; I didn't look at it as failing one of every twenty customers. Looks like you just raised the bar on me. What else should I think about differently?

"I only mentioned customer orders for the paying customers. You also need to apply that thinking internally in Cosmetics Products. Apply the thinking to manufacturing and purchase orders as well." Greg looked a bit perplexed by that challenge, but nodded.

"But let me go back to customer service for a minute. The competition in my Home Products market hasn't been sitting still. Five years ago if I delivered 90 percent performance, I was at the top of the tree. But now, my competitors are routinely hitting 95 percent, and my customers are asking why I can't do that well, or better. That's why I began thinking about all this.

"So since 95 percent is 'unacceptable' to my customers, using your word, I started thinking about getting to 99.5 percent performance, meaning one failure in two hundred orders. Frankly, even that's not brilliant, is it? But I can grow my market share significantly if I get that performance level cost effectively, and grow even more if I can lower costs and prices at the same time!

"Greg, I'm not knocking 95 percent performance, especially when it's achieved at lower cost through Capable Planning and Control. It's a sign that the supply chain and the management processes are working together adequately. Lots of companies starting out with poor or costly customer service would consider 95 percent customer service a great achievement. But it can't be the end of the journey, can it? There has to be more.

"That's why I was interested in getting input from Effective Management; I wanted to hear what they were saying and hear what other industry executives were saying. I wanted to learn to do something different, to create a new paradigm, in order to get different results. As my friend, Kelly, who worked for a high-tech company in Colorado once said to me, 'If you do what you've always done, you'll get what you've always gotten.' I could then, but can't any longer afford to get what I've always gotten." Roger moved to his sideboard and poured them each a cup of coffee. This would take some time now that Greg was engaged.

"I attended that Effective Management Supply Chain Seminar I mentioned earlier. They talked about a top management process called Integrated Business Management that goes beyond Sales and Operations Planning. I used to delude myself into believing that we ran S&OP in Home Products. We didn't. We simply held what was at best a forecast and production volumes information meeting that the planners attended once a month. Integrated Business Management, as I began to learn about it, sounded more like a powerful way to manage and direct a business. They talked a good deal about Class A Business Excellence as defined in their latest Checklist and about how Integrated Business Management tied together all the business processes. I listened to the presentations and talked with people from different businesses and industries. Slowly it all began to make sense. I picked up a copy of the Checklist a few weeks ago. I've been going through it, not reading cover to cover, but looking through it to get a flavor of what this all means. At first the scope of Class A Business Excellence seemed daunting to me, but I've already learned that you have to approach Class A as a journey, in defined steps called *milestones*, which are based on your company's competitive priorities. My priority, like yours, is to get control of my internal supply chain and customer service. The 'Capable Planning and Control Class A Milestone' addresses that challenge and is also one of the first milestones that many companies undertake.

"Just listening to Effective Management presenters and some guest speakers helped me begin to understand what I could do in Home Products. One of the speakers at the seminar, Glen Smithers from Holwarth Engineering, could have been talking about Home Products. He talked about transforming Holwarth to achieve leadership in their markets using 'Class A' business processes and best practices. He also talked about the benefits from their first implementation success in Capable Planning and Control. He said that Effective Management presented them a Class A Milestone Award as independent confirmation of their success. For Holwarth it was top priority to get their supply chain in control, improve costs, and increase customer service results above 95 percent. With the help of an Effective Management Diagnostic Assessment to start the ball rolling, Holwarth went on to study the '*Class A Checklist*' in order to understand business excellence standards, at a macro level, for their business processes and results. After identifying their obvious gaps during the Diagnostic Assessment, they asked the coaches from Effective Management to help them define an action plan to meet their strategic objective of becoming the leader in their industry segment. They are following Effective Management's 'proven path' methodology to achieve their objectives.

"Glen walked into a real mess when he became Chairman of Holwarth. But by the time he retired, Holwarth had made a huge improvement to their bottom line through a series of Class A Milestones; the company's stock price increase reflected that improvement. To say he is an advocate of Holwarth's Class A journey would be a gross understatement; he was the driving force After they got control of the supply chain and customer service, they kept going. They implemented a series of additional milestones addressing specific business objectives and, along the way, used approaches and techniques such as Lean, Six Sigma, and Agile to drive continuous improvement of their results. Glen's address at that Seminar was inspirational. He caused me to do a lot of thinking about the state of affairs here in Home Products."

"I can tell that you were hooked by these guys, Roger, as I would be if I could see a way to control my supply chain and improve customer service. What happened next?"

"Unfortunately my enthusiasm didn't translate into action. Our results at that time were meeting our commitments, so we didn't give it much priority. We already had a long list of other projects underway. Despite serious nonstop browbeating by my Supply Chain VP, I decided against taking on that additional initiative. I simply didn't think we could handle much more change at the time. Since then, I've had second thoughts about that decision. I now believe there could be significant benefit for Home Products, and undoubtedly even more in your division, given what you've told me. So I'm now toying with launching a Class A journey. Better late than never, as they say."

"Roger, if I could come up with an effective solution to my customer service problem, and start to regain market share I'd start now! But I'm still skeptical about using consultants."

Roger nodded, "I can only imagine the pressure you're under. But I know you could get some important insights, and direction from Effective Management."

"That almost sounded like, 'Trust me, I'm a consultant.'" They both laughed.

"Listen, Greg, here's what I'm saying. I was very busy, and was under pressure from Amalgamated's leadership, although not as much as you, to increase Home Products' contribution to the company. But I still invested a day in attending that seminar. Over the years, I've learned that in our positions, we can't possibly know everything. Yet the quality of our decisions is directly proportional to the knowledge and information available to us. We must have and rely on trustworthy people, processes, and supporting technology to provide that knowledge."

That comment took Greg a different direction. "I suppose an ERP system falls into what you call 'supporting technology.' Roger, my people tell me that our ERP system doesn't support the Cosmetics business; in fact it appears that they only use it to store information and record decisions made outside the system."

"I've heard the same story from my people, but they've got it wrong. An ERP system does exactly what you tell it to do and only what you tell it to do. If you tell it to do the right things, that's what it'll do. If you tell it the wrong things to do, well, guess what it'll do! I've talked with a good many CEOs about this. I know that Amalgamated's ERP software is being used successfully by some pretty big players out there. Interestingly, the most successful users are those who have made it a part of a Capable Planning and Control implementation. I'm convinced the ERP system is not our problem. There's something we and our people are missing, and we had better get to the bottom of it." Greg was very thoughtful; Roger's forceful response struck some familiar chords in his mind. Roger continued more gently.

"The challenge we have as leaders of our businesses is to determine what we need to learn and to do ourselves, and what others on our staff need to do for us. As Presidents we create and drive business goals and strategies; that's where we are accountable. Of course, we must manage the business from the top, put good people in the right places and provide leadership for the whole business, especially during periods of major change. We have lots of good managers to help us manage the business, but we own leadership. To succeed, we need to develop our strengths in areas like creating a vision of the future, creating business strategies and, even more importantly, driving those strategies into the operating plans to achieve them. As Joel Barker once said, 'vision without action is called dreaming.' Management alone can't make the organization move toward our vision. Leadership can, and must, lead." Greg nodded in acknowledgment.

"Greg, you don't have to do what I'm thinking of doing with Effective Management. Let me give you some case studies that might be helpful to you. These are copies of what I collected from Effective Management. You can read about companies like Holwarth that implemented Class A processes in various areas of the business. Most are not all the way to Class A yet, but the case studies are a quick read and could be great preparation for attending an Effective Management seminar. Here's a flyer I received last week. The seminar is designed for executives interested in implementing best practices to achieve business performance improvements. And who doesn't need that? I've personally worked with one of the presenters in the past and can vouch for her effectiveness. I know it's short notice, but I would recommend that you attend with your Supply Chain VP. It certainly meets your objective of getting fresh perspectives from outside the industry." Greg thought in silence for a bit. Roger could almost hear the gears turning.

"What you've said, Roger, has helped me make a decision. David, my Supply Chain VP, has also been prompting me to learn more. Fortunately, you're both pushing me in the same direction. You've piqued my interest and the timing is right for me. I'll talk with David and see if we can attend together. Once again, I appreciate your ideas, your coaching, and your just being there as a sounding board for me. And thanks for the case studies, Roger. I'll have a look at them tonight."

Greg talked about the upcoming seminar with David Simpson when he returned to the office. David was surprised and excited about the opportunity to attend with Greg. He had heard good reports about the company hosting the seminar. But of even greater importance to David was that Greg was showing real interest in learning about the business process improvements David had been advocating. They both cleared their schedules for the event, and Cynthia made their travel arrangements. Greg and David would fly to Orlando the following Monday afternoon. David reviewed the agenda and liked what he saw. He was excited also about the opportunity to see what he could learn from the other companies attending.

Greg read the case studies that evening. He found them straightforward but disappointing in that the improvement steps reported by the companies seemed to be nothing more than applied common sense. That made him reflect for a few minutes on just how uncommon 'common sense' seemed to be in Cosmetics Products. From talking with many people in the business, he knew that Cosmetics Products already appeared to be doing some of the things described in the case studies. How effectively they were being done was an entirely different question.

When he talked about his day with Penny, she also encouraged him to attend the seminar. "Despite your reservations," she said, "if you keep an open mind, you'll learn something useful." Greg was not convinced of that, but he trusted Penny's judgment.

Greg was beginning to look forward to the seminar but was skeptical about how much he could learn from someone outside the cosmetics industry. At the least, he rationalized, he could learn about issues people in other companies were facing and how they were dealing with them. He would take fresh perspectives and ideas wherever he could get them.

6

. . . AND LEARNING

*The pace of change in business is faster today than ever in history,
but is slower today than it ever will be again.*

*I also have a concern that what might work in one company,
might not work in another.*

*Culture change will occur only when it is led from the
very top of the organization.*

Greg and David arrived in plenty of time to select the best seats but sat near
the back, reflecting Greg's subconscious uncertainty about the event. There
was a book on each seat. Greg just read the word "checklist," and put it to
one side. At the beginning of the seminar, they learned that their hosts for the
day, Stan Stevens and Mary Medford, were part of the same consulting group,
Effective Management, that published the case studies Greg and David had
read. They also learned that Mary had been working closely with Holwarth.
That fact rekindled Greg's skepticism about finding the answers he needed
from an engineering firm. The agenda promised some input on business excellence principles from the hosts and some presentations by "real people," as
Greg saw it, from industry.

As the seminar began, Stan and Mary described their backgrounds and
work experiences in a number of industries. They had each worked as employees of companies that used Effective Management to help turn around declining business results. Before being invited to join Effective Management,
Mary had been an operations manager and, later, the Supply Chain Director
for a pharmaceutical company. Stan had recently retired as Marketing Vice

President in an electronics company. Both Mary and Stan had been key players in their company's business excellence initiatives. They explained that all Effective Management coaches had been similarly involved in transforming their company's performance to at least the "Capable Milestone" level before being invited to become part of Effective Management. For that reason, all their coaches could empathize with the concerns, doubts, and challenges their clients might face in transforming their companies' results.

Greg found it interesting that Stan always referred to himself and his colleagues as *coaches* rather than *consultants,* and that he focused more on education and mentoring than on consulting. Stan's primary objective was to share with others the importance to the bottom line of integrating all aspects of managing a service or manufacturing business.

After introducing themselves, Stan and Mary had all the participants do likewise, describing their current challenges and listing their reasons for coming to the seminar. While Greg's reason for attending was simply to gain new perspectives about improving business results, others had much more specific objectives such as understanding what opportunities "business excellence" might uncover, getting greater benefit from their ERP systems, relating business excellence to Lean and Six Sigma, breaking down functional silos, and learning ways to reduce working capital while not sacrificing customer service. Two companies appeared quite advanced in their supply chain processes (98 percent Customer Service; 10 inventory turns) and made comments that meant very little to Greg. One participant stated, "We're ready to move into Phase 2 business excellence, and we're trying to gain a broader perspective of what challenges we'll face." While Greg hadn't offered up any specific objectives, he began to think that almost everyone in the room was talking about his company. He seemed to be facing every challenge mentioned by the others.

Stan led off the formal presentation. "It's our experience, and I think you'll agree, that all organizations are on a journey to improve business performance." Stan looked around as everyone nodded in agreement.

"A journey has a starting point, steps on the way, and a destination. But many organizations don't understand and can't articulate their journey other than in the most general terms. Over the years, we have come to understand that in transforming a business on a journey to excellence, there are multiple routes that a company can follow. But the best route is always defined by a company's competitive priorities. We've learned also that companies must go through some enabling steps to reach their envisioned future. Many companies become enamored with the latest fashionable ideas. They try applying a bit of Agile here; a bit of Lean there; some Six Sigma initiatives elsewhere. But these companies don't realize that every journey has a correct sequence of business developments and initiatives that will lead them to sustainable transformation. Additionally, they may not have an effective process to drive the company along that journey in a manner that integrates and leverages all the improved business processes. This is where the Integrated Business Model comes in." [Figure 6.1]

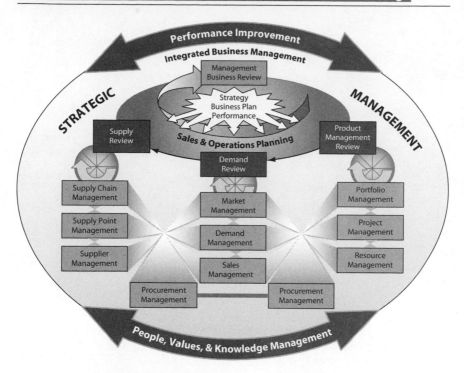

Figure 6.1   Integrated Business Model
Source: Oliver Wight. Copyright Oliver Wight International, Inc. Used with permission.

"This model shows, from right to left, product management, demand management, and supply management as three vertical 'legs' in the center of the diagram. Each leg is capped by a preparatory 'wheel' of activities showing the sequential activities required during the month to prepare for all the Integrated Business Management reviews. By the way, Integrated Business Management, which I'll discuss in few minutes, has as its core an advanced evolution of the process that in the past many of you might have known as Sales and Operations Planning. We go into great detail about the activities within those preparatory wheels during detailed education sessions with those teams, so I'll skip over them for now.

"When companies implement something like this on their own, individual elements within each leg often are loosely integrated. We nearly always find competing internal objectives and turf battles. And almost always integration of information and activities across the three functional legs is weak at best.

"In contrast, companies that follow Class A principles, exhibit Class A behaviors, and reach Class A standards of performance have all these functions fully integrated. They achieve and exhibit a multifunctional focus on achieving their business strategy and on continuously improving business results through the

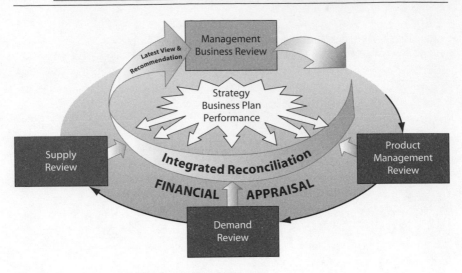

Figure 6.2 Integrated Business Management
Source: Oliver Wight. Copyright Oliver Wight International, Inc. Used with permission.

portion of the Integrated Business Model that we call Integrated Business Management [Figure 6.2].

"I want you to notice first that at the heart of Integrated Business Management, depicted by this ellipse, are strategic and business plans along with continuous financial review and reconciliation of issues and imbalances. Successful companies use Integrated Business Management to deploy their strategic plans and objectives through the entire company and to link strategy to execution activities. Senior managers review actual and projected business results formally, regularly, and thoroughly in this process to make sure all functional activities and results remain on target and on strategy. The process culminates in a single operating plan and empowers people at all levels of the company to make good business decisions from day to day, week to week and month to month. Smart decisions are made faster, and good information flows top down, bottom up, and across all functional areas continuously.

"At the very top of the Integrated Business Management diagram is the Management Business Review. This review is the culmination of each month-long Integrated Business Management cycle. It is a crisp and concise monthly executive review of recommended plans and includes presentation of recommended solutions to resolve significant issues. If all preliminary work is done well, it is a quick and focused meeting. Often, however, there is important debate allowing senior managers to test recommendations and evaluate current business conditions and strategies. In the end, it is a decision-making meeting resulting in a single set of integrated product, demand, and supply management plans with financial implications covering a rolling 18 to 24 months. Decisions are made approving or modifying the plans presented, resolving current issues, and avoiding future problems. Approved plans are then quickly and broadly communicated throughout the company. Functional leaders are held accountable for executing the approved plans and for delivering the planned outcomes. With this process in place, everyone in the organization is on the same page and works against the same objectives. The company's strategy is now solidly linked with functional strategies and with planning and execution processes.

"Having briefly reviewed Integrated Business Management," Stan continued, "I have described one portion of the Integrated Business Model. But the Checklist you have in front of you is built to support the entire model. If you have looked at the Checklist, you'll have recognized the chapter headings as the key business processes depicted in this model. Chapter 4 'Integrated Business Management' is a good example.

"Here's a fundamental problem many companies face. They simply don't know exactly where they are on their improvement journey and can't properly articulate their destination. They are unclear about their next step, and even more unclear about the steps that should follow. Nevertheless, management is under pressure to do something. Too often, they choose to implement the latest management fad or whatever seems to have worked in the past. So each manager, with the best of intentions, independently initiates improvement initiatives based on his or her functionally myopic reading of the situation. These initiatives are almost always intended to optimize functional outcomes, are strategically inconsistent, and conflict with each other. As a result, leadership direction is unclear and progress against the strategy is slow at best. People across the company are confused by what we call 'initiativitis,' the launch of multiple initiatives and completion of few. People become confused, make poor day-to-day decisions, deliver suboptimal results, and hope they can outlast the latest 'improvement program of the month'. Anyone recognize this condition?"

Several attendees offered horror stories describing ineffective initiatives of all sorts. Some were amusing and broke the tension in the room. Greg listened to the stories and laughter, but didn't engage. He recognized some of his own behaviors in the stories. He began to see this method of consulting, and the consultant, as having a degree of credibility.

Stan went on to explain how his company has been modifying the definition of business excellence over multiple generations of its *Class A Checklist*. "This Checklist has been translated into several languages and has become an internationally recognized standard of excellence. Assessment of a company's current business processes against this standard helps companies understand where they are and enables them to begin to quantify the gaps against those standards." He also explained that his company facilitates high-level diagnostic assessments of a business with its executive team, and then helps the team define a desired direction and destination. What Stan said next caught Greg's attention.

"The pace of change in business is faster today than ever in history, but is slower today than it ever will be again. This means to you that integrating your business processes has become critically important. Much of manufacturing outsourcing to lower-cost economies is a symptom of the inability or unwillingness of businesses to integrate their management processes, keep pace, or lead. How to respond to this situation is the question. Companies and people are paying the price, and we feel the need to throw them a lifeline.

"While previous editions of the Checklist have provided useful incremental upgrades, we recognized that to meet today's challenges, we had to pool our considerable worldwide resources and start again with a blank sheet of paper. So the current edition was constructed around the journey to business excellence. Note I said *the* journey, not *a* journey; that's significant. Along with the Checklist, we've defined levels of business integration with our *maturity maps*. These help you understand where you are as well as the nature of the journey ahead of you." Stan put up the next slide [Figure 6.3].

Greg listened as Stan explained Effective Management's definition of the four phases of business maturity, with Phase 4 being the ultimate level. Stan mentioned that there are very few Phase 4 companies in the world, and very few more that actually need to move into that phase. Greg got only a rough idea of what Phase 4 entailed. For him, it was an interesting concept but seemed light-years beyond his current needs. Phase 3 sounded to him somewhat like the best of the Japanese auto manufacturers he'd read about; more interesting, perhaps, but still beyond Greg's agenda. Stan's description of Phases 2 and 1 had far more relevance. In sequence, the journey to the top of Phase 1 meant 'Eliminating unplanned events and doing routine things routinely'. Greg thought, "Now that would be too good to be true. Nothing has been planned or routine since I joined Amalgamated!"

Stan continued by saying that Phase 2 is built on a foundation of Phase 1 and can be described as 'Eliminating failure in business processes'. Lean, Six Sigma, and Agile techniques can be very helpful, Stan told them, but only after a company reaches the top of Phase 1.

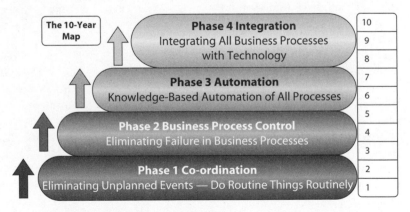

Figure 6.3   Integrating the Business: Maturity
Source: Oliver Wight. Copyright Oliver Wight International, Inc. Used with permission.

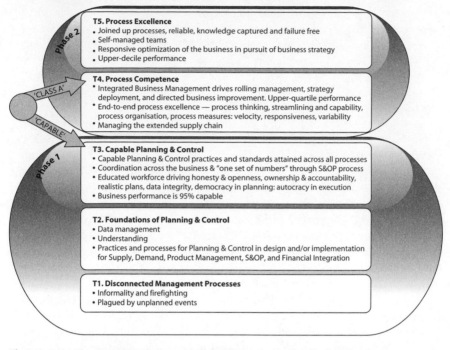

Figure 6.4   The Maturity Journey: Transitions through Phases 1 and 2
Source: Oliver Wight. Copyright Oliver Wight International, Inc. Used with permission.

Stan then divided Phases 1 and 2 into more detailed levels using what he called 'Transitions'. Greg groaned when Stan introduced the topic. "More concepts," he thought, "when what I need are some solutions to my problems." But when he saw the next slide, it didn't seem quite so conceptual [Figure 6.4].

Stan asked them to read through each of the five transitions, and to decide, as company teams, the transition best describing their company, recognizing that a company was rarely at a single level. A company might find itself mostly in Transition 1, at the bottom of the diagram, but have some pockets within the organization operating at higher levels. In that case, the current position on the chart might look like the shape of a pear if drawn on the chart. People studied the diagram, and the energy of the room increased markedly as attendees from companies huddled together and debated their current positions. Greg talked with David about where Cosmetics Products would fit. He doubted they would be anywhere in Phase 2 from what he'd seen. He suggested that their center of gravity was probably around Transitions 2 and 3. David disagreed forcefully, providing convincing examples that caused Greg to reconsider his initial conclusion. In the end, they agreed Cosmetics Products was firmly entrenched at

1. Managing the Strategic Planning Process
2. Managing and Leading People
3. Driving Business Improvement
4. Integrated Business Management
5. Managing Products and Services
6. Managing Demand
7. Managing the Supply Chain
8. Managing Internal Supply
9. Managing External Sourcing

Figure 6.5 *Class A Checklist* **Chapters**
Source: Oliver Wight. Copyright Oliver Wight International, Inc. Used with permission.

the bottom of the maturity map, in Transition 1. When Stan called for a report from the teams, Greg tried to look invisible. "We're probably the only business in this room with such a lousy starting point," he told David. Much to his astonishment, apart from a couple of companies that were in Transition 3, most companies reported that they, too, had placed themselves in Transition 1 with some Transition 2 characteristics.

"As you can all see, most of us are in Transition 1 and Transition 2," Stan summarized. "That's quite normal. It is no help to know where you are if you can't articulate the next level maturity characteristics that would help resolve your business problems such as poor customer service." Greg felt exposed, as if Stan had just spoken directly to him.

"So this is where the Integrated Business Model and the Checklist come together to help you establish the path toward your destination," Stan said. "Class A Business Excellence is recognized at the top of Transition 4. For those of you in Transitions 1 or 2, that's a big jump, too big to make in one step. So the foundation step toward Class A, or even higher, is at the top of Transition 3. We call that the 'Capable' level, as in 'Capable Planning and Control'." Greg had heard that phrase before, and could now begin to see the gap between that level and the starting point for Cosmetics Products.

"Each Checklist chapter covers a key element of the model [Figure 6.5]. That is by design, as I mentioned earlier. We use documented maturity maps for each of these chapters when facilitating diagnostic assessments, much as we did in the workshop we just completed. I'll talk more about each chapter in a few minutes.

"Before I do that, however, I suspect that you may be wondering what you might get out of starting this journey to Class A [Figure 6.6]. So, here are some benefits our clients describe from achieving their first milestone, Capable Planning and Control." Stan discussed each of the bullet points on the slide, and then finished by saying, "Importantly, the real benefit reported by each of our clients is significant bottom-line benefits, the real reason for starting the work."

Stan went back to the Checklist to describe, briefly, the contents of the book, its individual chapters, and highlighted examples of included best practices and behaviors.

- Leverage of full business integration
  - Enhanced predictability and sustainability
  - Business productivity through process reliability and integration
- Time to focus on strategic direction for growth and success
- More responsive to:
  - Customers and stakeholders
  - Market changes
  - Supply chain network
  - Change/cost control
- Significant bottom line benefits
- Enhanced competitive capabilities
- Integrated Improvement programs relate to a common journey:
  - Ensure alignment of initiatives versus competing
  - Identify resources to ensure on-time completion
  - More effective — improve the whole versus parts
- Upper-quartile performance across the business
- Platform for even more advanced business processes

Figure 6.6   Benefits of Achieving Class A Business Excellence
Source: Oliver Wight. Copyright Oliver Wight International, Inc. Used with permission.

"For most of you here, I'm describing a lengthy journey. Although to some it will seem impossible, it becomes possible when you break the journey into smaller, logical steps shaped by your competitive priorities. There are many routes to achieving Class A, and after working with our more advanced clients, we've defined the most common and logical routes as milestones. The journey is not restricted to the defined milestones. We recently tailored a milestone at Capable level for a CEO whose top priority was to instill the company values across the organization. To do this we collated relevant parts from seven of our defined milestones, but this sort of tailoring is rare. Each step is marked along the way by milestones. This approach breaks the journey into truly manageable steps. Each milestone, such as 'Capable Planning and Control' and 'Capable Integrated Business Management,' has a template describing what must be accomplished for successful milestone attainment. Each completed milestone establishes the foundation for a subsequent milestone. I'll show you a graphical summary of all the currently defined milestones and common routes to Business Excellence." Stan went on to describe the milestones and some of their characteristics [Figure 6.7].

Greg's discussions with managers and executives from several other companies during the breaks suggested that Stan's message was hitting home with nearly everyone.

After the break, Mary Medford took over from Stan. Asking whether there were any questions about the presentation so far, she was barraged with questions about the process, the effort to get started, time to get the processes

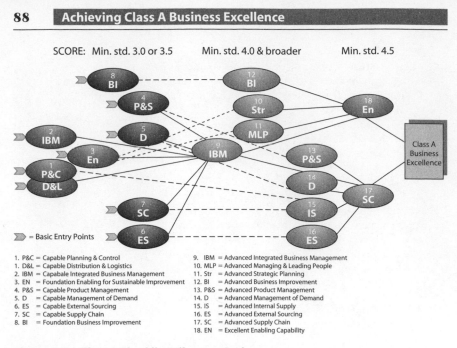

SCORE: Min. std. 3.0 or 3.5   Min. std. 4.0 & broader   Min. std. 4.5

⟫ = Basic Entry Points

1. P&C = Capable Planning & Control
1. D&L = Capable Distribution & Logistics
2. IBM = Capabale Integrated Business Management
3. EN = Foundation Enabling for Sustainable Improvement
4. P&S = Capable Product Management
5. D   = Capable Management of Demand
6. ES = Capable External Sourcing
7. SC = Capable Supply Chain
8. BI = Foundation Business Improvement

9. IBM = Advanced Integrated Business Management
10. MLP = Advanced Managing & Leading People
11. Str = Advanced Strategic Planning
12. BI = Advanced Business Improvement
13. P&S = Advanced Product Management
14. D   = Advanced Management of Demand
15. IS = Advanced Internal Supply
16. ES = Advanced External Sourcing
17. SC = Advanced Supply Chain
18. EN = Excellent Enabling Capability

Figure 6.7   *Class A Checklist* **Milestone Paths**
Source: Oliver Wight. Copyright Oliver Wight International, Inc. Used with permission.

redesigned and the time to deliver business benefits. She responded to each question in general terms, and then returned to the agenda.

"Now, let me turn to a common and very important question," Mary continued. "How do you change your company's culture and create the environment needed to improve business results continuously? Asked another way, how do you actually achieve and sustain what we call Class A Business Excellence?"

Mary responded to her own question. "Over the past 30 years, working with more than a thousand clients, we've developed a methodology to implement those best practices; it works time after time. It's a structured approach that we call our 'Proven Path.'

"This path to success begins with awareness. You could be made aware that there is a better way to run the business from a discussion with a colleague or with someone from another company who has been involved in a Class A initiative. You might learn about Class A from a book or an article about the subject or from attending a presentation or a course. The fact that you are listening to me today tells me that you've already begun your personal journey to success. Your interest has been aroused. Awareness can also come from very poor and even job-threatening business results that compel you to seek a new, more effective way of managing your business." Again Greg had that very uncomfortable feeling that the presenter was speaking directly to him.

"Most of the people who come to this seminar come as a result of business colleagues or friends recommending Effective Management. Why? Because

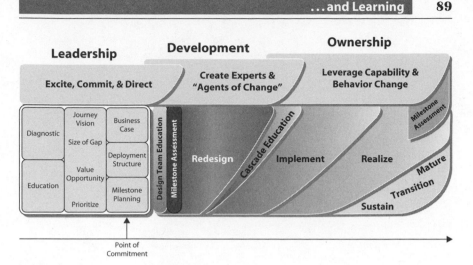

Figure 6.8   The Proven Path
Source: Oliver Wight. Copyright Oliver Wight International, Inc. Used with permission.

they've experienced how we coach them to get control of their business and drive benefits to the bottom line. We don't do the work for our clients; we transfer our knowledge and experience to them. I believe, from my personal experience as a client, that's why our clients become our strongest advocates.

"Companies experiencing problems have three choices: ignore them, delay a decision to do something about them while hoping that things will improve on their own, or decide to do something about the problems. If they decide to do something about them, our Proven Path, which Stan mentioned earlier, provides a proven improvement methodology. Let me show you our Proven Path and walk you through some of its key elements [Figure 6.8]."

Mary identified the Leadership, Development, and Ownership stages and the elements of each stage very briefly. She then directed their attention back to the Leadership stage and said, "I want to focus on the first stage of the model—the stage labeled Leadership on the next slide [Figure 6.9].

"The fundamental change you need to make is essentially a change of corporate culture, which requires leadership, excitement, understanding, commitment, and direction from the very top of the company. This leadership responsibility can never be delegated. I'll say it one more time. Culture change will occur only when it is led from the very top of the organization.

"The Proven Path Leadership work begins with a Diagnostic, an assessment much like you conducted with Stan this morning. It is a cost-effective business analysis at an overview level. This requires the executive team to revisit the company's vision, strategy, and the value proposition—the reasons customers buy from your company again and again.

"The Diagnostic assessment begins with an introduction to the concepts and principles of Business Excellence, such as you are experiencing today.

Leadership

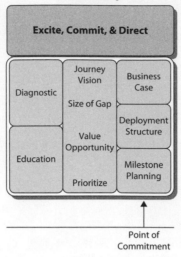

Figure 6.9   Leadership Engagement in the Proven Path
Source: Oliver Wight. Copyright Oliver Wight International, Inc. Used with permission.

That introduction is followed by a facilitated analysis of the business using maturity maps. This morning we used a maturity map for the overall journey, but in the Diagnostic we use specific maturity maps for each of the key business processes. During this maturity analysis, we explain the meaning of each map and executives reach consensus on their current transition level for each. Through our facilitation and the inevitable animated discussions that occur among the executives, we begin to develop a sense of current organizational behaviors and norms at work in the company. The executives can then determine if those current behaviors and norms truly reflect the vision, mission, strategy, value proposition, and espoused values of the organization. More often than not, there are gaps. The executives participating in the Diagnostic begin to understand and appreciate the gaps from best practice within each of their key business processes. In the Diagnostic, we look for answers to these questions: Is there a meaningful vision? Are there strategies covering a suitable strategic horizon? Is there a process to drive the strategies into the business at all levels? Are the executives leading, or reacting? Do the company's processes allow management to lead, or are the processes fragmented and reactive? Where there are processes, are there formal procedures and are they followed? Are people working together to eliminate failures, or does an adversarial climate prevail?

"Many of the concepts and business processes we examine are poorly understood within a company. Yet, to lead such a change program, management must understand them. Assuming the Diagnostic stimulates a positive response, and it usually does, then the next step is to provide executives the necessary education. That education enables them to understand the concepts and principles of business excellence in their company's terms and structures so that they can provide educated leadership on a Class A journey. Simultaneously, key operating managers and influencers are provided a more detailed business excellence course focusing on the integration of middle management's day-to-day activities required to meet senior management's strategic objectives. Using the outcomes of the Diagnostic assessment and subsequent education, senior management can begin to grasp the possibilities and business benefits and to make an educated decision to proceed to the next step, specifically defining the 'journey vision' for the initiative.

"In a workshop that we facilitate, senior managers define their vision of the business as it will be changed by the work. They identify the pressing competitive business needs that the initial milestone must address. So far, so good?" Mary's question was met with silence, meaning either everyone understood the fundamental, common sense steps to this point, or they were deep in thought wondering how to get the ball rolling when they returned to their companies.

"At this point, much of the detailed work required to launch a journey to Class A begins. Completion of the remaining elements of the Leadership stage of the Proven Path can and should be accelerated through facilitated workshops involving the senior and middle managers who attended earlier education events. A review of the findings and gaps from the Diagnostic is followed by facilitated discussions to align on the company vision and mission to achieve the journey vision; to agree on the value of the work in defining the value opportunity—meaning the potential cost, benefits, and opportunities of the journey; to agree on the competitive business priorities; to develop a business case; and to define at least the initial milestones that will address the strategic and business imperatives identified in the earlier steps.

"The selected milestones have templates defining the portions of the Checklist that will be in play. Knowing which milestones will be undertaken also helps determine the deployment structure that will be needed. I'll get into that later, but the deployment structure typically includes the executive management champion, steering team, implementation leader, and milestone and business process design teams.

"With the journey vision, deployment structure, value opportunity, and business case all defined, senior management can now make an informed decision whether or not to launch the work that will complete the first milestone. Senior management can terminate this Leadership stage at any time, but a decision to go forward marks the 'point of commitment' on the Proven Path. Execution begins in earnest at that time.

"The initiative is formally launched; the teams just identified are formed and chartered, and they begin their education. They receive a much more detailed education in their specific business processes and milestones than has been provided up to this point. Following education, the teams assess, with our facilitation, the current processes for which they are responsible against the details of the Checklist. Assessment results determine the gaps to be closed and help the teams identify the resources needed to accomplish the milestones.

In the Redesign phase, process design teams begin to refine design scope and deliverables, benchmark industry leading business results, create action plans to close the gaps, and deploy measures. These measures are used by the teams to track progress and ensure their redesigned business processes meet Checklist requirements and deliver required results. As these new processes are deployed, business process teams develop Cascade Education to provide education and training on the concepts and details of the new processes to those affected by the changes. In the Implement phase, new processes are actually implemented and results of the implementation are tracked. Finally, business benefits are delivered in the phase that we call Realize.

"When the first milestone is nearing completion and the defined business problem is being successfully resolved, companies choosing to continue the journey begin working on their next predefined milestone and business improvement objective, again using the Proven Path. All the work we do with clients focuses on helping them resolve their business problems. After achieving several milestones, many companies decide to continue the journey with the ultimate goal of achieving Class A Business Excellence processes and results throughout the business. This journey to Class A develops the people, processes, and tools required to ensure continuing excellence within a company's industry."

At this point, Mary introduced the two clients who would talk about their experiences in the first stage of the Proven Path.

Charlie Deveneau, Marketing Director for a footwear company, explained that during his company's Diagnostic, the executive team determined its highest competitive priority at that time was improving Product Management performance. In their fashion industry, they were just not fast enough to market, always ending up with excess stocks of products no longer fashionable or of interest to their customers.

Yet another moment of introspection as Greg once again thought the speaker was addressing him personally!

In Charlie's case, Manufacturing was not the biggest problem; the culprit was Sales and Marketing's poor Product Management processes. His executive team decided to target the Capable Product Management Milestone. Charlie described the implementation and benefits, which included faster time to market and increased market share. The completed process improvements made them faster, but still not fast enough to gain a competitive advantage. They discovered weaknesses in their planning and control processes, and began work on the Capable Planning and Control Milestone. Looking ahead, the executive team decided they would next undertake the Advanced Supply Chain Milestone.

Charlie fielded several questions and turned the presentation over to Sanjeev Patel, CFO of a specialty engineering company. As a result of their Diagnostic, Sanjeev's executive team realized that its vision was of the 'motherhood and apple pie' variety, inspiring no one. Their idea of strategy was to have operating plans covering the next three months. A longer-term strategy was undefined, but assumed to be understood. Consequently, individual executives and managers were making personal decisions based on what they believed the strategies should be. They concluded that their competitive priority could be addressed with the Strategic Planning Milestone and its prerequisites. He used a few slides to share their process, developed with the help of Effective Management. The result was an exciting, energizing vision, compelling mission, and supporting strategies that, according to Sanjeev, transformed the executives into a true team and inspired the CEO to lead the business with a long-range view. They now were in discussion about their next milestones, most likely Capable Integrated Business Management and Capable Planning and Control.

At this point, David interrupted, "Aren't you going to be stretched to the limit attempting two milestones at the same time?"

Sanjeev replied that one project would involve the executive team and senior managers, the other, middle managers. They were certain they could pull it off because the work was being led with passion from the CEO. No one argued about priorities or importance. He also explained that these two milestones are synergistic. They have many common elements, and some elements had already been implemented with the Strategic Planning Milestone. The milestones, he said, actually build onto and into each other. As one milestone is completed, there is less work to do in the next milestone because of those common requirements.

During every break, Greg and David spoke with people from other companies and learned that Cosmetics Products was not unique in the problems and challenges they faced. The president of another company said he had heard about this seminar from a colleague who was working with one of the other coaches from Stan's company and was making great progress. That comment opened up a new possibility for Greg.

Greg approached Stan after the seminar ended. "I have to admit, Stan, I was very skeptical about what I could learn from this session. You've hooked me, however, and that's not easy to do."

Stan was pleased. "We find education sessions like this to be critical in setting the stage for a culture change. If Mary and I have caused you to think about your business in a different way, we'll call this a successful day. But this seminar is only the tip of the iceberg, Greg. Education is never ending in a Class A journey. We have many public and tailored private classes that I recommend you look into. If you decide to move forward with this work, you should schedule your people into appropriate classes to give them a good foundation in all the business processes we discussed today."

"Thanks for the information, Stan, but I'm not yet ready to commit at this point. Besides, it sounds pretty expensive to me. We do have a library in the company with books on some of the subjects you discussed; in fact, I think some of them might have been written by your colleagues. I'm sure if we read them, we can apply the techniques and make the progress we need. There is something, however, that would be very helpful to me." Stan got pen and paper ready to make a note of Greg's request.

"Do you happen to have any clients I might call or visit in the next few weeks? Intellectually, I can see how Class A could help a company improve its results, but I learn better when I see those concepts and principles being applied. I also have a concern that what might work in one company, might not work in another. I'll have a much better sense of how to apply what you're telling us if I can actually see it in action."

"I appreciate your skepticism, Greg, and thanks for all your questions during the day. About your comments on the classes, however, I would still recommend that you take advantage of them. We have written a good many books that provide insight and improvement techniques, but classes and workshops provide an entirely different depth and interactive method of learning, and an opportunity to test ideas. I know you're not ready to move forward yet, but don't write off the possibility of utilizing formal, instructor-led classes to jump-start the effort if you decide to take the next step.

"Now, about speaking with some of our clients, I do have some who are willing to talk with others and are sometimes willing to host visits from other companies. I'll need to check with them first, however, to see if they can meet your timing. It sounds like your sense of urgency is high. I like that! I protect my clients so they don't get overwhelmed with requests, but I find visits by senior managers like you are almost always welcomed. I think you'll find most Class A companies and those on the journey are proud of what they've accomplished and are eager to help others. I'll let you know when I've contacted a couple of them. Then you can call them and create a mutual set of objectives to make it a beneficial visit for both companies."

Stan called Greg later that week with the Class A contact information. "I spoke with two companies yesterday, Greg. They would be happy to host a visit for you and a couple of your key people. The first company is Capital Equipment, a billion-dollar manufacturer of machine tools and construction equipment. Bob Radcliff is the President and Chief Operating Officer. He called us shortly after he joined Capital and was the top management champion of their Class A journey.

"The other company is Tender Care Pet Products. It's a smaller company, about $500M in sales, that makes pet food and pet care products. Shannon Stillwell is President and COO, and has been with Tender Care for most of her career. She first called us several years ago and is nearing the end of her Class A journey. Tender Care is in the consumer goods business, like you are, but in noncompeting product areas to the best of my knowledge. At Tender Care, you can see how a Class A consumer goods company handles challenges very similar to those you face with Cosmetics Products.

"Both Bob and Shannon are expecting your call and look forward to meeting you, Greg. Please give me a call after you've visited with them. I'll be eager to hear what you learn and what you see as your next steps."

OBSERVING

*Be careful not to allow a little information seem like a revelation;
it might lead you to an unenlightened solution.*

*We often refer to the way we used to make decisions as our
'ready, fire, aim' era of decision making.*

*Seems that every time I get an answer to a question,
I learn there is even more that I don't know!*

Greg called both Presidents as soon as he ended the conversation with Stan. Each was happy to talk with Greg and made arrangements for a visit within two weeks. Greg then phoned Susan to update her on the seminar and on his planned visits to other companies.

Visit with Capital Equipment

Capital Equipment's site was in Nashville, Tennessee. Greg invited Sara Miles and David Simpson to accompany him on the trip. Before they left, David briefed Sara on the Class A seminar he and Greg had attended. On entering Capital's lobby, all three received visitor badges and were escorted to Bob Radcliff's office, where they were introduced to Bob and to Dan Rogers, Vice President Supply Chain. Following introductions, Bob distributed the agenda for the day and kicked off the meeting.

"We've shaped the agenda to address your questions and interests. We'll start with an introduction to our business and products; then we'll tour our facilities to give you a feel for how things work here. Beyond that, we haven't prepared a formal presentation. You came here to learn from us, but I can tell you that we intend to learn from you as well. We've captured each of your requested topics on the agenda. I'll be with you for the first session and again at the end of the day. Dan will be your host for the remainder of the day and will have others join you as appropriate. Greg, please call me at any time if you have further questions after your visit with us.

"We can empathize with your position and probably your skepticism, too. We were in exactly the same position almost four years ago. We had a profitable business at the time, but looking back from a perspective of what we've learned since them, we really had no technical right to be that profitable and should have been far more profitable. We were disorganized; we used brute force to run the business; we burned out and blamed our people for mistakes that were caused by the management system we created; we buried our problems with inventory. At the same time, we had a terrible customer service record; our costs were increasing; and we had systems and processes that people paid lip service to while they ran the supply chain from spreadsheets. You told me a bit about your challenges, Greg. Let me tell you that we had every one of them and then some when we started our Class A journey. But before we get into those details, let's have Dan give you an overview of the business."

Dan Rogers projected a series of slides describing the history of Capital Equipment, including its recent expansion into new product lines, and reviewed its organizational structure. In the final portion of the presentation, Dan covered the changes in business results Capital attributed to the Class A initiative. "We justified the expense of the Class A journey based on our estimate of bottom line business benefits," Dan said. "Because we were still a bit skeptical, we were very conservative in our estimate of those benefits. I'm happy to report that we far exceeded what we thought we could deliver. Frankly, we were astounded with the improvement. Let me show you what I mean."

"Before we began the work, our customer service was terrible. Only 68 percent of our shipments were delivered on time, and that performance was based on a very loose standard. We considered 'on-time delivery' as a shipment delivered on the requested date or up to five days after that date. We were absolutely incapable of delivering early and rarely hit the requested date. Today, our customer service level is regularly more than 98 percent on time and complete. And what's even more remarkable about that result is that we now consider a delivery to be on time when it is delivered complete on the day we promised the customer."

"That is absolutely awesome, Dan!" Sara chimed in. "Before we leave here today, we must learn how you did that!" Greg and David echoed Sara's comment.

Greg's mind was doing more than just echoing Sara's comment. He thought to himself, "That kind of improvement will save my job if what they've done here will work at Cosmetics Products. I'm not going to get my hopes up, however, because we'll probably find that it won't. But I'd better listen carefully just in case."

Dan continued, "I wish I could give you a simple answer. Fact is, there was neither an easy nor quick solution to our customer service problem. But I think we'll give you a good idea before you leave today of everything we had to go through to accomplish that improvement. Closely associated with that measure, and absolutely counterintuitive to our thinking at the beginning of the initiative, we were able to reduce our inventories by 45 percent."

Greg interrupted, "Wait a minute. Did you say 45 percent?" Dan nodded.

"Up until that point in time, we always assumed that to improve customer service you had to increase inventory. We learned, to our amazement, that the traditional industry paradigm was absolutely wrong. We found that when we built products to increase inventory, we usually built products our customers didn't want. That no longer happens. We are now much better at building what the customers want and when they want it. We keep inventory, to be sure, but we now are clear and disciplined about what kind of inventory we keep, meaning finished goods, assemblies or component parts, how much we keep, why we keep it and where we keep it."

Greg interrupted again, "Hold on a minute, Dan. I recently directed our Manufacturing organization to build inventory to improve customer service. Now you're telling me my directive was exactly opposite of what I should have told them to do? Are you saying that when I get back home I should have David cut inventory by 45 percent? Pardon my cautious nature, but that sounds like a prescription for disaster in my company. We would be out of business in a week if we slashed inventories like that."

"That's a great observation, Greg, and it's a good lead-in to what we need to talk about. Along a Class A journey, be careful not to allow a little information seem like a revelation; it might lead you to an unenlightened solution. We were very good at doing that in the past. In fact, we often refer to the way we used to make decisions as our 'ready, fire, aim' era of decision making. We did not cut inventories precipitously at the beginning of the Class A work. That would have been a disaster for us, too. At the start of the first initiative, the Capable Planning and Control Milestone, we didn't have the processes in place to cut inventory of any kind, except for obsolete and defective items. By not having the people, processes, and tools working together, we were bound to have high inventory levels."

Greg had heard a similar comment before and was now beginning to recognize that inventory might be an outcome of some of the tangled interdependencies he was learning about. He knew he'd need to understand better at some point and made a mental note to talk about it with David.

"Our forecasts were poor, our manufacturing processes were unpredictable, we had quality problems, and we never trusted the inventory numbers in our planning systems. Sound familiar, Greg?" This time the presenter was, indeed, addressing Greg personally; Greg nodded. Dan explained, "Periodically, we would reduce inventory when our Controller made a fuss about how large our inventory had grown. Each time we did it, customer service would suffer and we would refill the warehouses with even more product than before, usually at the insistence of Sales, and always using manufacturing overtime and expedited material shipments. It took us a while to learn why and where we need to keep inventory, and even longer to discover how much to keep. It also took time to improve performance on everything from forecasting through shipping so that we could demonstrate the technical right to reduce the working capital we had tied up in inventory without degrading customer service.

Inventory came down steadily with each improvement in our internal supply chain, and at the same time, those improvements led us to a better than 95 percent customer delivery performance. And here's another unexpected benefit. We continuously modified our business model in the ERP system to reflect our internal supply chain process redesign. Slowly but surely, the planners gained confidence in what the system was recommending and moved away from their spreadsheets. They began doing all their work inside the ERP system and delivered even greater benefits."

David looked visibly relieved. "Thanks very much for that clarification, Dan. You just saved me a huge headache. I was having this horrible vision of getting back to the office and having Sara and Greg tell me to cut my inventories to the bone!"

"You're quite welcome, David. Keep in mind that results don't improve overnight; Class A is a change in the corporate culture that takes a good deal of time. Sure, you get some early improvements from harvesting low-hanging fruit, but there's a ton of work to do on business processes and people's behaviors before you see the type of benefits we realized. A key part of that change for us executives was implementing the Sales and Operations Planning process that we later evolved to Capable Integrated Business Management. I presume Stan talked quite a bit about Integrated Business Management during the Seminar." Greg and David nodded in agreement again, and Dan continued. "You'll find that most of the behaviors needing modification have been in place for years. Those of us in senior management needed the results improvements and pushed other people to change the way they worked. But, as we discovered, we ourselves were among the worst at being able to change what we always did. It seems to me that people generally embrace change so long as it is someone else who needs to change. When we started seeing the new processes working, and people following the processes with discipline, the results began building synergistically. That's one of the benefits of real process integration."

"Just look at the impact of our performance improvements on sales volume. Because we reduced lead times and could provide outstanding customer service, our sales increased by 21 percent. That improvement provided top-line growth to go along with significantly reduced costs. Bottom line, we saw a 268 percent improvement in profit over the past three years. Other projects going on at the same time contributed to the improvement, but we are absolutely confident our Class A Milestone implementation either delivered directly or enabled most of these benefits. The improved control of our business achieved through the Class A work gave us the time we needed to work on other improvement projects. Otherwise those initiatives would still be on our wish list."

At this point, Dan suggested a tour of the facility so they could get a feel for some of the changes made by Capital Equipment. Following the tour, the group returned to the executive conference room to continue the discussion. Greg commented first.

"That was a useful tour, Dan. I was really impressed with the people we met. Everyone was positive and very knowledgeable about customer service and production priorities. I also liked the fact that everyone sensed the importance of their individual performance in executing plans and in meeting the needs of customers. I'm not sure how to describe what I felt when I was touring, but it seemed like things were happening routinely out there. I didn't see people running around expediting customer orders like we do. But I suppose what impressed me most was how proud everyone seems to be about their accomplishments. Is that different from what it was in the past, or has that always been part of your corporate culture?"

"I can't begin to tell you how big a change that has been for us, Greg. You just described a critical part of the culture change required in what you've seen and heard today. Had you visited before we began our Class A journey, you would have seen a negative, even cynical, organization. We provided a good deal of education to a broad spectrum of the company's population, including our executive team and managers. People learned how everything they do must be focused on meeting the needs of the customer. We also learned how functional barriers compromise our ability to serve those customers. In the past, Sales, Manufacturing, Purchasing, Engineering, and Planning were always at each others' throats. Everyone now has a much better perspective of how the company works from one end to the other, and how what they do affects everyone else. As I said before the tour, these changes, especially the culture changes, don't happen quickly. But when they happen, the whole company begins to perform better."

Sara asked, "What are people doing differently today to deliver these enviable results you shared with us?"

"Good question, Sara. Let me give you a few of the most important changes. We now have very formal and documented business policies, processes, what we call procedures, and in some cases even detailed work instructions. These define *why* we do things, *what* we do, and finally *how* we do our work. Executives and their direct reports own the 'why.' The senior and middle managers own the 'what.' And the people who perform the work develop their own procedures and work instructions, the 'how.' The why, what, and how are all integrated so that there are no rogue 'personal' procedures at work undermining formal processes. This is completely consistent with ISO9000 guidelines that we follow here in Capital Equipment. Each project team worked hard to create these processes, made sure they were fully integrated with the policies, processes, and procedures created by the other project teams, and then trained all the appropriate people on the changes they made.

"Here's another equally important difference, maybe the most important. The business is now driven from a single set of operating numbers and plans.

This starts with our Integrated Business Management process through which we produce an approved set of product, sales, supply, and inventory plans that support our customers and business strategy and are driven down through the entire supply chain, even into our supplier base. Everyone knows what he or she is accountable for in achieving those plans."

"That sounds quite rigid to me. Doesn't it restrict your flexibility and responsiveness? I get a sense that our customers might be quite a bit less predictable than yours."

"I wouldn't bet that our customers are any more predictable than yours, but we had a similar initial reaction, Greg. Then our coach explained a simple truth to us. I've got the slide here" [Figure 7.1].

"If you believe in continuous improvement, you have to believe in standardization. To improve any process sustainably, you have to control it first. That's where standardization comes in. When it's in control, you can implement process improvements while retaining or redeveloping control. We were asked to consider this simple analogy: What is two times two times two? Answer, eight. All the factors are in control, so the outcome is consistent. It's always eight. Now how about this: two times two times v, where v is a variable? There is no definitive answer. There is a range within which any answer might lie, but you can't run a supply chain cost effectively with uncontrolled variables. The level of control we have today enables our 98 percent customer service level. Now we're looking at completing our Class A journey and know we'll have to do an even better job of controlling variables to enable 99.5 percent customer

1. You must *Standardize* to gain *Control.*
2. You must have *Control* to make *Improvements.*
3. You need *Discipline* to ensure the *Standard* is followed.
4. You need *Creativity* to continually *Improve.**
   *Using the principle of: 'my second job is to improve job #1.'

This is a cultural issue that management owns.

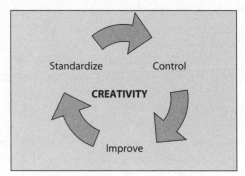

Figure 7.1   Sustainable Improvement
Source: Oliver Wight. Copyright Oliver Wight International, Inc. Used with permission.

service. We know without question that we'll have to do an even better job of refining our processes and behaviors.

"There's another change, Sara. We've implemented a suite of measures and continuous improvement analytical tools that allow people to track performance and identify actions necessary to improve their results. We no longer just report a bunch of numbers; we now use measures to drive improvements. That alone is remarkably different for us.

"As a result of the single set of plans, the suite of measures, the continuous improvement tools, and the fully integrated business processes, trust has improved dramatically within the company and with our customers and suppliers as well. People believe the numbers they see on their computer screens, they don't second-guess the forecast, and they believe that others will do what they say they will do. We no longer have to waste time double-checking things or checking up on what people committed to do. If there is a problem, people speak up immediately. We operate under the principle of 'silence is approval.' If you don't speak up, we assume you can and will do what you said you would do. When you put all of that together, it's what we sometimes call 'Integrated Supply Chain Management.'"

David and Greg exchanged a knowing glance with each other at the mention of "silence is approval." They had joked on the way home from the seminar that Stan Stevens had used those words a hundred times.

David commented, "What you just described is a totally different world from ours. I can now see what you mean by culture change and appreciate the amount of time it required. I can't even imagine how we would get there from where we are today."

"I had exactly the same concern when we started the work, David. It takes time and effort, but we used the well-tested 'Proven Path' methodology for making the transformation. Don't let the gap discourage you. You'll begin seeing improved business results with every milestone long before you reach Class A. With outside education and coaching, we succeeded. The rewards have been well worth the effort."

Greg stood, walked over to a serving cart and poured himself a cup of coffee while he determined how to raise a nagging concern. "You know, Dan, what you've accomplished is amazing. I see how what you've done works in your industry. Sounds to me that you pretty much make products based on orders from your customers, but we don't have that luxury in Cosmetics Products. You mentioned how well the Integrated Business Management process works for you. I know a little about that process from Stan Stevens' seminar, at least enough to know that there is a heavy reliance on forecasting. In the cosmetics industry, it's nearly impossible to forecast what consumers want. We work a lot on forecasting, but our customers and their consumers change their minds about what they want at the drop of a hat. A particularly effective advertisement, a coupon in the Sunday newspaper, or even a casual comment on a late night television talk show can change everything. That's one of the reasons we need so much inventory. In addition, our products are constantly changing. If we don't say 'new and improved' on our products and packages, our customers lose interest and buy some other company's 'new and improved' product. And very often, our competitors drive the timing of those changes. When they introduce a change to one of their products, we have to respond quickly and try to leapfrog their design during our next cycle of product changes. All in all, we're in completely different businesses."

"I can certainly understand your concerns, Greg. I also had Stan as an instructor in the class I attended. I enjoyed the class and his presentation, but was a little dubious about the whole thing. I don't know how many end items or stock-keeping units (SKUs) you have to plan and forecast, Greg, but for comparison, given the number of options we offer our customers, we have well over a million different end items. Actually, nearly every end item is unique, so we assemble our final products on the basis of our customers' orders. Rarely do we get an order for multiple copies of the same end item. Even though we assemble products to order, we still must forecast the business to have the right components, assemblies, and capacities available when orders materialize. When we realized the importance of dramatically improving our forecasting ability, our demand manager was ready to submit her resignation. We had to change our forecasting strategy and techniques. Since then, we've increased forecast accuracy from 22 percent to 65 percent and it's still improving. Our demand manager has also made great progress on narrowing the range of forecast variability, another important measure we're now tracking.

"Based on the coaching we received, we also changed how we master schedule. By modifying our process and adopting a more Finish-to-Order approach, we reduced the mountain of end items and parts we had to master schedule to a small but significant mound. We also have to deal with customers who change their minds right up to the minute when we ship an order. Our Manufacturing Director jokes that if he can catch the truck before it reaches our customer's dock, he can still fulfill a customer change request." Greg still looked doubtful.

"I admit there are probably some similarities, but your business is far different from ours, Dan. Your planning and supply processes are undoubtedly so different that they just don't translate to our environment. I really wish we could apply them directly because we certainly need the improvement you've delivered, but I just can't make the connection."

"I wouldn't jump to that conclusion, Greg. I visited a Class A manufacturer and distributor of meat products about four years ago and reached the same conclusion that you just reached. Over time, however, I realized that their basic business processes—forecasting, demand planning, master scheduling and production planning—are similar to ours. They have things like bills of material and routings, just as we do. Our products are significantly different from theirs, as are the ways we had to apply the concepts and principles of Class A, but their fundamental business processes are almost identical to ours.

While we were both performing the same business processes, the company I visited was executing those business processes far more effectively than we were at the time. When I finally woke up to that fact, I could get past the 'my company's different' thinking that had been blocking my creativity."

"That's an excellent point, Dan. I know that I have to think differently about my business, and you've certainly given me a different perspective on how a company can operate more effectively. Guess I'm resisting change, too!

"You told us there was a big effectiveness gap between you and that meat products company when you began your Class A journey. You also said something about a methodology you used to help close that gap. Tell us more about that methodology if you can." Dan paused for a moment to compose his thoughts.

"A couple of us had heard about Class A from business associates. We made arrangements to visit the meat company I mentioned, and later bought some copies of the *Class A Checklist* that they used to guide their improvement effort. We really thought we could get to Class A on our own, but over time realized we were stumbling around in a disjointed effort. That's when we called Effective Management (EM) and spoke with Jim Clark. We were in trouble, needed to get better results quickly, and just couldn't afford to waste any more time on our own. As with other EM people I've met since then, I found Jim to be very knowledgeable. What he said on the phone made a great deal of sense. I learned that Jim had been part of a Class A initiative as a senior executive with a client company before he began consulting. Since then, he's educated and coached many more companies to Class A. I phoned a few of his Class A clients who recommended him highly, so we asked him to work with us. He and a small team from his company brought clarity to our efforts and took us through a very disciplined and structured approach to achieving excellence. He and his colleagues got us aligned on a common vision and enabled us to move in the right direction quickly. In fact, had we been better listeners and stayed away from our 'we're different' excuses, we would probably have achieved Class A much sooner. You know, Jim and his team were pretty tough on us. They wouldn't do the work. Instead, they educated and coached us on best practice processes and behaviors so that we could do the work more effectively and efficiently ourselves, and so we could realize sustainable benefits sooner. Jim said over and over, 'You have to do the work yourselves so that you know what to do when we leave'. If it weren't for Jim and his team, we would still be stumbling around and undoubtedly would have given up without achieving the benefits. Had we not turned around our results, we might not even be here today. I'm sure you heard Stan Stevens say, 'If it isn't your blood on the pavement, you won't be successful.' We weren't sure what that meant at first, but soon realized it meant that to be successful, we would have to roll up our sleeves and do the work ourselves."

Both Greg and David chuckled, but realized the wisdom and the challenge of that statement.

Greg, Sara, and David spent the rest of the visit asking more detailed questions about the objectives, results, business process changes, and the methodology recommended by Jim Clark. They had time to meet with their counterparts at Capital and found them open and eager to share what they had learned. They heard a good-news story—one that they desperately needed to duplicate in their own company. They wrapped up the day with Bob Radcliff, who said, "Let me just add one other thought. We did our Class A work using an earlier edition of the *Class A Checklist*, but continuous improvement is also alive and well in Jim's organization. Effective Management is on a journey to excellence as well, and constantly incorporates new and improved best practices into their Checklist and into their coaching. Their latest edition is far more comprehensive and more broadly business oriented than the last one. We're still learning about it and have Jim coaching us on how to incorporate the latest ideas into our business processes. We've become a learning organization. With our continuous improvement culture, we never take a 'time out' from learning. If we did, we would quickly slip to the back of the pack among our competitors." Bob went on to summarize the benefits realized by Capital Equipment and again invited the group to call with any follow-up questions they might have.

On the way back to Atlanta, Greg, Sara, and David compared notes and impressions. The visit was enlightening and caused them to think differently about the challenges they faced. Capital was a company that had faced similar challenges and pressures several years ago. Capital not only survived, it prospered as a result of its Class A initiative. Greg, Sara, and David wondered privately whether changes similar to those made by Capital could produce the same outcome for Cosmetics Products. They saw for themselves what Capital had accomplished, but still had no real idea how to implement the required changes in their own company.

For Greg, there was also the concern about using outside consultants. For a long time, he held a personal bias against relying on people outside his own company, but Capital was singing the praises of Effective Management and how its approach was different from that of other consultants. Apparently they operated more as educators, mentors, and coaches than the others. They seemed first to focus on education and then coached Capital to Class A processes and results. One of Greg's personal development objectives was to open his thinking to new possibilities and challenge some of his personal paradigms. But he was still reluctant to use a consultant; changing his long-held views was proving difficult.

Visit with Tender Care Pet Products

During the following week, Greg, Alexandra Templeton (his new Sales and Marketing Vice President), and Matt Rutherford visited Tender Care Pet Products in Kansas City, Missouri. This visit presented Greg an opportunity to see how a consumer goods company, more like Cosmetics Products, approached the challenge of achieving business excellence. Before they left for Kansas City, Sara and David briefed Alexandra and Matt about what they learned from Capital and on what Greg and David learned from Stan during the EM seminar.

Shannon Stillwell, President and Chief Operating Officer of Tender Care Pet Products, and Allen Burke, her Operations Vice President, hosted the visit. They greeted the team from Cosmetics Products enthusiastically and immediately began a tour of the headquarters and plant facilities. Following the tour, they settled in the executive conference room. "That was an eye-opening tour," Greg began. "I'm not sure what I expected to see, but I was surprised by the cleanliness and orderliness of your operations. I was also surprised to see very little inventory in the production areas. Everything seemed to be moving so smoothly compared with what I see in our operation. I don't know how to describe exactly what I mean, but I sensed something different, perhaps a different rhythm than what I sense in our company, or perhaps a different level of focus and control. Things seemed to be 'humming,' although that doesn't describe effectively what I felt during the tour."

Matt and Alexandra nodded in agreement. "I would expect you have some rather impressive results coming from that level of focus and control. By the way, why did you choose to go after Class A, Shannon?"

"That's an interesting observation and good question, Greg. Regarding why we decided Class A was right for us, I wish I could say that it was leadership brilliance on our part, but in reality we were in deep trouble. In retrospect, we should have initiated the work much earlier, but you know the old saying—'necessity is the mother of invention.' We implemented new ERP software in the fall of 1999. Our old software was rather archaic anyway, and we were worried about potential Y2K problems affecting our ability to run the business. We invested more than $50M on software and training, and saw no benefits. Six months later, people were still running the business using spreadsheets and the same procedures as before the investment. If anything, our ability to service the customer was worse because everyone had been distracted by the software implementation project. We missed product launch dates because we were too slow creating bills of material. We missed shipments because we promised deliveries based on what the system told us, and then couldn't find the product that was buried somewhere in the warehouse. We ran out of raw materials. We couldn't ship product because the information required by the computer was incorrect or missing. We couldn't pay our suppliers because of corrupt data in our supplier and material masters. You name it: it happened to us. Customers were getting poor service, we had some suppliers refuse to do business with us, and we had a few of our best customers actually fire us."

"Shannon, your description is eerily familiar. You just described our company. I guess the good news, besides your success in solving all those problems, is that I now know we are not a uniquely dysfunctional company!"

"We are living proof, Greg, that you are not alone. There are lots of companies profitable enough to stick their heads in the sand and cover up problems with either money or inventory," Allen Burke interjected. "I know that for a fact, because we did it for a long time. We had some 'designer' lines of pet food that were so profitable they covered up our problems. Our motto at that time was, 'Denial is a river in Egypt.' We weren't so much in denial about our problems as we were simply blinded by our success. We couldn't appreciate how much money we were wasting in operating the business that way. It finally caught up with us when a few competitors improved their products and supply chains, lowered their prices, and beat our customer service level. We lost some long-term customers. All this happened at a time when we were still paying for our ERP system investment. We raised prices a couple of times, watched our inventory spill out into additional warehouses, and found ourselves right in the middle of a crisis. Had we been using Sales and Operations Planning at that time, we would have seen what was coming and would have taken corrective action to prevent the worst of the problems. At the time, we thought that long-range planning meant looking at next month's forecast. We had major problems and were totally unprepared to deal with them. We didn't understand that our business processes could deliver good functional results and, at the same time, undermine our overall business results. We had a Cadillac of an ERP system, but had no idea how to make it work for us."

"Allen has described our situation very accurately, Greg. We didn't know whether we could recover in time to avoid bankruptcy. Just out of curiosity, are the problems Allen described really that similar to the problems in your company?"

Matt was first to respond. "I can only echo Greg's earlier comment that you have just described Cosmetics Products perfectly. We have all of those problems. Let me ask you this. When you realized you were in trouble, how did you come up with a game plan for recovery?"

Shannon thought for a moment. "A few of our supply chain experts kept trying to tell us that we couldn't fix our problems with a new ERP system alone. They told us that we needed to focus on improving our business processes first and needed some outside help. Our leadership team, however, was convinced that we knew what to do, and that we were smart enough to solve our problems. Of course, we were distracted at the same time by product launches, budgeting issues, and myriad other priorities called 'running the business.'

"We had been a successful company and had little interest in the changes our supply chain experts said were needed. We paid a big price for that decision. But it was only when the CFO pushed the numbers in front of us and actually shouted, 'You better do something about this now!' that we admitted we were in crisis and asked for recommendations. We talked with our own experts, not for the first time mind you, but for the first time we really heard them. They told us about Class A and about all the work that we should have done before implementing the new software system. They told us that we needed to reimplement the software, but this time doing it properly. I have to confess that I said to them, 'Okay guys, go do it; you have my blessing.' They just stared at me. One of them finally and quietly spoke up and told me that the core of the problem was me, the executives, and senior managers. He told me that the executive team needed to implement Sales and Operations Planning (S&OP). I was a bit perplexed and told him verbatim, 'We manage the business; we pay others to be planners.' Looking back, I can't believe I said that. Know what they did? Have a look. This is what they handed to us. It's a definition of Planning. I keep this on my wall in the office as a reminder of that day:

> Planning is the first step in management. It consists of setting measurable objectives and deciding how to achieve them. Planning is a prerequisite for execution and control. Without plans there is no basis for evaluating the results achieved. Planning not only provides the path for action, it also enables management to evaluate the probability of successfully completing the journey. Planning, execution, and control are iterative processes that should occur continuously.
>
> *Source:* Donald W. Fogarty, John H. Blackstone, Jr. and Thomas R. Hoffmann. *Production & Inventory Management,* 2nd Edition (Cincinnati, OH: South-Western Publishing Co., 1991).

"You see? 'The first step in management.' That really hit home. Of course we're planners. So I decided to implement the latest evolution of S&OP—Integrated Business Management, at the Capable level—and led the Task Team myself, with the help of Effective Management, of course." David smiled. Greg was certain he knew what David was thinking. Shannon continued.

"They suggested that we needed to revisit the company vision as a first step, and say it in two sentences! I thought this would be easy, but when the executives met, we discovered that each of us had a different understanding of the vision. That was a revelation and an important first step for us. You know the sayings, 'If you don't know where you're going, any road will do!' and 'If you don't know where you are, a map won't help.' We asked individuals at all levels to state the company vision. That was enlightening and more than a little disappointing. Even those of us on the executive team couldn't pass that test. Unfortunately, that's who we were at the time.

"We had to reexamine our leadership and who we are as a company. As a result, we established and communicated throughout the company a clear vision and mission; then we renewed our business strategies and our strategic business objectives. We literally reevaluated how we want the market to view us by restating our Value Proposition so that everyone in the company, and outside the company for that matter, can understand our distinctive contribution in the marketplace. At that point, we knew where we were headed.

"As to 'where we were' at the time, we took a different path. We needed a meaningful assessment. Two of our people had been in Class A companies earlier in their careers and presented a compelling case for outside, professional help to ensure the assessment would be useful and objective. We began working with a small EM team led by Roxanne Barnes."

Over the next few hours, Shannon and Allen described Tender Care's transformation. They shared the remarkable turnaround of their bottom line business results. "In a two-year period we first set our sights on the 'Capable Planning and Control' and 'Capable Integrated Business Management' Milestones. Then we expanded that work to include the 'Foundation Enabling for Sustainable Improvement' Milestone to improve our people and continuous improvement best practices. And we've just recently completed the 'Advanced Supply Chain' Milestone. As you can see, we focused our efforts on becoming a benchmark company that all our competition would envy. Our customer service climbed steadily from 88 percent, to 95 percent, then 98 percent, and is now routinely above 99.5 percent." Greg and his team gasped audibly at this statement.

"Greg, I'm not finished," Shannon said. "Our sales volume grew by 34 percent; cost of goods sold dropped 9 percent; inventory was reduced by 23 percent; and profit increased by 66 percent."

The story, the approach, the method and tools used, and the results improvements were remarkably similar to what they had heard from Capital Equipment. Matt and Alexandra took copious notes, while Greg mentally compared the similarities and differences between Capital and Tender Care. Greg then moved on to considering the similarities between Tender Care and Cosmetics Products. Despite the obvious differences in products, the message from Capital was nearly identical to the message they were hearing from Tender Care. Either because Greg was hearing it for the second time, or because Tender Care and Cosmetics Products were both in the consumer goods industry, the message was getting through.

As they wrapped up the visit, Greg said to Shannon, "If you can, I'd like you to summarize the three things that enabled you to deliver the incredible results you've shared."

"I really wish we hadn't made it sound that easy, Greg. Listing three things would sell short what we had to do. I won't even try to get it down to just three things, but I suppose the first key step was to select a standard of excellence against which to measure our performance." Tender Care had used the same standard as Capital Equipment, the *Class A Checklist for Business Excellence*, and they also studied benchmark performance levels of companies in their industry.

"Until that point in time," Shannon explained, "we always measured ourselves against what we had done in the past and against the budget.

"Next, we brought in the outside counsel to educate and coach us about excellence and how to achieve it for ourselves, not to do the work for us. Roxanne and her team caused us to be disciplined, and gave us a structured approach to achieving excellence. That turned out to be critical to our success.

"We educated a broad cross-section of the organization on those best practices, what they mean and the power of integrating them. We also conducted two types of assessment to determine where we stood against Class A companies. Roxanne Barnes called the first type of assessment a Diagnostic assessment of the organization. She facilitated that assessment for our executive team using maturity maps as calibration benchmarks. This set of maps covers the full scope of business excellence as defined in the Checklist. That helped us get a feel for where we were at the time, specifically our level of development or organizational maturity in each of the business process areas. I have to tell you that the maturity maps enabled us to reach consensus quickly on our overall company's effectiveness. In most business processes, we found ourselves pretty much in the firefighting mode when we started. The Diagnostic identified the areas where we were the weakest and where we needed to focus our efforts to solve our highest priority problems. It also enabled us to begin defining the sequence of improvement milestones against which we would target our efforts.

"After we had agreed on the initial milestones, we worked with our coaches to define the project behind each improvement milestone, formed cross-functional project milestone teams, and charged them with closing the identified gaps and improving specific business results.

"With those milestone teams in place and chartered, our next step was to educate the teams and some additional subject matter experts at a much deeper level. This education prepared them for the second type of assessment, a detailed assessment of our business processes against Checklist elements relating to the Capable Planning and Control and Capable Integrated Business Management Milestones. In those assessments, we involved the milestone teams and our own subject matter experts for each of the business processes. They compared our current procedures and behaviors to the details contained in the Checklist. We needed to know specifically where we stood against the best companies.

"We did a couple other important things differently in the areas of education and measures," Allen added. "We now recognize that people in planning roles must be professionals just like people in sales, marketing, product development, and engineering. Seems pretty logical, now, but it didn't occur to us in the past. After all, planners are the people who must balance our capabilities with the ever-changing marketplace needs. We've learned that is no small task. The planners need to know our customers and their requirements, our products and services, our internal capabilities and the capabilities of our suppliers. They must be knowledgeable in the concepts, principles, and techniques of production and inventory management. For that reason, we started putting highly capable people in planning roles. First we brought them up to speed with current knowledge and best practices by using Effective Management courses. This was a fast process. For longer-term maintenance of knowledge, and to increase the professional status of our planners, we insist that all planners work steadily against a personal goal of achieving certifications from external Associations. This takes longer, but reinforces our commitment to planning excellence. Additionally, we have some senior supply chain people now involved in several supply chain forums.

"We also require our planners to be expert in the use of the ERP planning systems. In the past, we moved people through those roles frequently, but we've learned how shortsighted that was. We now have career paths in planning and logistics enabling people to be recognized and rewarded as experts in those areas.

"Turning to tracking performance measures for just a moment, in the past we had all kinds of measures, but they were mostly functional measures. With the help of our coaches, we developed a set of integrated measures that allow us to better monitor the health of our business processes. That, in turn, caused us to examine how well we were driving those improvements to the bottom line. Our measures are now more forward looking. We structured the measures so that we can predict what our business results will be in the future and prevent rather than react to crises. It was quite a challenge to define and implement the metrics behind each measure, meaning exactly where, when, who, and how to get the necessary data; what calculation to use; how to make the results visible; and how to integrate these back up to the Executive Dashboard. You'd be amazed at how many exceptions were being 'forgiven' in our old measures. We had been fooling ourselves about our reported results for years! But those days are gone.

"I'll give you a few examples of our new measures. Sales plan performance, forecast accuracy, bill of distribution accuracy, bill of material accuracy, routing accuracy, master supply schedule performance, inventory accuracy, and supplier delivery performance are all measures that we didn't have in place a few years ago. They've now become so important to us in monitoring the health of the company that we can't imagine trying to run the business without them.

"We used to take enormous pride in our skills as crisis managers. We thought that was the ultimate mark of a successful manager. Some of our best crisis managers were legends in their own time. We were probably among the best at that in any industry, mostly because we had so many opportunities to practice. Talk about an expensive way to run a business! With this new set of measures we've become skilled in listening to the business through the measures and taking action to avoid most of the crises altogether. That's not just a major change in our culture; it's a major improvement in relationships among our business partners and in the quality of work life for all of us. I'll give you an idea of just how much a change it has been. We've had to learn how to recognize and reward people's ability to prevent problems and avoid crisis management heroics. That's not as easy as it sounds. It's much easier to see and reward people running around and reacting to a crisis than it is to see the creativity involved in avoiding one."

"That's well said, Allen," Shannon interrupted. "We now use the measures and our balanced scorecard almost like a panel of aircraft instruments. We no longer have to 'fly blind' or by the 'seat of our pants.'

"From a business perspective, some of the improved bottom line results are attributable to a solid Integrated Business Management process, and the single set of operational plans and numbers used by everyone to run the business. We trust the numbers we see and make better data-based decisions. We also trust each other to do what we say we will do all along our supply chain, both internally and externally. And we have the ability to do scenario analyses, and more recently some modeling, to test the implications of decisions before we execute them. Our people now let the computer crunch the numbers while they spend their time working on ways to improve the business. That's many more than three things that we did, but I hope we answered your last question, Greg."

"You did indeed, Shannon, although you used a number of terms, especially the measures you referenced, that I don't understand. Seems that every time I get an answer to a question, I learn there is even more that I don't know!

"A concern with what I've heard so far is that I've had some disappointing experiences in the past with consultants, and I want your opinion. I'm more inclined to rely on internal experts, but both you and Capital Equipment, whom we visited last week, told us that using outside resources has been a critical success factor. Speaking specifically about Effective Management, how do you rate the people who worked with you? And, based on your experience, would you recommend I call and set up an appointment with them?"

"Yes, without any reservations. You'll find that their personnel have a real passion for what they do because they have been through it themselves as clients of their consulting firm. So don't expect a bunch of people who tell you what you want to hear. I can promise you from firsthand experience, they will tell you what you *need* to hear. The real enlightenment and improvement, however, came from *our* doing the work, with their coaching, and applying what we learned to create breakthroughs in business processes and results. Our people really take pride in what they accomplished.

"Our coach was Roxanne Barnes. She asks difficult questions and has tough standards that she insists you meet. On occasion, she gave me some pretty straight feedback about my own behavior. From time to time, some of our project team members didn't like her very much because she held them accountable for their results and accepted no excuses. But she enabled all of us to deliver some pretty remarkable improvements.

"Let me give you a little more to think about, Greg. Since we began our journey to Class A business excellence, we can see that we have even further to go; it's a never-ending journey. We intend to keep improving and to become one of the most effective companies on earth. To that end, we've asked Roxanne and her group to continue coaching us toward full Class A Business Excellence so that we can move on and mature as a company. That's probably more than you want to think about now, but if I were in your shoes, Greg, I would call her, or one of her colleagues, as soon as you get back to your office and hope that one of them has some open time in their calendar to work with you."

Matt and Alexandra seemed as excited with what they observed at Tender Care, as did Sara and David at Capital. They were eager to produce the same turnaround as their host companies, but knew they would need help if they were to be successful. Greg sensed that among his leadership team he was creating a critical mass for changing the organization, but was still a little reluctant to involve a consulting firm.

That night when he arrived home, he shared the details of the trip with Penny. "You know, I'm becoming painfully aware of just how much I need to learn and how little time I have to learn it. I've now seen two companies that used to be in just as much trouble as we are. But based on what we observed firsthand, you would never believe they were in that kind of trouble a few years ago. It gives me a lot of hope that we can do the same thing, but I'm still not sure how to do it. You're aware of my bias against consultants, but both company Presidents said the people who worked with them were critical to their success. They must have found consultants who work differently from those I've worked with in the past." Penny smiled; she knew that Greg was already beginning to open up to new ways of thinking.

"Sounds like you've had a good couple of weeks to me. You may not yet have the answers you're looking for, but I hear more optimism and excitement in your voice than I've heard in a long time. I know you enjoy learning, and I sense you are on a pretty steep learning curve right now. But why not give the consultants a chance? What do you have to lose?"

"You couldn't be more right about that, Penny. The good news is that I seem to be on the steepest learning curve of my career. The bad news is that it may be the longest learning curve of my career. I simply have to learn faster; perhaps this Roxanne person can help me with that. I'm just not completely comfortable, yet."

Later that week during his Leadership Team meeting, Greg and those who accompanied him on the Class A company visits summarized what they learned for the others. They discussed the challenges involved in making the changes needed, especially the resistance they would have to overcome with the amount of change ahead of them. They also discussed the obvious risk of doing nothing and quickly concluded that doing nothing was not an option. At least now they knew there was a tested and proven path forward. What they didn't know was how, specifically, they could achieve the needed results. One thing was clear. They did not have the knowledge and expertise to get there on their own, at least quickly enough to survive. Greg's staff knew that they needed the outside help suggested by both Capital and Tender Care, but they could still sense Greg's hesitation. They asked him to articulate the specific concerns fueling his resistance.

"I'll be straight with you. In part, my concern is purely personal and emotional, and I'll admit that. Susan brought me here to solve our problems. Hiring a consultant is an admission that I don't have the answers. I know full well that neither Susan, you, nor anyone else expects me to have all the answers.

Nevertheless, that I don't have the answers is an admission I don't like to make. That consideration gets in my way, and I know I have to get over it."

Sara was the first to respond. "Greg, I think I can understand your concerns. Most of us have worked with consultants in the past and probably share some of those concerns. And not one of us in this room likes to admit we don't have all the answers. Having said that, I didn't pick up on any evidence of what you're concerned about during the visit to Capital, and I didn't hear any negative comments from your trip to Tender Care either. Sounds like the consulting group that these companies used has a unique consulting model. I'd recommend having one of them come to see us. Let us address your concerns head-on and find out how the consultant proposes to work with us. Now, let me ask you a direct question if I may, Greg. What's our alternative? We've been unable so far to solve the problems on our own despite our best efforts. We've seen two companies that we could try to emulate, but we don't have time to do the necessary research and learn all the details about what they did to achieve their results. Don't forget, they said they tried it on their own and failed. I think we are just flat out of big ideas about what to do next. So what's our next step if we don't bring in this consultant?"

The others nodded in agreement, and Greg replied, "You've made a good point, Sara. If we invite a consultant in for a visit, we could at least have that person address my concerns. We know that Roxanne Barnes has been successful in helping another consumer goods company and, to be honest, I just feel more comfortable working with someone in our industry. I know that's probably wrong, but it's just how I feel. I also feel comfortable knowing that Roxanne is highly recommended by the Chief Operating Officer of Tender Care. Since you put it to me straight, Sara, I know I need to make the decision about what to do next and make it soon. I'll call Roxanne tomorrow and will let you know what I find out."

Early the following morning, Greg called the cell phone number given to him by Shannon Stillwell and spoke directly with Roxanne. Greg introduced himself and told Roxanne about his visit with Shannon and her staff at Tender Care. After recapping all the good things that the company had to say about her work, he shared with Roxanne some of his concerns about working with consultants. He also assured her that he was impressed with what she was accomplishing with Tender Care and might need her help in delivering similar business improvements for Cosmetics Products.

Roxanne explained that there was a proven process to help Greg and his team at this early stage. She outlined for him what she called a "Facilitated Diagnostic" through which they would collectively gain a better understanding of where they were and insight into where they could be. She explained why this would take at least two days, a heavy commitment for executives.

Roxanne proposed an agenda for the 'Facilitated Diagnostic.' "I'll be using a set of our simple, but powerful, maturity maps as a tool to help you define where Cosmetics Products is today. At the beginning of the first day, I'll want to hear from you and your team the nature of the problems you're dealing with and your business objectives. I'd also like a tour of the facility, especially if you have supply operations there, just to get a better feel of how the organization works. I also need time alone with some of your key managers from across the Division during the day. Toward the end of the day, I'll facilitate the Diagnostic for you and your Leadership Team, and also share my initial observations. Then on day two, having talked about the gaps, I'll give you some insight into our business excellence expectations, so you have a better view of what Cosmetics Products could look like in the future. You'll also see more clearly by then how my colleagues and I could work with you. We can then talk about the potential costs and the benefits of a Class A journey and discuss what your next steps might be."

Roxanne offered Greg a few dates, the earliest of which were at the end of the following week.

"Our need is urgent," said Greg, "So I'm going to bite the bullet. Next week it is. I appreciate your ability to respond quickly and look forward to meeting you."

Greg already had an opening on Thursday of the following week, but had to free up Friday, which he anticipated would not be a problem. Greg now had to break the news to his team and get everyone else to clear those days. He could only imagine the groans he would hear from them.

After the call, Greg was a bit less apprehensive about working with a consultant. He was also more energized since he had put in place at least one step toward improved results. He notified his Leadership Team and asked them to clear the following Thursday and Friday for meetings with Roxanne. At the end of the day, Greg called Susan and further updated her on his visits to the other companies and on his plan to meet with Roxanne.

Greg also closed the loop, as he promised, with Stan Stevens to thank him for the contacts, to review the results of his company visits, and to let him know that he had invited Roxanne for a visit.

8

POSSIBILITIES

Let me ... assure you that the problems you face are not unique.

When you're up to your neck in alligators, it's hard to remember your mission is to drain the swamp.

Facilitated Diagnostic—Thursday

Roxanne Barnes arrived a few minutes early and was escorted to the Cosmetics Products Executive Conference Room. Cynthia had the room set up with audiovisual equipment and refreshments. Greg and Roxanne spent a few minutes sharing backgrounds and discussing the situation at Cosmetics Products that precipitated the invitation. After Sara, David, Alexandra, Matt, Gabriella, and Zachary had joined them, Greg introduced Roxanne and reviewed the objectives for the day.

"I want to thank Roxanne for joining us for the next two days, and thank the rest of you for clearing your schedules. Our business situation is well known to everyone here. Today, we'll share more of the details with Roxanne. Here's the agenda. We'll start with our business objectives and the problems we're having in achieving them. Then Roxanne will take a quick tour of the Atlanta manufacturing facility just to get a better feel of what we make and how we make it. After the tour, she'll meet with each of you alone. Later we'll meet here again to conduct a structured Diagnostic assessment. Roxanne will help us through this so we can articulate and understand our problems better and begin to see what we need to do. Tomorrow I want us all here for a bit of education about business excellence. We've all started to use those words, but I for one would certainly welcome the opportunity to understand what they really mean.

Roxanne will give us an idea of the potential costs and the benefits that we could expect and discuss what next steps might be appropriate. Does that sound like an appropriate agenda to everyone?"

Everyone nodded in agreement, so Greg continued. "It's important, everyone, that we answer Roxanne's questions openly and honestly; by that I mean be straight. Don't try to put a positive spin on information that might not be pretty. At the same time, it's equally important that we get straight observations from Roxanne about what she hears and about how she would work with us if we agree to take the next step in our relationship." With that, Greg turned the meeting over to Roxanne.

Roxanne thanked the team for inviting her. She provided information about her background in industry and as a coach with Effective Management. She then asked the Leadership Team to introduce themselves, explain their current roles, background, and familiarity with business excellence and Class A standards and principles, and finally to state their personal objectives for the day. Roxanne listed their individual objectives on a chart pad and then resumed her comments. "I'll ask lots of questions and will need those straight answers, as Greg requested. They'll enable me to make a better assessment of your issues so that I can explain how a journey to business excellence could help. Please let me know if I ask a question that gets into the area of sensitive business information. I don't intend to do that, and I certainly don't need that kind of information at this point." With that clear start, she continued.

"Let me move back to the chart pad so that I can record your business issues, concerns, and challenges. This will help me organize my thoughts and help us later as we consider potential benefits and next steps. Let's start with the commercial side of the business, meaning Sales, Marketing, and Finance, the organizations charged with creating and building the business, interfacing with customers, and managing the financials. Greg, Sara, and Alexandra, what issues are you are dealing with today? What keeps you on edge and, on occasion, awake at night?"

As Roxanne recorded their comments, the list of issues began to take shape. Poor customer service was at the top of the list followed by poor product availability, especially during the launch of new products. The list continued with high product cost; long product development lead times; long supply chain response times; poor information with which to prepare sales and financial forecasts; and financial surprises, especially at quarter-end and fiscal year-end.

"That list provides some real opportunity for improvement," Roxanne commented. "Let's now turn to the supply and technical sides of the business. But first, is there any disagreement with the list so far?" A uniform shaking of heads was the only reply, so Roxanne continued. "Then let's move ahead. What supply and technical issues are you are facing?"

The issues list grew rapidly as David, Matt, and Gabriella dominated the airtime. Inaccurate and frequently changing forecasts; large inventories; last-minute new product design changes; poor manufacturing reliability and missed schedules; material outages; unreliable suppliers; high premium freight costs; high overtime costs; excessive firefighting and expediting; frequent short notice emergency customer orders; excessive swings in production schedules caused by spikes in sales; periodic plant layoffs caused by those wide swings in sales volume and mix; low morale; and high plant staff turnover caused by the layoffs. The combined list filled several pages now lining the conference room walls.

Greg noted that Roxanne listened intently as his team offered up and discussed concerns that made it onto the issues list. She asked clarifying questions and summarized their comments to make sure she heard them correctly, but she did not make judgments or launch into any canned solutions while she recorded the comments. "If my previous experience of consultants is repeated, however," Greg thought, "she just got from us what she will put in her report. If she does that, she'll reinforce my concern that she won't add much value to our initiative, and I'll really need a Plan B."

At the end of the opening session, Greg and David drove Roxanne to the Atlanta plant so she could see the operations and talk with some of the plant personnel. Brion Smith, Atlanta Plant General Manager, met the group and led the tour.

David recapped the morning's meeting for Brion and encouraged him to be open in response to all Roxanne's questions. As they toured, Roxanne asked about what appeared to be a large amount of inventory on the shop floor and in the warehouse.

"It seems like a lot, Roxanne, but it isn't, really. We've been working overtime to build inventory to improve customer service. We're not there yet, but we should see those results improve soon," Brion responded.

Roxanne asked to view the master supply plan and shop floor schedules. She spotted several products being packaged that were not on the day's published schedules. Brion responded that the production departments were still trying to catch up on last week's past-due orders. Additionally, one of the products was the result of a district sales manager's call direct to the production supervisor with an important customer order. "We take a great deal of pride in being able to do whatever it takes, whenever it's required, to service our important customers. Of course, that can wreak havoc with the schedule as you just discovered, but we view ourselves as a 'can-do' organization." Roxanne made a note for later comment.

Roxanne asked Brion whether there were ever material shortages and, if so, why? "We have fewer outages now than we used to. Several months ago, we put an extra week's worth of all raw and packaging material inventories into the warehouse. That didn't solve all the problems, but it helped considerably. Don't misunderstand, we still get surprised more than we'd like. Last week, we learned a new formulation had been approved and added to the schedule, but it was too late to get all the new materials we needed. A week before that, we were caught by a stock record error. A warehouse rack of packaging materials contained mixed shipping containers, but our records showed that the storage rack contained only one part number. I suppose those things happen to every company, don't they?"

Roxanne avoided answering the question directly and instead asked, "That brings up an important question. What is your current level of inventory accuracy, Brion?"

"Overall, it's pretty good, Roxanne. Over the past three months, we've lost less than 0.5 percent of the dollar value of inventory. That's well above our performance last year, better than my target, and close to an all-time record for this plant."

"I suppose that's good, Brion, from an accounting standpoint, but what is the accuracy of your inventory system records for individual items stored in specific locations? Is it at the same high level as the accounting record?"

"To be truthful, we don't measure it that way, Roxanne, so I can't give you an accuracy measure for individual materials, if that's what you're asking. However, when I think about it that way, I'd be surprised if it were the same as the accounting result. Our accounting measure is an aggregate calculation that nets all the individual gains and losses while a measure by location or by item would not." Roxanne smiled, nodded and made another note.

"Looks like that packaging line is being worked on, Brion, what's happening?"

"We're changing from one product to another, and this particular change includes a package size change as well."

"How long does this change take until you are back running at the standard rate?"

"This changeover normally takes about six hours, but we've had problems with some of the change parts and tools. We are going on eight hours now. After we get the lines back together, start-ups are never smooth. It often takes us several more hours to work out the bugs after the physical changeover is completed. That's the main reason we prefer long production runs. It's really a good strategy for us. Our efficiencies and productivity results are much better when we do that, as is our overhead absorption. I can show you the results if you'd like to see them."

"Perhaps later, Brion, when we have more time. Do longer production runs also provide good customer service? And let me ask you a second question. What is the overall cost effect of longer production runs?"

"Well, our intent is to improve customer service, but we're not quite there yet, as I said earlier. There has to be a trade-off."

"Please explain what you mean by trade-off?"

"Certainly, Roxanne. We are still working on building a large enough inventory to provide good, long-term customer service levels. While we do that, we've had to live with some product outages. As I mentioned, the strategy of long production runs really helps with my efficiency and productivity costs, and will eventually help with customer service results as well. I'm not sure how to answer your question about overall costs. I can tell you that our unit costs are better. Certainly there is a cost associated with holding more finished product inventory, but we in Manufacturing aren't accountable for that. You probably need to speak with Finance or Marketing to get that answer. I'm accountable to David for things like efficiency, utilization of resources, productivity, manufacturing unit cost, and overhead absorption."

Greg and David overheard Brion's response and cringed. They realized they had much more coaching to do, and some serious analysis of their reward system.

After the plant tour, everyone returned to the executive conference room where Roxanne spent a few hours in one-to-one meetings with members of the Leadership Team and in preparing notes for the first day's wrap-up.

Greg's team reconvened later in the day. "I know you are under a good deal of pressure to reverse your business results," Roxanne began, "but I do have some very good news for you." Eyebrows were raised around the conference table as people leaned forward in anticipation. They hadn't had any good news in a long time. "First, on these lists I believe you have captured most of the symptoms of your problems accurately. Notice I said symptoms. You haven't really defined the issues, root causes, or the solutions, but at least you recognize you have some serious problems. Next, you are not looking for scapegoats. Finally, as the Leadership Team, you are deeply dissatisfied with the status quo and accept accountability for making the necessary improvements. Said another way, you are trying to improve things, not trying to make things look better than they are. From my perspective, those are three very good signs of a healthy leadership team. That may not seem much like good news to you, but there are many leadership teams out there not nearly as willing to address their issues as openly or honestly.

"Let me also assure you that the problems you face are not unique to Cosmetics Products. My colleagues and I see them in many, many companies. You can read about them in the newspapers and trade journals every day if you are willing to read between the lines and past the spin. There are also many smart and enlightened companies who have addressed these problems and solved them; you met a couple of them recently. They turned their weaknesses into strengths. Based on what I've seen today, I'm confident you have what it takes do the same.

"Now let's get down to the Diagnostics part of our meeting. I've handed out a set of maturity maps with transitions for the business as a whole, and for each of the key processes. I didn't include any Phase 3 or 4 maps because that probably won't be on your radar screen for several years, if ever, in your industry."

Roxanne guided them through the high-level "Integrating the Business: Maturity" map [see Figure 6.3].

"As I said before, Class A performance falls in what we call Phase 2. All the companies we work with, with rare exception, are in either Phase 1 or 2. Phases 3 and 4 represent a rarified atmosphere of companies that have virtually completely predictable world-class business processes integrated with automated knowledge systems across entire global supply chains. They rarely need our help. But only a very small number of companies can, or even need to, operate in Phase 3 or 4. Even then, it's important only in limited parts of those companies. Many companies seem to want to jump right to those rarified levels. In fact, some Phase 1 and 2 companies try to implement Phase 3 and 4 processes and tools because the initiatives sound exciting. They believe that by trying to use these advanced techniques they can market themselves as being progressive. But nearly all those companies, as I said, are still struggling to achieve basic coordination and business process control. We observe over and over that if a company does not work step by step up the maturity map, eliminating any deficiencies and improving processes along the way, it cannot sustain improvements, cannot possibly automate knowledge systems, and will never make significant progress.

"Let me add a little more definition to Phases 1 and 2 for you. The least developed companies in Phase 1 waste much of their time in chaos and fighting fires. They never seem to know what's coming, live a reactive existence, and are continuously surprised by unplanned events. Plans and decisions are based on history with a hope that the future will look something like, or a little better than, the past. Functional behaviors predominate with functional leaders spending much of their effort protecting their turf. To these companies, 95 percent performance levels seem, and in fact are, impossible. They're more likely to be in the range of 40 to 80 percent performance with resulting high operating costs. Now, there's quite a range of maturity within Phase 1. As they move to the top of that phase, companies develop much more control and begin to do routine things routinely. Firefighting is nearly eliminated in the best Phase 1 companies, especially those that accomplish the Capable Planning and Control Milestone. They are characterized by routinely delivering better than 95 percent performance and reduced costs.

"Phase 2 companies have much more appreciation of people and knowledge as valuable business assets. These companies focus on eliminating variability in all processes since process variability restricts further significant progress. Through reduced variability, empowered people, and increased organizational knowledge, Phase 2 companies can create even more precise, predictable, and reliable business processes. These companies begin to demonstrate an ability to respond to market changes much more quickly, and deliver right first time products and services by the hour or even minute when that is necessary. This predictable performance then enables them to employ more advanced planning systems including optimizers and simulators or modelers, with event reporting and management capabilities. The 'second job' of every individual becomes finding even more improvements in planning and executing the business. True collaborative planning for the extended supply chain becomes possible at this point with potential synergistic cost benefits for all trading partners.

"Phase 2 companies also routinely benchmark best-in-class companies across a range of industries and, as a result, periodically raise their own acceptable performance bar. Their extended supply chains are collaborative and synchronized, and are driven from a common set of performance indicators.

Events such as annual budgeting become significant non-events driven from rolling, forward-looking plans integrated across all functions and across the entire supply chain. Phase 2 companies typically operate at a 99.5 percent performance level.

"Based just on what you see and what I've just described, in which phase of business maturity would you place yourselves?"

David offered the first response. "Is there a phase somewhere below Phase 1? Seriously, I see us at the very bottom of that phase. We are constantly surprised by the marketplace, by our suppliers, and by our own performance failures. What you've described is both helpful, in that it provides some structure to my thinking about where we are, and depressing, in that we have a mountain to climb and have no idea how to take that first step. I'm glad you didn't describe Phases 3 and 4. It would be demoralizing to learn about companies who are that far ahead of us."

Others nodded. Greg added, "I'm relieved you said that almost all the companies you see are in Phases 1 and 2. I would have to support David's assessment that we are near the bottom of Phase 1. Is that where you see us as well, Roxanne, or are we being overly critical of ourselves?"

"Based on the nods of agreement, it appears that you are all in basic agreement. I think you're about right, although to be certain of that, we need to identify the gaps and gap closure priorities. In other words, we need to do a much more detailed assessment. We have maturity maps and also detailed transition descriptions for each of the nine business processes in the Checklist. We'll next use those maturity maps to define a baseline on which to build improvement plans and milestones.

"It's late, so let me summarize. Companies of all sizes, in all countries, and in all industries have problems similar to yours. You've seen living examples, from two completely different industries, of companies that recognized there was a better way to run their businesses and did something about it. Both of them applied the same business excellence and Class A concepts and principles and are now delivering outstanding business results. Beyond seeing the results of their transformation, you saw that they are still dissatisfied with where they are on their improvement journey. They continue to improve their business processes and results aggressively every day. They know that if they don't improve, a competitor will pass by them and take some of their business."

There was a very thoughtful silence, and then Roxanne closed the session. "That's enough for today. We'll save the Diagnostic for tomorrow." Greg thanked her for a stimulating, if at times disheartening, first day.

Facilitated Diagnostic—Friday

Roxanne opened the session. "Let me show you a simple model of what you described to me yesterday." She used her computer and projector to display a diagram on the conference room screen [Figure 8.1].

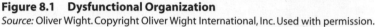

What are we trying to accomplish?

Figure 8.1 Dysfunctional Organization
Source: Oliver Wight. Copyright Oliver Wight International, Inc. Used with permission.

"This is what I saw—an organization in chaos, a dysfunctional organization. People are working very hard; they are dedicated and are doing their absolute best to help the company. You are fortunate; you seem to have great people. They may be great people, but great people aren't enough. They're working, as the diagram suggests, at cross-purposes. It doesn't matter how hard they work; they cannot succeed. We often see this when business leaders have neither created nor broadly communicated a clear strategy and vision; we also see this when companies haven't integrated strategies with execution processes. We see it when an organization is in crisis and is doing everything anyone can think of to keep the business afloat, and also when functional priorities take precedence over business priorities.

"I witnessed a recent example when the Marketing department of a company was planning to increase revenue by launching lots of new products and promotions while the Supply organization was releasing staff to reduce costs. Each was doing its best to increase profitability, but in ways that were conflicting. The challenge ahead of you is to create and deploy a compelling vision and strategy, and model the leadership behaviors required to align conflicting activities. Your leadership function then is to cause the entire organization to begin moving toward that clearly defined vision, as depicted on this slide [Figure 8.2].

"Alignment occurs in one of the earliest steps in a Class A journey. There has been a common misunderstanding of Class A as a goal in itself and an event to recognize a company achieving excellence. Over time, we and our clients have come to recognize that there is no end to the journey. There may be occasional pauses, but it's a never-ending quest that you are beginning today. Please note that when I refer to Business Excellence I mean as we define it in our *Class A Checklist*.

Greg interrupted and asked, "Can you tell us a bit more about that Checklist? Specifically, I'd like to know how you are certain the contents represent 'best practices.'"

Got it!

Customers Employees Shareholders Society

Figure 8.2   Transition to Business Alignment
Source: Oliver Wight. Copyright Oliver Wight International, Inc. Used with permission.

"Sure, Greg, let's do it now." Roxanne took a sip of water and continued.

"In the latest Checklist, all the tried and proven basics of previous editions are now stated in a business, rather than an operational, context. We and our clients learn together how to continuously improve their results. And when we observe a breakthrough, we update the Checklist. But the most compelling reason we believe the Checklist contains best practices is that companies implementing Class A business processes and achieving Class A performance deliver outstanding business results from that journey. That's exactly what you experienced when visiting both Capital and Tender Care.

"In this latest edition, expected performance levels have been raised, and attaining Class A Excellence requires a company to operate consistently in the upper quartile of all companies in their industries. A formal and robust continuous improvement process essential for remaining an industry leader.

"We have broadened the latest edition to include both manufacturing and service companies and more of the end-to-end supply chain.

"One more thought about the credibility of best practices. The more advanced companies with whom we piloted the new edition agreed with our definitions. They reported that the new edition was helping crystallize their thoughts about achieving even better business results. Most of the pilot companies were already Class A certified under the previous edition but struggled in achieving the new broader and tougher criteria in this edition. Since then, some of their divisions have been recertified at the 'Capable' level against these tougher criteria. A few fast-moving consumer goods pilot companies have even been certified in some Advanced level Milestones. At every step on their journeys, these companies delivered improved business results. Did I answer your question, Greg?" Greg agreed, and Roxanne continued.

"Class A is in Phase 2, as shown in our maturity model. It is not the end of the journey; it's a platform for never-ending business excellence and continuing progress. But so far we've only examined your business at an overview level. We are about to dive into another level of detail.

"I'd like to spend our Diagnostic time helping you place Cosmetics Products on these remaining maps. The first one takes the same business maturity map into more specific 'Transition' characteristics [see Figure 6.4].

"As you can see, there's a lot more detail here covering just Phases 1 and 2, and Transitions 1 through 5. We define the 'Capable' performance level to be at the top of Transition 3, and full Class A at the top of Transition 4. I'd like you to look at the descriptors and identify the Transition that best describes your company. Greg, I suspect that Stan took you and David through this in the seminar you attended, but I think your entire team should go through this exercise. I'd like you to work as a team."

The team spent a few minutes reading through the text before Greg said, "Okay, team. Tell me the truth. Where are we?"

All offered Greg their opinions, at times seeking clarification from Roxanne. She occasionally had to refocus them when they started making excuses for their performance and raising themselves to a higher Transition. She reminded them that neither their customers nor shareholders would accept their excuses. "Nor Susan nor our Board, I suspect," added Greg. The team reached a consensus view that matched what Greg and David had concluded during the seminar.

"I just marked up a copy of this maturity map where you placed Cosmetics Products, and added a few brief notes that might be of help at some future point. Now, let's turn to the nine key business processes represented by the Checklist chapters [see Figure 6.5]. Each chapter has at least one maturity map and Transition Chart associated with it. For example, when we talk about 'Managing the Supply Chain' (Chapter 7), I'll include an additional maturity map covering Distribution and Logistics. For now, however, we'll concentrate on eight maturity transition maps. I'm holding one back because it requires special emphasis."

The Diagnostic assessment and analysis utilizing the eight Transition maps filled the next several hours. Roxanne guided the team through discussions and to consensus about their current state of affairs. Roxanne then displayed the annotated slides. "This is how you've diagnosed your current state."

"With more than a little help from you, Roxanne. Thanks for keeping us on track as we went through them. It was too easy for us to get off on a tangent and start trying to come up with solutions. We seem to be pretty good at coming up with solutions for symptoms. It's one of the team behaviors we need to change!"

"My pleasure, Greg. How did you find this exercise? I hope not too depressing."

Greg quickly responded, "You know the saying, Roxanne, 'The truth sets you free, but it can also hurt at first.' I believe I'm beginning to see our problems in a completely different light, and that has to be just the first step to developing effective solutions. Before today, I could see most of the symptoms and was pretty quick to fire from the hip as they raised their ugly heads. Now I realize I'd better live with those problems at least long enough to understand their root causes and eliminate *those* so that the symptoms don't return. I believe this Diagnostic has allowed us to begin our work. Does that make sense and ring true for the rest of you?" Each in turn expressed agreement and shared personal reactions to the Diagnostic. Roxanne took charge again.

"Now that you've identified the major gaps in your current state, there is a good deal more work to do, including determining the bottom line benefits from closing those gaps. We're going to tackle that in a few minutes, but first, let's go back to the list of problems we recorded yesterday and quickly reread them." She paused for a few minutes allowing everyone to read through all the chart pad pages displayed on the walls. "Are there any issues we didn't capture yesterday?"

"I am already in overload," Sara commented. "I don't think I could handle any more negatives on that list." No one disagreed.

"Now that you are thinking about where you are today, I want you to think about what might be possible in terms of the bottom line benefits. I'll begin by just briefly summarizing the Integrated Business Model [see Figure 6.3] and the specific steps in the Integrated Business Management process." Roxanne described them much as Stan Stevens had described them in the public seminar, but used her own words. She could tell that the Cosmetics Products' Leadership Team was beginning to realize just how much they would need to change for the company to match Tender Care's achievements. They were listening intently.

"In the Diagnostic, you described your position in relation to best practices. Now let's see what benefits might be available if you progressed to the 'capable' business process level. I'm going to ask you a series of questions and record your consensus responses as we go. First, let's assume you are suddenly able to meet your customers' requests 99.5 percent of the time. Hold on. Let me change that to 95 percent given your starting point today. In other words, with 95 percent reliability, you deliver the right product to the right place, at the right time, in the right quantity and quality. Let's say also that, as a result, you become recognized as a preferred supplier to your key customers. Would that mean anything for your business?"

Alexandra was the first to answer. "If we started delivering at that level of performance, my customers would think it was accidental and unsustainable. But in short order, my Marketing team would get more creative and stop holding back ideas to build the business. Our poor customer service has really dampened their creativity over the past few years. Our Field Sales folks could stop wasting their time apologizing and making excuses for poor performance. They could turn that effort into value-added business building activities. Beyond that, they could at long last be effective in selling promotions and displays, and could land some new customers. Most importantly, we would have a much better chance of getting our customers to take new products, which always give us higher margins. I'm excited just thinking about the possibilities. Conservatively, I suppose we could leverage that kind of customer service into at least a 10 percent across-the-board volume increase. Possibly even more if the increase translates into fewer outages on the shelves and display pegs in the stores. Our marketing effectiveness and salesforce productivity would soar, as would morale. And those things are contagious. Come to think of it, staff turnover would probably decline as well."

The general consensus of the leadership team was that Alexandra's estimate, although a bit conservative, was about right. Roxanne recorded the result. Sara started her own list and began using her computer to log the potential financial impact of the improvements.

Roxanne posed the next question: "Suppose the improvements allow you to hold your costs flat over the next two years and even allow you to lower your prices slightly without loss of profit compared with today. Would that help you expand the business?"

This time Sara responded. "We certainly see sales and revenue spikes when we offer temporary price reductions in our promotion calendar. We have price reduction promotions and use coupons to increase trial usage with the hope of building long-term business. In reality, as far as I can tell, volume increases are short-lived and just tend to pull future business forward—that's if and when we actually deliver the product! But based on that effect, and the fact that we're in a price-sensitive industry, I'd expect a permanent price reduction just might give us a 5 percent volume increase. We could expect a competitive response, so the increase depends on the size of the reduction, our ability to make a splash in the trade news with the pricing change, and the response of our competitors. Without knowing any more details, I would think up to a 5 percent increase is reasonable."

Greg offered his support. "I know how Blackstone buys, and they're not all that unique. We'd have to make our pitch before our competitors heard about it, and present a compelling story to the trade buyers. Our ability to present a compelling story depends on our ability to clean up our customer service act before we approach the customers. Given all that, I think your 5 percent sounds about right."

Roxanne and Sara noted the consensus 5 percent effect, and Sara continued to log the potential financial benefits.

"How agile is your supply chain? In other words, how quickly and effectively," Roxanne asked, "can your supply chain respond to sudden volume and mix changes requested by your customers and consumers? Another related question: what is your lead time for developing a new product and getting it into the market?"

Matt responded to the second question. "Lead time depends on whether the product is what we call a *flanker*, an item that extends a product line in a way that provides a new consumer benefit yet keeps the same brand name; a packaging change; or a totally new product. If you're asking about a new product, it can easily take us 18 months to develop the product and the advertising campaign, get it into production and out to our customers. We know a lot of that time is wasted because we get into a 'catch ball' cycle of Marketing, Development, Product Management, and Manufacturing change requests between our functional groups. Those change requests put Product Development in a seemingly endless redesign loop that often delays the launch or limits the amount of product we can ship. All in all, we're making some improvements and trying to get more disciplined, but our product launch process is still pretty much broken."

David added, "It's a similar story for a sudden volume increase. Invariably the demand spike catches us in the wrong part of our production cycle. We either stay on cycle and absorb some customer service failures, or we break into the cycle and try to respond the best we can. Either way, we usually fall short of satisfying the entire demand spike. Whichever way we respond, there is almost always a negative effect on our business results."

Roxanne continued. "Suppose your market intelligence were improved and your product development and supply organizations were leaner and more agile. Suppose you could respond more quickly and effectively to changing consumer needs. Suppose you could beat the competition to market on new products and still have the improved customer service we talked about a few minutes ago? Any business benefits in that case?"

"That's a real stretch, Roxanne. I'm having trouble visualizing how that would ever happen given our current situation," David said somewhat sarcastically. "What you described would constitute an enormous paradigm shift. However, if you mean that we could respond in a reasonably sane and disciplined fashion, we would probably see a significant increase in our business. If we could simply have done a good job of executing our promotions last year, we would have had at least a 5 percent increase in shipments."

Alexandra added, "I think that's way understated, David. If you add to your promotion estimate an ability to present a believable case to our customers when we launch a new product or promotion, and also come up with those products before our competitors, I'm guessing we would see increased market share and realize at least a 10 percent volume increase. Remember, too, that those new products usually give us a real profit boost as well."

Sara and Greg strongly supported Alexandra's estimate. Sara and Roxanne recorded the increase.

Greg interrupted the process. "Roxanne, let me get clear about something. We've already talked about increasing our volume and revenues by 25 percent. Are you saying you can guarantee that you'll actually deliver that kind of improvement if you work with us?"

"I can't guarantee that, Greg, because I won't be doing the work. You and your team will be doing the work. I can tell you, however, that our clients always realize a dramatic improvement in their business results and bottom lines.

For now, I'm far more interested in your thoughts about what you can deliver in the areas you've described as business opportunities. We'll come back to the average improvements from a client survey we conducted, but for now, let's keep addressing your opportunity areas."

Greg nodded, and Roxanne continued. "Let's turn to your ability to forecast sales. How accurate are your forecasts, and what business improvements would you expect if you could improve forecast accuracy?"

David jumped in immediately. "What is an adjective that means something worse than horrid? Whatever it is, that's the word I'd use to describe the accuracy of our current forecasts. Nothing personal, Alexandra. I know your group is working hard to give us good forecasts, but you could save a lot of time and just use a random number generator for forecasting."

"David, you're not trying to fill Tony's shoes in the cheap shot department, are you?"

"Sorry, Greg and Alex. That was not my intention, but I think Alexandra will agree that we don't even have a decent method of measuring accuracy. The lack of accurate forecasts is costing us a fortune. We have tons of inventory from building products that don't sell and from keeping products just in case they do sell. I expect that we could reduce finished goods inventory by at least 20 percent if we had a better handle on what our customers were planning to buy from us. There are other effects, too. Last-minute forecast changes or orders that exceed forecast cause us to run with too much overtime—over 30 percent in the past three months. And we spend far too much money on premium freight, both inbound and outbound. Last year alone, we spent more than $1M on premium freight. Much of that was airfreight to meet emergency orders. Too many times, we air freighted component materials to the plants and built products on weekend overtime only to have it sit in our warehouses for days, weeks, or even longer. That doesn't even count the money we spent on overtime in our planning organization to rework schedules, count inventory and expedite all kinds of materials and trucks. I don't know how good the forecasts are in Class A companies, but if we had reasonably reliable forecasts, I expect we could get back to my goal of no more than 5 percent overtime and could reduce premium freight by at least 50 percent, if not more. I would also expect that our manufacturing and planning group productivity would increase by at least 10 percent if we could eliminate unscheduled last-minute product changes on the shop floor."

"Those would be impressive improvements in plant operations and costs, David. But think across your supply chain for a minute," Roxanne prompted. "Would there be any potential benefits to your customers or suppliers?"

"Good point, Roxanne. If we had better forecasts, we could stabilize our production schedules, which would lower our costs just as I said. That alone would contribute to lower prices and better product availability for our customers. And if we had more stable production schedules, we could stop calling our suppliers at the last minute with emergency material needs.

I'm sure they could reduce their costs to some degree as well and, perhaps, the price they charge us for the materials we buy from them. I really hadn't thought much about it before, but our calling the suppliers with last-minute changes is no different from our getting last-minute orders and forecast changes from our customers. We know last-minute changes are expensive for us, so they must be equally expensive for our suppliers."

Zachary Zellers, who had been quiet to this point, asked, "Do your Class A companies actually see any material cost savings from more stable schedules, Roxanne?"

"Good question, Zachary. The Class A companies participating in the surveys said that they realized significant material price reductions for two reasons: from providing more stable supplier schedules and from giving their suppliers better visibility of *credible* future needs. Class A respondents have reported anywhere from a 9 percent to 13 percent reduction in the prices they pay for noncommodity raw and packaging materials."

"Good heavens!" Sara exclaimed as she added those numbers to her list. "Do you have any idea how much money that would drive to the bottom line for us? It's over $5M for that savings item alone! I'm not confident enough to say that we could save all of that, but half sounds reasonable." Sara logged an additional $2.5M to her list of potential savings. "You have responsibility for the external sourcing contracts, David. Are you comfortable with that number?"

"I don't know about that, Sara. Our people have been real pros at squeezing our suppliers. We get them to bid against each other pretty aggressively. They know that if we aren't happy we can pull their contract at the end of the year, and we do that pretty often. I don't see how we can save another $2.5M, but for the sake of argument, go ahead and add it to the list."

Roxanne thought for a minute, and then turned to David. "I can't help myself. I've been trying to refrain from intervening in the process we're engaged in, but this is a real teachable moment I can't let pass. What you have just described, David, is the traditional and adversarial relationship many companies have with their suppliers. I agree with you totally that in an adversarial customer-supplier relationship you couldn't save much money. In that kind of business relationship, neither party trusts the other enough to make a long-term, win-win commitment. But when companies achieve a high level of business excellence, they have supply chain relationships that are more like alliances. Those companies have long-term trading-partner relationships focused on driving waste out of the entire supply chain to the benefit of all partners. You would need to build that kind of supply chain relationship to get the savings, but I am confident you can do it. Any other supply chain benefits that you see, David?"

"I'll take your word on that for now, Roxanne, and I'll need to understand more about how that kind of relationship might work. To answer your question about other supply chain benefits, I have some thoughts, but I wouldn't attribute these to poor forecasts or to other unplanned changes. On occasion, we run out of materials we thought were in the warehouse and are forced to make some unplanned changes that I attributed to forecast inaccuracies. I'll now come clean and admit many of the unplanned changes are self-inflicted wounds. Also, we frequently have to change schedules because our supply operations are not as reliable or predictable as I would like. The stability of long-term material forecasts that we occasionally give some of our key suppliers is even worse. Several suppliers have asked for better long-term information. I have to tell them that we can't provide any better information because our own forecasts are so poor. Sorry about that, Alexandra. All those problems add probably 5 percent to our cost of goods sold, but they are not really part of Class A improvements, are they?"

"I'm glad you added those, David. They certainly are part of a business excellence journey. You can't really plan anything if you don't know what's in the warehouse. And you can't send a valid production schedule to your supply organization if you don't have a predictable manufacturing operation with well defined and demonstrated capacities. These are some of the foundational building blocks of a company on a journey to business excellence." Sara added the 5 percent cost of goods sold reduction to her list as Roxanne continued. "Is there anything else in the supply area?" Hearing nothing, she switched topics.

"Next, I want to highlight important changes required in the way we manage and lead people" [Figure 8.3].

"This is the Transition map I held back earlier because I said it needed special attention. As with the others, Class A Business Excellence on this chart is at the top of Transition 4. Look at the details and tell me where you would place Cosmetics Products on the 'people' journey?"

After studying the descriptors for a few minutes, Greg replied, "I'd like to think we are doing quite well on the subject of people, perhaps Transition 3? I know that Susan, our CEO, takes this subject very seriously. In fact she sometimes refers to herself as the 'Chief People Officer'. What do the rest of you think about our division? I've not been here that long." The silence was a little too long for comfort. Zachary broke the silence.

"I'm glad you put this one in front of us, Roxanne, for two reasons. Thinking about our people, I have some serious concerns. Thinking about our business, I think we've overlooked a big area of potential savings. The way we operate causes serious morale problems. We run around the clock and through the weekends for a while, then we sit idle and have to lay off some employees. That pattern has caused much higher employee turnover than I like. When we lay off skilled people, we can't expect them to sit at home by their phones waiting for us to call, or expect those who come back to be highly motivated. Lay me off and I'll look for employment in a company that values and keeps its people, especially if I have a family to feed.

"Losing a skilled person is more expensive than we think. Hiring and training new people is expensive, and it certainly reduces productivity when they

Phase 2

T5. Self-Managed Teams: people working for the goals of the project
- Problems anticipated and resolved before they become a problem
- Teams set their own goals, select the most appropriate leader and times
- Problems anticipated and resolved throughout the Extended Supply Chain
- Proactive, boundaryless, empowered, and success-driven people

T4. Multifunctional Teams: people aligned to Company processes & working together
- Boundaryless mindsets and process focus enables cross-functional cooperation
- Culture wholly positive
- Extended supply chain constitutes the team opportunities
- Business needs seen to be more important than functional or personal

Phase 1

T3. Functional Teams: people aligned to functional processes and work together to improve
- Teamwork and teambuilding activities based on functional/process needs. Suppliers involved
- People starting to work with and for each other within their functional home
- Business status and plans communicated and understood. Team briefs. Two way
- Soft management techniques used to complement the "hard." Limited blame culture between functions
- Trust, honesty, openness, and humor lubricate the organization via regular communication

T2. Task Oriented: functional bias, however, the individualism has moved to departmental
- Hard management still reigns, however, management using "Problem-Solving Teams" to modify
- Blame culture exists but more between departments and toward the suppliers rather than individuals
- Teambuilding commencing to enable task teams to operate more effectively
- Communication improving but ad hoc and only one-way transmission
- Education requirements based on individual and company needs being developed and implemented

T1. Individualism: strong links back to the Functional Home "Silo Mentality"
- Autocratic management — We say you jump. People may act through fear rather than good reason or understanding
- No teamwork — "blame culture"
- Company culture developed through rumors, cliques, poor communication, and limited education
- Qualities such as trust, honesty, openness, and humor are not established
- Hard management issues rule

Figure 8.3 People Maturity Journey: People and Their behavior

Source: Oliver Wight. Copyright Oliver Wight International, Inc. Used with permission.

start on the job with no experience. It reduces productivity and costs even more if we have employees who are disgruntled when they return from a lay-off. How could we expect someone like that to have any loyalty to the company or to show commitment to improving the business? We operate this business like an aggressive driver who constantly shifts from the gas pedal to the brake. I can't give you a number in terms of the impact to the bottom line, but I bet we could figure it out without too much difficulty."

"Is it really that bad, Zach?" Greg asked.

"I've been conducting an employee survey. Not all the returns are in yet, but I've seen enough already to know that we are in Transition 1."

David added, "I agree with Zachary, Greg. With all the pressure we've been placing on people to increase output, maybe we haven't been as careful or car-ing as we should be. That's not a criticism, just an observation."

Greg looked concerned. "What do the rest of you think?" They provided examples that supported the comments of David and Zachary.

"I know you're not criticizing me, personally, but I own the people issues in this division, with coaching from Zachary, of course. My wife warned me that the pressure I'm putting on myself has been affecting the family. Guess it's affecting all of you and everyone else in the business as well. I've started pay-ing more attention to that at home. I'll have to pay more attention here as well. You'll be happy to know that, thanks to Penny, I've become coachable. You'll also be happy to know that Penny agrees I need coaching." They all smiled and asked Greg to thank Penny for them that evening.

Roxanne quickly took control of the agenda again. "By recognizing this issue, you can do something about it. You've identified another common char-acteristic of companies near the bottom of Transition 1. You know the saying, 'When you're up to your neck in alligators, it's hard to remember your mission is to drain the swamp.'" Her comment brought a welcome laugh. "Just recog-nize that you and Zachary are going to be busy understanding the people jour-ney, and in making the necessary changes fundamental to supporting a culture change." Greg and Zachary both noted Roxanne's comment.

"I should have been more aware of this earlier," Greg commented. "High turnover, inexperienced employees, and unhappy people have to be con-tributing to operating errors and quality defects as well. That has to lead to increased costs and contribute to poor customer service results. Zach, I'd like you to work with Sara and David to come up with a good estimate of the finan-cial impact of these shortcomings. I'm sure it's costing us a lot more than it appears at first glance. And Sara, how about any other Finance-related ben-efits? Do you see any potential there?"

"Well, Greg, I would think that if we had all these problems under con-trol, we'd do a far better job of creating budgets and financial forecasts. How much time do we spend creating and modifying our budgets and forecasts? That's a rhetorical question, but it has to be expensive and doesn't show up directly on the bottom line. It must show up indirectly, however, as a result of our spending expensive leadership time on massaging numbers rather than on building the business." Everyone around the conference table nodded in agreement and sat silently for a few minutes.

Roxanne walked back to the chart pad. "It sounds like you're beginning to run out of gas. We've probably captured most of your biggest potential business benefits for now. Sara, you've been keeping more detailed notes, and I've seen you punching away furiously on your computer. What do you see?"

"What I see is pretty unbelievable! We haven't put a dollar value on some of the benefits we listed, but even at that, between increased profits from the higher volume and the operating savings, my bottom line benefits list is approximately $12M, plus nearly $15M in cash from the conservative one-time 20 percent inventory reduction David mentioned. Do you realize what we could do with the cash from a $15M reduction in working capital alone?" Roxanne smiled.

"Now that you've answered my questions, I'll give you a reference point with which to compare your rough estimate. Some time ago we conducted a survey of clients who were engaged in an effort to reach Class A levels of planning and control. This survey involved companies using an earlier version of the Checklist, where the old Class A roughly equates to the current Capable Planning and Control Milestone. The companies were from different industries. These averages are based on their survey responses [Figure 8.4].

"As you can see from the slide, companies that had already reached the Capable level reported an average 26 percent improvement in customer service and 30 percent inventory reduction. Now, those percentages seem counterintuitive to most people who work in companies that haven't integrated best practices into their business processes, but all our clients report similar results.

Based on Survey Results

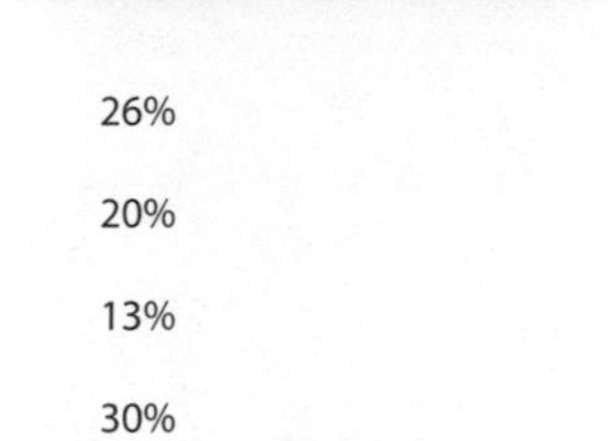

Class A Benefits

Customer Service	26%
Productivity	20%
Purchase Cost	13%
Inventory	30%

Figure 8.4   Capable Planning and Control Business Benefits
Source: Oliver Wight. Copyright Oliver Wight International, Inc. Used with permission.

In fact, results being reported by clients more recently, using the latest Checklist, actually exceed these improvements. You can certainly use these benchmarks as a 'sanity check' for the savings numbers you just compiled."

"Those benchmarks are very helpful, Roxanne," Sara responded. Turning to address the team, she continued, "You know, I believed what the folks at Capital told us, but have to admit that I was still a bit skeptical. What's amazing to me is that everything we've talked about today seems achievable. I've no idea yet how we make it all happen, but I'm beginning to have confidence in Roxanne's ability to help us figure that out. I'm usually a pretty patient person, but our business is dying before our eyes. We can't afford to waste any more time. If \$12M in annual bottom line benefits is about right, and I see no reason to doubt that number, it means that every month we delay getting started is costing us one million dollars; that's a one with six zeros behind it. That means for every day we delay, we lose about \$50,000!"

Greg decided he had better get Sara back under control. He had never seen her quite this animated, and he wasn't ready to make a commitment to Roxanne. "I agree that the numbers Sara just shared with us would solve many of our problems, but starting today is a bit premature. I, for one, have a couple more questions for Roxanne. For example, what's the cost of taking this business excellence journey? I'm certain you're not volunteering your services, and I'm also certain there are other internal costs involved in making the changes you've described. A second question involves the probability of success. We saw two of your client companies. If I were you, I would make sure we visited only your most successful clients. What's the failure rate of companies beginning this 'journey' as you call it? Third is how long would it take to realize the kind of results we've been talking about?"

Roxanne responded, "Assuming your ERP system supports your type of business without further investment, and I believe it does, you'll be investing the time of your people, the very people who are going to make it all happen. Some companies include people costs in their estimate, others don't. In addition you'll be investing in education and coaching from us. We put together a package covering the initial work plus the first milestone, or milestones, including education, workshops, facilitation, and coaching services. Is it expensive? Depends on what you call expensive, but price is a traditional consideration. Our clients look at this work as a high value investment, especially when they begin seeing the benefits. The value has proven to be quite remarkable for our clients, Greg. We provide that value because of the work we do to continuously update best practices and keep our people on the leading edge, even though they came to us initially with personal Class A experience. That value is there because our coaches know how to get to the heart of issues quickly without needing a lot of expensive investigative work up front. I can't give you a number today, for either the cost or the benefits because we haven't talked yet about your competitive priorities or your first milestones, although I think I have a pretty good idea what they might be.

"After you decide on the initial milestone, we can quickly come up with a package price based on the size of your company, the number of people requiring education, the number of teams that will need coaching and the requirements of the milestone implementation template. If your initial improvement plan includes two Class A Milestones, you achieve some economies of scale since the milestones will have some common requirements.

"When you have the business case, the journey vision, the milestones and the deployment structure steps in the Proven Path in place, you'll have all the information you need to make an informed decision whether to launch the work. At that point, we would begin to provide education and workshops for your milestone teams and others in the company. Your teams will then conduct a facilitated, but more detailed, assessment against their specific milestone requirements to determine the nature and size of the gaps, and a sense of just how much change may be required. Those assessments help us refine our earlier estimates of who and how many people from our group might have to be involved, help you further refine the cost-benefit analysis and assign responsibility for delivering those benefits. We can help with any benefit or cost analysis through use of our value calculator if you wish.

"You didn't ask specifically, but I want to assure you that we would have a small number of people engaged with you, and that they would be here only when needed to support the improvement efforts of your people. We don't come in with a large group of consultants and overwhelm your organization. That makes our involvement cost-effective for you. Our coaching style is extremely focused. That's a distinctive characteristic of our company, and is a key contributor to the high value reported by our clients.

"When the cost-benefit analysis is completed, you'll be in a position to make a well-informed leadership decision on whether to embark on a business excellence journey toward Class A performance standards and results. For the purpose of today's discussion, let's consider what we've already documented to get a ballpark, or 'feasibility-grade' estimate of the benefits. To give you an idea of the potential benefits, it has been the experience of our Class A clients that their return on investment has ranged from 300 percent to as much as 3000 percent; they almost always report far greater benefits than they originally estimated. Based on your estimated potential benefit of $12M per year plus the $15M working capital reduction, and the experience of our clients, you can get an idea what your cost might be. And my guess is that your potential return on that cost will be far greater than your ROI project acceptance hurdle. I should also add that the savings you just estimated are not unusual for a company your size. You can put a cushion around each of those estimates, on the high side for the cost and on the low side for the benefits, and then decide as a group whether you want to pursue the next step in putting more definition around what is required to begin the journey and in refining the cost-benefit analysis.

"I'd like to address your second question, Greg, about the success rate. I can tell you that you're right about the two companies you visited being very successful. Those two are very proud of what they accomplished and are willing to share their experience with others who are serious about making similar improvements. But there are many others equally successful. I'm not talking about companies who pick up our Checklist on their own, or attend a couple of classes and then begin a self-guided journey to business excellence. The failure rate of those companies is high. Those companies who come to us for education and coaching, agree to follow our Proven Path, and visibly commit to business excellence at the very top of the organization have a high rate of success. I've had only a handful of companies not achieve Class A status. There are two primary reasons why companies fall short of reaching Class A. The first reason is that the president or general manager waits too long to take the necessary improvement steps. By the time improved results begin to materialize, corporate management has lost patience with its management team and replaces the manager or managers in charge of the business. The new management team immediately begins undoing what their predecessors began, which undermines those actions that were just beginning to produce improved results. The second reason is when there are serious discontinuities in the external environment, and their parent company's board or leadership team stops all work not directly related to running the day-to-day business. I won't mention the names of any of those companies, but I can tell you that in the latter case those involved in the journey knew the parent company's decision was shortsighted. They just weren't successful in getting the decision reversed. Aside from those few, each of my clients has been successful.

"Regarding the time frame, it depends on the milestones you select and to an even greater degree how focused and committed you and your team are to completing the milestones. Let's assume that on-time delivery is where you want to focus and you select as milestones Capable Integrated Business Management and Capable Planning and Control. We've seen clients start getting benefits in as early as three months, but a few others, without true leadership commitment, take years to get the results, if ever. Considering what we I've have seen during this visit and the enthusiasm of your leadership team, I would think you should get significant results in six months and reach Capable level results in about a year. Again, I just can't emphasize enough the commitment of this team in getting there.

"I hope that addresses your questions, Greg."

Greg nodded his acceptance of the answer, but thought to himself, "If it weren't for Susan's support, I just might end up being one of those failures in the former category. I just hope for the sake of everyone on this team that we haven't waited too long. We need to begin delivering to our customers on time. If we can just make a start at improving our delivery performance in the next three to six months and reach 95 percent consistently in the next year I know I can count on Susan to run interference with the Board long enough for us to deliver some of the other improvements Roxanne is suggesting. But I'm not all that confident about the Board's patience. I'll need to put together a communications strategy so that Susan gets the information she needs to help me with the Board."

Roxanne continued. "I would close by saying that I've seen a clear business need here these past two days. I've also observed the strong leadership commitment needed for a successful business excellence journey. Finally, I remind you of Sara's comment about the cost of delay being nearly $1M per month. Regardless of whom you choose to coach you, I urge you to get outside counsel and get started as soon as possible."

Since there were no more questions, and since it was well past 6, Greg and his staff thanked Roxanne for visiting with them and for staying so late.

Roxanne looked at her watch and then apologized for keeping them. "Sorry about the time; I usually do better at time management, but since this is one of the few places I visit where I don't have a plane to catch, I just lost track of time."

Greg and his team were also surprised that the time had flown by so quickly. They thanked Roxanne and agreed to contact her within a week to let her know of their decision.

Greg reassembled his team after a short break.

"I know it's very late, but I have two questions for us to consider," Greg began. "First, do you believe we can manage two milestones, Capable Planning and Control, and also Capable Integrated Business Management? And secondly, do you think we could begin to see improvement in three months, and achieve 95 percent on time delivery to our customers in a year? Sara, I think we already know your position, so I'll turn to the others for their opinions."

Matt began the series of responses. "The only question I have is about the timing. I'm concerned about being able to see improvement in our results in just three months. I think six is a bit more realistic. If it takes us a couple years, I agree with Roxanne, we probably won't be around. Beyond that reservation, I believe we need to move ahead and move quickly. Any further delay won't help us."

"I think Matt has a valid concern," David responded, "but the companies we visited both told us that they started seeing some positive results within a few months. I certainly agree with Matt that we should get started. Perhaps we can get more information about the timing of the savings from Roxanne or from Tender Care. I say, let's get that and move ahead quickly on Capable Planning and Control. I'm not sure about taking on Capable Integrated Business Management at the same time though."

Greg didn't respond to the comment about the second milestone. He would give it some additional thought. He was concerned about the timing. Three months seemed optimistic to him, too. He certainly didn't want to go to Susan with an objective and then not achieve it. "Let's build the implementation plan with a goal for improvement in six months and to reach 95 percent in a year. We'll have to quantify both in detail, but that seems realistic to me and, based on your comments and body language, to the rest of you as well."

Alexandra and Zachary were both supportive and had nothing further to add to the discussion.

"I've been pretty quiet to this point," Gabriella Jemison stated. "From a quality, safety, and regulatory perspective, I can certainly go along with a yes decision, providing we do nothing to compromise quality, safety, or any regulatory requirements. So far I can't think of anything I heard today about the journey to business excellence that causes me any concern. Just know that I'll be looking closely at any business process changes. Now if we also implement continuous improvement programs such as Lean, Agile, and Six Sigma to further improve quality and reliability, I could get very excited. I see those programs working together. One other thought. If we decide to proceed, everyone in this room has to be totally committed. If we are, let's get started."

Greg responded, "That's about as close to a unanimous opinion as I've seen in any discussion since I joined Cosmetics Products. So Sara, I'll ask you to contact your counterparts from Capital and Tender Care and ask about their cash flow profiles when they started the work. Separately, I'll agree that we take the next step to define the process better and to refine the costs and benefit of the journey. Now, here's my last question. Should we proceed with Roxanne, or should we invite some other consulting companies in so that we have a comparison of costs, methodologies, and approaches?"

"As the head of the external sourcing organization," David began, "I suppose my position almost has to be to get some comparisons. I like what I heard from Roxanne, but we could be shortsighted if we just accept the first offer on the table."

Matt jumped in. "I agree with David. I would never authorize the purchase of a piece of production equipment unless we had competitive bids and an idea of what various manufacturers had to offer. This shouldn't be any different. I have to admit, though, Roxanne makes a great deal of sense, and we have an endorsement from Tender Care. Nevertheless, I am reluctant to recommend just jumping on the first proposal."

"I'm not so sure we should wait" Alexandra offered. "On the one hand, we have someone we just spent a couple of days with, and we believe she knows what she's talking about. On the other hand, we have some clear procedures about competitive bidding. I could probably be swayed to go along with David and Matt." Zachary nodded in agreement.

"Let me bring you back to a very harsh reality," Sara said with some edge in her voice. "Just how much time will it take to research other options, visit other companies, and reach agreement on an approach? One month? Two months? More like three months? Let me remind you that every month we delay, we are wasting about one million dollars and creating even more animosity among our remaining customers. Wake up, people! We are sitting here self-destructing; our business is dying! I can't believe what I'm hearing. I can't believe there isn't a greater sense of urgency in this room. Let's get off our butts and make a decision to do something other than schedule a lengthy delay and talk some more about how bad our business results are. I can tell you without question that our financials will be worse in one month than they are today. They will be even worse than that in two months, and again in three months. In addition, I called my counterpart at Capital, the VP of Finance, whom I met with while we were there but ran out of time before we could get through my list of questions. I asked him for the straight answer about the Class A work from his perspective. He supported everything we heard. And then, he had an additional startling comment. He said that when they had their business processes aligned with Class A best practices, the Sarbanes-Oxley audits were a piece of cake! You know how much work we've done on compliance and all the consulting help we've needed? What else do we need to know? We don't need any more information. We know Roxanne; we've seen the results of her work; we have a glowing endorsement from one of her clients; and we've visited another client coached by someone else in her group. We already know how they work. Make the decision now. The decision isn't irreversible. Neither is our continued employment with Amalgamated. If we don't act today, we might not even have much of a future. How much do we have to invest to do the assessments Roxanne mentioned, put together Milestones, review our vision, decide who will work on the team, and refine the cost/benefit analysis? It's an amount that I can cover easily with our contingency budget. Besides, that's when we'll be at the real decision point for moving ahead. Roxanne said that herself, if you were listening. Greg, it's your call to go without competitive bidding, but I think it would be absolutely irresponsible to delay taking the next step by even one more day."

"You're right, Sara" David responded. "There is nothing that says we can't move ahead. I'll cover the technicalities with my sourcing group. As the Supply Chain VP, I agree we can't afford a multimillion-dollar delay. My recommendation must be that we move ahead as quickly as possible." Others shifted their position to moving ahead immediately as Greg went around the table. Despite some minor reservations about the competitive bidding aspect and some of Greg's rapidly diminishing concerns about using consultants at all, the leadership team reached a unanimous decision to move to the next step with Roxanne.

Greg closed the discussion. "Thanks for your thoughtful discussion; and thanks, Sara, for bringing us back to reality. You all know that I had the greatest reservation about using outside consultants. I appreciate all of you helping me get past that barrier, which was affecting the entire business. I'll call Roxanne tomorrow and ask her to return as soon as possible to help us map out what will be required, organize the next steps, refine the Value Opportunity, and get us to that Point of Commitment on her Proven Path. I would think refining the Value Opportunity will take a good deal of your time Sara; just be prepared to do what Roxanne needs. The same is true for all of us. I don't know what will be required exactly, but my guess is that all of us will be involved.

"It feels like we just made a big step forward; I hope it is the first of many effective steps. No question about how far we have to go, but I think I see a possibility that didn't exist even last week at this time."

9

BEGINNING

We get brilliant results from average people managing brilliant processes.
Focus on the obstacles and that's all you'll see.

"Roxanne, we'd like you to come back and help us understand what we should do next." Greg had reached Roxanne on her cell phone with his first call the next morning. "Specifically, we want to know more about the implementation process, how we should organize to do the detailed assessments you mentioned, how to go about developing milestones, and the details associated with a cost/benefit analysis so that we can make an informed decision about the value and opportunity ahead of us. Just to be clear, we're not yet committing to any further work with you beyond the next visit. We'll consider what's next after that visit. How soon do you think you could meet with my leadership team again?"

"I have to admit, Greg, I'm surprised to hear from you so soon, but then I suppose I shouldn't be. I had a really good feeling at Friday's meeting. Your team has a strong sense of urgency and a desire to learn. All too often following a first visit, leadership teams waste weeks, months, and in some cases a year or more determining what to do next rather than quickly taking action. Given the cost of delay we discussed yesterday, I think you just saved a bunch of money! And given your sense of urgency, I'm going to reschedule a couple of personal engagements so that I can be available Thursday and Friday of next week to meet with you if you want to move that quickly. We'll need two days to conduct some additional education, clarify the steps needed to help you solve some of those business problems we discussed, go through the maturity maps, and define at least the first improvement milestone to begin moving your company ahead. I know that's a lot of time for your team, but there is a lot to accomplish. Can you make the session fit into your schedule?"

"I'm going to make those days available. Cynthia will probably give me some grief about rearranging my schedule, but I believe we must keep moving now that the dog thinks he's seen the hare! I'll do everything I can to have the entire team here, but even if we're missing someone, I still want to move ahead. We need to get a handle quickly on what to do next."

By sheer coincidence, Roxanne had three days of vacation scheduled at that time but no specific plans that couldn't be changed. Her husband would be working that week; but she had planned a few down days just to relax and get caught up on domestic responsibilities. She agreed to meet with Greg and his team on such short notice because she knew Greg wanted to get started quickly on an improvement plan. She also knew from many years in business that she had to respond promptly to her clients' enthusiasm before it waned. Her downtime could wait, but she had now blown her weekend plans as well, given the time it would take to prepare a presentation to meet Cosmetics Products' needs. With Roxanne, as well as with the rest of her colleagues, income is necessary but her real motivation and excitement lies in helping companies and people like Greg accomplish more than they ever thought possible. That's the real reward for her; and she had an especially good feeling about the opportunity with Cosmetics Products.

Fortunately, all Greg's direct reports were in town and cleared their schedules for the two-day session. They were already assembled when Greg and Roxanne entered the conference room. Following a few minutes of getting reacquainted, Roxanne jumped into the agenda she and Greg had prepared.

"Our objective over the next three days is to take you to another level of education and understanding about the concepts and principles of Class A, to continue the Diagnostic assessment to determine in more detail your organizational maturity, to agree on and clarify the first business milestone or milestones you need to attack; and then to decide on the next steps you need to take as a leadership team. Agreed?" There were nods around the table. Roxanne continued. "I'm sure Stan Stevens talked about the People, Processes, and Tools diagram in his seminar. Greg and David, do you recall the three overlapping circles, the 'three balls' as he may have called them?" They nodded their heads.

"When a company embarks on a significant business and culture change such as you're contemplating, you need to understand why that model is so important."

Roxanne went to the chart pad and wrote:

1. Tools
2. Processes
3. People and Behaviors

She turned to the team and said, "When related to managing the business and the supply chain, which of these three elements is most important to the successful operation of a business?" The discussion that followed got the team quickly involved, but no consensus emerged. So she asked individuals to vote for just one of the three. As she recorded responses, it was clear that *People* and *Processes* both came ahead of *Tools*.

"So you're telling me that of the three, Tools such as your ERP system, is of lesser importance. Fine. I can accept that. Now let me ask you another question.

"On which of these three have you spent the most effort, money, and management attention?" The nervous laughter in the room told Roxanne that she had just made her point. "Your reaction tells me that, like most companies, you spent most of your time and money on the element that you ranked least important. I'm not saying you didn't spend a good deal of money on *training* your people in how to use the tools, but I want you to consider these questions:

- How much did you invest in *educating* your people on what you were trying to accomplish with the tools, and why you were headed down that path?
- How much time did you spend *educating* your people on the principles and concepts of integrating your business processes *before* training them on how to configure, implement, and use the software?
- How many of you *educated* yourselves and your people on Supply Chain Management, and what that actually means?"

After a short pause, Roxanne continued. "Like most companies, you probably weren't even aware that you needed to do these things. Here's the hard truth: if you didn't provide this education, you have little hope of effectively using such powerful tools, or of generating the benefits you may have been counting on."

These rhetorical questions resulted in even more discomfort and a good deal of quiet introspection. Greg couldn't relate to most of the questions, because he wasn't around Cosmetics Products at that time. But it was clear to him that that their ERP implementation must have been exactly as Roxanne described. It certainly was not an education-led implementation of a more effective way of planning and managing the business.

"All three of these elements require attention, and must be integrated fully in your organization. That's why our slide for this shows three overlapping circles, one for each element. More correctly, this is a *Venn diagram* providing a visual representation of the relationships and interactions among the three elements. Each circle represents the set of characteristics of the element name; for example, the set called 'People and Behaviors' represents the influence people and behavioral aspects can have in contributing to the overall model." Roxanne projected the model, the Venn diagram, showing the three overlapping circles [Figure 9.1].

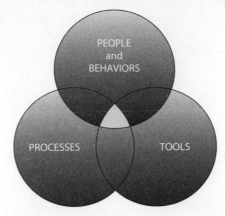

Figure 9.1   People and Behaviors, Processes, Tools
Source: Oliver Wight. Copyright Oliver Wight International, Inc. Used with permission.

"You can allow the elements to interact naturally, without control, but your results will be variable and unpredictable. In business, we can't afford that kind of unpredictability. As leaders, your job is to ensure that desired results are delivered predictably and routinely. Consequently, you must have control over these interactions. Let's examine what I mean using customer service, a topic close to your hearts. When People, Processes, and Tools elements interact naturally, the customer service performance would average at about 50 percent, meaning the service level could vary between 0 percent and 100 percent for any individual customer. That's not the kind of performance that will build a loyal customer base! To control the outcome, companies must integrate these three elements to achieve good results regularly, such as 95 percent to 100 percent customer service. The three elements must not be managed as if they were independent. They must be managed holistically with interdependent process rules to drive performance toward the desired result. I'll be the first to tell you that integrating all three effectively is a challenge, but helping you achieve that is a specialty of ours at Effective Management. If you don't integrate them well, you'll suboptimize your business results. In plain English, you'll make a lot less money. If you simply focus on only two of the three elements, you'll be ignoring the reality that the third element is still operating." Roxanne pointed specifically to the Processes and Tools circles. "Let's just suppose you focus on these two, as many companies have, and deeply regretted before long. There's every likelihood you'll automate the current ineffective business processes. Or you may bring in new processes, and implement the supporting tools without the people. In either case, the people won't understand the new, and often more complex processes, and won't use them. End result, you'll alienate your people, because you'll make their work more complex in ways that won't help them run the business any more efficiently or effectively. And they will be the first to know it." Roxanne looked out at the team.

"By the way, if you seem to be mired in a 'program of the month' syndrome, always looking for the next silver bullet to fix your problems, chances are pretty high that there is absolutely no integration of the three elements. In that case, your organization is probably suffering from what I call 'functional myopia'; it has both a weak vision of the future and a weak operating strategy. Decision making will be focused almost totally on near-term functional priorities. Your employees more than likely are just waiting for the last improvement program to fade into oblivion as you frantically try to implement the next and latest management fad." Greg painfully recognized this to be one of Cosmetics Products' issues as Roxanne continued.

"We have seen all of these situations; they are all unsuccessful. We've seen technology investments, in the form of software, of twenty million to well over one hundred million dollars written off as a total loss when, in fact, the software was never the problem."

Discussions during sessions and breaks that morning clearly indicated that Roxanne's messages were hitting home. Greg began to see and recognize some of the natural conditions that existed in Cosmetics Products. And he began to understand how they were suboptimizing his business results.

Roxanne continued after a break. "Companies with a track record of success do a great job of recognizing and integrating all three elements. This skillful integration of People, Processes, and Tools [see Figure 9.1] is essential if you want to excel as a company and be a leader in your industry."

Roxanne pointed to the overlap of the three circles. "Later, we'll talk more about this area of excellence where all three circles overlap and where we can see the combined impact of the three elements coming together. These elements can be greatly disturbed in a change initiative where their interactions are not understood. You must manage the elements ahead of, or at least in parallel with, the initiative if your change is to succeed.

"Not only must you address each of the three elements; you must address them in a specific order. Most companies don't understand this and begin their implementations with a focus on the Tools element. I'll give you a common scenario.

"Let's consider a specific company that recently implemented an Enterprise Resource Planning (ERP) software system. First, the company selected a software package with a selection process led by Information Technology (IT) and Finance. They then configured the software, making literally hundreds of decisions to structure how the system would work. Software integrators from outside the company, with the company's IT organization, led this configuration exercise. They had little participation from the company's own operating personnel who were either too busy handling operational problems or too busy running the day-to-day business. Even worse, the operating people who were

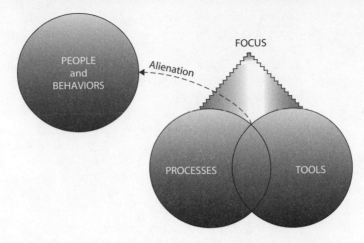

involved were not educated on the concepts and best practices needed to integrate business processes properly. Much as they might have hoped it would, the software simply wouldn't do the integration for them. The result was that the configuration ended up emulating the current processes. Their method of software implementation simply reinforced current ineffective business practices and results, but at a greater cost—the additional capital investment and software training expenses.

"Even though the company configured the software to emulate its current practices, they later discovered that the current operating procedures had to be modified to support the requirements of the new system. So the company changed the procedures and retrained its people to use the new software [Figure 9.2]. Remember the alienation scenario that I mentioned earlier?

"That's exactly what took place in this example. Now let me summarize the sequence in which my example company pursued its change initiative [Figure 9.3].

"The sequence on this slide—Tools, Processes, and then People and Behaviors, is always a guaranteed road map to failure. The desired and expected business results used to justify the project will never be realized." Greg could see that his team recognized the path they had taken in implementing their ERP system. It was exactly as Roxanne had just described.

Roxanne continued, "Successful business improvement initiatives involving technology follow the exact opposite sequence [Figure 9.4].

"Here's the logic behind the correct sequence. Taken together, your people know everything there is to know about your business. They know 'what you do'—the key things you must achieve to get product through your supply chain and out to customers. They know 'why you do it'—the company value

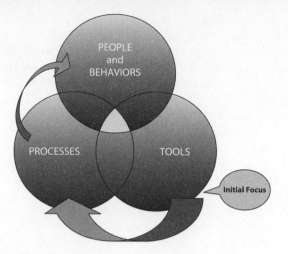

Figure 9.3 It Never Works ...
Source: Oliver Wight. Copyright Oliver Wight International, Inc. Used with permission.

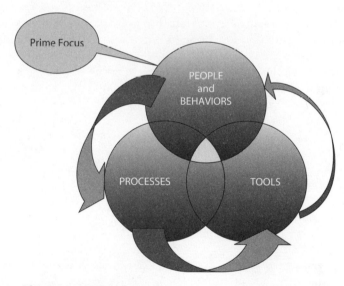

Figure 9.4 The Correct Sequence
Source: Oliver Wight. Copyright Oliver Wight International, Inc. Used with permission.

proposition, the financial targets, and the growth strategy. And they also know 'how you do it.' Unless there's very weak strategic planning in your company, the thing you're going to change with the implementation is the 'how you do it.'

"Following some extensive education, your implementation team will compare how you do things today with what they learned about Class A concepts, principles and best practices to determine the gaps between today and where they need to be. Because the team knows your company well, they can quickly redesign and integrate your business processes to be in line with best practices as they are applied to your unique facilities, assets, and products. This is why we say change must start with addressing the people issues up front. And to rally the people around the need for change, executive management must present a compelling case for what they are trying to achieve and why they believe it is critically important to the company. You have already been quite clear, Greg, about the importance of delivering at least 95 percent customer service, routinely and cost effectively." Greg acknowledged that was indeed the heart of his intention.

"So, Greg, I'll follow that customer service objective in my example as we move on. The process would be similar if your objective were any other milestone, such as improve Product Management." At this point, Greg smiled.

"You know, Roxanne, that just might be our next priority after we've fixed customer service!" Roxanne gave Greg a knowing look, as if she'd read his mind, and continued.

"A key element of such an initiative is the supporting tool, the ERP software system. For most of our clients this is already in place, but not used properly. So the company faces implementing significant, and for some, worrisome changes to the current business processes and configuration of that ERP system. To get input and buy-in into the implementation, without getting mired in too much detail now, your people would be organized into various task teams; educated on the possibilities; and then asked to redesign and integrate the business processes that will deliver your targeted business results. While there would be a small full-time team leading and pulling it all together, most involved on the Process Design task teams would be engaged part time. When I was working for a company as a client of Effective Management, I wanted no more than two days a week on the project for most team members, because I wanted those people interfacing with their colleagues discussing what they'd been learning and doing. In this way, a huge number of people were informed and contributed to the work in one manner or another. Given your urgency for improvements, you might need some people for three or four days a week at times.

"Having redesigned your processes, and documented the new desired way of working (the new 'how we do it'), then, and only then, should you look at Tools. It is at this point in the work that you know what functionality you need to support your new way of managing the internal supply chain. If the ERP system selection has been made already by another part of the organization, you'll know how to modify or reconfigure what you have so that the tool works for you. Either way, the full-time implementation team would lead configuration or reconfiguration of the software. They might have to incorporate certain corporate requirements, such as financial settings, but most of those would already have been incorporated into the redesigned business processes.

"When the software has been configured, this team would demonstrate running the business with the software by using credible skeletal data, scenarios, and volumes. This is to demonstrate goodness of fit and confirm that the new way of managing, planning, and scheduling the business actually works.

"After the successful demonstration, you would establish your education and training modules. Education is formal; we would provide the concept education for your managers and project teams. But you, the executives and managers (with help from your team), would lead training on the new policies, procedures, and work instructions through what we call *cascade education*. So you would educate and train all your people, first in the concepts, then in the new processes, and finally in 'how to use' the tools to support those processes."

Greg interrupted to check his understanding of what Roxanne had been presenting. "What I am hearing you say is that technology, such as an ERP system, is simply a tool that can't be properly used until considerable education and process redesign have been completed." Greg turned to the others, "How close did we get to this sequence?" The others agreed that they were nowhere near the process Roxanne had described, especially since their ERP implementation had been a Y2K defensive initiative. Greg continued, "I suppose I could conclude, then, that the approach we used is the main reason we're still struggling with the system and not getting the business results we expected. The approach Roxanne talked about sounds more like a complete redesign of how the business operates and a significant change in the business culture, not just a software implementation. Roxanne, I need to deliver a quick turnaround of our business results, but delivering a culture change is a lengthy process. Have I interpreted what you've said correctly?"

"From what I've seen and heard, Greg, it sounds like you are exactly on target with your analysis, except for the lengthy process part. We have a good many clients who did exactly what your company did. Like Cosmetic Products, they installed the software without examining their culture or business processes. As you just stated, company executives must understand that software is only a tool, not a solution. Don't get me wrong; it's a necessary and powerful tool, but it does only what you tell it to do. If you tell it to do what you are now doing, the software will be happy to do that, and do it incredibly fast—often much faster than your people can keep pace. If you are currently delivering unsatisfactory results, the software will help you deliver those same unsatisfactory results even more quickly, and more expensively than ever.

"You couldn't have said it better, Greg. A software implementation project, or any other significant change initiative, must be part of a culture change. That kind of project requires leadership from the very top of the organization. The culture and the behaviors of executives and down through every level of the organization, even into the supplier base, must be examined and changed where they do not reflect best practices. Approach the implementation correctly and you'll improve the way you do business for the next 20 years. More important than that, you'll deliver bottom-line benefits beyond what you ever thought possible.

"What we talked about after the Diagnostic last week in which we identified your business problems was that you should prioritize those problems. Then you can examine and improve the processes that will deliver the improvements you want. Don't try to eat the whole elephant at one time. Let me explain that in a little more detail." Roxanne pointed again to the screen.

"Let me go back for a moment to the area of overlap in the diagram [see Figure 9.1]. This is the area we refer to as the 'sweet spot.' It's a sports analogy; those of you who use a baseball bat, a tennis racquet, or almost any other racquet, bat, or club will know the term. In tennis, if the ball hits the sweet spot of the racquet, it sounds different; and the ball is returned with a lot more power and control. So it is with the sweet spot in this diagram where the correct synergy between the three elements can enable outstanding performance. The synergy comes about when integration of the three is based on the best practices in our Checklist.

"In summary, the three elements, the circles, are addressed in a specific sequence by excellent companies. First they educate their people in the concepts, principles and behaviors of business excellence and best practices; next, they enable those individuals to redesign, integrate, and implement business processes conforming to best practices; finally, they configure appropriate tools to support their new business processes.

"I need to say a few more words to define what I mean by 'business processes.' Dan Jones defined it very effectively in his article, 'The Beginner's Guide to Lean,' published in *Manufacturer* magazine in December 2003. He said that a business process is 'a sequence of events or steps that must be carried out in a proper order to create value for the customer, and managed as a whole, not separately.' You see, the focus of the definition is not on functional responsibilities; it's on business processes and how they work together to deliver value" [Figure 9.5].

"This is what Dr. Deming called 'the system'; he stressed the need to *optimize the system,* and to subjugate *the parts* to the success of the system. The quality of the business process itself is also critical. To paraphrase Dr. W. Edwards Deming again, he often said in public seminars, '93 percent of the time the problems come from the processes, or system design, and not the people.' Let me state clearly that the 'system' and design of business processes are management's responsibility. If management is not getting the results it wants, management must not immediately blame the people who work in the system; rather, they must reassess the effectiveness of the policies, procedures, and processes they put in place for others to follow. In that same *Manufacturer* article I mentioned earlier, a senior executive from Toyota said, 'Brilliant process management is our strategy. We get brilliant results from average people managing brilliant processes. We observe that our competitors often get average results from brilliant people managing broken processes.'" This was a revelation to Greg and his team. Roxanne let it sink in; then she continued.

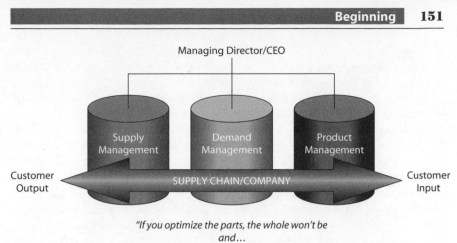

*"If you optimize the parts, the whole won't be
and...
If you optimize the whole, the parts won't be."*

Figure 9.5 "Optimize the Whole": The "System"
Source: Oliver Wight. Copyright Oliver Wight International, Inc. Used with permission. Based on *Out of the Crisis*, by Dr. W. Edwards Deming, 2000, Cambridge, MA: MIT Press.

"I'll give you some examples of business processes later, but for now, I just want to remind you that the answer to improving your business results lies in your people and in your business processes. The answer does not reside in newer and ever more sophisticated tools—in this case software packages— although you absolutely need software to support the people and processes. I'll say it just one more time, at least for today: the key to improving your business results lies in having well-educated people and integrated business processes supported by an effective business planning tool all aligned and driven from a clear vision, a supporting business strategy, and a single set of operating plans and objectives." Roxanne paused—then looked at Greg. "So what is your vision, Greg, for Cosmetics Products?"

"I have a desk drawer full of vision statements that I inherited. For now, Roxanne, I suppose it's pretty simple: survive and grow the business."

"Okay, Greg, I didn't mean to put you on the spot like that, but I did want to make the point that most company vision statements look like they came from a book of standard vision statements for beginners. And they are—pardon me for saying this—boring!" Greg cut his response short because he agreed. Now he understood why he left the inherited vision statements in his drawer. He decided there and then, to feed them to the shredder before he went home!

"If a vision or mission statement does not inspire others to action, it has no value whatsoever. I see four types of vision statements, but only one that inspires. You have the 'rambling vision,' lots of words that don't say anything; much like a politician's promises, they are well-meaning maybe, but just words. The 'parody vision' is characterized by statements such as 'we'll be number one' or 'the supplier of choice'; it might as well add, 'we'll be good boys and girls, and eat all our vegetables.' Then there's the 'self-reward vision' that looks inward to what the company wants for itself without regard for its customers, such as 'we'll be a ten-billion-dollar company' or 'we'll financially outperform the competition.' Do any of these inspire you? Would any of them help you make decisions, or guide the way you work?"

David summed up the reaction of his team, "Now that I think about it, no. I know of lots of companies that use words like those in their vision statements, and you're right; they are boring!"

Roxanne agreed, "Aren't they? A common characteristic of the most successful companies, especially successful start-up companies, is that they have a burning desire—not for their success—but to meet the needs of their customers and consumers. They have a loudly proclaimed *purpose* for their business that energizes and engages their people in making a difference for their customers and the marketplace. As a result, they succeed. I picked up a lot of these insights from Mark Earls in his book, *Herd: How to Change Mass Behaviour by Harnessing Our True Nature* (Hoboken, NJ: Wiley, 2007). A more useful way to think about vision might be to think of it as a *purpose statement*. Some companies have both, but purpose needs to be an outward-looking vision. A good affirmation of its effectiveness appears when your customers relate to your purpose, often actively, as in the case of the iconic Apple iPod. Other manufacturers sold technology; Apple sold a fashion extension, or expression of the individual. Sure it's got the technology, but Apple appealed to their customers' need for self-esteem—and won. The customers still revel in their needs being met. And at the time, iPod belonged to the people—it was theirs, not Apple's.

"You may have heard this before, but without a clearly communicated purpose-driven vision, which I'll simply call purpose-vision for now, you have nothing for your people to get excited about. And by the way, don't just state it or post it on the walls; as executives, you must live it." Greg interrupted, "Team, sounds like we need to spend some time on this. I could do with a bit of energy and excitement. Roxanne, can you share any relevant examples?"

"Sure can. I carry this with me, and it's highly relevant to your industry. It refers to the Unilever Dove brand of products. The Dove marketing team was unhappy with traditional ways of marketing beauty products—twenty-year-old slim women in their prime, promoting beauty and fashion products. They felt this portrayal of their consumers was exclusive, not inclusive of ordinary women one meets everyday. So they decided to differentiate Dove products from its own company's and its competitors' 'beauty brands' very successfully. Most beauty product companies' brand visions are of the self-reward type, citing market share, being number one, and so on, internally focused. They promote their brands from their own perspective, usually on the basis of a perceived physical ideal of youth and beauty that few women can relate to, me included. Sadly, research studies show that this type of advertising leaves ordinary women feeling even worse about their own appearance. And companies are doing that to their own customers! This brand team chose to avoid induced misery and self-loathing because they didn't want it for their customers, for whom they had great respect and empathy. This paradigm shift took shape in their revolutionary purpose-vision statement:"

> To make more women feel more beautiful every day, by widening today's stereotypical view of beauty and inspiring them to take great care of themselves.

"This memorable statement inspired the team to recreate the brand image, and to change their advertising to include all ages, shapes, sizes, and ethnic groups. Their ads began featuring women who look like the wonderful, normal, happy women who are all around us every day. The brand has become very successful, and has a loyal following that embraces everybody—or 'every body,' if you prefer."

Sara and Alexandra clapped and cheered. "So we're no longer being forced to compare ourselves with twenty-something fashion models!" Roxanne built on their response. "Your reaction is exactly what a customer-focused purpose-vision is supposed to elicit. It captured your attention, engaged your mind, and generated excitement in you. Greg, that's exactly what an effective vision can do for your people, and also for your customers when you effectively communicate it through your advertising copy." After a short silence, Roxanne knew she had made her point and wanted it to soak in for a while. She suggested they break for a few minutes.

Roxanne continued following the break. "A vision on a piece of paper is useless—like those Greg has in his desk drawer. So let's examine ways to build a purpose-vision into the company's infrastructure [Figure 9.6]."

"Following along this diagram, your vision (hopefully, a purpose-vision) needs to be translated into your strategic plan covering the next five to ten years. Anchoring that vision are quantifiable and time-phased Strategic Business Objectives (SBOs). These become the drivers of your core marketing, product, operating, and financial strategies. Technology-dependent companies also have a technology strategy. From the strategies, each function develops its tactics—the specific and, often dynamic activities that can change from time to time—but keeps the thrust toward meeting the strategies in the dynamic marketplace and business world. This is very different from the common strategies and tactics that meet functional needs but don't fit together to meet business needs. The Integrated Business Management team is accountable for ensuring that all the parts fit together and enhance the whole.

"You must pay particular attention to your core business processes because they help distinguish your company from all your competitors. Don't get me wrong. All business processes are important to a company, but you must identify your core processes carefully, and ensure they have strategies tightly integrated to your overall business strategy. The business competencies required to support

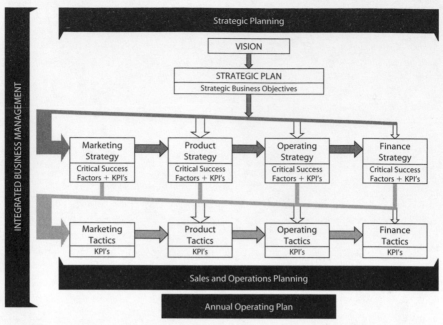

KPI = Key Performance Indicator

Figure 9.6 Vision → Strategies → Tactics: Cascade
Source: Oliver Wight. Copyright Oliver Wight International, Inc. Used with permission.

the core processes must be carefully nurtured and developed to maintain your strategic competitive advantage in the marketplace. You can face a lot of potential people issues here. Having the right packaging designer with the right knowledge database can make or break a brand in some industry segments. You would be reluctant to outsource these core processes as long as they, in fact, remain core to your business. Outsource a core competency, and you'll quickly risk losing your competitive advantage. Every company must understand which are its core processes and its core competencies—how effective they are and how they are being continuously developed. You must also pay attention to your competitors' core processes and competencies, as far as you are able. Are they more relevant or less relevant to the market than yours today? in the future? Is there a competitor exhibiting weaknesses in one of its core competencies that might open a door for you to expand your strategic advantages and erode theirs?

"All this becomes easier when your value proposition, business strategy, markets, and customers have been defined by executive management.

"A company must determine its desired value proposition—the benefits it wants its customers to experience when doing business with it. The value proposition defines why customers come back again and again. Coincident to the value proposition, the company must choose from among the three value disciplines: price competitive, product leadership, or customer/client unique solutions, sometimes referred to as *customer intimacy*. The value proposition, along with the associated value discipline focus, establishes the company's unique positioning in the marketplace. Bringing this home, Cosmetics Products' marketing and sales folks, and the rest of your organization for that matter, must be absolutely clear about your company's espoused and actual value proposition and value disciplines. You must structure and organize your entire supply chain, and I mean all of your activities, to deliver them, especially when trying to achieve Capable-level performance. You must focus on one of the value disciplines but you can't afford to ignore the other two. Even price competitive companies must offer quality products that meet or exceed the needs of their customers." Greg and his team were jotting down notes and appeared a bit dazed as they contemplated the amount of work ahead of them.

"Now, because it's so critical to the success of any company, I want to change direction for a bit and go back over some ground we covered in our last session. You've had some time to think more about the Integrated Business Model and Integrated Business Management [see Figures 6.1 and 6.2]."

"Let me revisit the 'Model,' the big picture of the organization command and control structure." Roxanne explained the model and the associated management roles. She provided examples of how implementation produced breakthrough results for companies that modified their structures and policies to conform to the model. Roxanne summarized her remarks: "With this model in place, everyone in the organization works toward the same integrated objectives. When the top management processes are integrated and direct the business effectively, you have what we call Integrated Business Management. It is, more than anything else, what produces alignment in the organization as depicted by the arrow diagram I showed you during our last session together [see Figure 8.2]. So, does the Integrated Business Model resonate at all with the way you manage your business today?"

"I think not!" David responded. "We do have many of the processes, but I wouldn't call them formal processes, or integrated. I don't see any semblance of the level or quality of integration you describe. Our executive meeting is usually just a debate about what we expect to sell next month. Among product development, supply, marketing, finance, and sales organizations, we haven't yet figured out how to work together constructively. We tend to throw semi-completed ideas over the walls separating our functions, and wait for the repercussions. You describe this Class A process as having an 18- to 24-month Integrated Business Management planning horizon. We're not even sure we'll be in business 18 to 24 months from now. We've never planned that far into the future except, perhaps, for new products. It's hard to even comprehend that kind of planning capability, given where we are today."

Sara added, "You also said something about people being accountable to deliver agreed-to plans, objectives, and performance measures. We share a lot of information and have lots of discussion, but we don't often make formal decisions, let alone commit to executing them. I don't see any real commitment; I mean, I don't see the kind of commitment that fires people up and makes plans happen, or else. That lack of commitment manifests itself as financial surprises and disasters, especially at the end of quarters and at the end of the fiscal year. I don't get much sleep during those closing periods."

"I agree with Sara. From a marketing and sales standpoint," Alexandra added, "I'm afraid I don't see us really committing to deliver the sales plans or forecasts we discuss. Now that I think of it, our forecasts are really only for information. They are semi-educated guesses to project our revenue and earnings, but even at an aggregate level, they're not all that accurate. My people would probably take exception to this comment, but in reality, we act more like marketplace victims. To be brutally honest, our mindset has been that we really can't forecast this business. We sell the products that are easy to sell and whatever the customer wants, rather than seriously trying to *influence* what the customer wants. What will sell itself, we sell; don't hold us accountable except for meeting those quotas that we need for our sales bonuses. For other than routine repeat business in some of our larger brands, we tend to be reactive and go after targets of opportunity that happen to materialize, irrespective of the forecast. We don't very often create sales opportunities. I suppose after the years of dealing with out-of-stocks and poor new product introductions, that shouldn't be much of a surprise. Sales reps are reconciled to that condition being irreparable. Our current way of operating is ineffective if not counterproductive. How will what you're describing help us change these norms?"

Before Roxanne could respond, Greg looked at Alexandra and said, "You know, Alexandra, I agree with you completely. What you've described is totally unacceptable and helps explain why our business is in such bad shape today. If we had the kind of committed business integration that Roxanne describes, we could see what is happening better, take corrective action and avoid some of the crises that have cost us customers. It would make a world of difference."

Roxanne added, "Greg, do you remember us talking about 'one set of numbers'? Are you getting the picture? What Sara and Alexandra described are proof that today you do not have one set of numbers you can believe in to integrate around. That's a major reason this journey is so vital for you to get control of your business—to make it what you want it to be."

Turning to Roxanne, Greg said, "I think the concepts are falling into place, Roxanne. Although I still have some reservations about how it would work in Cosmetic Products, I'm expecting my reservations will be taken care of as I learn more."

"I'm expecting to address your residual concerns over the rest of the day, and I would take you into the detail for how it could work in Cosmetics Products if we work together. Let me start with how Integrated Business Management works. For the moment, I want to show you a slightly different version of the Integrated Business Model [Figure 9.7]."

Figure 9.7   Integrated Business Model: Cascade
Source: Oliver Wight. Copyright Oliver Wight International, Inc. Used with permission.

"When implemented effectively, management decisions cascade everywhere through the organization, even into Human Resources which has the responsibility to provide the right people and the right skills for the future. That's for starters. To digress for a moment, I'd like to tell you about a brand-new COO I worked with. When he got into his job and experienced some significant frustration, he asked me, and this is a direct quote, 'Where the hell's the steering wheel?' He realized that he had no direct process to convey board-level decisions through the organization to the people carrying out the work. He quickly became the energetic champion for implementing the Integrated Business Model. Changes in strategy and business plans at the top of the model cascade down through every facet of the model; changes at the bottom must be communicated up so that plans throughout the entire organization remain synchronized. Some of our coaches refer to this model as 'organized common sense.'

"Given your customer service issues, Greg I'm going to focus on the planning and control aspects of demand and supply. We'll touch on other aspects as we go; after all, the model is integrated! A change in one element of the model directly affects other elements of the model. As I've said before, planning and control of the business must start at the executive level with strategic plans and financial plans. Most often these plans look out into the future at least five years. Depending on the industry, that planning horizon could be much longer.

"The executive team must also determine in the Strategic Planning Process, after it is clear about the company's value proposition and value disciplines, what kind of player it wants to be in its business sector. Does top management intend to be a local, regional, national, or global player? Do the executives want the company to become the industry leader? Another decision; what are the revenue and earnings objectives and desired rate of growth? Specific objectives are usually annualized and stated in financial terms or percentages. These high-level questions can only be answered by the senior executives. The answers provide general direction for the company, but not in enough detail for making good day-to-day decisions about the types of products and services to offer, the types of marketing and sales efforts to fund, the manufacturing strategy to be employed, or the resources required. These details begin to take shape in the two to three-year business plans, annual budgets, and operating strategies developed at the next level in the organization, as depicted in this model.

"At the business plan level, annual revenue and earnings objectives for the next two to three years, market share, types of products and services, cash flow, and other more detailed, but still annualized, objectives begin to take shape. This can be thought of as the annual budgeting process where business leaders make commitments on revenue and profit to corporate leadership. These objectives become the annual scorecard, so to speak, for the senior leaders of the business units.

"Although they are more specific and detailed, these objectives are still annualized numbers, not nearly detailed enough for running the day-to-day business. Suppose that Amalgamated's CEO told this leadership team that your annual revenue commitment for the business is $220M. Would that information alone let you know in what direction to head? Would it tell those who report to you what plans they should be executing? Of course it wouldn't. We haven't yet developed a business unit strategy or an operating strategy to guide us in day-to-day decision-making. Let there be no mistake, people will get very busy, create department goals and objectives, create personal objectives, make action plans, and work like crazy to carry them out. Will they deliver the business strategy? What business strategy? You'll have organized chaos until you have more specific direction from the business leaders. By the way, does that way of operating sound familiar to you?"

Greg was the first to respond. "You already know us too well, Roxanne. It sounds exactly like that dysfunctional diagram you showed us, the one with the arrows going every possible direction [see Figure 8.1]. From my perspective, that sounds very much like us."

"That's exactly what I was thinking, Greg. So let's begin to bring order out of the chaos. Let's move to the next level of the model below strategic planning, that is, to Integrated Business Management [see Figure 6.2].

"This diagram includes all the elements of Sales & Operations Planning, and it's on these I'll focus. You saw the well-respected S&OP process depicted in the previous model as well, but in practice it would be even more integrated in the form of Capable Integrated Business Management. Here you can see a little more clearly how product, demand, and supply are managed together, and are integrated with strategy, company plans, and annual budgets. In this way, the core supply chain processes are monitored, measured, and analyzed for consistency and performance. In Integrated Business Management, business unit management organizes its products and services into families, usually somewhere between five and fifteen of them."

Greg interrupted, "Seems like these families may be our product categories. Do you agree?"

"Could be, Greg, but we'll get to that a bit later; for now, just stay with me conceptually."

Roxanne continued with her description. "Typically, if there are fewer than five families, management won't have enough detail to determine if the business is under control and on strategy. If there are more than fifteen families, management will spend too much time mired in detail that is better managed by their subordinates. For each family, management develops objectives, goals, strategies, and measures to support its overall business strategy. For example, should this family grow? If so, by how much and when? What are its customer service objectives? Should we promote this family? How much advertising? When, if ever, should we launch new products in this family? What kind of capacity or inventory should we carry for this family? What is our capacity strategy? Should we wait until actual demand exceeds current capacity and we are on backorder, or should we build capacity in anticipation of market growth? Those sorts of decisions are required."

Greg thought they probably had many of these details in mind, but not coordinated in the way that Roxanne described.

Roxanne interrupted Greg's thoughts. "In Sales and Operations Planning, plans and objectives are documented in aggregate family volumes for sales, and for the agreed production volumes, balanced of course against resource constraints; and also for agreed inventory or order book levels. These same plans are visible in financial terms. The 'Family aggregate' definition could be by product groupings, categories, brands, market segmentation aggregates, or even key customers. It's whatever makes business sense, especially for Sales and Marketing, and can be supported by the supply organization for planning using a common unit of measure. Family plans are detailed by month for each family over a rolling 18- to 24-month horizon.

"The detail necessary to make day-to-day decisions is now beginning to take shape. Executive management can tell in the monthly Management Business Review if the overall business and the individual families are on strategy. They also can accurately determine whether action must be taken to ensure that financial commitments to corporate leadership, and to the financial markets, will be met. But even this information does not yet provide the level of detail necessary for the supply chain, meaning the plants and suppliers. We'll talk about how that works much later. For now, I want to move into how input is prepared and fed into the Integrated Business Management process. I also want to describe what happens with the output of the Management Business Review. For that, we need to move to the model's next level.

"Preparation begins each month with the work leading up to the Product Management Review, followed by Demand, and then Supply [Figure 9.8].

"I'd like to start with what happens during preparation for the Product, Demand, and Supply Reviews, as depicted in the preparatory wheels on this diagram. As you can see, the current status, issues, performance, and future proposed plans are developed during the month. As you can see from the flow from Product, to Demand, to Supply, all the activities are interdependent. When conflicts surface or a lack of synchronization exists, the objective is to resolve the issues within the core process prior to the Management Business Review. Let me give you an example to clarify what I mean. If there is inadequate supply to meet projected demand, the supply manager would attempt to resolve the imbalance with alternative supply scenarios. If, and only if, there is a remaining mismatch would the imbalance be referred to the Integrated Business Management Process Leader, who is responsible for coordinating and facilitating Integrated Reconciliation, and later the Management Business Review. That person would bring the appropriate parties together to develop and decide on a viable solution. If the recommended solution is beyond the decision-making boundaries for those individuals, or has strategic implications, they would present their recommended solution(s) to the executives for decision in the Management Business Review."

Greg turned to David, "Roxanne has been mentioning several roles I don't recognize: Product Coordinator, Demand Manager, Supply Planning Manager, and now a Manager for Integrated Reconciliation. We don't have anyone in those roles, do we, David?"

"Well, Greg, we certainly don't have a Demand Manager or a Product Coordinator. I suppose Janice Hackworth, who runs my supply chain team, is the closest to being our Supply Planning Manager. As for integrated reconciliation, that sounds like yet another addition to my responsibilities. Lucky me!"

Recognizing the distraction caused by this separate discussion, Roxanne took control. "Let's delay that topic and come back to those details if and when you implement. The message I need you to get is that these processes are hardwired to each other and so operate across the entire business using the same numbers. And that it's an ongoing process."

David interrupted, "You know, managing to the same set of numbers in this team would be a tremendous advantage in managing our supply chain. Greg, we need to do this."

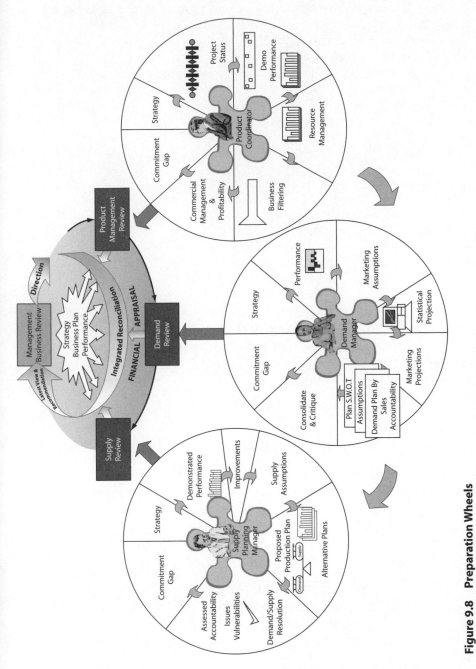

Figure 9.8   Preparation Wheels

Source: Oliver Wight. Copyright Oliver Wight International, Inc. Used with permission.

"Hold your horses, David; I need to understand more about all this before I commit to anything." David sat back in his chair, slightly disappointed at Greg's obvious reluctance.

Roxanne grabbed the reins again. "Let's take a second to prepare your thinking for the next important point. You need to consider this model [Figure 9.9]."

"I want to place all these planning levels in the context of a time horizon, as this model shows. Strategic Planning never resulted in anything actually being made. Integrated Business Management is about resourcing aggregate families of products to meet market and financial expectations. As with Strategic Planning, the Integrated Business Management process never made product either. So where does the real planning that creates products or services take place? Well, it happens in two interconnected processes called demand management and master supply planning—or for clarity it's often called master supply planning over the mid-term to long-term; and master supply scheduling over the cumulative lead time. The figure shows time breaks where management of the business passes from superaggregated strategic planning, to family aggregated Integrated Business Management, to end item planning in master supply planning and scheduling. These time breaks are points where the next level of the organization becomes empowered to plan the business details, although constrained by the numbers from the previous level at the point of empowerment. A master supply scheduler is free to create detailed end item plans for SKUs comprising a family, typically over the first 13 weeks. When the detail is aggregated, however, it must be within $+/-2$ percent of the previously agreed aggregate monthly family volume. If there is a need to schedule more or less

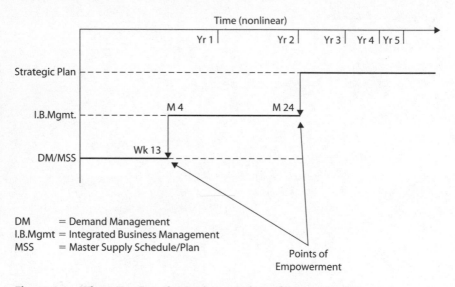

Figure 9.9   Where You Run the Business: Points of Empowerment
Source: Oliver Wight. Copyright Oliver Wight International, Inc. Used with permission.

than that amount, the decision must go back up to the higher planning level for approval.

"Notice that when we talk about Integrated Business Management, we're actually talking about months 4 through 18 to 24, or perhaps even longer if necessary. Weeks 1 to 13 are not actively managed through Integrated Business Management, as we can see. Changes within 13 weeks at end-item level can be extremely disruptive and expensive, although sometimes necessary. The aggregate plans in that period have been agreed to and handed over for the more detailed weekly and daily planning processes.

"A key process throughout the entire time line is Demand Management. Demand Management develops sales plans by family within the Integrated Business Management process horizon; also develops the more detailed end-item demand plans; and manages order entry against supply capability.

"Supply's responsibility is to ensure there is enough overall capacity and resources to meet the predicted demand, or to provide alternative capacity solutions to offset any shortages. This balancing act ensures that family sales, production, inventory, and financial plans presented to executive management are valid, meaning the production volumes are needed and can be executed. I won't yet get into measures used to monitor and improve this process for now. Just know that we measure accuracy of all these forward-looking plans carefully."

Sara asked about the source of purchasing plans. Roxanne replied, "This is where Material Requirements Planning (MRP), the core module of your ERP system, comes into play. When you have an approved master supply plan, it is transmitted to your ERP system's MRP module. Assuming all the foundation data is accurate and that the demand plans and master supply schedules/plans are valid, MRP does the number crunching to create plans for all materials, from intermediate components produced in your plants to purchased components and raw materials. At least, that's what should happen. But the way you described your ERP system implementation, you are undoubtedly doing most of this work manually."

Greg stared intensely at David, "Does this mean we could be doing all this with our system?" David nodded in agreement with Greg's question. "So why haven't we done this already? It's why I pay you, isn't it."

Roxanne stopped this conversation abruptly. "Greg, that's water under the bridge. Your implementation was designed to avoid a Y2K problem, not to meet supply chain objectives, as was pointed out earlier. But it's not too late to recover that capability as you'll see as I move to the next slide [Figure 9.10]."

"I want to focus on the Supply Review and the work that leads up to it. The boxes in this diagram represent work processes that support and feed information into the monthly Supply Review. You may remember that I said you seem to be missing the links between the boxes. The way your system is configured, and the way you work outside the system using spreadsheets, negates all those links. The circles on this diagram represent the foundation elements

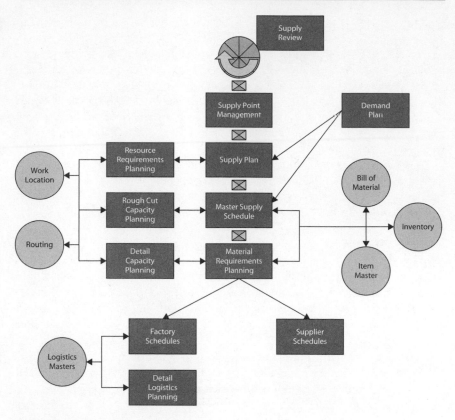

Figure 9.10   Supply Point Model
Source: Oliver Wight. Copyright Oliver Wight International, Inc. Used with permission.

for any ERP system. Some would refer to them as the business rules for each link in the process flow; we call them master data. As powerful as it is, MRP can only follow your rules. So the links and resulting output will be valid only if your master data is accurate. To be of value, the planners must do their work within the system using the messages or recommendations produced by the system. We won't get into the detail of MRP with this team, but that's how it's meant to operate."

Sara, VP of Finance, spoke up. "I need to back up for a moment. We don't have a Demand Manager. We don't have a Supply Manager as far as I know. We don't have people with the title of Master Supply Planner or Material Planner. What about it, David?"

"Don't be too tough on us, Sara," David, the VP Supply Chain and Manufacturing, responded. "We do perform most of those functions and tasks; we just don't have people with those specific titles. We do have master supply schedulers in each plant. I'm quite certain, however, that people performing some of the activities Roxanne described don't understand their responsibilities in the way that she just described or have them integrated very well. At the very least, we need to fill those roles formally and invest in the education and training of the people filling them."

"I can echo what David just said," Alexandra contributed. "We have a forecaster, but I certainly wouldn't call her a 'Demand Manager.' Demand Manager sounds like a much more responsible position than we have thought about in the past, even in my former division. Our forecaster is one of the senior market analysts, Roxanne. She works hard, but we're still not convinced it's possible to actually forecast this business, let alone manage the demand as you described. When it comes to forecasting the business by units and by week and by shipping point, as I've heard you talk about, forget it; we're not even close." Sounding more than a bit defensive, Alexandra continued, "By the way, David, how do you go about deciding what products to ship to our distribution centers (DCs)? Given our poor customer service levels and high inventory, it doesn't sound as if you have a very effective process either."

Roxanne jumped into the fray. "People, this conversation is not productive. You are where you are, and must decide as a team how you can work together to solve your problems. I'm giving you points to consider, not ammunition with which to assign blame!" Seeing his team looking duly chastened, Greg was impressed that Roxanne didn't hesitate to take them to task.

Greg said, "Let's take a fifteen-minute break and then resume our discussion over lunch."

When all had filled their plates and returned to the conference room table, Roxanne continued.

"I want us to stay focused on the supply functions for a bit. It's the responsibility of the senior supply executive to ensure that the supply plans presented in the Management Business Review are valid. Capacity planning takes place at every step from strategic planning to detailed planning to ensure that schedules can be met across the supply chain over the days, weeks, months, and years. We realize that the mix of SKUs actually produced and shipped within the families may vary during the month, but the focus of Integrated Business Management is the total volume for each family. In supply planning, we ensure that there is a plan in place to provide the required product and resources when they are needed.

"As with demand planning, where forecasts are done at both the SKU and family levels, supply planning uses the same approach. In each area—demand and supply—SKU plans are created and must roll up and match the aggregate family numbers. In both areas, all necessary resources such as people, equipment, marketing plans, sales incentives and component material must be available to support the plans. Remember, Class A companies run their businesses with one set of operational numbers.

"With approved aggregate plans for each of the families in products, sales, production, inventory, and finance, the supply chain can now begin its work to execute the details of those plans."

Alexandra interrupted Roxanne. As I've said before, Roxanne, I'm still having a little trouble with the concept of forecasting SKU shipments by week from each of our DCs. We do a poor job of forecasting total sales revenue by quarter. I really think forecasting by week is overkill in this business, if it's not totally impossible."

"I'm really glad you made that comment, Alexandra, because it gives me an opportunity to clarify what I mean. If the Demand Planning Manager does not provide the weekly forecast, then someone else will! Manufacturing has to decide what to produce each week, and each day for that matter.

"I can assure you that someone in Cosmetics Products is estimating weekly shipments, even if the method is as crude as dividing the monthly forecast by four. That responsibility needs to be within the Demand organization. Here's a fundamental principle in excellent companies: forecasting must be done in one place by one group; that group must be as close as possible to the customer. The Demand Planner has far better knowledge than supply or distribution planners as to what's going on in the marketplace. Have your Demand Planners forecast by week. Initial results will not be good, but they will soon be better than anything you've had in the past.

"I don't want to get into too much detail at this time, but you'll need to consider several methods of forecasting to find the model closest to your customer experience. As an aside, if you have rapidly changing portfolios, then 'probability' forecasting might help." Alexandra made a note to get back to Roxanne on that. "That's just one example of a number of techniques that can be employed when traditional forecasting produces soft numbers. Based on the experience of our clients, your results will begin to improve rapidly because your Demand Planners will gather the information and document the assumptions needed to improve forecast accuracy continuously. When you gain control of your supply chain, at least at the capable level, we can talk about an excellent advanced process to improve forecasts by week and even by day. Collaborative supply planning actually links your forecasting and planning activities with those of your key customers. But that can come only after you've achieved a capable level. Does that help, Alexandra?"

"I'll have to take your word for it now, Roxanne, but it's a leap of faith for me. We'll have to make sure people know that the measure of forecast accuracy is to be used to drive improvement, not to punish the forecasters."

"Fair enough. Thanks for your candor. That's a great point, by the way, about the forecast accuracy measure being used to improve performance. I don't want to get into all the required measures now, but most functional groups will need to put measures in place to track progress toward delivering desired results. Whatever the measure, it must be used to assess business process effectiveness and improve business results, not to assess the performance of individuals. That is a tough culture change component for most companies.

"At this point in the Integrated Business Model [see Figure 6.1], your planners have the information they need to run the day-to-day business with the support of your software. I won't get into any more of the details of the supply planning process or how the software works to support the planners. That's more detail than you need now, but I'll briefly describe what goes on in your supply chain as a result of having weekly SKU forecasts.

"The entire process is designed to answer some very straightforward questions:

- What does the customer want?
- What do I have already?
- What do I need to make, and when do I need to make it?
- What does it take to make it?
- What components do I have already?
- What do I need to get, and when do I need to get it?"

"We often refer to these as the *universal manufacturing questions,* first articulated by the late Oliver Wight. They are the same questions you must answer whether you plan cosmetics products, automobiles, magazines, patient care in a clinic, or a holiday dinner for your family.

"Let me ask you this question." Roxanne went to the chart pad and wrote, 'What do I have?' "David, what is your current level of inventory accuracy?"

"I don't think we have a formal measure for that other than the overall monthly financial variance, Roxanne. Oh, and we do a physical inventory count every quarter, when we can fit it in."

Roxanne recorded a question mark next to inventory accuracy. She next wrote, 'What does it take to make it?' "Well then, David, what is your bill of material accuracy level?"

"How do you measure that, Roxanne?"

"Good question, David, but let's not get into that amount of detail now. For the moment, I think your question answers my question." She recorded another question mark and asked, "Any idea of the level of accuracy for item masters, work locations, routings, logistics masters, customer masters, supplier masters?"

David held his hands up in mock submission. "I give up; please show some mercy! I haven't a clue, and I'd bet the ranch that we don't measure accuracy of those records at all."

"Thanks for your honesty, David. If you aren't measuring the accuracy of these critically important foundation elements, I'm quite confident that accuracy is poor. In turn, the planning system can't create valid material plans, nor support your planners by giving them useful information or realistic recommendations. That means that your planners are forced to work outside the ERP system. Poor data integrity of the foundation elements may not be the entire problem with software acceptance, but it's a big part of why you've failed to get the expected value from your ERP system and control of your customer service."

Sara offered her insight. "That also explains why the financial analysis we do in the system often doesn't make much sense. If the system would give us believable data, we would rely on it, do more effective financial simulations and be able to close the books more quickly. Instead, we spend countless hours trying to reconcile data in the system with the data in our spreadsheets."

"It's now clear to me that we have even more work to do than I thought," Greg said. "I don't pretend to understand the details of Master Supply Planning, MRP, or any others of those three-letter acronyms you rattled off, Roxanne, but I know that we all have lots to learn. I'm beginning to see that we're not close to having Class A processes anywhere, but I'm most interested in those business processes that will solve our immediate problem—delivering to our customers on time. Later we can think about the rest of the Integrated Business Model and Class A. Trust me; I badly want the business benefits we estimated in our last session, but first things first."

"If you're in agreement, Greg, let me address three related topics: benchmarking, organization maturity, and the *Class A Checklist*. I think those are useful topics to get at your 'first things first.'"

Greg and his leadership team all nodded in agreement.

"When you have selected the appropriate milestone, we recommend you start by using the *Class A Checklist* as a benchmarking tool for best practices for the key business processes and their subprocesses.

"Hopefully you recall that we looked at your position on the various maturity maps last week [see Figure 6.4].

Greg thought to himself, "How could I ever forget that humbling exercise!"

"As I said then, to be certified as Class A, companies must progress to the top of Transition 4. From a performance standpoint, results for those companies fall solidly and continuously in at least the upper quartile of results in their industry for a range of performance indicators described in the *Class A Checklist* across all nine chapters. Additionally, by the time they are certified, Class A companies must have delivered most of, if not all, the business results and bottom line improvements that they predicted at the outset of their journey."

"I think we're doomed, Roxanne," Zachary Zellers, VP Human Resources, commented, only half-jokingly. "We agreed that we are solidly in what you call Transition 1. I can't imagine how we get from Transition 1 to Transition 4 in my lifetime. It seems like a mountain to climb, and we can't even see the foothills yet." Unspoken agreement presented itself as visible gloom on the faces of the leadership team.

"Wait just a minute, folks. I didn't intend to depress you. It is possible for Cosmetics Products to get to Transition 4, and get there within your lifetime, Zachary. Remember the riddle, 'How do you eat an elephant? One bite at a time!' Don't forget that members of this team have already seen two companies that were certified using our previous Checklist edition and are nearing recertification against the current Checklist. Many companies have had the same issues you are confronting when they started their work. It's important to take on bite-sized portions of the Checklist aligned against specific business objectives. Those are what I've been calling 'milestones.' Your most pressing business need and competitive priority seems to be achieving improved on-time delivery and improving customer satisfaction causes us to lean toward Capable Planning and Control and perhaps Capable Integrated Business Management as your first milestones."

Greg interrupted, "You can say '*is* improving Customer Service,' not 'seems to be,' Roxanne. I just want to remind us of that."

"Okay, Greg, 'is.' So we seem to be firming up a recommendation to align first at least on the Capable Planning and Control Milestone. As you make progress against this milestone, you'll begin to realize the bottom line benefits you estimated during the Executive Briefing last week, and probably more than what you estimated. There will be tough challenges along the way, but remember that saying, 'Keep your eyes on the prize.'"

"This is about the point I thought we would reach on day one, so it's a good place to stop. We can focus on the Checklist in a bit more detail tomorrow."

"Perfect timing, Roxanne. I think we need some time to internalize what we learned today. You've given us a lot to digest. Talking of which, we'd love for you to join us for dinner."

Roxanne gladly accepted Greg's invitation, looking forward to an informal and relaxed environment over dinner. But she knew the questions would continue.

Her instincts were correct. As dinner moved along, the conversation became more animated; challenges to what she had covered during the day were emerging. Much to her surprise, every time a concern or doubt was voiced, another member of the leadership team jumped in with a response. Several times, Roxanne clarified a point she'd made during the day or deferred the question to the next day when she would address it in depth. What was most encouraging was the absence of cynicism among the people in the room. There was a clear sense among the team members that doing nothing was not an option. They had to move forward quickly.

10

HOPE

*If you think education is expensive, try calculating
the price of ignorance!*

The leadership team was gathered in the conference room over a continental breakfast early the next morning following their team dinner when Roxanne arrived. Team members questioned Roxanne about how companies organize to make the leap from Capable to Advanced levels of performance. They also asked her detailed questions about the time commitments and cost required to make the journey she was describing. She responded in general terms since they had yet to assess their starting point fully and define their gaps to business excellence. Roxanne agreed to cover the path to excellence in more detail later that day. The sense of "doom," as Zachary had described it, had mellowed to a healthy nervousness at the enormity of the task, but also a sense of excitement about the possibilities. They were finally getting an idea of the path they could follow to improve business results.

"Thanks for your questions this morning, everyone. I was deliberately general in my responses, but keep the questions coming. I intend to answer some of those questions in detail as we go through the structure of the Checklist and the implementation methodology we call the 'Proven Path.' First, let's turn to the *Class A Checklist*. At my suggestion, Greg purchased copies of the book for each of you. Let me hand these out, but try not to dive into the book yet. Isn't that the most difficult thing anyone can ask you to do? People are inherently inquisitive, and already several of you have flipped through a few pages. No harm, but let's close the books for a few minutes, please.

"First, a bit of background. For Effective Management, our passion is to support companies seeking to be consistent winners by aspiring to excellence. This Checklist is the comprehensive statement of excellence in business today. It embraces every part of the business to be pursued for business excellence, and sets out those business processes and practices that we see over and over at the heart of successful and excellent companies. It is written so that your people can see for themselves what excellence is and what each of them has to do in order for the company to be excellent. Its chapters align with core business processes and the enablers of those processes, covering the entire business. Simultaneously, it is demanding and rewarding—very demanding at times—but true excellence never comes easily. Class A companies operate consistently in the upper quartile of companies in their industry in each of the processes, or chapters, below." Roxanne paused after this introduction as the team took in her message.

"There are nine chapters in the new Checklist [see Figure 6.5]. The first four are 'priority chapters':

1. Managing the Strategic Planning Process
2. Managing and Leading People
3. Driving Business Improvement
4. Integrated Business Management

"In these chapters, we've brought together the processes and practices that are common and fundamental through all other business processes, and that enable the entire business to be excellent. The remaining five chapters address the processes that distinguish each company in the marketplace:

5. Managing Products and Services
6. Managing Demand
7. Managing the Supply Chain
8. Managing Internal Supply
9. Managing External Sourcing

"I suggest these chapters cover the entirety of your business."

David responded first, "Although I'm not familiar with all the detail in the Checklist, I can see our responsibilities as individuals and as the executive team falling within these processes. So I agree with you." The others agreed. Roxanne continued.

"I'll not get into much detail yet; I'll just say a few words about each chapter, but understand that all the chapters are interdependent.

"*Chapter 1, Managing the Strategic Planning Process:* You have to be clear about your business vision and strategy for your people to plan what they must do to get there. This chapter challenges your process for the longer term planning of the business. It demands the setting of business priorities and clear communication when deploying your plans and your business excellence program throughout the business. You've probably gathered by now that I'm passionate about vision, strategy setting, and planning. It's a simple equation: no vision and strategy = no direction = excellence impossible. And good luck because you'll be facing some very stormy seas out there!"

"Been there; done that; got the scars to prove it!" Greg thought to himself.

"We ask you to establish and manage the process for setting purpose-vision, strategy, and direction to become an upper quartile company. The chapter requires that this purpose is reflected in all plans, projects, and actions throughout the company. Chapter 1 is not about how to create a strategy so much as it challenges you to set your direction and your value proposition, and then your supporting value discipline focus. You then ensure there is alignment with Amalgamated's corporate vision and strategy. When that's complete you must deploy Cosmetics Products' business vision and strategy throughout your organization, even down into your supplier base. Then everyone will be—no, make that 'must be'—engaged in delivering that strategy and living your value proposition. In this chapter, you'll find references to the benchmarking process we discussed yesterday. The importance of strategy, once you have developed it, is knowing where you are heading and keeping that vision clear and meaningful in the face of changes in the business landscape. The strategy must be dynamic and energizing. Your job is ensuring that the strategy remains relevant, and that it is actually executed.

"*Chapter 2, Managing and Leading People:* People are the ultimate differentiator as the marketplace becomes more demanding and competitive. This chapter leads you to think through your business values and organization for the tasks ahead. The chapter requires that you are clear about the company culture and behaviors needed, and that you design supporting programs to develop the competencies of your people for the challenges ahead. It challenges your processes for knowledge management, and your culture of leadership and teamwork. It also challenges your style of leadership, your commitment to respecting and developing your people; and among other topics, how you ensure a safe and healthy environment for your employees and society. It underscores the reality that the only sustainable competitive advantage a company has is its people.

"*Chapter 3, Driving Business Improvement:* This chapter articulates an approach for assessing the maturity of your business and its processes. It then challenges how you prioritize your business improvement program to secure the early gains that create a solid foundation for the future. This chapter challenges you to walk before you try to run, and to give value to those everyday issues that are at the heart of excellence in business. Driving Business Improvement establishes the improvement architecture that underpins and generates the company's overall business performance improvement program. Chapter 3 focuses on driving out waste and variability to increase velocity in all business processes, and to establish a culture of sustained results and continuous improvement. In addition, it helps steer the company as it grows from a culture of defensive behavior and the chaos of never ending unplanned events, to a culture of cross-functional continuous improvement across the entire business with a clear focus on meeting and exceeding the needs of the stakeholders—investors, customers, employees, and society.

"*Chapter 4, Integrated Business Management:* This chapter articulates the continuing, natural evolution of the Sales and Operations Planning process. It has been designed and developed over many years, building on client needs and experiences in all sectors, and in all parts of the world. Integrated Business Management is the unique, yet now de facto standard approach to managing the gap between company strategic goals and everyday activity. It is the prime tool for keeping all parts of the company aligned to a common agenda and set of priorities. Integrated Business Management allows the company to manage the entire business through one set of numbers and ensures timely decisions to maintain management control. It drives gap-closing actions to address competitive priorities and to deliver management commitments. In fact, it is the critical process in deploying the business strategy throughout the company. In essence, Integrated Business Management is the process with which executive management links strategy to execution.

"So these are the four priority chapters. They must be addressed directly by you as the executive team. You could say that they define quite simply in four nuggets your role in the organization."

After answering a few questions for clarification, Roxanne prepared to move ahead when Greg commented. "I like the idea of nuggets—pieces of gold—it expresses my, and our, accountabilities well. I can see that I need to know more about this to do my job better."

David added, "And it gives us a clearer view of our accountability as a team as well."

"Good points, Greg and David. Now we move on to the five chapters covering the processes that distinguish each company in the marketplace."

"*Chapter 5, Managing Products and Services:* In every business sector, product life cycles are getting shorter. Portfolios require an increased frequency of new products and services and a carefully planned phase-out of old. This chapter establishes best practices for how you establish your product portfolio and manage your products and services. It expects you to have a clear supporting technology strategy as well. It challenges your practices for delivering sales and profit to your business through an increased number of successful products and services introduced into your market. It also defines the latest practices in Program Management for large complex projects."

Alexandra couldn't hold back. "Take me to that chapter—right now!" Everyone laughed and commented in agreement. Roxanne continued.

"May be a bit premature, Alexandra, but I agree this chapter would help you because it focuses on aligning product and service activities to business strategy and market needs while not forgetting about making money through an intense passion for customer success. While under the leadership of Marketing, overall process governance and linkage to supply and execution processes is achieved through the Integrated Business Management process. This way, the resulting product plans are completely integrated with company operating plans.

"*Chapter 6, Managing Demand:* Greater understanding of customer needs and of your marketplace leads directly to increased predictability in your short-, medium-, and long-term business requirements. Best practices in Managing Demand enable better understanding and planning of your position in the marketplace and the creation of order-winning plans that are consistently more successful. This chapter challenges to improve how you create and plan demand. It also challenges you to improve your control of supply and demand in the short-term through sales activities. Managing Demand is a marketing-led process for delivering strategic and business plan requirements by ensuring that planned and predictable revenue streams are realized. While all companies find forecasting and demand planning to be an inexact science at best, Class A companies become very good at getting closer to their customers. Through this linkage, they collaboratively develop better demand plans. They also do a much better job of influencing customers and consumers to match their requirements with the company's capabilities whenever there is a supply constraint. Class A companies treat a forecast as a request to create products and services, not just as a casual prediction. Class A companies create products and services when they are needed; deploy finished goods inventory, if needed; and then quickly turn the resulting inventory into cash."

"Okay, Alexandra, there's your job description," Sara piped up, to general laughter.

"*Chapter 7, Managing the Supply Chain:* As technology evolves and your target market expands, you face an increasing challenge in delivering your products and services to the point of use. This chapter challenges your understanding of your extended supply chain. It establishes best practices for improving your strategic and tactical extended supply chain design to deliver optimum customer service and bottom-line performance. It challenges you to build an increasingly responsive supply chain that plans, integrates, links, and shapes the supply planning and execution processes so that they deliver competitive advantage, leading to consistent upper quartile performance. Don't panic when you read through this chapter! This is what we call a 'Phase 2' activity. Much of it is not possible until you have made significant progress in your internal planning capability, as defined by the Capable Planning and Control Milestone. You need to understand now what's in the chapter so that you'll have a vision of what is beyond the capable level. Chapter 7 also deals with creating a supply chain strategy that supports supply and demand segmentation, and then redesigning the supply model to permit complete integration of the end-to-end supply chain. The final challenge presented in this chapter is to provide equitable benefits in service, inventory, capacity, costs, and benefits for all extended supply chain partners. Everyone must be a winner. You'll also find collaborative supply planning, six sigma, agile, flexible, and lean approaches at work in this chapter.

"*Chapter 8, Managing Internal Supply:* While business focus is moving to the extended supply chain, excellence in core supply activities remains vital in meeting the needs of customers and consumers, and in meeting the challenge of global cost competition. This chapter challenges your internal operating groups that make and deliver goods and services to understand just how quickly they must be able to modify and execute internal supply plans in response to changing marketplace demands while optimizing costs. Managing Internal Supply challenges your current paradigms for managing internal capabilities and resources. It asks you to plan and execute business and supply strategies through integrated supply planning and control. Internal supply processes feed required information into the monthly Supply Review, and are linked directly to performance tracking, and financial planning and reporting with one set of numbers. It's really about people creating valid plans inside the company, and then executing those plans to satisfy customer commitments with optimal inventory, effectiveness, and cost. Fundamental elements of this process include master supply planning and scheduling, material supply planning, logistics (through Distribution Resources Planning), supplier planning, capacity planning, asset management, and maintenance management. There is a fundamental, underlying expectation that all related data has a high level of integrity and accuracy.

"*Chapter 9, Managing External Sourcing:* The trend of a rapid increase in products and services and a wider market present new challenges to the make/buy decision-making for products, components, and materials. The challenge extends to sourcing strategies that follow those decisions. Technology offers new procurement approaches with major savings potential, and has significantly advanced the use of total cost of ownership consideration in procurement decisions. This chapter sets new standards for assessing excellence in your procurement processes and in planning and coordinating the movement of goods into your supply chain. It also questions the way you manage sourcing to create competitive advantage and consistently operate in the upper quartile of supply chains in your industry. The expectation is that you balance risk and total cost of ownership, rather than focus your analysis on purchase price variance."

David interrupted. "We rely almost solely on purchase price variance to manage our purchasing spend. I've heard of total cost of ownership, but I've always thought of it as a theoretical consideration. I obviously need to understand its implications much better than I do today."

"Thanks, David, for your honesty. It helps to get all the issues on the table so that we make the best decisions about where to focus our limited resources. To continue, in this chapter you'll find the best practices for developing strong relationships with companies that can effectively and efficiently supply the goods and services you need to create your products and services. By that I mean relationships in which the principals act more like partners on your journey to the future you envision. These are very different concepts from the all-too-present outsourcing to suppliers offering the lowest purchase price. You'll find suppliers who want to be your preferred suppliers, but you need to hold up your end of the agreement. You need to be a preferred customer if you intend to operate most effectively.

"By the way, how often have you asked your suppliers how good a customer you are?"

"Interesting concept," David replied. "I don't think we've ever asked our suppliers that question. I know for a fact that we haven't asked since I've been in the business. We're quick to criticize and squeeze our suppliers, however. I realize that we are a difficult customer. There probably isn't a single day when we don't ask at least one supplier to jump through hoops to meet our changing needs. In fact, we believe a good supplier is one that can meet an unreasonable request without whining. I take it, Roxanne, that you would not define us as a good customer."

"If that is really your concept of a good supplier, David, you couldn't be more right about not being a good customer. The kind of behavior you just described increases supply chain costs significantly. Class A companies have long-term relationships and work closely with their trading partners to continuously improve quality, reduce variation, and eliminate waste in the supply chain. Perhaps the most overlooked aspect of being a good customer is providing your suppliers with reliable forward visibility of your needs. No matter how good a customer you want to be, unless you have robust planning and control processes in place you just can't provide your suppliers with that kind of information. There are significant savings to both trading partners in that kind of relationship." David nodded in agreement.

"As I said a few minutes ago, I don't want to get into the details of the best practices in each chapter at this time. If you decide to work with us on a program to improve Customer Service—that would be our Capable Planning and Control Milestone and, perhaps our Capable Integrated Business Management Milestone as well—you will become familiar with the Checklist details that support reaching those milestones. If, later on, you decide to undertake the journey to business excellence and want to achieve Class A performance standards, you'll have to become familiar with the content of the entire Checklist. For now, I want to turn to implementation—how you get there from where you are today."

"Perfect segue, Roxanne," Greg said. "We're beginning to get a better understanding of business excellence; we understand more about the transitions we'll go through; we know more about the best practices in the *Class A Checklist*; and we know that Zachary doesn't think we can get there in his lifetime. But we have only a limited amount of time to deliver breakthrough customer service results or we'll all be looking for new careers. How do we do it?"

"Thanks for the setup, Greg; let's pick that up after we take a break for lunch."

After lunch, Roxanne continued, "With your last question, Greg, you've directed our attention to the final subject for the day. Stan Stevens, one of my partners who, with Mary Medford, presented at the seminar you attended, talked about what we call our 'Proven Path,' our proven methodology for helping companies transform their culture, accomplish milestones along their journey toward business excellence, and ultimately achieve business excellence operating at Class A performance levels. What he discussed was a fairly conceptual model. What I want to discuss with you now is our approach in helping clients reach their milestones and, ultimately, Class A status. Based on the extensive experience of all of our colleagues, we can say that our 'Proven Path' to business excellence works every time it is followed diligently and is supported by senior management" [see Figure 6.8].

"You're now in the middle of the Leadership Engagement phase [Figure 10.1]. All the work leading up to the Point of Commitment is the responsibility of the executive leadership and sets the stage for successful implementation and completion of the milestone(s) along the journey to business excellence. The implementation clock starts at the Point of Commitment. I want to be completely clear that in Cosmetics Products it is your team Greg, that has accountability for completing the Leadership phase and for deciding whether to commit. You can and should have other people to work with you in this phase of the Proven Path, but when it comes to the final decision to

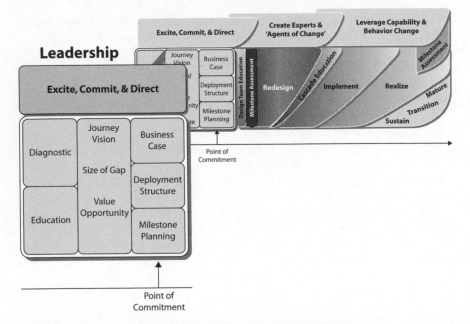

Figure 10.1   The Proven Path: Leadership Engagement Phase
Source: Oliver Wight. Copyright Oliver Wight International, Inc. Used with permission.

proceed, it is yours and yours alone. Let's look at those Leadership elements, in which you begin to build excitement and commitment among the leadership team and set the direction for the organization.

"To begin the work, we recommend education for the executives and potential initiative leaders, as we've done this week and last. You've already been through a Diagnostic assessment of all chapters to assess your current state, and you've had some exposure to a desired future state. More detailed education is needed for those who will participate in the milestone assessments so that they understand the concepts and principles of business excellence related to the selected milestone templates. Based on what you've told me so far, I'm quite certain your first initiative will be all about improving customer service. When you've decided which milestone or milestones will best address that issue, we'll provide the required education for a larger assessment team and facilitate a detail assessment of the associated business processes and behaviors. That work, however, will come after the Point of Commitment [see Figure 6.8]. The detail assessment helps you determine and quantify quite precisely the specific gaps between current business processes and behaviors versus Checklist best practices, information critical to accomplishing the initial milestone(s).

"It's important that all who participate in the detail assessment receive education similar to what you are receiving, but in much greater depth. As you'd expect, we have a complete portfolio of courses to fit education needs at all levels of the organization involved in such an initiative. For each milestone, we educate management and key non-management leaders first, and then at the right time we provide more specific detailed courses supporting the milestone to your process design teams. I want to be clear, we provide *education* to your people; you will then conduct *training* or retraining classes related to process changes coming from your design teams. Our objective is to transfer enough of our knowledge to enable you to design your business processes for success, and then for you to train your people in how to carry out those processes.

"Your process design teams must be deeply involved in what we call 'facilitated detail assessments,' against the Checklist topics and descriptions referenced in the milestone template. Our facilitation allows the assessment to be completed quickly and ensures accurate results. We guide your people in comparing current processes with those in the template, provide clarifying comments, and ask probing questions. We provide insight into the meaning of the Checklist, subjects, and definitions; but we ask your people to determine assessment scores. Our calibration ensures that your teams are neither too critical nor too easy on themselves. I got a bit ahead of myself talking about the milestone detail assessment. Just let me remind you that the design teams' education and facilitated assessments are conducted after you have passed the Point of Commitment.

"To help you reach that point in completing the Leadership phase, we would facilitate for this team a pretty intense two-day workshop. The first deliverable of that workshop is a formal milestone initiative mission statement designed to keep the team focused. This statement must support the corporate and Cosmetics Products' vision/mission statements for the business. The initiative mission statement, however, is focused specifically on the business excellence work and on what you want to accomplish with your initial milestone." Greg interrupted.

"Actually, Roxanne, I'm pretty much convinced after considerable thought that our first initiative must be customer service, and to accomplish that, we must include two milestones—Capable Planning and Control and Capable Integrated Business Management."

"Good for you, Greg. You need to be careful you don't stretch beyond the resources you can deploy, but those seem well within your capabilities. Keep in mind that a journey to business excellence is not a sprint; it's more like a relay race. There are many distractions along the way, so it's good to break the journey into bite-size chunks aligned with our milestones; that approach will allow you to better focus your resources on the most important business issues at the time. So it's important to keep your initiative mission statement in front of everyone. Use it in making decisions about priorities. An ongoing part of your team's work, Greg, is to maintain meaningful business-level vision and mission statements. This initiative would be one of the resulting strategic business objectives. By making these visible, your people should challenge you when your decisions don't seem to support your business vision or objectives.

"Having made the decision about your initial milestones during the workshop, it is important to be clear about the value and opportunity the work presents. In an earlier session, we have already seen that for Cosmetics Products the potential benefits far outweigh the best-guess implementation costs. However, you need to go through that analysis more thoroughly using your standard cost/benefit procedures.

"Organization is next. Each milestone would have a team accountable for achieving that milestone" [Figure 10.2].

"This slide is a good representation of the organization our successful clients use to manage their initial milestone when they're starting in Phase 1—and they mostly are. Realistically, only companies already at the top of Phase 1 are in a position to decide to pursue the entire journey because they have some enablers in place that make it more feasible. Whatever the initiative decision at this early stage, you, Greg, must be the champion. Within the initiative, each and every milestone supporting that initiative also must have a top management champion at the executive level. The milestone champion keeps close touch with the project work, clears away barriers and keeps the executive team on track when the going gets tough. The champion has to be a real enthusiast. In your case, since your first milestones are likely to be Capable Planning and Control and Capable Integrated Business Management, and since they are so critical to your division's success, I suggest you consider David as the champion of Capable Planning and Control and Alexandra as the champion of

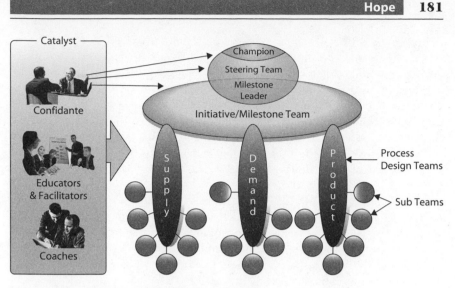

Figure 10.2   Organization for Change: Phase I
Source: Oliver Wight. Copyright Oliver Wight International, Inc. Used with permission.

Capable Integrated Business Management. The Effective Management coach works closely as a mentor and confidante with the initiative and milestone champions. Together, they are catalysts for the change effort. The coach also works with members of the Steering Committee to keep the effort on track. I presume that in your case, the people in this room would constitute the Steering Committee for any identified milestones and for the journey in general. Each steering team member, by the way, is expected to serve as executive sponsor for one or more of the business process design teams. The EM coach also serves as confidante and personal coach to the steering team members in their support of the milestone teams. Our role is to help you accelerate the flow of benefits to the bottom line.

"As you see, the steering team includes a member called the 'Milestone Leader,' who coordinates the efforts of all the business process design teams related to the milestone, as dictated by the milestone template. Ideally, the milestone team is made up of the milestone team leader and the business process design team leaders for a specific milestone, plus any enabling subteams.

"The Milestone Leader also works closely with the executive management milestone champion and the outside coach to ensure that proposed improvements meet the milestone requirements and to ensure that milestone work remains on schedule.

"The coach works closely with the Milestone Team and with the individual process design teams. The routine points of contact with Effective Management would be the milestone champion and the Milestone Leader. Normally Process Design Team Leaders forward design questions that their teams cannot answer to the Milestone Leader who may be able to answer the question. If not, or to validate a response, the Milestone Leader can contact the EM coach to coordinate a reply.

The Milestone Leader is responsible for ensuring that the overall design remains technically sound and integrated across all teams. The milestone team has accountability for achieving the milestone, but most of the groundwork to accomplish that milestone is done by the business process design teams. We provide a good deal of education to the teams, and then rely on those teams to train the rest of the organization as they redesign their operating procedures and work instructions. This is all part of our operating principle of knowledge transfer. It would be easy and profitable for us to train everyone in your organization. We would enjoy that the opportunity, but that would limit your ability to sustain the results after we leave. Instead, we prefer to coach your people to the point that they can continuously develop those who move into new assignments or are new to the organization, and have you call us when you need public education to bring someone new aboard or to provide some refresher education privately for your company.

"If you choose to work on more than one milestone, someone must ensure that the efforts of all the milestone teams are in alignment and integrated with each other, and that the company is efficiently utilizing its resources. We therefore recommend an initiative leader in addition to an initiative champion.

"Looking ahead, having reached the top of Phase 1, the Capable level of your selected milestone, we hope you would choose to embark on other Phase 1 milestones to broaden your capabilities, and then go on to a Phase 2 milestone that could take you to an Advanced level, on the way to full Class A.

"As you can see, before each decision to go further we would help you define your competitive priorities and business case for each additional step in the journey [Figure 10.3]. This isn't a jigsaw puzzle where you put in milestones to make a pretty picture. Assuming that people and empowerment aspects have been addressed, you would begin to see a rather different organizational model. By this time, you will be organized as process teams—cross-functional, empowered, and maybe self-managing. This aspect of integration will become an integral part of your culture. When they reach this point in their 'People' maturity journey, companies find it impossible to understand how they ever managed their business without these teams.

"You can see in this slide [Figure 10.4] that the process teams are even more cross-functional since the advanced milestones are truly focused on process, rather than on any particular function. Having achieved business integration, the process teams become more and more self-managed with guidance and coordination from the Business Excellence Leader, who, as you see in the model, leads Phase 2 initiatives, and steering team. Nevertheless, for each milestone in either Phase 1 or Phase 2, an important responsibility of the executive team is to establish and prioritize performance objectives and goals. Each template includes the critical goals and the minimum levels of performance required. Early on, these may satisfy your needs. But as you progress I would

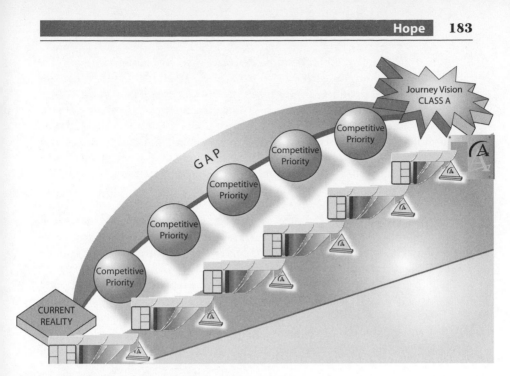

Figure 10.3   The Proven Path Steps to Class A
Source: Oliver Wight. Copyright Oliver Wight International, Inc. Used with permission.

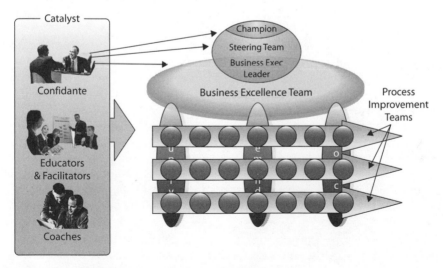

Figure 10.4   Organization for Change: Phase 2
Source: Oliver Wight. Copyright Oliver Wight International, Inc. Used with permission.

also expect that you might have additional objectives and goals resulting from benchmarking other companies in your industry. In the later milestones on the journey, you'll need to achieve results consistently in those defined areas in the upper quartile of your industry. You'll also need to define and achieve the bottom line business results that you have defined in the Leadership portion of the proven path. We can provide coaching and workshops in all those areas. It's important for you to review and understand all performance goals and business objectives for each milestone up front so that you don't surprise and demoralize your milestone and business process teams with new requirements at the last minute. One word of caution: beware of trying to carry forward today's performance measures that don't fit in the integrated environment. If you think you need an extra measure, or you think a measure in the template is redundant, please call us first. Most often it's a misunderstanding that can be resolved quickly.

"When you've completed the leadership tasks, you'll be well positioned to decide whether to proceed with the first milestone or milestones. If you choose to proceed, you'll schedule a formal kick-off event marking deployment of the initiative. In that meeting, you can communicate your vision of the future, the mission for the team, the performance objectives, the organization including the milestone and process design teams and the Milestone Leader(s) responsible for success of the effort, and, most importantly, the bottom-line improvement objectives such as costs, customer service, inventory, and savings.

"The first job of the teams as you move into the second part of the Proven Path [Figure 10.5] would be to lay out a time line, based on the steps in the Proven Path, and bounded by management's delivery expectations. The time line would include the initial detailed education for both milestone and process design teams.

"Here is a list of the typical teams companies need to support Capable Planning and Control [Figure 10.6]. In assigning the process design team leaders, do not select people who are easy to free up. The better the people you select, the better the results you'll get. You'll get faster and more sustainable results if you assign the managers of the associated areas to the project. If they aren't your best people, perhaps you don't have the right people in management. Have the Team Leaders recruit their cross-functional team members. Since these are the people who will redesign your business processes, you need people you can trust to do a conscientious job. As quickly as possible, the executive team should charter and commission the milestone and process design teams, and provide whatever internal orientation and business case education necessary to begin to get people excited and up to speed. That would give us time to schedule your people into our public courses and arrange for private courses to fit in with the teams' needs and your timetable."

Greg interrupted. "Don't get too far ahead, Roxanne. We haven't yet decided to move ahead with this initiative."

Development

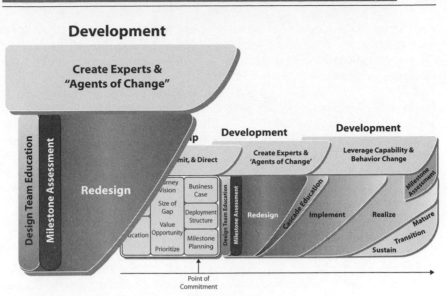

Figure 10.5   The Proven Path: Development
Source: Oliver Wight. Copyright Oliver Wight International, Inc. Used with permission.

- Integrated Business Management
- Product Management
- Demand Management
- Supply Management
- Master Supply Planning, MRP, and Capacity Planning
- Production Operations
- Supplier Scheduling and Purchasing
- Finance
- Inventory Records
- Data Integrity—Master and Dynamic Data
- Performance Measures

Supported by IT and Documentation Specialists

Figure 10.6   Typical Process Design Teams for Capable Planning and Control

Roxanne noticed her look of exasperation as Sara said to Greg, "Like, what else do you propose, Greg? The Plan B you've been talking about?"

Roxanne intervened. "Hold on, Sara. Greg's absolutely right. You all need to sit down and create a proper business case, however rough-cut, and consider how you're going to free up resources; set out a rough time line; assign budget, and then decide whether to go ahead. If you bypass these, you'll be missing a vital step in reaching your formal Point of Commitment. Remember the Proven Path? You need to work on the business case, then the deployment structure, and then do the milestone selection and planning.

"I did get a bit ahead of myself. My apologies, Greg, but I know you'll forgive my enthusiasm!" Greg acknowledged Sara's apology with a smile. Roxanne continued.

When teams are formed and a timetable created, that's the point at which we would begin a series of courses for the business process teams and others who will be working closely with them. This education focuses on how to achieve best practice processes related to the selected milestone, to begin closing the gaps identified during the Diagnostic assessment, and to prepare the teams for the detail assessments. It enables the business process design teams to develop a common language and understanding, and to begin developing their work plans.

"If you are wondering why I stress education, it is because education is the key to your success. Employees must understand *why* they are being asked to do something differently. You may have noticed that I said Effective Management would educate your teams; but I didn't mention the rest of your people for a good reason. That part is your job, internally, through what we call 'cascade education.' And remember, when we're no longer here to help, you will be responsible for sustaining your people's knowledge of how you want your integrated processes to operate, and why. This need for education is especially relevant when a senior manager joins the team. Just for your information, Greg, turnover among leadership team members is far and away the biggest reason that companies experience an erosion of their procedures and lose their performance edge."

Greg interrupted Roxanne. "I agree with you, Roxanne; you talk a great deal about the importance of education, as did Stan Stevens and Mary Medford in the seminar David and I attended. There must be a less expensive and less time-consuming way of educating people than by sending them away to courses. We have smart people; can't smart people simply read technical books and get the same information?

"There are lots of ways to learn, Greg. People should take advantage of every learning opportunity including reading books, attending courses and seminars, using e-learning for technical training, acquiring specialist certifications and talking with peers at professional association meetings. All of those methods are good and important throughout a career. But where speed is of the essence, where you are seeking a culture change and you want the best and the most up-to-date information, you need the sort of education we provide. Our clients tell us that the education we provided was critical to transforming their organizations. We'll help you save time to achieve bottom line results. I believe it is a question of value, not cost."

Roxanne continued. "Let's table that discussion for now and follow up with further discussion offline. I want to go back one slide and spend some time discussing the Development phase of the Proven Path [Figure 10.5].

"Following education, the teams are ready to participate in detailed assessments against their milestone template. Because people have had the education and received our help in facilitating the event, they begin to see and quantify gaps against best practices. And, because they know your current processes, they begin to develop some initial thoughts about the redesign. We keep them calibrated against the best practice concepts and goals, and provide insight and guidance where necessary.

"Then the fun work begins. Teams redesign their processes, test, revise, validate goodness of fit to the business, and begin to determine how best to configure the ERP system to support those new processes. Then they finalize their new designs and formally document their new business processes. The milestone team ensures there is integration between the process teams' redesign efforts, and keeps the design teams on schedule. When all that work is complete, there is a formal design review with the steering team to ensure that the final design is fully tested and integrated, to answer the executives' questions, and to convince the steering team that the new design is ready for implementation.

"Around this point, it is often helpful to convert a slice of the business to the new processes in order to demonstrate that they work and deliver the expected early benefits. After this first cutover, rapid implementation across the whole business is required by the executive team, which is counting on the improved results across the board.

"Implementation is the process of training all affected people on the new business processes, establishing ownership, developing the capabilities and competencies of the people involved and ensuring that the required new behaviors are in place. That is when the results begin to really flow to the bottom line."

Greg interrupted. "Roxanne, you said it typically takes three months to start seeing results and a year before we would be 'Capable.' I'm still concerned about how much time we really have left to solve our customer service problems. I need to fix those problems now!"

"Assuming you reach the Point of Commitment and make a 'go' decision, I would assign a small team of coaches—two or three, plus myself to support an urgent implementation. We could begin working with your people very soon after that if you can free up some of their time. Between us, we should be able to complete the design teams' education, workshops, and milestone assessments within a matter of weeks. The rest of the Development phase, specifically the actual redesign and the beginning of cascade education, depends on the size of the gaps, the complexity of your company and, again, the focus of your steering team. Quite frankly, the biggest factor regarding speed to results often seems to be the commitment and attention span of executive management.

"Benefits follow as work is completed; the more focused the effort, the sooner on-time delivery improves, revenue and profits increase, and customer service improves. Regardless, improved performance won't come instantaneously, but improvements in planning the business internally will soon work their way into improved customer service results. Of course, global companies take longer to get to the redesign, maybe as long as six months, given the realities of geography, regional differences, and logistics.

"When the Steering Team stays focused, many companies begin to see the first signs of improved customer service and financial benefits about three months after the Point of Commitment. Greg, it's my experience, and that of my colleagues, that if the path to business excellence is followed, milestone results and targeted bottom line benefits are achieved as predicted and often exceeded. But there's no magic wand to wave and there is no quick fix; don't let anyone tell you otherwise. I hope that answers your question, Greg."

"It does, Roxanne. Of course I'd like to see immediate improvement in customer service but your answer makes sense. We took about three years to screw it up; it's going to take some time to put it back together correctly. The way your company approaches the work as knowledge transfer and culture change probably requires a bit more time up front. But I see how it can accelerate the realization of improvements and reduce the total time needed to get the benefits. More importantly, I can see clearly that the resulting improvements would be more self-sustaining. What would you suggest we do next?"

"As individuals and as a team, you have some serious thinking to do. Some rhetorical questions come to mind. Are you going to focus on the Capable Planning and Control and Capable Integrated Business Management Milestones? Have another look at that rough-cut business case and determine if it's close enough, or if you need more economic analysis? How quickly can you reach the Point of Commitment? How quickly can you set up the organization structure for change? Who will be on the various teams? How soon can you free up some of their time? Will your team lead aggressively and support the effort required?

"Greg, you and your team have to answer these questions. If and when you decide to 'go', we'll be right there to help you get going, to provide education, the relevant facilitated milestone assessments, mentoring, and coaching. Then we'll step back so your redesign teams can develop and own their redesigns. I'd normally come in every month for a few days to assess progress and provide help as necessary, and also to coach you through any tough spots. Members of my team would be here as often as necessary to speed up your redesign and accelerate the transfer our knowledge."

"Roxanne, before we break, just run over the next steps following Point of Commitment. I want to see if I've got it right."

"Okay, Greg. When you've assigned and freed up your teams, we'll provide detailed education in two parts. First, an overview of business excellence for the milestone team, and any other managers you'd like to put in the loop at that time. We would then start the milestone template assessments, so by then you'll also need your executive champion in place.

"I'll facilitate your milestone assessment with David and Alexandra. You'll begin to understand your business as never before, I promise you. At times you'll be shocked by what's common practice today. You'll have to bite your tongue and just make a note of it and remember that the current processes have been, by default, sanctioned by today's management. Overview education and facilitated assessments would take two to three days each. I'll then spend a day with that same team in a high-level workshop on areas for redesign. If you discover that there may be some other implications of the design such as safety or quality, the milestone team could charter a subteam to look at those issues.

"Part two of the education is usually more detailed private courses on best practice concepts, process by process, for each of the redesign teams. To remind you, the people on process design teams would typically spend two days a week in team activities. As I said before, given your urgency, it sounds like you'll want to put in more of their time, maybe three or four days a week, but not 100 percent. Education for the design teams would take one or two days for each, depending on the gap from best practice. That's about twenty education days, probably covering about 100 people in your case. Before you say it Greg, if you think education is expensive, try calculating the price of ignorance!" Greg smiled, "I'm sure I've heard that before," and nodded in agreement.

"Then it's up to your steering team through the Milestone Leader and executive champions, to drive the redesign activities to conclusion. As a reminder, when a process redesign team has completed its redesign, it is disbanded, leaving the milestone team to take implementation forward. Is that enough information for now?"

David spoke first. "That gives me a much better sense of what's involved, especially with the facilitated detail assessment. I can see redesign will follow as a natural next step." Greg spoke next.

"That helps me a lot too, Roxanne. I'm beginning to see that this could really work for us."

Greg brought the day's session to a close. "Roxanne, I like the idea of getting a more definitive estimate of the cost and the benefits of completing the first milestone, and maybe the next one or two. You can guess pretty well where I'm headed, but first I would need a costed proposal for the use of Effective Management's services if we go ahead with you. Price your proposal as if we will pursue both the Capable Planning and Control and Capable Integrated Business Management Milestones. That'll give us the information we'll need for going after just Capable Planning and Control, or both."

"Sure, Greg, and I'd like to include your expenditures to date as well so you see the big picture. We use common milestone program templates with all our clients as a starting point and adjust it to individual company needs.

I'll get that to you next week—but only as a starting point for further discussion until we complete the detailed assessment. The good news is that our program pricing template assumes everything is wrong, so usually we can reduce it a bit."

"I'll believe that when I see it, but I'm impressed with your approach."

"Greg, my company's purpose-vision is 'to help clients make themselves successful through sharing our experiences in a committed relationship.' We want, passionately, for our clients to be winners. We work closely with and alongside your project teams to ensure client success. As I said earlier, we are successful only if our clients are successful in meeting their business objectives.

"I've come full circle back to the start of this monologue. I would really enjoy working with you. Your potential for success, from my vantage point, is enormous. Regardless of whether or not you choose to work with Effective Management, I will be happy to be an ongoing resource and sounding board for you, Greg, and for the rest of your leadership team. I don't have anything else to add at this time, except that you can expect my proposal within a week. Do you have any final questions for me?"

There were no questions, so Greg closed the day's meeting. "You've been very helpful, Roxanne. I appreciate your candor, insight, encouragement, and your willingness to stay with us until this late hour. We'll get back at it on Monday, team. We'll see if we can make a decision or at least come to grips with what else is needed to make a decision quickly."

Later that evening, Greg shared the events of the day with Penny, and then phoned Susan. "Sorry for bothering you at home, Susan, but I want to bring you up to date on the meeting with Roxanne Barnes. I need to review her proposal for the next steps, but I don't think that will be a barrier to moving forward. I'm really encouraged. Specifically, I've asked her for a proposal to provide initial education to a cross-functional group of people from our business offices and plants. That education would prepare those people to participate in a detailed assessment, with Roxanne's help, of our current business practices against what are called the 'Capable Planning and Control Milestone' and the 'Capable Integrated Business Management Milestone' based on Class A best practices. You'll find out more about these terms when we can sit down together. Alongside the diagnostics we've already run as a management team, that would give us a clear view of what's broken, and needs attention; what's not effective and needs to be improved; and what's good that we don't want to lose. We can then determine accurately the cost and potential bottom-line benefits of putting in the Class A processes required to achieve our customer service objectives. We'll then be able to decide whether to proceed.

"My confidence is growing that we can get the customer service problem behind us. However, I know just lurking around the corner are other issues to be addressed, including profit objectives. Let me tell you what I found staggering. Based on some benchmarks, and please don't hold me to this yet, we did a very rough estimate of potential benefits. We came up with annual, reoccurring savings of about twelve million dollars plus another fifteen million dollars in a one-time reduction of our growing working capital investment while at the same time increasing customer service to at least 95 percent."

"Impressive! Tell me honestly, Greg, do you really believe those numbers? Is Roxanne capable of delivering that kind of financial windfall?"

"She was very clear with us that we would be responsible for delivering those savings. She and a very small number of her colleagues would coach us, but they insist that we learn the concepts and principles of business excellence that will lead us to Class A performance levels, implement the required culture changes, and deliver the results. Now, to answer your question about her capability, I would say unequivocally, she is capable. Roxanne has a grasp of the supply chain that even impressed David. She has been through similar business excellence journeys as a member of a leadership team before becoming a consultant, and has a wealth of knowledge about how other companies faced and overcame challenges similar to ours. I need to stay objective as I review her proposal, but I haven't been this encouraged about turning the business around in a long time. I really can't wait to get started."

"I like it when you get passionate about a plan, Greg. Sounds like you had a great session this week. Please let me know when you've reviewed Roxanne's proposal. If you choose to proceed, let me know your plan. I'll need some details, especially about when we might begin seeing the twelve million dollars on the bottom line. Needless to say, the Board is still looking for a return on their investment in Cosmetics Products. By the way, if you go forward, I'd like to meet Roxanne."

11

DECISION TIME

I've been feeling good about laying out a plan for survival, but not for excellence. That's a sobering revelation.

The sooner we get started, the sooner we stop the hemorrhaging. We just can't waste another day without doing something to stop the loss of customers, revenue, and profit.

Remember, you can't make an omelet without breaking the eggs!

Greg remained optimistic throughout most of the weekend. The difference was obvious to his family. He talked with Penny about the way he had been feeling about work.

"You know, Penny, Roxanne made a lot of sense the way she spoke about total integration of the business. I didn't completely understand some of the details, but the way she talked about integrating the efforts of people across the entire supply chain, and the way she described the path we could take to improve our results was eye-opening. It was exciting. She gave me the confidence that I haven't had in a good while. We started thinking differently about the business.

"And, Penny, thanks for being a good listener again, and for putting up with me the past few months."

Early Sunday evening the house was quiet. He and Penny were relaxing while reading recent best sellers. Greg was distracted by his thoughts as he read and was getting excited about a future with improved customer service results. He realized the path he was on would make Cosmetics Products competitive again, but wouldn't make them the preferred supplier he wanted them to be. He remarked aloud, "How could I possibly have missed that fact?"

193

Startled, Penny said, "What is it, Greg?"

"I just realized that I've been feeling good about laying out a plan for survival, but not for excellence. That's a sobering revelation to me!" Penny simply shook her head and went back to her book. But for Greg, the seeds were sown for Cosmetics Products to continue on the complete journey to business excellence. He would keep his plan to himself for a while so that his executive team would stay focused on the work at hand.

When he returned to work on Monday, Greg noticed an increased level of energy and enthusiasm among everyone on his leadership team. On Monday afternoon, he received an e-mail from Roxanne with her draft proposal. He sent it on to his team with a note that it would be on the Tuesday afternoon team meeting agenda for the following week. But when Greg arrived at his office this Tuesday, early as usual, he was surprised to find David pacing impatiently outside Greg's locked office. He followed Greg through the office door.

"Hi, David; couldn't sleep?"

David snapped back, "Greg, we need to talk. Oh, and good morning."

Greg closed his office door and motioned David to take a seat. "Okay, what is it?"

David sat, but then stood up again and resumed his pacing. "Greg I'm getting really frustrated with your holding back on fixing our customer service problems." Greg looked at David, taken aback, as David turned and faced him. "We've got to get on with the Capable Planning and Control and Capable Integrated Business Management Milestone. Let's make the decision today so we can start cleaning up the mess we're in. We can't wait until next Tuesday! Let's get honest with ourselves; there is no Plan B. I don't understand what you're waiting for. It's the right thing to do. They are no smarter than us over at Capital or Tender Care, so I'm convinced we can start quickly to make a difference in our results. Roxanne hinted any number of times that you need to make the decision and lead the effort. We're fiddling while Rome burns. What can I do to persuade you? The cost can't possibly be an issue, given the return on investment (ROI) we estimated."

Greg motioned for David to sit down again. "Take a breath and let me collect my thoughts for a moment." After a pause, Greg continued. "I've learned to trust your opinion, David, and I value especially your frank comments. I agree with you completely. I'll get Cynthia to arrange a 9:00 A.M. meeting today for the executive team."

David looked relieved. He had taken a risk confronting his boss and hadn't been reprimanded. "Thanks for listening, Greg. I couldn't hold back any longer; it's been keeping me awake at night."

The team assembled, except for Zachary who was off-site for the day. They were puzzled by Cynthia's request for an emergency meeting with no stated agenda. Greg got straight to the subject.

"Folks, David just took me to task this morning; on reflection, very appropriately. Thank you, David." They all wondered what was coming next. "Okay, David, you take it from here and explain our conversation." David gathered his thoughts and addressed the team enthusiastically.

"What I said to Greg is that I've heard enough; I don't need any more convincing. We need to start the Capable Planning and Control and Capable Integrated Business Management Milestones now. We need to make our decision today and stop wasting time. We have the draft proposal from Roxanne. Let's get back to her and get on her schedule as soon as possible. We can clear up any procedural stuff that we need to address over the next couple of weeks, but, meanwhile, let's get started with the milestones and stop the hemorrhaging."

Everyone began talking at once. Smiling, Greg raised his voice, "Hold on everyone! I love the excitement in your voices, but we need a little structure. This is an important decision for all of us. I'd like you to spend the rest of the day doing three things. First, I need your consensus recommendation on 'go' or 'no-go.' If the answer is 'go,' your second task is to tell me in ballpark terms what it means in the way of people resources. We have to agree on the initiative, confirm what milestones we are going to address, and assign champions and leaders. We'll not get the urgency we need with a part-time person trying to do his or her regular job and be Milestone Leader at the same time. We'll also need to assign a number of others to the various task teams. We don't want the people you can spare, or who have time to do it. If we're going to change our business culture and practices, I need to be assured that you're going to put the best people we've got against it; I want people who will get the work done and done well. And third, I want a draft announcement that we'll finalize today to let everyone know our direction and that it will be a top priority for us and for them. If we don't show our unified commitment, it won't happen."

Several people began explaining conflicting appointments for the morning, but didn't change Greg's new-found resolve. "If this is worth doing, it's worth doing well. Anyone have a scheduled meeting with a customer today?" Alexandra had an afternoon meeting scheduled with a key customer. "Okay, keep that one. Anyone have a personnel issue that can't wait? No? Then let's get on with it. Remember, you can't make an omelet without breaking the eggs! We'll meet again in the executive conference room at 3:00 P.M. That'll delay the start of our regular executive meeting agenda, but it can't be helped given the urgency."

Greg had turned David's challenge into a leadership opportunity; he'd sent them off with a new sense of excitement and energy. Greg next called Susan who asked if the decision to proceed had been made. Greg explained that it hadn't been made yet, but that he was confident about what his team would recommend. Susan expressed her support and wanted to communicate to the Board that turnaround action plans were being executed. Greg suggested it would be better to await the formal announcement, but was pleased with Susan's enthusiastic support.

Greg's executive team, who recently had begun to think of him as "Greg the Hesitant," would have been speechless had they listened in on his next phone call. In anticipation of his team's recommendation, Greg phoned Roxanne. She answered on the second ring. Greg surprised her. "You know, I've been thinking about this all weekend, Roxanne. I believe the executive team has to be more directly involved, and that we need to be more aggressive. I really want to do Capable Integrated Business Management as well as Capable Planning and Control. What problems do you see?"

She first expressed her delight that Cosmetics Products had chosen to proceed. "I'm glad you've decided on Capable Planning and Control and Capable Integrated Business Management. From where I stand, they're your obvious priority. Although they focus on the business management and the internal supply chapters, there are some requirements across all chapters. So you'll need good participation from all the supply chain functions to cover the design teams we talked about.

"As to your question, let's think through the implications. First, I'd hate for you to spread yourselves so thin that you aren't successful. Do you believe you can manage that scope with your team? I know you have the capability, but can you make the time?"

"The answer is yes. If we don't make the time to do both milestones, all of us may have more free time on our hands than we want. I am determined to show by example that I'm leading this business turnaround. It'll be my success, or my failure. Taking on both milestones won't be easy, but I simply don't see an option. We'll have to figure it out."

"If you remember, in our last session I agreed that there might be a need to include both milestones in your effort to get the customer service results that you want. I think you can achieve both since some of their of requirements overlap. Given your commitment and that of your executive team, I believe you pull it off. I'll have to round up a couple of my colleagues to help educate and coach both teams. Some of the education is common to both milestones, so I'll take that into account.

"You already have my draft proposal. When will you need it finalized, Greg?"

"Why don't you give me an update of the draft and outline project plan by the end of today if that's possible. I can wait for a few days for the final proposal."

Roxanne said she would spend the day freeing up available days in the near-term calendar to help Cosmetics Products get started quickly. The longer-term scheduling would be a simpler matter. She would alert her intended supporting colleagues immediately to provide their availability over the next six weeks as a starter. "Remember, Greg, for the Capable Integrated Business Management milestone, you'll need involvement of your executives, including a fair amount of your own time."

Greg felt relieved that a plan for action was taking shape at last.

Meanwhile, David had suggested that the rest of the team begin their meeting at 10 A.M. to give everyone time to reschedule appointments. They agreed to meet in the Finance conference room since it was convenient and available.

Sara welcomed the team to her conference room. She had arranged refreshments and a catered lunch so they could work steadily until their meeting with Greg. As they sat down, Sara commented that she had received Roxanne's draft estimate for supporting both Integrated Business Management and Capable Planning and Control Milestones, and that it should cause no funding concerns. "If we agree to launch this initiative, I'll have to submit some paperwork, but that shouldn't delay us. The numbers I have at the moment are close enough and show that the project will easily pass our financial hurdle rate, even if the cost increased by 50 percent."

David was next. "As I see it, Roxanne offers us the only way I know of to get out of our customer service mess; the approach is logical and direct. There's a proven path that we saw actually work in a couple of companies. I think she called the approach 'organized common sense', and I certainly agree with that description!" They then spent a little time discussing potential players they would have to free up for the teams, and how they would backfill their responsibilities. The discussion was open and positive. After lunch, David brought the meeting to order. "A while ago, Sara just answered the only question I had, which was about the budget. So, are we ready to agree to a 'go' recommendation?"

Back in his office Greg was smiling. Roxanne had just called with some good news; she and two of her colleagues were finishing early with another client and had two days open at the end of the following week. "Because of the size of the group and the need to be available for some design workshops, including a separate workshop for your leadership team, I'll need the help of a couple of my colleagues for the meeting. I want them to be present on the first day to listen to your issues, become familiar with the people and the challenges, and have your people begin to get comfortable with them. On the second day, they'll help directly with the workshops. The two I have in mind are Tom Wilson and Dan Evans. Tom has an extensive background in consumer goods, both in operations where he earned his Class A credentials, and as a coach in our group for the past five years. Dan spent his career in the pharmaceutical industry, specifically in sales and marketing, and worked on Class A project teams in two different companies. He joined our group nearly ten years ago and has been a coach for companies in chemical processing, heavy equipment manufacturing, and also in the electronics industry. I know both Tom and Dan will do a good job in the workshops and will be very helpful as you go forward. I included the cost of three of us in the proposal, but didn't indicate specifically who would be involved. Is their participation acceptable to you, Greg?"

"Works for me. If you're confident about their ability to help, I welcome their participation."

When he reflected on the conversation after the call, he thought, "Was that me welcoming a consultant? Guess I've already started changing my behavior!"

Roxanne had told Greg that these two days would be used to help Cosmetics Products set up the work, and requested that the initiative champion, initiative leader, milestone champions, and milestone leaders be assigned prior to the workshop. Depending on progress, the executive Champions might not be needed for all of the second day; but should join in for a wrap-up. At this point, Greg felt a bit alarmed to be excluded from that part of the workshop. He thought to himself, "Gotta' let go; gotta' trust them; gotta' stop micromanaging." This was a new concept for Greg. He was continuing to confront and change his own counterproductive behavior.

The executive team, looking upbeat, reconvened at 3:00 P.M. Greg spoke up, "Okay folks, what do you recommend: 'go' or 'no-go'?"

David replied, "We have a recommendation, Greg, but first we need to give you our rationale. Sara, take us through it."

"Greg, I took notes for the team and David helped me summarize our thinking. There should be no surprises." Sara spent ten minutes running through half a dozen slides.

David followed Sara's presentation. "Greg, our recommendation, and we are unanimously committed to this, is 'go', and go quickly."

Greg paused a moment, making eye contact with each of them, before saying, "Good! I expected that decision. How should we announce this? We need to make sure Alexandra and Zachary know of our decision before they learn about it through the grapevine."

But within a few minutes Alexandra entered the conference room. "Sorry I missed the first part of the reconnect. Where are we?" David filled her in and said they were about to look at the proposed announcement.

Sara put up the proposed wording on the screen. Greg read it silently, and then frowned. "Well, that does cover all the points, but there's no fire in it. Remember your feelings when I asked you for a recommendation? You were excited and passionate about moving forward. We need the rest of our people to be just as excited."

"Maybe we make this more like a declaration of our intent." David continued, "You know, like an official proclamation; something like, 'We the Cosmetics Products team . . . are committed to . . . to achieve . . . so that we . . . by doing this . . . it's our top priority project.' That sort of thing. And maybe we can all sign it and make copies to display around this place, even in the plants, Field Sales offices and distribution centers. And let's create a communication package so we can schedule department meetings to explain the new direction." The excitement increased, and Greg decided it was time to demonstrate his commitment as well.

Before he could speak, Alexandra said, "We need a name for this initiative so that everyone from the Board to the shop floor to our customers can understand and relate to it. I suggest we make it simple and just call it the 'Customer Service Initiative.'" Everyone nodded in agreement.

Then Greg spoke. "Well, while you have been enjoying a free lunch, I've been busy. I've already contacted Effective Management and reserved some of their time." Their surprised faces showed that Greg had just scored a home run with his team. There was a buzz of approval and discussion in the room. "Okay, so I jumped the gun a bit, but I was confident about what your recommendation would be." He paused for a moment, "Now the other news. I need you to clear your calendars next Thursday and Friday, and think about others who should join us for an executive and initiative team kick-off meeting. According to those slides of yours, you've already started to think about who should be on the teams. That's great! Invite them to come along when you've finalized your choices. And we should also include our own subject matter experts. Roxanne's coming in with a couple of her colleagues to help us get going. They'll be here to take us through the milestone templates in detail, and to facilitate our job of setting up the initiative." The excitement turned to anxious mutterings about how they would clear their calendars with such short notice.

Alexandra interrupted. "I've just been talking this afternoon with a key account. We're this close to being fired by yet another customer. I can't think of anything on anyone's schedule that should take priority over the initiative kick-off. Greg, I'll make sure our key marketing and sales managers will be there—no excuses. The sooner we get started, the sooner we stop the hemorrhaging, as David so appropriately put it. We just can't waste another day without doing something to stop the loss of customers, revenue, and profit."

Greg smiled. "Here's my next piece of news. Alexandra, you will champion of the Capable Integrated Business Management Milestone and David will champion for the Capable Planning and Control Milestone. I will be the champion for the overall Customer Service Initiative." David nearly choked on his coffee. "I think you all agree with me that Alexandra and David are the right ones to lead the milestones." They agreed readily since David and Alexandra both had already demonstrated their passion and leadership. "You'll both need to free up some time to get this show on the road and get a project plan in place."

The team agreed that achieving this initiative was their top priority, and asked Greg to let them know who else he had volunteered from the executive team. This was the opening Greg needed.

"Well, actually I've volunteered the entire executive team to lead the work in achieving the Capable Integrated Business Management Milestone in parallel with the Capable Planning and Control Milestone." This brought another flurry of questions all being asked at the same time until Greg raised his hands to quiet the group. "First I heard you tell me that getting our business sorted out is the top priority. I fully support getting customer service fixed, but I'm equally committed that we don't slip back again to where we are today. I want us to have the most robust executive business management process anyone has ever seen. I want customers to want to do business with us. Together, these milestones will move us in that direction and provide a superb launch platform for taking on additional milestones in the future."

The meeting continued longer than anticipated as they discussed the implications for current business; how to provide support for the milestones; and how to engage themselves in the Integrated Business Management Milestone—all at the same time. Most of the discussion was about potential candidates for the initiative and the milestone leaders, the persons driving the project teams day to day and hour by hour, and about possible cross-functional task team members. They concluded one person full time could be the initiative leader and lead one of the milestones but they would need another leader for the second milestone. Time and again they challenged each other to release people each regarded as key to the business, rather than offer up good but second-best candidates. Following additional discussion about the remaining elements of the Leadership phase of the Proven Path, and completing an abridged Leadership Team meeting agenda, they finished the long but exciting day at 7:30 P.M.

Greg phoned Roxanne the next morning to report the formal decision and the leadership team's reactions. He told her they would call it the "Customer Service Initiative," and that he'd asked the leadership team to round up their best people from which they'd select the milestone teams.

"Good," Roxanne responded. "In addition, I think you should make an opening statement at the workshop before handing the agenda over to us. Initially we'll cover much of the information from the facilitated diagnostic that I already shared with your leadership team, Greg, but we'll get into more of the Checklist details. You should purchase a sufficient quantity of Checklists so that everyone will have easy access to it. The workshop will prepare them to begin working on the Customer Service Initiative. It's important that all attendees take away from the session a clear sense of what they'll need to do next. You'll be surprised how much education will occur during the next couple weeks. The team sessions during the workshops will give us an opportunity to see whether the participants have the right mix of background and capabilities to identify and close the gaps to best practices. By the way, having your leadership team present for the two days will speak volumes to the others about the priority and importance of this effort. I really hope all of you can attend."

"Not only can we attend, Roxanne, we'll make sure there are no cell phone calls or any other interruptions. In fact, I think I'll have the meeting scheduled off-site. It's too easy to get distracted when we're here in the main office. I trust that's acceptable to you?"

"Perfect, Greg. We'll need everyone's complete attention. I really like the way this is shaping up. The most important foundation element in any culture change effort is the commitment of the leadership team. You and your team are demonstrating exactly what we need. That's why I am so confident that Cosmetics Products will be successful in solving your customer service problems through these milestones. I'm also confident in your ability to complete the entire journey to business excellence successfully if you choose to go on after completing these first two." Meanwhile, Cynthia had been busy and managed to hire a good venue.

Roxanne and Greg checked their calendars and planned logistics for the meeting, which would be held at the Marriott Marquis in downtown Atlanta. Greg selected that location so that the participants would recognize the importance of the event and to minimize interruptions. Greg would tell everyone at the beginning of the meeting to turn off cell phones and any other communications devices, a previously unheard of request in Cosmetics Products. He wanted the beginning of the culture change to be apparent from the first day. Roxanne suggested that in his opening address he should include the business case, why those present were invited, and what it would mean to them as individuals and to the future of the company. They also agreed to schedule a Thursday evening dinner to which Greg would invite Susan as the keynote speaker. Roxanne had heard a good deal about Susan and welcomed the opportunity to meet her. Greg couldn't wait to get the ball rolling.

12

KICK-OFF ...

*We've discovered that our planning process is broken
from the top to the bottom.*

*Now is the time for you to either get on the train or decide you don't
want to be part of the journey and get off, because the train is leaving
the station this morning!*

Greg was preparing an e-mail message to Susan, updating her on the meeting and requesting her participation at Thursday's dinner when he heard "You've got mail." Ironically, the incoming message was from Susan asking him to attend a 10:00 A.M. meeting in her office on that same Thursday. With some reluctance, Greg phoned Susan to request a special dispensation and also to request her appearance at the dinner. Susan agreed that his workshop was too important for him to miss and changed the date for her meeting. She also enthusiastically agreed to be his keynote speaker. Susan ended the conversation by once again encouraging Greg to do whatever was necessary to make Cosmetics Products successful.

On the following Thursday, Roxanne, Dan, and Tom met Greg for an early breakfast at the Atlanta Marriott Marquis to get to know each other and review the agenda. At 7:55 A.M. they went into the ballroom where nearly 50 invited participants representing Sales, Marketing, Demand Management, Manufacturing, Supply Chain, Quality, Engineering, Logistics, Purchasing, Finance, Product Development, Technical Services, Human Resources, and the full Leadership Team had assembled. Greg stepped to the podium precisely at eight o'clock, another visible sign of culture change, welcomed the assembled group, thanked them for rearranging their schedules on such short notice, introduced Roxanne, and began his opening remarks.

"I have been looking forward to this day for a long time, perhaps without knowing it, since the first day I joined Cosmetics Products. I believe this could turn out to be the most important day in our history because it's the day we begin to transform the division into a preferred supplier to our customers. We are calling this transformation the 'Cosmetics Products Customer Service Initiative.' Today, we take the first steps in what I anticipate will be a rapid resolution to our customer service challenges, and the first step in a longer journey to business excellence. We are meeting off-site, away from our daily jobs and routines, so that we can begin to think differently about who we are and what we can accomplish . . . beginning now. So, cell-phones off." At this point Greg held up and switched off his own phone.

"It's a rare opportunity to have so much talent assembled together in one room. But despite our collective talent and our uniform desire to be successful as individuals and as a company, we're facing a serious challenge. It comes as no surprise to any of you that revenue and profit are declining, that customer service can only be described as poor, despite large and growing inventories, and that we recently lost some important customers. Our job—yours, mine, and ours collectively—is to reverse these trends and to do it quickly. I'm confident we can do that. I am confident that we can become a preferred supplier and even a leader in our industry after we've solved our immediate problems. I am confident for several reasons. First, we certainly have the motivation, the proverbial 'burning platform'—dissatisfied customers. We can't continue on our current path and survive as a company. Next we have the talent, meaning those of you in this room, to accomplish the required transformation. Finally, we have recently learned about a path to success that companies facing similar challenges have followed. It has enabled them to become extremely successful despite what seemed to them to be overwhelming odds at the start. This path is not just theoretical. The methodology those companies followed has been proven time and again by companies in nearly every industry. Some of our Cosmetics Products Leadership Team members visited two companies that followed the path and have become successful. That's why you're here today. You're here to learn what we've been learning over the past month during visits to other companies and in discussions with Roxanne Barnes, and others from Effective Management, our chosen consultants, or rather coaches, for our journey. Notice I said 'our' journey."

Greg went on to provide the backgrounds of Roxanne, her two associates, and Effective Management.

"You'll find out over the next few days that our Customer Service Initiative will be guided by Effective Management's Class A concepts and principles. Class A, as I've come to understand, entails a great deal of common sense. As you'll soon learn, it enables companies to become focused in accomplishing their business strategies and objectives by following a single set of operating plans and common objectives across the entire supply business. Roxanne will take you through some of the details today and tomorrow, as she has done with us over the past few weeks."

Greg continued. "The Leadership Team is inviting you to work alongside us in solving our customer service problems and in changing the image of Cosmetics Products in the eyes of our customers. We will use today's education and tomorrow's workshops to prepare us for setting up what are termed milestone teams—teams of people who will design and implement the new business processes to comply with best practices. The Customer Service Initiative is comprised of two milestones: 'Capable Planning and Control' and 'Capable Integrated Business Management.' These milestones, a name you'll become familiar with, bring together all the elements of the *Class A Checklist* that will enable us to deliver our initial customer service objective of 95 percent on-time delivery in full. I'm the Executive Sponsor of the overall initiative, David Simpson is the Executive Champion of the Capable Planning and Control milestone. Alexandra, our VP Sales and Marketing, will be Executive Champion for the Integrated Business Management milestone team. Other appointments to the team will follow. This will mean some tough culture and behavior changes for all of us. And the 'us' who must change behaviors applies equally to our executives. Be assured, this is not a labor reduction project hiding under a different name, although there will be some changes in all our responsibilities. We'll all be stretched to the limit designing and implementing these new processes. Once implemented, however, they will allow us to meet our strategic objectives."

Greg could see and feel the concern and discomfort of his audience. Change is never comfortable. "Hands up for those who think seriously we can continue on our current path and survive?" Not one hand was raised. "That's the same conclusion reached by the Leadership Team. Trust me; our jobs will change more than yours. We're going learn how to plan the future of this business. I can't believe I just said that we're all going to have to learn to be planners!" Laughter filled the room and broke the growing tension, but Greg didn't smile. "You heard correctly, Cosmetics Products is going to become a learning and a planning organization, starting at the top. It is management's responsibility to plan the future of this business. But don't worry. We're not going to do any of the detailed planning you're involved in today. We've discovered that our business planning process is broken from the top to the bottom. We are going to get some coaching so that we can fix our part of the process and provide you the coaching resources to fix your part of the planning process. With the support of Roxanne and her team, we will become a world-class organization and preferred supplier to our customers!" That statement brought forth an enthusiastic round of applause.

The energy in the room was now building as Greg began to convince most of the people by presenting the business case for change. He knew that there would be some die-hard resistors of change, but he and the rest of the Leadership Team would deal with that resistance as it surfaced.

Greg held up a copy of a book. "This is called the *Class A Checklist for Business Excellence*. It's the book in front of you. You'll become very familiar with the book's contents over the next few weeks. It has been in continuous development over the past 30 years and is based on the work its Effective Management authors do with some of the best companies across the globe. Today and tomorrow you'll get an introduction to the contents of the book and to the scope of best practices within it. Then we'll start talking in more detail about how it will help us improve customer service. During these two days, the executives will also be finalizing who, from among the members of this group, will be assigned to our milestone teams.

"I want to emphasize that any discussion about today's gaps against best practices will focus on the capabilities of our processes. It will not be a finger-pointing exercise to assign blame to individuals. Roxanne has made this point repeatedly with the Leadership Team. This work is not about finding blame; it is about getting better at what we do. This is an important point and worth repeating. Our performance as a company can be only as good as the processes we've designed and require you to follow. We need to learn how to improve and integrate those processes so that we can deliver a superior level of customer service.

"And finally, since I'm your President, I'm accountable for the success of this project, and I happily accept that accountability. So now is the time for you to either to get on the train, or decide you don't want to be part of the journey and get off, because the train is leaving the station this morning!"

That last statement was a shock to those who suspected that this was just another management initiative and would fade away over time.

To strengthen the leadership's commitment further, Greg described briefly the Capable Integrated Business Management Milestone that would be running in parallel with the Capable Planning and Control Milestone. Greg explained the Leadership Team would be the Steering Committee for both milestones to ensure control and integration. He finished his remarks and invited Roxanne to take over the agenda.

Roxanne thanked Greg and the Leadership Team for the opportunity to address the assembled group. She began by emphasizing that at any time during the next two days questions from the floor would be welcome and, indeed, necessary if anything said was not understood. She described how she had been working with the executives up to this point, and how that team had completed a Diagnostic assessment of the business recently.

She then moved into a discussion of the history of Class A business excellence, covering the concepts, principles, and benefits of integrating the entire business. She also described the Proven Path methodology with which they would structure their journey to solve their most pressing business problems. This journey would lead to improved results and the organizational maturity common in companies that achieve excellence and deliver Class A business results. She could see that many were skeptical about their ability to take on such an enormous venture. That led her to discuss the concept and purpose of milestones in creating manageable steps toward the goal of improved customer service.

"Does everyone here recognize that Cosmetics Products' customer service must improve? The word 'must' is the operative word in my question." Her audience fidgeted uncomfortably, but heads nodded in agreement. Most thought they were in for another lecture and began to think defensively, but Roxanne surprised them with her next statement. "Let me share with you an important fact. Your poor customer service performance is not your fault; you are not to blame. It is the fault of the processes you use to manage your internal supply chain." She cited both W. Edwards Deming and a top executive at Toyota to reinforce her statement. This revelation eased the tension and allowed people to be less defensive and open to the message Roxanne was delivering. She continued. "Your current planning processes, similar to so many companies that engage us, have developed over time in isolation. They are often more complex then they need to be and simply don't fit or work together. As the late Oliver Wight used to say, our job is to help you simplify and integrate them. Your President and the executives have asked us to coach you in designing and implementing more effective and integrated processes. These will give you the chance to raise your 'on time to the day and in full' delivery performance to at least 95 percent against first promise to the customer. With your knowledge of the business, participation, and commitment to the initiative, you will succeed."

She talked briefly about the Capable Integrated Business Management and Capable Planning and Control Milestones, their scope, their relationship with the Checklist and, more importantly, how they would contribute to solving the customer service issues.

"You are going to build the 'Planning Spine' [Figure 12.1]. This analogy refers to the role of the spine in the human body, holding it together and carrying the central nervous system that gathers information and coordinates our activities and responses purposefully. An effective supply chain must operate with exactly the same purposefulness and integration." Then, referring to roles on the chart, she continued.

"The Demand Manager brings to the Supply Chain the demand picture: current products and new products, as planned demand numbers, forecasts, and orders. The Supply Planning Manager works with the Demand Manager to create the optimum supply plan. All detailed supply plans and activities are driven from this supply plan. We'll talk later about how they deal with an imbalance of demand and supply.

"The Planning Spine is like a neuro-network that communicates seamlessly up and down the material supply structure. You use it to hardwire resource plans to the master supply plan and to hardwire the master supply plan to forecasts and customer orders. We'll get into the details of how these integrated processes must be designed and operated when we work with your process design teams. I suspect there are some considerable changes to be made."

Roxanne changed subjects. "And your managers won't be getting off the hook either! You'll need direction and resources to match the company's

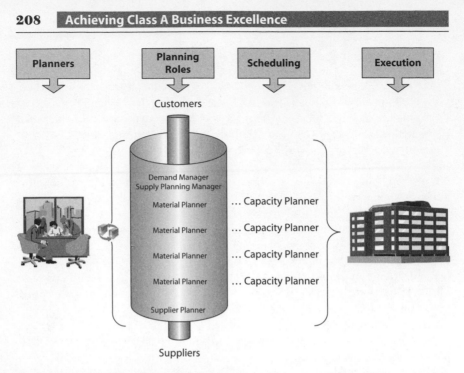

Figure 12.1   The Planning Spine Concept
Source: Oliver Wight. Copyright Oliver Wight International, Inc. Used with permission.

ambitions in the marketplace. Said another way, management must establish the company's strategic intent and provide the resources and capabilities required to achieve their strategic objectives. To do this, the Leadership Team must manage volumes and timing of new products, demand, forecasts, inventories, manufacturing, purchasing, people, capital assets, and cash. Their process for managing all of this is called Integrated Business Management, which links the company's strategies to the resources and operating plans."

From the back of the room, a brand manager commented. "Based on what we've already heard about the work required in Planning and Control, I don't see how we can take on this Integrated Business Management work at the same time. After all, the real problems are in the plants. Seems like that's where we should be focusing our efforts to fix things." There was a predictable din in the room as supply participants volunteered their displeasure at the brand manager's comment.

Greg brought the meeting back to order as he stood and responded, "Charlie, I think there are plenty of problems to go around! I've thought about this a lot, folks. Frankly, we must accomplish the Capable Integrated Business Management Milestone since we have no effective integrated process for steering the company. When we looked at what would be involved running these two milestones in parallel, we could see that it was only incremental extra work for us, I mean for the Leadership Team. Lots of you will be involved with designing the related business processes, but the executives and I will need to do a majority of the work with this milestone. I am confident that we can, and that we will, make it happen."

Over the course of the day, Roxanne followed a similar agenda and used many of the same examples that she had used in introducing the Leadership Team to the Class A work. Tom and Dan frequently interjected comments and additional examples to clarify and emphasize Roxanne's points. She covered the structure of the Checklist, the purpose of each chapter, and elements from the Proven Path [see Chapter 10]. She also pointed out the progress of Cosmetics Products on that path [see Figure 10.5]. They were beginning Development, would soon be into Milestone Planning, and soon thereafter begin educating the process design teams. Roxanne explained that they had passed the Point of Commitment, and that the clock had started ticking. She shared examples of how other companies educate their people, redesign business processes, and utilize planning tools appropriately both to support long-range business and supply chain planning and to support more tactical day-to-day activities. Her explanations included excerpts from the Checklist that enabled her listeners to begin to understand parts of the text.

As she discussed managing internal supply, two of the distribution planners asked questions regarding the relationship between processes and planning tools. They were unhappy with their planning system, which was giving them unreliable recommendations. Addressing their questions, Roxanne described how planning systems must support formal planning processes. She described that they access forecasts and orders to drive warehouse replenishment through a distribution network using Distribution Resource Planning (DRP). This linkage to forecasts and orders allows companies to increase customer service while decreasing overall inventory, so long as there is also a link to an effective master supply plan. She explained then how master supply planning works to decouple demand from internal supply. For the system to work effectively, however, she explained that all data in the system must be extremely accurate.

A district sales manager suggested that decoupling would make the plants unresponsive to customer needs. Roxanne responded to the statement with some questions for the sales manager.

"First, let me ask you a question. Do your customers read your forecasts and buy according to those numbers?"

Once again laughter filled the room. The sales manager was eventually heard above the noise saying, "I wish. The customers just buy whatever they want whenever they want it."

"Of course. I'd expect that to be the case. So demand is variable day-to-day and week-to-week, sometimes extremely variable. Let me tell you a secret. Your manufacturing plants, taking into account current material lead times, began procuring materials for this week's packaging schedule about 12 weeks ago, based on the forecast they had at that time. Now if you could manufacture your products on the same day that you receive a customer order, perhaps you could just set up resources and people, and wait for the customer's call. Would that work?"

The Atlanta Plant Operations Director called out, "We'd probably need to triple our resources, labor, and equipment capacity, to do that. The cost would kill us." Another Manufacturing Department Manager added that she couldn't make products on the day of an order receipt since the manufacturing operation was not that agile. Roxanne was pleased with the responses since they allowed her to continue building her message.

"Fair enough. So you are telling me, I believe, that to keep the 'cost of goods sold' down and make a profit, you must manage your supply resources carefully to optimize your cost, while factoring in your customers' needs and your competitors' pricing and responsiveness. So, today, your solution to this balancing act must be to decouple demand, with its volatile dynamics, from supply that is less agile. Customer demand can and does change rapidly; a single phone call from a customer can change everything. Nearly all supply chains operate at a much slower pace, almost stationary by comparison. Your only option at this time is to protect yourself against the variability of both demand and supply with safety stock. However, companies operating in what we call Phase 2 have become much more agile and responsive, and can respond faster, and with less inventory. But that subject is for a later time, after you've completed these initial milestones. You need to build that foundation first."

Roxanne went on to describe how the Planning Spine [Figure 12.1] must be supported by a properly configured ERP system. None of the processes she mentioned were new to people, but her explanation of how they were meant to operate together was illuminating.

During the lunch break, many people welcomed Roxanne, Tom, and Dan personally and mentioned that they liked what they were hearing. Several also shared their concerns that the company's leaders really didn't understand enough about their problems and wouldn't support all the major changes required to make the business successful. It was obvious to Roxanne that people were paying attention and were serious about delivering better customer service results. It was also obvious to Roxanne that the presence of the Leadership Team in this meeting was just as important as she had predicted from experience with other clients. Their presence was establishing a visible commitment in the eyes of those they led.

When the group reassembled, Roxanne projected a list on the screen. "As the Leadership Team worked with me over the past couple weeks, they documented a list of challenges facing Cosmetics Products [see Chapter 8]. They also decided that they would pursue the Capable Planning and Control Milestone and Capable Integrated Business Management Milestone to address these challenges."

The attendees were in agreement that the list created by the executives was thorough, accurate, and brutally honest. Many told her that they understood the importance of these first milestones, and were in agreement with their objectives. This was an important indicator to Roxanne that Cosmetics Products benefited from open and honest communications, and a willingness to share bad news as well as good. This openness was further reinforced throughout the day by the level of engagement within the group. No one seemed reluctant, even in the presence of Greg and his vice presidents, to ask questions or to challenge Roxanne or others in the group. Neither were they reluctant to share examples of behaviors that violated the concepts and principles of business excellence. In general, the comments confirmed for Roxanne that a lack of organizational focus, poor cross-functional alignment, and uncontrolled and frequent last minute changes to products, plans and schedules were causing poor customer service, poor product management, high inventories, declining morale, and high costs.

After the next break, before Roxanne could get into her stride, one of the young department managers from the Atlanta plant challenged her. "I agree with others that what you've been telling us seems logical, but I'm not sure it's necessary. I'm in an MBA program and have been studying Kanban, Lean, Agile, and Six Sigma. One of my professors said that these modern techniques eliminate the need for the kind of supply chain planning and coordination that you've been discussing. He said that these new methods are so responsive to customer needs that companies no longer need a forecast from the sales organization. He said that long-range planning should go the way of dinosaurs. Business today is all about velocity and pulling materials through the plant only when they are needed. That makes a lot of sense to me, Roxanne. We already have a Six Sigma Black Belt and some Green Belts in our plant. If we just continue to use them to increase plant velocity, much of what you've been promoting would be unnecessary, wouldn't it?"

Several people spoke at once; many others raised their hands, but before Roxanne could respond a brand manager stood and joined the fray. "I've been sitting here biting my tongue for a long time, but I just have to get this off my chest. It's also crystal clear to me that you don't have a clue about the difficulty of forecasting the kind of products we produce, Roxanne. It would be easy to forecast products with long lead times such as tractors, or home appliances where you have a leading indicator such as housing starts. You just don't understand that ours is a volatile industry with lots of influences outside our ability to forecast. If the product isn't there, the consumer will buy some other company's product. Having product available to ship is a Manufacturing responsibility. If they can't do their job and the resulting absence of products on the store shelves affects customers' buying decisions, then we can't be held accountable for that failure. You have to realize that if our Product Development friends give us a poor design, there's no way we can move that product despite our best efforts. Or if some MTV celebrity mentions a product on the air, our sales could either skyrocket or dry up entirely. Don't expect us to forecast any of that. Look, we take a good shot at creating a sales forecast, but it's hardly worth the effort; no one in this industry can do it. The customer service problems aren't our fault, by any means. I'm telling you right now that it's not possible to forecast any better than what we are doing now. Why don't we just implement those tools that the professor described, and do it now? The supply organization just needs to get serious, stop whining and making excuses for their ineffectiveness. It would be really helpful if they would provide the products when our customers need them!" The room erupted with people trying to talk or shout over each other to make their points, either to support the brand manager or to take serious exception to his inflammatory comments.

Greg rose to his feet with arms raised to regain control of the group. When everyone quieted, Greg spoke. "I'm glad to see this much passion regarding issues which are critical to our success. From my standpoint, it's extremely important to get these issues out on the table. Thanks for sharing your opinions, Jamie and Ted. Unless we recognize and define the issues, and stop being in denial about them, we'll never solve them. I'm sure we have as many opinions about these particular topics as there are people in this room . . . maybe even more. But before we lose total control and come to cross-functional blows, let's give Roxanne an opportunity to respond to the questions raised in the past few minutes."

"Thanks, Greg. Let me respond quickly to each concern, and I promise you that during the detailed education to support the milestone teams, and in later work, we'll spend all the time you need, and maybe more than you want, discussing them.

"First, let me address the issue of forecast accuracy. I'll tell you that there is no such thing as a perfect forecast. One of my colleagues says, 'There are two types of forecasts . . . lucky forecasts and lousy forecasts.'" This brought some laughter and the people relaxed a bit. "While I don't necessarily agree with him on that point, his comment does frame the difficulty of predicting what a consumer is going to do when he or she is standing in a supermarket or pharmacy aisle looking at a vast array of products and presentations. By the way, forecasting also has its challenges even for those long lead time products and heavy equipment industries you mentioned. Those customers are not as predictable as you might imagine. I can assure you that many companies in your industry have learned how to improve the accuracy of their forecasts by using a variety of techniques suited to your situation. One of our clients changes more than 50 percent of its portfolio every three weeks!" That comment got the attention of the brand management participants. "Try traditional forecasting techniques in that business! So they don't use traditional forecasting techniques. When we get together with the Demand Process Design Team, you'll learn about other possible forecasting models. But all techniques provide better forecasts when forecast assumptions are documented, debated and reviewed after the fact. There's too much time spent arguing about numbers when the numbers are simply the consequences of those assumptions. Do you document and track forecast assumptions in your business?" Shaking heads indicated that they did not. "So hold on to your doubts until your process design team has had some additional education.

"Companies are also improving their forecasts by getting closer to their key customers. There are some proven techniques for getting your plans synchronized with those of your customers. But before you can leverage any of these forecasting improvements, your internal supply planning processes must be at least at the 'capable' level.

"We haven't yet mentioned ways of managing demand or using demand market levers to influence customers, and even consumers. Companies are also getting much better in managing demand through more effective design and targeting of marketing programs, selective advertising, packaging design, and promotional activities. We'll talk later about these and other processes that enable companies to significantly improve their forecasting and demand management capabilities.

"As we continue our education, you will come to understand that Six Sigma, Lean, and Agile techniques can only be effective if applied to capable planning and control processes. If not, they just cannot deliver sustainable improvements. In fact, we recognize Agile, Lean, and Six Sigma as enablers for more rapidly achieving advanced Class A attributes that result in full business excellence and Class A performance. If I can be permitted to simplify the comparison, excellent companies plan, integrate, stabilize, and control the business over an extended time horizon from one end of a supply chain to the other. They predict and provide the necessary resources required to enable people to do what they say they will do. They have processes in place to make sure that all activities are driven from customer demand, and that all plans are valid and achieved. They have both short-term and long-term views of resource requirements so that the appropriate resources, even long lead-time capital intensive resources, and required new technologies and competencies, are available in every functional organization at the time they are needed, not before they are needed, and not after they are needed. Achieving and sustaining Class A standards of performance also requires an ongoing, formal and aggressive approach to continuous improvement. No matter how good a Class A company's performance is at the time of certification, everyone in that company knows there is a better way to do their work and a potential to deliver even better results. In today's hyper-competitive environment, if you don't deliver better business results tomorrow than you did today, you might find your competitors passing you by. If you don't figure out how to obsolete your own products and services with better products and services, someone else will, and you'll lose market share. All this requires long range planning and visibility, and short-term market insights. The need for long range planning is not going away.

"Let's now talk about Agile, Lean, and Six Sigma, and I want to mention Flexibility as well. First, I'll start with the typical meanings of those words. *Lean* is about eliminating nonvalue-adding waste anywhere it occurs in the business. *Six Sigma* is about reducing process and product variability to levels that, until you need to implement automation and robotics, or bio-technology, are experienced as virtually invariant. *Flexibility* is the ability and speed of the supply chain to respond to volumes changes. *Agility* is the speed and ability to respond to product changes, usually caused by customers' choices. All of these, and the associated aspects of people and teams, are included in milestones as companies approach full Class A business excellence. All of them require a paradigm shift. No longer would we talk about the percentage of products with quality defects or a percentage delivery performance. Class A companies measure defects or performance failures in parts per million, recognizing just how big a problem even 99.5 percent compliance presents. Let me ask you. Do you consider 99.5 percent a good level of operational or quality performance?" There was a uniform positive response to Roxanne's question. One of the participants mentioned that she would be ecstatic if they could even get to 95 percent.

"The day you have to compete against a Class A competitor," Roxanne responded, "you just might not be in business much longer. I can almost guarantee that some of your competitors are speaking in terms of fewer than 100 parts-per-million (ppm) levels of performance defects or failures. Just to remind you, 99.5 percent is 5000 ppm. Could you compete against less than 100 ppm especially when it's achieved, almost certainly, at costs lower than yours?" There was absolute silence in the room.

"The good news is that your Six Sigma resources will be invaluable to you when you move beyond Capable milestones to Advanced milestones. As a matter of interest, how many of you knew you had Black and Green belt resources available to you?" About 10 of the 50 people in the room raised their hands. Some of the executives looked a bit sheepish about their own lack of awareness.

"Your company, like most we meet, provides lots of education and training, but with only a minimal change in the organization's culture or in the behaviors of its people. Education and training programs should be based on clear performance or behavior change objectives. The programs should provide the knowledge and skills required to develop the competencies and behaviors necessary to achieve strategic objectives. That's how *we* approach education. As we go through the assessment, we'll help you to identify gaps. We'll then provide appropriate education and training when it's needed to help the process design teams close those gaps and improve business results.

"There is one other thing I want to reinforce. Class A is not just compatible with Lean, Agile, and Six Sigma; it requires their consideration as you move into more advanced milestones. You already have some knowledge of the concepts of Agile, Lean, and Six Sigma and some trained resources. That puts you far ahead of many companies, but to be really effective, those resources and techniques must be applied to business processes that are already stable and delivering predictable results. Getting to that point is the purpose of Capable milestones."

Following the afternoon break, Roxanne described how Cosmetics Products would implement Class A business processes at the Capable Level. She led the group through the proven path to business excellence paying special attention to the first few elements, as she had with Greg's team.

"Tomorrow you will work in teams for much of the day. With David's help, we've grouped you as potential members of the Capable Planning and Control and Capable Integrated Business Management process design teams. The Leadership Team has already selected the design team leaders. David will share the names tomorrow morning after he's had a chance to talk with the individuals. Tomorrow we'll begin the day together in this room, and then break up into the design teams to begin the work. You'll be helping the milestone leaders create the first cut of the Project Plan." She handed the meeting over to Greg.

"And so tomorrow, we'll begin in full session in which Roxanne, Tom, and Dan will describe in more detail what you need to accomplish. They'll give you a brief overview of the purpose and content of the nine chapters in the Checklist. Then you'll break into your process design teams [see Figure 10.6].

"Before we break up today, I will hand out the Capable Planning and Control Milestone Template which includes the scoring guidelines. My team will receive the Capable Integrated Business Management Template. Reviewing these is your homework for the evening. The templates list the elements of the *Class A Checklist* needed to achieve our milestones. We'll discuss them in more detail tomorrow. Design Team Leaders, you need to become especially familiar with the elements linked specifically to your business processes. So, for example, the Demand group will mostly be focusing on the requirements of Chapter 6, Managing Demand.

"You'll have your team leaders in place by tomorrow morning, and you'll also need to appoint a scribe—not your subject matter experts please—to take brief notes of your reactions to the Checklist and templates. Please create a list of questions, comments, or challenges for our coaches.

"Later, when the design teams are finalized, Roxanne's team will provide the business process education you'll need for assessing and redesigning our business processes. They'll also be around to coach you through the inevitable choices and problems.

"Unless you have additional questions, this brings us to the end of today's formal meeting. Thanks, Roxanne, Dan, and Tom, for your hard work and for another enlightening day. As many of you know, Susan Barnett, our CEO, has agreed to join us for dinner tonight. She slipped in at the back of the room a little while ago. Welcome, Susan. Would you like to say anything to the group?"

"Thanks, Greg. I was thinking about your meeting all day and finally decided to come down and eavesdrop for a few minutes. I'll take the opportunity to address the group after dinner, if you don't mind."

"Not at all, Susan. I know Susan will be eager to hear your comments about today, so please feel free to speak candidly with her. And now we'll stand adjourned until dinner at 6 P.M."

Susan had intentionally arrived early so that she could observe the end of the workshop and determine for herself the level of interest and engagement among the participants. As people began to leave the ballroom, Greg introduced Roxanne, Tom, and Dan to Susan. She was also greeted warmly by many others who offered encouraging words about the day's events. Susan sat down with Roxanne, Tom, and Dan to learn more about their backgrounds, the work they were beginning with Cosmetics Products, particular opportunities Roxanne had already discovered and, specifically, their recommendations about what Susan could do as CEO to best support Greg and his team. Susan also wanted to know if the work was compatible with and transferable to the other Amalgamated businesses. Roger Winchester, President of Home Products, had introduced Greg to the concepts of business excellence and had mentioned a number of times over the past year the possibility of a Class A journey in his Division. However he hadn't yet made the decision to begin.

Susan wasn't surprised that Greg had acted first, since she knew Greg's ability to recognize opportunities and apply new ideas successfully. She also suspected that the most important reason Greg moved so quickly was the pressure he was feeling; Roger didn't have that same business pressure.

To see Greg so excited about the journey to business excellence told Susan that there was a high probability of success. If her instincts were right, she wanted to position Amalgamated to realize similar improvements in all its businesses, not just Cosmetics Products. She then wondered to herself why most people were so reluctant to change until the pressure to change became intolerable and, too often, past the point of recovery. Probably goes back to the old saying, "no pain no gain," she thought. "Perhaps I should figure out how to create more pain so that others like Roger will develop Greg's sense of urgency!"

Later that evening, as dinner drew to a close, Greg took the opportunity to welcome Susan officially. "As you finish your dessert, I want to thank all of you for your participation today and for the creative work I expect you'll accomplish tomorrow. I also want to thank our CEO, Susan Barnett, for joining us tonight. I've had the privilege of working with Susan for many years and have often told her how much I appreciate her vision and her ability to inspire others. Most of you know that Susan invited me to join Cosmetics Products, but that should in no way be a reason to question her judgment!" A ripple of laughter followed that comment. "If you haven't yet had the opportunity to meet her personally, please introduce yourself after dinner. I've asked Susan to address the group, so with that I'll turn the microphone over to the Chief Executive Officer of Amalgamated Consumer Products Corporation, Susan Barnett." Polite applause greeted Susan as she stood to address the group.

"In the short time I've been here today, I've spoken with a good many of you, including Roxanne and her colleagues. Your energy level, optimism and confidence really impress me. You've already convinced me that you have what it takes to overcome the challenges and barriers to success. Of course, you still have to develop a detailed plan of action and deliver bottom line results. But I know that you'll be successful.

"You have my complete support and also the support of my Executive Team for the changes you'll need to implement. It's important for me to make that point, because I heard some concern about the willingness of senior management to change. I stand in support of Greg and his Leadership Team on this issue. Greg's track record is that he is not only willing to change, but is a driver of change. It's no secret that the Board is counting on him and all of you to make Cosmetics Products successful. I look forward to telling them what I've heard tonight and will keep a close eye on your progress so that I can continue to update them regularly.

"Thanks for inviting me to dinner. I can't wait to learn about what you accomplish tomorrow."

Susan received a standing ovation as Greg joined her at the podium. "Thanks very much, Susan. Well, this brings us to the end of the first day. Get a good night's rest, everyone. We have lots of work to do tomorrow! We'll have a continental breakfast here at seven o'clock and begin tomorrow's agenda at half past the hour. Good night, everyone."

13

INVOLVEMENT

You don't have enough time to be patient to a fault.

Whenever everyone is accountable for something, no one is accountable.

Greg, David, and Alexandra met with Roxanne and the team leaders for a 7:00 A.M. breakfast meeting to review David's proposal for design team membership. After brief discussion, and with only a few changes, they reached agreement. Cynthia joined the group for breakfast and had prepared the Initiative organization charts for Alexandra, David, Greg, and Roxanne; and lists of team member names for each team leader.

The remaining meeting participants arrived in time for a continental breakfast, and were in their seats for the 8:00 A.M. start in the main ballroom. Greg greeted the assembly. "Thank you for being here on time. I'll hand the meeting over to David and Roxanne to fill you in on today's events … David."

"Today we're going to divide into a number of process review teams. I'll introduce each team leader, and then each leader will let you know who should report to his or her team [Figure 13.1]. Each team will be reasonably cross-functional. There will be suppliers of input to the process, process experts, and customers of the process output. This structure will give you an objective view of how the processes are really working today." After David introduced each team leader, the team leader in turn called out the names of people on that team, and asked them to gather together at specific tables. At the end of the 20 minutes required to identify all the teams, six managers were left looking confused since their names had not been called. Alexandra eliminated the confusion.

"Those of you whose names have not been called are on my Capable Integrated Business Management Milestone team. You'll remain here when

219

- Integrated Business Management: Alexandra Templeton
- Product Management: Yanitza Gonzales
- Demand Management :   Jeff Black
- Supply Management: Janice Hackworth
- Master Supply Planning, MRP and Capacity Planning :   Sandy Bar-Nestor
- Production Operations: Bill Bates
- Supplier Scheduling and Purchasing :   Pauline Powell
- Finance: Gordon Fast
- Inventory Records: Francis Brandon
- Data Integrity (Master and Dynamic Data):   Sally Kennings
- Performance Measures: Angus Martin

Figure 13.1   Assessment Teams and Leaders

the other teams go to their breakout rooms. You weren't forgotten after all!" This caused some nervous laughter in the room.

The noise level picked up as the teams formed and were given time to introduce themselves to each other. David allowed plenty of time for this knowing that the first team interaction would begin to open up the communications channels allowing them to work together. Finally David called for order and handed the microphone to Roxanne.

"Just so you know, each of the eleven teams has its own breakout room. The list of teams is shown on the screen. Room assignments are on the chart by the door on your way out of the ballroom.

"Dan and Tom are handing out additional copies of the Capable Planning and Control Scoring Template for those who forgot to bring them this morning. You're not yet ready to perform a formal assessment. Today's work is primarily to educate you on the requirements of your milestone. We want you to become conversant with the terms and requirements and get an initial sense of major gaps, without trying to be precise. You will look at and try to reach consensus on a score for each chapter's elements included in your milestone template. In some cases, you will know how the process is working only in your area and not across Cosmetics Products. That's fine; just use the information you have to try and reach a consensus for the business. For other elements, you just might have no knowledge at all. If so, mark that as "don't know" and move on. You won't have time to research records or reports back at the office. We want you simply to consider what is working well and not so well in comparison with the best practices on the templates. This exercise will help you begin to understand the size of the gaps as a basis to help you put together a time line for your work. Over the next few weeks, after we've provided additional education to each process design team, we'll be asking you to go back and formally score the starting point of your part of the milestone. We'll introduce and use our *e*List web-based milestone tracking system for that assessment, but that comes a few weeks down the road.

"Before we go any further, I need to describe the *Class A Checklist* structure:

- *Chapter*—there are 9 chapters [see Figure 6.5].
- *Definition*—a high-level view of the best practice.
- *Description*—a detailed view of the best practice.
- *Business performance measures*—key indicators of the performance of the business processes in supporting the performance of the total company. Measures become increasingly demanding for advanced milestones and full Class A levels, but we don't need to concern ourselves with those at this point.

"The Planning and Control Template lists, chapter by chapter, all the Checklist definitions and descriptions that need to be considered. Each definition will have one or more descriptions—the detailed aspects to evaluate how close you are to meeting the definition requirements. It also indicates, for each definition, the minimum score to meet the Capable-Level standards.

"As an example, let's look at Checklist pages 104–105. You'll see that we're in Chapter 5. I want you to look at Definition 4. There are four descriptions underneath the definition, *a* through *d*. But only Descriptions *b* and *d* are within the Capable Planning and Control Milestone scope. When your Leadership Team gets to the Integrated Business Management Template, however, they'll find a requirement to consider Definition 4, and all its descriptions. So between the two milestone teams, you'll have this requirement completely covered, but at scoring level 3.0, which is the Capable-Level performance, rather than the full Class A requirement of a minimum of 4.5 out of 5.

"Don't worry too much about these details now. Tom, Dan, and I will be available to answer your questions as they come up during the day.

"Now here's the agenda for today:

1. All the teams, except for the Capable Integrated Business Management team, will review the Capable Planning and Control Template as a whole, referring to the Checklist for the definitions and descriptions.

2. Discuss each definition, and its associated descriptions, and try to estimate where you think you are; use the 0–5 scoring scale as detailed on the handout you just received, where 0 means Not Doing, and 5 means Excellent. Please refer to page xxiii in the Checklist book for interpretation of the scoring. These will not be official scores, but will give us some practice with scoring and some insights that may be enlightening. What will be equally or more important are the comments recorded by your teams. There are fifty-five definitions on the Capable Planning and Control Template, and obviously even more descriptions—between one and eight for each definition. That means you'll need to cover at least ten definitions an hour to leave here at a reasonable time. That's perfectly

possible if you don't get too hung up in detail. This exercise is only meant to be rough-cut, or even best-guess. When you need to close the discussion around a definition, team leaders should decide the score if the team members are unable to reach consensus.

3. Record your scores and comments and bring them back to the ballroom to share your key insights with the rest of us.

"Now you know why we wanted to wait until this morning, when you are wide awake, to cover these details! A final important reminder: this is not an assessment of people, how hard they work, or their commitment to your company's success. It is an assessment of the business processes as they work today. From my observations as an outsider, everyone here is working hard and wants the company to succeed. So don't get caught in the trap of taking criticism personally, or we'll not get the information we all need."

One of the Dallas Plant's Material Requirements planners asked whether his team should look just at the MRP-related questions. Roxanne responded that at this stage, each team should review the entire Capable Planning and Control Milestone Template to get a sense of all the business processes within the scope of that milestone. She reminded everyone that they would focus on their specific responsibilities during the official assessment later.

The Capable Planning and Control process design teams then moved to their breakout rooms with instructions to reconvene in the ballroom at 3:00 P.M. At that time, they would report their conclusions about significant opportunities. Lunch buffets were arranged for each of the breakout rooms.

Roxanne stayed with David, Greg, and the other executives and senior managers to assist with a review of the Capable Integrated Business Management Template. She suggested, given the time available, that they focus first on the executive management aspects of their template since other teams would be covering almost all the other requirements. She also reminded them that at this time they would be comparing themselves to Capable-Level expectations.

"You need to start in Chapter 1, Strategic Planning since no other team has that responsibility." They got down to work.

Milestone discussions continued through the working lunch and into the afternoon. At times the discussion was lively; at other times it seemed depressing, as people still perceived that their individual performance was being criticized. It was hard work, too, for Tom, Dan, and Roxanne, as they moved among the teams to keep them focused. At 2:00 P.M., Tom advised all teams that only one hour remained. Some of the teams were startled that time had passed so quickly with still so much to do, but teams whose leaders had good time-management skills were on schedule. At the end of the hour, with a few seconds to spare, everyone reassembled in the ballroom.

Greg stood up and addressed the group. "If you're like us, your heads are spinning, you've not taken a break, and you're wondering what's next. So, let's stop all team activity now and take a fifteen-minute break. Step outside if you want some fresh air to clear your minds, but no calls on your cell phones. And you'll find fresh coffee, soft drinks, fruit and snacks on the buffet tables at the back of this ballroom. Back in exactly fifteen minutes!"

The announcement of a break was well received. People drifted off in all directions but came back on time, ready to take part in the feedback. Dan started the proceedings.

"Let's get right into the team feedback. Each team will have ten minutes. I'll stop you if you run over. Team scribes, please send your team's lists to David's assistant so that he has them in his office by 8:00 A.M. Monday. Now, I have two rules in addition to the time limit.

"First, you may ask questions only to clarify understanding, not challenge observations. Got that?

"Second, when you listen, I want you to 'assume innocence.' That means assume that no one is taking shots at you or your department. Don't get defensive, just listen."

Greg smiled at this point and spoke up, "I've never thought of a two-by-four as a facilitation tool, but knowing us, you'll probably need to use one. Dan, you have our agreement."

"Thanks Greg. We'll take the Integrated Business Management team's report last. David wants to hear the perspectives on Planning and Control from everyone before giving you the executives' views."

Product Management Team: Leader, Yanitza Gonzales

"We spent more time on the Chapter 5 definitions than the rest since that reflects the primary expertise of the group. But going through the Capable Planning and Control Template for all chapters, here's what we concluded:

- *Strategic Planning:* Not sure, certainly doesn't flow through to us. Score 0–1.
- *Managing and Leading People:* Although the results aren't that dramatic, we felt good about this. Score 3.
- *Driving Business Improvement:* Well, we think there are some encouraging signs like this meeting. But before these last two days, we have done nothing but firefight. We're not aware of any initiatives affecting us. Score 0.
- *Integrated Business Management:* Sorry Greg, but whatever processes there are, and we know you hold some forecast meetings, they don't seem to do anything for us. The Checklist reads like they should. Score 1.
- *Managing Products and Services:* Where do I start! We found the concepts and practices being referred to are exactly what we need, but we don't have any of them. Integration of plans is nonexistent. We're in a totally reactive mode. We each use our own version of project planning,

and we have no mechanism to plan for resources except to work harder even though we're already on overload!" This brought an unsympathetic groan from the other participants. "We just try to do our best, but we don't really track progress or spending as the Checklist suggests. We usually catch major quality problems prior to launch, but have to correct a good many after launch. The Checklist refers to a Stage and Gate type development process that Charlie in our group has used in another company, but poorly, as he explains it. I can't say we have any process that meets those Checklist criteria. And as for project planning milestone performance, what milestones? We're almost off the scoring scale, and I don't mean on the high side. All in all, we felt fairly depressed until Dan came in and helped us stop flogging ourselves over our shortcomings. If we've understood correctly what's required, we'd have to score ourselves 1.

- We didn't know enough about the other definitions to score, except *Demand Management* where we concluded there was none. Score 0."

This brought some very defensive comments from Sales and Marketing people. Dan intervened and reminded them of the rules. And since they were next up, he asked the Demand Team not to retaliate, tempting though it might be.

Demand Management Team: Leader, Jeff Black

"First we'd concur with what Yanitza said about the Chapters 1, 2, and 3 definitions. We scored them just about the same as her Product Management Team:

- *Integrated Business Management:* We do a lot of work each month pulling together our numbers, and initially scored ourselves 3. But later, Tom came in and asked us to reread the definitions and descriptions. It didn't take me long to change my scores. Others on the team, with varying degrees of reluctance, changed their scores as well, with one notable abstention." David made a note and would try to determine who that was. "We do hold a type of Demand Review each month, but where we fall way short of the requirements is that we spend all our time talking about the hot products, backorders, and anticipated volume for the next few weeks. Some questioned the value of thinking further ahead since it's just a theoretical exercise. We'll have to resolve that concern later." Roxanne intervened and said the upcoming education would cover all these process issues, and she stressed the word "process." Jeff continued. "It all went downhill from that point. Tom stayed with us during this part of our meeting. It was very helpful to get his clarification as we went along. We have both demand and supply planning activities, but as for being integrated . . . I wish. We have no policy document for reference. I could go on and on. Greg, bottom line, we just aren't doing Demand Management. We do some forecasting and then hope like crazy the customers do what we forecast! Scoring was problematic; a few people thought that from a simple demand perspective we were doing fine. The rest of us thought that you couldn't take an isolated demand perspective. So our score is 0 or 3 depending on the perspective. You choose!

- You've heard about *Managing Products and Services* from that team; I guess overall we concur with their comments, although we scored it 0.

- *Managing Demand:* Before we read the through the definitions, we thought we'd score 4.5 (excellent), or even 5, on the first requirement, definition 6.10, about having an 'Unconstrained Demand Plan.' We are expert in asking for all the demand we want and then some!" This brought some raucous laughter from the others present. "What brought us back to earth were the requirements at the next lower level of detail, the descriptions. A few of us thought those requirements were unreasonable, and I noted that on our summary for David. But most of us began to see something new and powerful in what we read. Personally, I found it exciting and inspiring. Without going on forever, we at best have poor compliance with ownership, accuracy measurement, horizon, and detail; and no compliance with assumptions and time fences. So I've recorded my view of the score, which is not a consensus, of 0."

A sales manager from Jeff's team interrupted at that point. "I haven't been convinced yet that it's even possible to forecast this business, so I want that definition removed from the template scope."

David jumped to his feet before Greg did, and before Jeff got caught up in the fray. "We'll certainly take note of what you request; I'm certain that it'll be an important topic when the Demand Process design team begins its work. Meanwhile I want you all to listen and let the reviews be presented. Keep going Jeff."

"Thanks David. We have no Demand Manager, and we're still not completely clear about the importance of that role or the need for it. I'm keeping an open mind, but for now, score it 0. In terms of sales plans and marketing plans, we're not convinced that marketing plans exist, although we're told they do. And our salesforce has incentives that encourage them to sell as much as possible; I would think that's good. Have to admit we have no monitoring process. Overall, we scored between 1 and 2:

- *Supply Chain and Logistics:* Distribution and warehousing is always reacting. We all recognize there are issues, but we're not sure of the root cause. So we scored 1.

- *Internal Supply:* I had to make the call on this one. Once again, it was interesting to actually read the definitions and descriptions objectively.

It's an area that's a lot more complex than I'd realized. We based our comments and score on what we think we know, so we gave it 1.

- *External Sourcing:* We had no idea about this in my team, so we didn't score it."

Supply Management Team: Leader, Janice Hackworth

"After some discussion, and with Dan's advice, we focused on the overall supply chain, and aggregate supply planning aspects of the milestone:

- *Strategic Planning:* There is little evidence that business strategy influenced the way the supply chain was designed and operates. So we scored it a 1.

- *People Processes:* Like the others, we enjoy working for this company and we get along well with senior management. Training is available for those who want it. There is a good deal of communication, but it is borderline frenetic and focused on the most recent crisis, which means we only hear the latest concerns and what we are doing wrong, not the broader picture of what we should be doing. Specifically, communication out of the monthly supply meeting is sketchy at best, and priorities that are communicated are often changed within 24 hours. Very recently, we have observed that the Leadership Team seems committed to change things for the better. Unfortunately we've heard this before. Nevertheless, we're hopeful and scored this area 3.

- *Driving Business Improvement:* When we looked at the requirements we could see that our history of firefighting and heroics stops any serious compliance with these best practices. Nothing is sustained. Score 1.

- *Integrated Business Management:* Some of us have experience with S&OP from our past in other companies. We used that experience to help us understand the questions. Our response to this section of the Checklist was a bit of a downer; we could see intention, but no execution. For example, we don't adequately include products and portfolio in the plans, and demand discussions are more about SKUs than about families. Supply numbers seem to be about unchangeable finished goods production plans. Our focus is always on surviving the next few weeks or months. There are no longer-term plans; resource planning is based on the 'give it your best guess' algorithm. The final killer for us in this area was the 'one set of numbers' requirement. We scored this 0.5.

- *Products and Services:* We don't have 'integration' of requirements; we have unilateral 'insertion' of requirements into our schedules, usually without warning. There is no 'New Product Master Plan,' and the modus operandi is reaction instead of planning. But somehow we do launch new products, albeit usually late and requiring postlaunch modifications. We gave it a 1.

- *Demand Processes:* These are weak or nonexistent; for example, there is no process to track assumptions. We sell products, but we don't manage customer order-promising, meaning we often fail. At the aggregate level, not aggregates by families, but aggregate for the entire business, there are numbers that probably aren't too far off. But numbers at that aggregate level are just not useful for planning. Score is 0.5.

- *Supply Chain Management:* Product does move through the supply chain, but more by luck than planning, and with huge inventories that usually seem to be of the wrong products and wrong components. We noticed that no one has mentioned Data Management. Not surprising because data management processes for the supply chain are informal. They are not managed, not audited, and not even on our radar. Some team members think we might be okay and that I am a bit obsessive about this. But I learned a long time ago that without validation of the accuracy of basic data, we won't know if it's accurate, and should suspect the worst—which is exactly what we experience. Score 1.

- *Internal Supply:* We covered the inputs and outputs, not what happens in between. We left that to Sandy's team who'll be covering this [see Figure 13.1]. Depending on which numbers you take, internal supply does a good job delivering against its own plans, but a terrible job against actual customer orders and warehouse replenishment requirements. From our perspective, this is 1.

- *Managing External Sourcing:* Since purchasing falls into the plants' planning responsibilities, you would think there should be some supplier plan stability. But there isn't because of all the emergency orders released inside lead times. And we're too busy to be proactive about incoming quality; we react to the occasional bad quality delivery by screaming at the supplier. As for supplier relationships, I'm sure if they didn't need our business they'd fire us! We threaten them with termination if they don't jump through hoops to get parts to us within days when the agreed lead time is weeks. Sadly we had to rate this 1. That's it."

David intervened, "Janice, that sounded like a pretty thorough review given the time you had. How did you manage to cover all that ground?"

"I guess it's just luck, David. We had on the team people who work cross-functionally, as well as some internal experts. So the language in the Checklist was not a problem for us." But David was confident that Janice was instrumental to the thoroughness of the review. He made a mental note to see where she might be best placed for the overall good of the initiative.

Master Supply Planning, Capacity Planning, and Material Requirements Planning Team: Leader, Sandy Bar-Nestor

"I guess as we go along, it gets easier. We could relate to the previous presentations, except maybe Demand. So I'd like to focus on the supply definitions, given the time constraints. We had some serious disagreements on our team, but it was from members who are either suppliers to, or customers of, our process. They don't understand how we really operate, so we didn't put much weight on their input:

- *Integrated Business Management:* We provide good numbers every month. We're not sure what others do with them but from our side we score this one 3.

- *Strategic Planning:* Since we haven't gotten any input about strategic planning from corporate in the past, Tony set up a process for us to develop our own operating strategy before he left the company. Tony always said the rest of the organization would do well to catch up to us. So, and not to boast, we gave ourselves a 4.

- *People:* We're a very effective team, except when Sales comes along with an unreasonable request. We work hard on developing our people, and have good communication processes among ourselves. Score 3.

- *Managing Products:* We experience the vacillations of poor decision making in the product area, but we've buffered ourselves with time and budget to cope with most of it. Score 3.

- *Managing Demand:* This is the bane of our existence. Demand is out of control, and we need to keep them at arm's length to stop them from disrupting our performance. Clearly their processes are very poor. Generously, we scored this definition a 1. In truth, we have internal processes to buffer us from their demand swings, but there's no integration processes. We work to meet the major plant objective of being productive and efficient. Perhaps the one exception is linkage to financial planning. I mean we get reports every month, so something must be working, although we often don't agree with the variances reported. Overall Score 2.

- *Supply Chain Management:* No real comment here. We ship product out when it's ready, but occasionally have nowhere to put it. After considerable debate we scored that a 2.

- *Internal Supply Chain:* This is where we spent most of our time. For the Master Supply Planning requirement, we have a master supply scheduling process, although we don't call it that, but it doesn't seem to match up to the definitions under this topic. That's probably because of the industry we're in. We do consider all demands, but we have to move around those that don't fit our planning model. All our plans are valid and conform to our utilization and overhead absorption goals, although for some reason these important objectives aren't mentioned in the Checklist. We do rough-cut capacity planning. We do use the ERP system. We enter our plans into the system every day after we have rebalanced our schedule in the Excel spreadsheets that Tony put together for us. We have to use those because much of the information in the system is inaccurate. The spreadsheets work well and we do load the schedules into it, so we feel pretty good about this area. As everyone knows, we have capable people, and we encourage them to get appropriate qualifications. Our Master Supply Schedule drives all our planning activities. We update it whenever we need to; we weren't sure what 'in a timely manner' meant, but we think we're okay. We're the experts, of course, at Material Requirements Planning. Clearly we're doing this or nothing would get out of the plants. We weren't sure what 'formal system' meant, but we guessed it meant 'done by the material planners,' so that's okay, too. We create purchase requisitions whenever stock hits a reorder point, and we tell our suppliers, so we're okay there, too. For Capability Planning, we don't use a finite scheduler, but we know what capacity we have and are scheduling longer production runs to maximize output. We're clearly capable in this area. As for demonstrated capacities, we tried creating schedules with them a couple of years ago, but that just didn't challenge production people enough, so now we create schedules that keep the pressure on production to raise the output to higher levels than in the past. Based on our experience, we know this is the right way to run our business and motivate production departments. The Checklist's wrong on the next point. It says the plan should be 'refreshed daily,' but that isn't necessary because we don't intend to change our plan. So we update the schedule weekly and completely revise it monthly. That takes much less time than what the Checklist says is required. As you can see, we think our processes are quite a bit advanced over the Checklist. We scored ourselves a conservative 3 since there must be ways improve our processes."

By now Greg was holding his head in his hands, grateful that Tony was gone. He didn't realize the depth and persistence of Tony's legacy. Any second thoughts he had about firing Tony were erased. David was listening and trying to hide his disbelief. He knew that this was one team leader he would have to replace.

Roxanne spoke up, "Sandy, how much did you actually refer to and discuss the Checklist in your team?"

"Well, Roxanne, we understand internal supply as well as any company, at least as it applies to Cosmetics production. I don't know if you've ever worked in our industry, but I can attest that our challenges are quite unique, and that many of your so-called best practices just don't apply to us."

"Thanks, Sandy." Sandy wondered why there was a rather long silence in the room before the next team leader stood.

Production Operations Team: Leader, Bill Bates

"We focused on our experiences downstream of all the other teams. We relied heavily on our team members from outside the production area to help us interpret their parts of the milestone. I think we are pretty much in alignment with what most of the other teams have reported:

- We work to the schedule, keeping a close eye on utilization, of course. We often need to resequence orders to reduce total changeover time. Despite our time fences, we still have too many changes. We'd prefer a four-week fixed zone, but we try to be flexible when it's really necessary. We respect the intermediate production schedules from the material planners even when we think they're wrong. We record all our activities on production logs that the supervisor sends back to planning every couple of days to put into the ERP system. So in that sense, we're definitely using the ERP system. As to safety and housekeeping, we have an extremely good safety record for our type of industry, including a Georgia OSHA award. We are strict about cleanliness and orderliness; we conduct housekeeping audits every week. We meet the latest schedule as closely as we think is reasonable, but efficiency and utilization goals have to be met. Most of us wanted to score ourselves 4, but the nonproduction people on the team disagreed strongly. So to reach consensus, we scored ourselves 3. That's about it."

Supplier Scheduling and Purchasing Team: Leader, Pauline Powell

"I have to admit that these reports have been eye-opening to me and a bit shocking to be quite frank. I've heard issues I didn't know we had. We seem to be isolated from the turmoil that is rampant elsewhere, except for frequent expedited material requirements. But anyway, given the strict rules and regulations we have in Purchasing, compliance with these best practices comes naturally to us. You know, I recall a material crisis with an FD&C colorant about three years ago ..."

Dan gave Pauline a hand signal to speed up. Pauline acknowledged the message and got back to the subject at hand. "Our processes were set up to control spending and ensure integrity. Going through the Capable Planning and Control Milestone Template reminded us that there's more to material planning than we'd appreciated. Of particular help were the insights provided by the finished goods planner on the team. Okay, now to our review—and I won't repeat too much of what's been said before so we can focus more on our purchasing role:

- *Strategic Planning:* We scored 1.
- *People:* We scored 2.
- *Driving Business Improvement:* Well, we only see very minor activity involving us. Score 0.5.
- *Integrated Business Management:* We know about the supply meeting, and occasionally get dragged in if there's an underlying supplier issue, but that's about it. It certainly didn't seem too close to what the Checklist says. Score 1.
- *Managing Products and Services:* We get yanked around by sudden changes of supplier, or a new supplier 'engaged' by Product Development people without our knowledge. I remember once . . ." But Dan interrupted again.

"Pauline we need you to keep on track; we'll save the horror stories for break time." Pauline nodded and moved on.

"The integration of Product Development with Purchasing ranges from poor to nonexistent. Score 0.5.
- *Managing Demand:* Most of the team has little experience with this; those who do say it's pretty bad so we scored it a 1.
- *Supply Chain:* What we see of distribution is sudden requests for their consumables, such as shrink-wrap, and emergency orders for marketing materials such as leaflets, handouts, and point-of-sales stuff. After we jump through hoops to get it, sometimes it's actually used. There's a whole aisle of the stuff in the warehouse gathering dust. It's full of outdated or never required stock of those materials. We scored this area poor, that's a 1.

Finance Team: Leader, Gordon Fast

"Tom reminded us that the net effect of everything we do as a company shows up somewhere in our books. If everything the *Class A Checklist* calls for were followed, we'd be looking to lay off about half our staff!" This statement elicited a gasp from most people, and a puzzled look from Greg. "You may be happy at the thought of getting rid of some bean counters, but with the mess we currently have, that ain't gonna' happen soon!" This was not being received well by the audience. "Let's face it; you can't even use the ERP system so we have to spend way too much time reconciling spreadsheets every month!"

Roxanne interrupted Gordon. "Sounds like your team had a tough session, Gordon, but I must ask you to only make statements that begin with 'we'; and to stick to the purpose of the feedback session." Duly humbled, Gordon started again:

- "You're right, Roxanne. My apologies. I let my frustrations get the better of me. We can tell you that only a small percentage of the data that comes to finance is usable without review and adjustment. Our numbers have to tie back to the only reality we are certain of: money in the bank. We have a start-of-month and an end-of-month number. What happens during the month has to tie those numbers together. Put simply, they never tie together unless we massage them. And there's usually no time, except for major variances, to explain why we're doing it. We spent so much time grousing in our session that we didn't have time to go through all the Checklist details, so we threw in an overall score of 1."

Angus Martin stood up next to present what turned out to be an assessment from three related Process Design teams.

Inventory Accuracy Team: Leader, Francis Brandon; Data Integrity Team: Leader, Sally Kennings; Performance Measures Team: Leader, Angus Martin

"When we got to our breakout teams, we found we all had the same room. Tom was waiting for us. He pointed out that although there would be three design teams, at this stage it made more sense to go through this together. We agreed since we have overlapping areas of responsibility and experience to bring to the table. I'm Angus, and I'm presenting this review on behalf of the combined group. At the end, I'll give you a combined summary, rather than by design team. I see we are about out of time, so here's a shortened version:

- *Strategy:* Agree it's about 1.
- *People:* We thought 2.
- *Improvement:* It seemed to us it was 'on hold' rather than active, so we scored 1.
- *Integrated Business Management:* We agreed with 1.
- *Product:* Nothing to add to the other presentations: score 1.
- *Demand:* Same deal, 1.
- *Supply Chain:* We've heard a lot about that, and we'd agree with most of it. Score 1.

- *Internal Supply:* Obviously we have a good deal of interactions with planning and production. Despite the upbeat comments from the internal supply team, from our perspective internal supply is pretty weak, so we'd score it 1.
- *External Sourcing:* Not a lot of experience here, so we opted to give it a 2.
- *Data Integrity:* Although not a chapter in the book, this is our favorite subject and the one we spent most of our time discussing. Some of us have been through ISO9000 audits in our previous lifetimes, and our view is that we don't have robust data processes."

David interrupted, "Is that static or dynamic data you're referring to?"

"Good question, David. It refers to both types and to our performance measures. For example:

- *Inventory Accuracy:* We don't measure it. We take a physical inventory each month and correct the ERP records. We make a lot of corrections; some big, most of them small, but all are significant. So our inventory accuracy is worse than a stopped watch; it's only right once each month, and that's only if you believe the wall-to-wall counts. Closely related, and probably one of the key causes of the poor inventory accuracy is a casual attitude about transactions. When we asked Tom what was meant by transaction timeliness, he explained that when anyone touches the inventory, the matching transaction should be in the system within fifteen minutes, if not instantly, at the Capable Level. We'd be hard pressed to guarantee it gets into the system within fifteen hours. It's not that people don't care, it's just because we haven't defined that expectation. Of course, we haven't provided the tools to make that kind of speed possible either. We're looking forward to learning how other companies meet this requirement. If we were to score at this level, we thought 0.5 would be appropriate.
- *Data Integrity—master and dynamic:* We covered a bit of the dynamic timeliness issues, but we have no rules or procedures around transactions. We know we could fix that with a little coaching. For master data, it's a mixed picture. Some fields on the data masters are managed with solid change control procedures, but others, such as supplier addresses and other contact details, are not. We believe bills of material and routings are managed reasonably well when first released to production but not so well from then on. Item Number 770864 Body Lotion Intermediate is just one example. We have trouble homogenizing this product, so we routinely add extra surfactant and a little more solvent with the verbal concurrence of Tech Services and Quality Control. We've requested a change to this bill twice, but it's never happened. To make the product, we just keep on using the extra ingredients. And the routing file calls for the wrong homogenizer. The product runs much better on the H-1000

in work location 14, not the H-500 series in work location 12. This is just one example of many where we've learned through experience what the process engineers didn't know when we set up the routing in the beginning. We don't measure routing accuracy, but we think it must be below 50 percent. Same sort of thing on stock location records, and most other data integrity areas. We start off following the newly created standards; then we improve the process or product to improve efficiency and quality, but the master data just doesn't get changed to reflect reality. Again, there's no blame here; there is just no clear expectation to keep the master files up to date after a formulation is released. We started out with a score of 2. After we'd talked more, we reduced it to 0.5. I'd love to be proven wrong on this one."

Greg spoke up, "Angus, I really appreciate your team's candor. We have to get this fixed as soon as possible. I've learned enough from Roxanne to know that if our master data is inaccurate, there's no way we can create plans to run the supply chain effectively. It is now perfectly clear to me why we don't use the ERP system. But we are going to get this under control and fast. This is so important for so many reasons that I want to keep a close tab on the improvement plans and results!"

"Thanks, Greg! We welcome your participation. No question about the priority of this work! I'll finish up in just a few minutes:

- *Performance Measures:* First we asked for a quick lecture on what was required. So, a performance measure represents relative performance against some desired minimum, or range. For all the measures we looked at, the requirement is to achieve a stated minimum or better. As we talked through our current measures, we concluded that we do have a number of the required measures such as 'customer service,' which we call our 'delivery performance.' But we are at about 50 percent on that measure as you know; that's pretty pathetic performance. But Dan sat through this discussion and made us feel even worse. He introduced us to the need to define what he called the 'metric' as opposed to the 'measure.' The metric is the way inputs to the measure are collected; the actual calculating algorithm, including any tolerances or exceptions; and finally the output number, usually a percentage. Customer Service was worthwhile pursuing, so we contacted some people back at the office and our IT resource to understand our metric. We all assumed we understood 'on time and in full,' but there must have been five different definitions for starters. Some thought the metric referred to the day; some included a day tolerance for late transactions; others called it a 'hit' if we delivered early; some made allowances when we couldn't make the product on time and so had to ship it late. Greg and David, our performance measures aren't always telling us what we think they are telling us, but I think we can say that 50 percent customer service is, at best, a guess at how well we are serving our customers. We concluded that very few of our measures and metrics are well defined, and that we are missing some of the important ones required by Checklist best practices. We scored this area at a 0.5 just to reflect that we are at least trying to measure our performance!"

Greg again interrupted, "Gabriella, I want you to keep in touch with these three teams. We have to get the measures and metrics right and get them in place quickly or we'll continue to steer this ship without a compass. These measures will give us the equivalent of a global positioning system (GPS)! Sorry to interrupt Angus ... do you have more?"

"No, that's about it, Greg."

David started to stand up to acknowledge the teams and their reports, but Greg beat him to it. He faced the audience and said, "David, if you don't mind, I'd like to wrap this up. As I see it, together we have made an extraordinarily compelling case for change. Anyone disagree? No? So there is no turning back. The change begins now!

"I want to thank all of you for your hard work over the past two days, and above all for being so open with each other and with the Leadership Team. Our Leadership Team has had the benefit of more education and exposure to the concepts of Class A, but you have provided the details of how things are really working today.

"I can tell you that, in our review of the Capable Integrated Business Management Template, we reached similar conclusions as the rest of you reached in your Capable Planning and Control review. We have an enormous challenge ahead of us with both milestones.

"This has been a tiring two days, but I hope you are as excited as I am about understanding better what the real problems are. Our next challenge, with Effective Management's help, is to learn how to fix them. Remember to send all your notes to David's administrative assistant.

"The next step will be the formal announcement of the process design team members. There may be some changes to the teams we had working today, so keep an eye out for that announcement. We'll also be scheduling the design team education that Effective Management will provide. We'd like the team leaders to stay a bit longer with the Leadership Team, but the rest of you are free to go with my thanks and appreciation for your work."

After a brief break, the Leadership Team, team leaders, Roxanne, Dan, and Tom reconvened. David sounded defeated when he said to the group. "That was a depressing experience; we are in a much deeper hole than I imagined."

Greg countered the defeatist tone in David's voice. "David, I'm far more upbeat and excited than I was two days ago, and you should be, too!"

"How can we be happy with what you've just heard? We're responsible for this mess!"

"As we've said before, 'The truth can set you free; but it can hurt a lot at first.' We've all been experiencing the pain, but I now understand, can articulate the problems, and have a much clearer understanding of where we need to be in the near future. Knowing where we are and where we need to be will allow us to chart a course to better customer service. And don't forget, we now have a room full of people who also understand and can help us get there! That's why I am so excited right now."

David sat up straighter, "You're absolutely right, Greg! I fell into the trap of focusing on what's wrong instead of what's possible. Must be tired. Let me start again.

"What's next on the agenda to get our room full of people engaged in reaching our customer service objectives?" The others in the room had just observed a lesson in leadership. They experienced the same paradigm shift as had David, and were beginning to focus on the future possibilities.

Roxanne now took charge. "As you said, Greg, you first need to formalize the team leaders and process design team membership. Where you think there is value in changing the makeup of today's groups, make sure you have one-to-one discussions with the individuals involved. You need everyone on board for the kinds of changes you're facing."

David realized that Roxanne was looking at him while she talked about the schedule, "The next task is to develop a formal project plan for each milestone and to make sure that the teams are coordinated in their work. You'll need to validate that you have the necessary resource availability. We can provide an initial project planning template for each milestone to help get you started. These should become working documents that the teams modify as they go along to reflect your plan. When those are in place, I'll review them with Alexandra for Integrated Business Management, and with David and the team leaders for Planning and Control. Then we'll set up Design Team education, which is mission-critical for a fast start. Anything else Dan and Tom?"

Tom responded. "Just one point, I don't think I saw any system analysts on the teams. It's a good idea to include them on at least the Master Supply Planning, Capacity Planning, and MRP Teams to facilitate the inevitable interactions between process and system experts."

"Thanks Tom, I'd forgotten that. Greg, can you follow up on that suggestion?"

Greg looked to David, "If it makes sense to you and Matt, do it. I'm sure Matt can find someone who understands both sides of the computer screen." Matt Rutherford smiled, and nodded agreement.

Greg stood up again, "Team Leaders, I hope you've gotten the message. We're putting our future in your hands. You are going to be empowered to change the way we run the business. Of course our Steering Committee is ultimately accountable for the changes we approve. You'll have to live and work with those new processes, so empowerment is a double-edged sword, as it always is. Any questions?" There were a few questions about freeing up time to do the work and about getting team members' managers on board to support their new responsibilities.

David got up quickly. "Team Leaders, let's meet Tuesday morning at 8:00 A.M. in the executive conference room. I'll keep it to under an hour, but we have a few things to discuss, including how we put together the time lines for your work. I have a feeling we'll be spending a lot of time together over the next year! See all of you then."

When the team leaders had left the room, Dan spoke up, "Based on some very limited data, there were a couple of people on teams I facilitated who were not as prepared, open, or engaged as others on the teams. I know Tom and Roxanne had similar experiences with some of their teams. If you think you can bring those people along quickly, you can avoid making visible and potentially embarrassing changes. If not, I agree that you will have to make substitutions. We'll do everything we can to help coach those individuals, but time can be your enemy. You don't have enough time to be patient to a fault. By the way, the team leaders in my teams were very well prepared and appear to be good candidates for taking on the responsibility for ongoing process ownership."

David thought to himself, "That's not entirely true for all the teams. I've got a lot of work to do with the Internal Supply Team. I can't even believe they presented what they did. More advanced than the Checklist? Actually saying in public that they discounted the nonmanufacturing team members' input? Incredible. I wonder just how much Sandy influenced the outcome. I need to talk with her first thing Monday, but I don't see how she can lead that team."

Greg made a note of Dan's comments and said, "Changing leaders is the role of the Steering Committee as I see it. We'll take care of that and any other issues as they show up."

Greg turned to Roxanne, "We want to thank the three of you for your help this week. I made lists of process and performance gaps that we hadn't even considered before this session. We'll be discussing some changes in team structure on Monday, based on what we observed today. I don't know about the others, but I've already started thinking about the business differently."

Alexandra Templeton was quick to reinforce the needed customer service improvement. "First and foremost, this work has to gain back the trust of our customers by improving our performance. I think 95 percent performance on an order line-fill basis would meet and exceed their customer service expectations of us, at least for a while. Some of our former customers tell me that 95 percent will get us back in the game. I've put on hold some other initiatives so my people won't make that more difficult. So for now our focus will be on 95 percent order line fill delivered on the date promised."

Roxanne interjected. "Good reminder, but tell me, who owns driving customer service performance to above 95 percent, is it Alexandra?"

"I suppose we all do, Roxanne."

"I understand why you said that, but it's not a good answer. Whenever everyone is accountable for something, no one is accountable. The desired outcome is rarely achieved. It is true that lots of people contribute to the successful accomplishment of that result, but the Leadership Team must assign accountability to one person. Ultimately, of course, it's you, Greg."

Greg arrived at home earlier than Penny expected. She thought he'd probably be back very late, as normal on Friday evenings since joining Cosmetics Products. Surprising their boys, they attended the boys' basketball game together, and then enjoyed a family dinner to celebrate the win over the team's arch rival.

14

EDUCATION, EDUCATION, EDUCATION...

*What other project ... will deliver $12M to the bottom
line and free up $15M in cash?*

*When our old customers come back to us, we'll
know we've been successful.*

*An opportunity to participate in a change effort
of this magnitude may come along only once in a person's career.*

*Integrated Business Management ... must be led
from the top, passionately.*

The two weeks between the teams' self-assessment and the overview education (Three-day Business Excellence Overview) couldn't have passed more slowly for Greg. During the two weeks, there were additional product launch problems and customer service issues, but Greg could already see that the people who participated in the Capable Planning and Control Milestone Assessment were beginning to respond and work more effectively across functional boundaries. There was a noticeable effort to develop customer-focused solutions to problems instead of functionally expedient solutions.

On a previous visit, David had been impressed when he saw Roxanne taking notes in an electronic, web-based version of the Checklist, called the *e*List, already tailored for Cosmetics Products' milestones. She demonstrated the tool for David and told him that, with a license, he and his Initiative Coordinator could use *e*List to document progress against every definition and description, and record internal assessment scoring results. Before each visit, she would then be able to review their latest status update from her office and conduct interim facilitated assessments to help them calibrate their scores. Later David explained the value of the system to Greg, and informed him that he had already purchased a license for the *e*List, at an insignificant cost, to enable the milestone teams to track their progress and scores.

David received notes from all the Kick-off meeting assessment teams and compiled the results on a spreadsheet, applying some judicious editing to the internal supply team's rosy view of their planning and production operations. To create a baseline in the *e*List, Roxanne agreed to have the scores and notes entered into the tool. From this point on, design and milestone team members and leaders would be trained to enter their own data into the tool. David later logged into the *e*List, reviewed, and then printed what Roxanne had called the "Cosmetics Products Baseline," the starting point from which all progress would be measured. The bad news was that most definitions scored between 0 and 1; the only good news, the People definitions scored 2.5, a reassuring assessment of this important organizational attribute. Cosmetics Products would need the continuing goodwill and support of its people to weather the early changes. They would need to bring along the silent majority to overcome the resistance to change that was bound to surface.

The Leadership Team used the two-week period to finalize team structures and to ensure team members could devote the time needed to support the initiative. Roxanne worked with the team to finalize the Capable Planning and Control Milestone structure and its links to the Integrated Business Management Milestone to avoid unnecessary duplication of effort. At a steering committee meeting, Roxanne asked who would be the overall Integration Leader for the initiative to coordinate the combined work of both milestone teams. David immediately replied that he had thought he would fill that role, but Roxanne challenged his conclusion. "David, this is a lot of work. Usually when we have two milestones supporting an initiative we find that one person can lead the initiative and one milestone, but no more. It's a full-time job. You're an executive; you still have to run the business and work on Integrated Business Management. I don't think it's feasible for you to take the Integration Leader role; do you, Greg?"

Greg responded. "I was thinking it would be David, but there's no way I can lose him to a full-time position. I do need someone I can trust to get the job done. Give me a moment." You could almost hear the gears turning as Greg mentally sifted through possibilities. Suddenly his face lit up. "Got it! The person for that job is Peter Bertrand. He fits the requirements of Initiative Leader and has the capacity to lead the Planning and Control Milestone as well. He's the perfect candidate for the job." Greg looked over at Matt Rutherford (VP Engineering, IS, and Product Development), who was also Pete's boss.

"Not a chance, Greg. Peter is managing several major projects. If I pull him off those, we risk delaying some important product introductions. I can't possibly give him up now. If that role took an hour a day it might work out, but I'm not even sure he has that much time."

"You know as well as I, Matt, that the Integration Leader role needs to be a full-time position. Remember, too, how Roxanne cautioned us that if the person were easy to give up, he or she probably would be the wrong person to lead this work? There's no question in my mind that Pete is exactly the right person. What do the rest of you think?" There was a little discussion, but none of it sympathetic to Matt's concerns. They all supported Greg's choice. Greg continued, "He has project leadership skills and some Class A experience from his last company, although that was about 10 years ago. Let me ask you two questions, Matt. What other project is anyone working on that will deliver $12M to the bottom line and free up $15M in cash? And is there anyone else in the organization who could lead that effort better than Peter?"

"You've got me there, Greg! Conceptually, I know you're right, but I have to tell you that this move is really going to hurt. I can't dump his projects onto the other project managers; they're already working 10-hour days. I may need your agreement to hire another experienced, and I mean really experienced, project manager."

"I'm not against hiring a project manager, Matt, but I don't think we can afford the time it will take to hire an experienced replacement for Pete. Remember our cost of delay is about $50k per day, which means delaying Pete's move into his new assignment will cost us big bucks. I agree that Pete's projects are important; that's why Pete was assigned to them. So let's not delay their progress and use the Class A work as an excuse. We can't afford more problems with product introductions. The only way I can see to get into the milestone work quickly and still have his projects move forward without delay is to give Pete's projects to someone already in the organization. You must have someone who's capable of leading those projects and is ready for promotion. When you've moved the appropriate people, hire a coachable, high-potential person at the starting level. You should be able to find someone with those credentials quickly, even right out of school. Forget trying to find that experienced, professional project manager who can take Pete's place; promote someone, Matt. We need Pete in the leading the Customer Service Initiative now!"

"That's absolutely the fastest and easiest staffing decision I've ever been a part of, Greg, even though it's not exactly what I had in mind. I can't argue with you about the difficulty of finding the right person quickly for a senior project management position. Last time I tried that, it took months and even then the person didn't work out. The guy had all the right qualifications on paper and talked a really good game. But he didn't work well with others and wasn't a good leader. Those are intangibles that are sometimes hard to detect during interviews. I agree with you; we don't have time to experiment.

"I'm going to have to sell this to Pete. What's in it for him when this initiative is over? Have you thought about that?"

Greg responded without hesitation. "When we successfully complete these two milestones, I expect we'll establish another milestone and push ahead. If Pete does as well as I believe he will with the Planning and Control Milestone and coordinating the Integrated Business Management Milestone, we'll probably want him to lead the next initiative and another milestone. And a pay-grade increase at that time would be a just reward. If we continue on the entire journey to Class A Business Excellence, we'll be at it may be five years or more, according to Roxanne. When we complete the journey, I don't think we'll have any issue with Pete's next assignment. Our business will be expanding so there will be plenty of room and some choice assignments available to him. If we're as successful as we think we will be, we'll be promoting lots of people—including Pete. If we aren't successful, Pete will probably get your job because you and I will be history!"

A wry grin crossed Matt's face. "You know, Greg, I've always been confident, at least on an intellectual level, that we would be successful in this Class A work, but I have to tell you that on a gut level I had some concerns. I wasn't absolutely confident about our commitment to do what it takes to transform the culture of this organization. You just eliminated most of my concerns about commitment with that staffing decision. It's always taken us months to make a decision like that. It's just like they say with the ham and egg breakfast: the chicken is involved but the pig is committed. Never thought of myself as the pig before, but I am now. Guess giving up Pete makes me committed!

"I'll talk with Pete first and then the rest of my staff about freeing him up, rearranging assignments and hiring a new person. We'll have all the bases covered by the end of the week, somehow. I'll review all the projects again and talk with you about postponing or even dropping some of the lesser projects. We'll minimize the impact. I'm thinking that this change might really get the development group energized again. It's been a long time since we've promoted someone and brought new blood into the group. It'll also send an unmistakable message that we are dead serious about improving customer service. I'm getting more excited about the work just thinking about it!"

Greg turned to Alexandra and said, "Now about the Integrated Business Management Milestone Leader."

Alexandra was way ahead of him. As soon as the conversation began, she knew where it was headed. No use trying to fight a losing battle. "I think that Bart Billings would be the perfect candidate for that." She had already made plans for his replacement anticipating that Bart would be consumed full time for several months.

Greg turned to David, "Talk to Roxanne and get Pete and Bart into the earliest public 'Business Excellence for Executives' course. We need to get them up to speed quickly."

"I agree with your intentions, Greg, but we need them in our own Business Excellence Overview three-day course and the workshops to follow as their top priority. They can pick up the executive course later." Greg agreed with that. Matt excused himself as he now had some personnel matters that needed his urgent attention!

Greg was thinking about the work ahead. The Integrated Business Management Milestone work would begin with a two-day *Integrated Business Management in Practice* course for the managers participating in the process, either in the preparation steps or through the monthly cycle of meetings. The would need two separate classes of about 20 participants each. There were five separate reviews (Product Management, Demand, Supply, Integrated Reconciliation, and Management Business) in the process. Each would need a small team to translate the concepts learned in the course into a process designed specifically for Cosmetics Products. The Product, Demand, and Supply Review work overlapped to a degree with the Planning and Control Milestone teams' work. The combination would deliver the integrated Customer Service solution. It had been difficult to set the course dates, but with few exceptions everyone adjusted their calendars in order to attend. The course would be followed a week later by four facilitated one-day design workshops led by Roxanne.

Roxanne's voice brought Greg back to the present. "From what I've heard about Peter and Bart, they sound like a good choices. I'll need to spend some time with them before the first initiative and milestone team meetings." Greg agreed and soon brought meeting to an end.

Greg wanted to add his personal encouragement and communicate his expectations to the milestone and process design teams as soon as possible. Although he would have preferred it, time constraints prohibited a face-to-face meeting. Instead, he sent an e-mail to all team leaders and to the people who would be doing the design work:

We are now entering the education and process design phase of our Customer Service Initiative. Collectively, you and we on the Leadership Team, have a great deal of work to do to improve our processes, to improve our customer service and to lead Cosmetics Products toward our ultimate goal of Class A Business Excellence. I know that together we will create a much brighter future for our company. One of our primary objectives is to overcome the resistance to change that we'll encounter throughout the organization and even within ourselves. I suggest you use the milestone baseline scores, and notes posted on our intranet <cp.csp/baseline> to help make your case with others. We're asking you—actually we're asking all of us—to become champions of change; to be inventors, creators, problem-solvers, teachers, facilitators, subject matter experts, entrepreneurs, and agents of change in this effort. At the same time, we're asking you to continue carrying out your responsibilities back in your home organizations. That's a tall order, as I know from my own involvement; but it can also be a rewarding one. I'm also asking you to consider putting many minor projects on the back burner for a year or so to free up people's time for the Customer Service Initiative. Let David Simpson have a list of projects that will be delayed, and projects that you believe should continue. David will help with priorities if necessary. We are asking you to help us transform Cosmetics

Products into a preferred supplier to our customers, those same customers we've been losing recently. When our old customers come back to us, we'll know we've been successful. An opportunity to participate in a change effort of this magnitude may come along only once in a person's career. It will be a challenging and an exciting time for all of us as we continue our journey to business excellence.

Greg Sanders,
President, Cosmetics Products Division

Peter Bertrand, now in his Integration Leader role, had invited the leaders of the milestone and process design teams to the first Executive Steering Committee meeting at Greg's request. "I know you've all seen the announcement, but I want to introduce Peter Bertrand officially as our Integration Leader for our Customer Service Initiative. On behalf of the Leadership Team, I want to thank Peter publicly for accepting this important role—and also to thank our VP of Engineering, Matt Rutherford, for jumping through hoops to free up Peter for this assignment. Peter is, from today forward, a member of the Steering Committee for this work, and he will also lead the Capable Planning and Control Milestone Team." Turning to his new Integration Leader, Greg said, "I'm counting on you, Peter, to keep us moving and on schedule."

He then turned to Bart and said, "I also want to introduce Bart Billings as our Integrated Business Management Milestone leader."

"You've undoubtedly noticed that Susan Barnett, our CEO, is also here for the start of this meeting. Welcome, Susan." They were impressed that she'd taken the time to attend the meeting and offer words of support.

"Thanks for the welcome, Greg, but I should be welcoming all of you to this effort. Your work will make a huge difference to Cosmetics Products and to Amalgamated." Susan reinforced the business situation and the urgent need to improve customer service. She explained to everyone how success with the first milestones would improve customer service and bottom-line business results, begin to meet the expectations of the Board and shareholders, and improve the quality of life for everyone in Cosmetics Products. Susan used a set of talking points that Greg prepared for her, but elaborated on them in a way that demonstrated her commitment and passion for excellence in managing the business. Her remarks reflected an inherent understanding of the concepts and principles described in the *Class A Checklist*. There was no doubt in anyone's mind that improving Cosmetics Products' customer service was important to Susan, and that she had a solid grasp of the significant challenge ahead.

Susan commented specifically about her team and its own education. "In fact, I am so interested in your Customer Service Initiative and what it can mean to Amalgamated that I've scheduled Roxanne to provide some education for Amalgamated's Executive Management team. I want them to understand what you're doing so they can be as supportive as possible. Even more important, I'm hoping they catch the excellence fever to the same degree as Greg."

Susan took a few questions primarily about the Board's support and management's willingness to change. She also dealt with some questions and concerns about the amount of time people on the process design teams would need away from their primary jobs to accomplish this additional work. Susan acknowledged the additional workload that would be placed on all team members. She assured everyone that Greg and Zachary Zellers, VP of Human Resources, had already spoken to her about adding the new responsibilities to their job descriptions and personal goals. She also assured them that they would be rewarded appropriately for success, as would their customers and the entire company. She then deferred to Greg, thanked the group, and left the meeting.

"Pete and Bart are the only people currently assigned to a full-time role in this work. Some of you might have full-time responsibilities for a short period to complete a critical portion of the design, but then you'll return to your regular work. We'll do this from time to time to get those critical tasks completed quickly. Pete will oversee the integration of both milestones. Okay, let's move on. Time is money; this Class A journey is making that very clear to us. Now, David, please continue."

"Thanks, Greg. Pete and Bart will attend all executive Steering Committee meetings for the overall Initiative, and I will try to attend at least one in four of your Planning and Control Milestone team meetings so that we hardwire our communications. Alexandra will do the same with the Integrated Business Management Milestone meetings. Please note that Pete, as the Integration Leader, is the primary contact for all of us and will schedule and facilitate Effective Management visits. Each of the plants also has a local Integration Leader, working under Pete's guidance. They can also arrange the details of coaches' visits to the plants, through Pete, and coordinate the efforts of the plant business process design teams. They will keep plant teams focused and on schedule, while Pete will coordinate their efforts as well as the overall efforts of all teams and coaches. Pete will also manage education and project activities, keeping them moving and on track when the coaches are not on site.

"He's the key person for tracking costs against budget, benefits against commitments, with help from Finance and Accounting, of course, and for establishing a method of communicating progress. He'll facilitate the monthly executive Steering Committee meetings. He and Bart will lead respectively their weekly milestone team meetings, and coordinate the schedule of weekly business process design meetings.

"Finally, as Initiative Integration Leader, Pete is responsible for making recommendations to the Steering Committee for budget and organization changes and, as a last resort, for changes to milestone schedules. Now, does anyone not understand why Pete's job is a full-time role?" There was laughter in the room and a few good-natured jibes directed at Pete.

"Both milestone teams will meet at least weekly, as will the business process design teams, at least until their designs are completed. The milestone teams will monitor progress against project plans, design and formalize all business processes associated with their milestone, and ensure their work is supporting all the design teams engaged in their milestone. Integration of all efforts so they fit together properly is key to our success. The milestone teams will oversee the cut-over to the new processes, develop and track essential measures, and track achievement of committed bottom-line business benefits.

"Occasionally, a design team may need to charter a spin-off task team to wrestle with specific questions or problems and to bring back their recommendations. As design teams incorporate those teams' recommendations into new procedures, we'll need to finalize, document and approve the procedures, and have all affected groups agree to follow them. Getting people to agree to change may be a challenge. And that's one of the Steering Committee's responsibilities—to support you. Pete, want to say a few words?"

"Thanks David. First I want to thank you for putting so much trust in me; I'll not let you down. I'm in catch-up mode at the moment, but already see the need and logic behind the Customer Service Initiative. I've spent a day with Roxanne, so I'm getting up to speed on the next three steps. Let's say they're education, education, education." This brought a few smiles from the group.

"Following the team's education, we'll go through the detail assessment process to re-establish our baseline from a more enlightened perspective. It'll help us focus on the gaps we're going to be working on closing. Then I'll be driving the team to create what we'll call the Cosmetics Products Planning Spine, the core of Capable Planning and Control. I've already e-mailed my milestone team a schedule covering the next few weeks, as has Bart; We're asking people to make sure our meetings take priority over other events. If there are any problems, bring them to me and I'll try to clear the way. I've also included a team list giving everyone's contact details.

"At the top of your schedule are the *Business Excellence Overview* course dates. We'll be running this twice, so you'll have some schedule flexibility, but attendance is mandatory. As process design team leaders, I'm asking you to have as many of your team members as possible attend with you. By the end of the week, we'll have our own 'war room' assigned with all the space and technology we'll need to work together away from our regular jobs. David, I don't know how you did it, but I've never seen such quick response from the facilities group."

"Unless there are any more points . . ." Greg looked around ". . . we'll end there. Thanks, everyone. This is going to get exciting very soon. I can smell it in the air."

Roxanne arrived the following Monday to present the first of the two *Integrated Business Management* courses to be run in the Atlanta Marketing Headquarters auditorium for the Integrated Business Management Milestone team. As planned, half the Leadership Team attended the first class; the other half attended the second class on Thursday and Friday. Peter and David arranged to be in the first class. The day between classes gave Roxanne an opportunity to coach Peter and Bart on the structure of the two milestones and to explain the templates to be used as the basis for their project planning, or program planning as Roxanne described it. Roxanne's personal coaching also alerted Peter and Bart to some common problems, such as the manager who behaves supportively in public, but who resists behind the scenes, or just doesn't get anything accomplished because of a reportedly "heavy workload," a major issue for many implementations.

Greg attended the first two-day course; Alexandra attended both courses in order that the two key players in setting up Integrated Business Management could have maximum exposure to the comments and concerns of the other executives, process owners' managers, and other key functional area leaders. Greg wanted attendance to be as inclusive as possible to help create a critical mass.

Roxanne led the participants through an agenda beginning with a high-level perspective of business excellence, through the key concepts, elements, and processes of Integrated Business Management, to the details of the monthly executive Management Business Review. The course took the attendees from concepts, the "what needs to be done and why," to the application of the concepts in Cosmetics Products, the "how to do it" in practice. The interaction among all present was lively and addressed many concerns and misunderstandings. Greg noted that he, Sharon, Alexandra, and David would have to agree early on who would fill the various process steps' coordinator/facilitator roles: Product Review Coordinator; Demand Manager; Supply Planning Manager; and Integrated Business Management Process Leader—this latter role includes Integrated Reconciliation and facilitating the Management Business Review. While it was clear that Greg would own and chair the Management Business Review, the other roles were less clear. They learned that Marketing had overall responsibility for Demand, as expected, but also for Product Management. This started a discussion about where Product Development, currently under Engineering, should fit in the process. Roxanne suggested they take that question offline as a design team issue that she would facilitate. She pointed out that Cosmetics Products did not currently have the Product Manager role properly defined, a subject for design consideration. Matt looked uncomfortable and said he'd make sure he was well represented in that discussion. Reluctantly they agreed to postpone that debate.

After some off-line discussion, the Integrated Business Management Process Leader role was assigned to Bart Billings. This role included responsibility for coordination and facilitation of the monthly Management Business Review, the final decision-making step in the monthly process. Roxanne wrapped up the course with an explanation of the organization for design and implementation of the new process.

During the following week, Effective Management ran the first of four three-day *Business Excellence Overview* courses for the Planning and Control Milestone team, all those directly involved in the milestone and business process design teams, planners, and various internal experts and managers who needed to understand the broader picture of integrated business processes.

This cross-functional education was an important step in breaking down internal barriers.

Peter introduced the presenter for each of the four courses. He then took a few minutes to explain the course objectives, why everyone was there, and the next steps for those on the business process design teams. Throughout the courses one or more of the executives would drop in to demonstrate their support of the teams and commitment to the changes the teams would be recommending. The presenters covered the same scope as the executives' course but in much more depth and detail. Participants were encouraged to take copious notes for later reference. In the executives' course, Roxanne had talked about aggregate plans driving the detailed plans; in this course, the presenters demonstrated the relationship between aggregate and detailed planning that led to scheduling and loading of orders on work locations and suppliers. They described dispatch lists, picking and shipping lists, and how reporting of actual transactions and results linked with financial reporting. There were descriptions of processes new to Cosmetics Products: Demand Planning, Demand Control, Master Supply Planning, and the use of time fences to stabilize schedules. They learned about the essential nature of data and transaction integrity and stock record accuracy. They called these records "enablers," without which the planning spine could not operate correctly and effectively. The attendees wrote notes feverishly and safeguarded their course notebooks as if their lives depended on them. There was too much to remember; they would have to rely on their notes over the coming months.

In total, 80 people attended the Business Excellence Overview courses over the two-week period.

Between classes, Roxanne worked with Greg and Alexandra to schedule the executive team's next tasks. The Integrated Business Management Team would go through a sequence of five one-day sequential workshops to determine how to prepare for and satisfy the needs of the Product, Demand, Supply, and Integrated Reconciliation Reviews leading up to the Management Business Review. Each of these workshops would involve, the executive responsible, his or her coordinator, and the key people who would actually prepare for that review each month. They would design a fixed day-to-day schedule of activities throughout each month to ensure a smooth flow of information from review to review. As an example, Roxanne explained that a key input needed to begin Demand Review preparation is the previous month's sales numbers. If that process input were delayed beyond the first few days of the month, the entire Integrated Business Management cycle would be affected.

Workshop output would be the proposed schedule and procedures, details of the input data needed for each review, and the sources of that data. Greg asked, "When should we start the whole process?" He was surprised at Roxanne's answer.

"You must start the first cycle one month after the workshops. This is a process that we call 'Fast-Track.' It works well when we have commitment from the executives. The clock's ticking; your customers don't have much patience left."

"I need just a little reassurance about starting so soon. I can't imagine we'll be ready given that we'll have had only four weeks to get ready for the first cycle."

Roxanne thought for a moment and then replied, "Let me answer by paraphrasing what I heard from a client of mine. Integrated Business Management is the process that integrates every aspect of your business and gives you the tools to win in the marketplace. So it must be led from the top, passionately. The sooner you get started, the better. Don't expect perfection in the first few cycles. Each month, you'll get better and better at it. You'll probably have incomplete data at first, but don't give up. Improvement will come from persistence. The most important objective is to transform the executives from a committee to a team—a high-performance team focused on business, not functional, success.

"To achieve that objective, the process must have the support of Sales and Marketing. We've found that the process is a natural for Manufacturing, but often meets resistance from Sales and Marketing. Greg, you may have to push Sales and Marketing to really engage. As soon as they realize that this process gives them better results, you'll see complete buy-in. The sooner you get started, the better. Those were my client's words, not mine; but I agree completely."

Alexandra interrupted, "I hear what you're saying about Sales and Marketing, especially if they haven't had any education on the process, Roxanne, but with us it's not a problem. If any of my people resist, they will hear from me directly. We simply must work together to be successful."

Roxanne smiled, "I stand corrected, Alexandra, and it's encouraging to hear you say that. The benefits of that cooperation are well documented. Independent surveys show that Integrated Business Management improves results in all business key performance indicators (KPIs) and bottom line results.

"You'll be able to see further into the future, steer the business better, ensure your strategy is deployed and know that management decisions will actually be executed. The last point is a double-edged sword. Your strategy and business decisions had better be good ones, because they will be executed, absolutely."

Greg and Alexandra followed up with a few questions for clarification. After a brief private discussion with David, Alexandra said to Greg and Roxanne, "We've decided we need to get on with it. We'll have our first cycle of meetings starting next month—that's three weeks from now— knowing that it won't be perfect. We'll learn by doing. We were very impressed with your client's advice; it was right on target for us."

Roxanne was pleased with their determination. "I'm delighted with your decision and have a last bit of coaching for you. If you find you're talking about the business over the next 12 weeks or so, you've got it wrong. The Leadership Team's contribution lies primarily in months 4 through 24. That's where you should spend your time. In your notebook from the last course, you'll find a typical Management Business Review (MBR) agenda and the required attendees. We'll help you determine your Integrated Business Management product families, which as you said, Greg, might be your product categories at this stage. David, you and your Supply Planning Manager will have to see if they make sense in terms of your supply chain requirements. If necessary, you'll have to create a matrix that translates the Integrated Business Management families into production families in order to understand the resource implications. After two or three runs, I want you, Alexandra, to ask Bart to get your team to assess themselves against the milestone template. Remember, you have an *e*List license so you can record scores there and keep track of your progress. About four months from now I'd like to sit through all the reviews. I'll put my assessment scores and comments into the *e*List so you can calibrate your own scoring with mine. Meanwhile, after we facilitate the design workshops, you'll be pretty much on your own except for periodic visits or if I get a call to come in and help with an issue. I want you to realize that this is your process, not mine."

"Let's try it" Greg said, "I know where to find you if we need advice."

Roxanne had previously reminded the Capable Planning and Control Milestone Team that their focus was on creating the integrated Planning Spine, from demand to suppliers. This would involve deploying robust and managed Master Supply Planning and Scheduling processes and driving integrated Material Requirements Planning (MRP), the heart of the Planning Spine, which was totally dependent upon absolute data integrity. The design teams didn't grasp the full meaning of this statement, but soon would as they participated in their specialist education and design workshops.

Dan and Tom took charge of specialty education for the Design Teams, each course including the leader of the related milestone team. Peter attended as many of these as possible to help him understand the complete picture. Courses had been tailored as necessary based on the gaps to best practice already identified. This wave of education was to provide each design team enough education to start their design work with best practices in mind. Specialty education, a combination of lecture and application workshops, began in earnest and included:

- *Product Management Team:* Two-day *Product Portfolio and Life-Cycle Management* course, followed by a two-day workshop, covering a wide spectrum of processes including marketing as the overall driver, product and market planning, idea generation, selection and prioritization development and launch, and measures such as time-to-profit.
- *Demand Management Team:* Two-day *Managing Demand* course, followed by a two-day workshop focusing on demand management processes.

- The *Supply Management Team:* Education was incorporated into the executive Integrated Business Management Team's education to ensure the links would be in place between aggregate and detail planning.
- *Master Supply Planning and Scheduling, Capacity Planning, and Materials Planning Team:* Three-day *Supply Planning in Practice* course, followed by a two-day workshop on Master Supply Planning and Scheduling, and for other planners two days on Material and Capacity Planning—thus providing the foundation of principles and practices for creating a planning spine.
- *Production Operations Team:* Two-day *Operations Scheduling and Control* course, and one-day workshop covering work location loading and job prioritization techniques, use of the official work location Production schedule (a.k.a. Work-to-List), and Production's responsibility to meet the plan.
- *Supplier Scheduling and Purchasing Team:* Two-day *Supplier Management* course and two-day workshop dealing with day-to-day practical issues of communicating material requirements, and working with key suppliers to drive waste out of the supply chain.
- *Inventory Record Accuracy Team:* A two-day *Sustaining Inventory Accuracy* course and one-day workshop covering best practices for first establishing inventory record accuracy, and then maintaining it at levels greater than 95 percent.
- *Data Integrity Team:* A two-day *Data Management* course that included Sara Miles, VP Finance; David Simpson, VP Supply Chain and Manufacturing; Gabriella Jemison, VP Regulatory, Quality, and HSE; and Brion Smith and Savannah Richmond, Plant General Managers as participants. The key message was that top management owns data integrity and has responsibility for creating a culture to deliver and value that integrity. This would be followed by a two-day workshop for the non-executives on item, bill, routing, and purchasing master data integrity, and processes for improvement, and standards and auditing.
- *Performance Measures Team:* A two-day *Performance Measures Overview* course and workshop covering two aspects of performance measures and the metrics—what to measure and how to calculate results.
- *Finance Team:* The Finance Team members were spread through all the other courses so that, together, they would see how all new business processes will feed provide more accurate and timely data and information to the finance organization.

This was the most intensive education ever undertaken by Cosmetics Products, or even Amalgamated. Given the scope of the education and all the new concepts presented, Greg now understood the importance of education before design and before software training. Because he needed Cosmetics Products to capitalize on their new learning as soon as possible, he met personally with each Process Design Team leader to state his expectation that the design teams begin meeting within the next week. He wanted a quick translation of the learning into process designs.

A few weeks later, Sara entered Greg's office with a financial report in her hand. "Greg, do you realize that with their latest invoices, we've already spent three quarters of our Effective Management budget?" Greg called David to his office for his perspective. "Well Greg, as Roxanne advised us, education is front-loaded. Don't forget that the teams have already accomplished a good deal of their design work in the workshops. Now they just need to refine what they've accomplished and get it ready to test, document, and implement. I brought a copy of the expected spending plan to show you. As you can see, it's not linear, and we're right on target." Sara and Greg expressed relief and now looked forward to designing and implementing the improved business processes.

15

PROCESS DESIGN

If you always do what you've always done, you'll always get what you've always gotten.

Roxanne spent a full day with the Planning and Control Milestone Team, but the first few hours were with Peter Bertrand to review the implementation plans, and listen to his thoughts about the team members. While Roxanne would form her own opinions, she wanted to know how Peter perceived the players' capabilities. Peter informed Roxanne that Janice Hackworth had been appointed leader of the Master Supply Planning, Capacity Planning, and Materials Requirements Planning (MRP) team replacing Sandy Bar-Nestor. David spoke with Sandy after her disastrous kick-off meeting milestone template assessment review. She was still a team member, but the team was informed that David decided he couldn't spare her for the team leader role. Peter knew privately that she had been confronted and coached to be more open to the possibilities presented by the Customer Service Initiative. Roxanne asked Peter to arrange 30-minutes with David at the conclusion of each of her visits. At 10:30 A.M., they walked to the team's new conference room. Modifications weren't yet complete, but it was theirs for the duration. David agreed to attend the team meeting for the first half hour.

Peter introduced Roxanne to the team members, although most had already met her. Since there were a few changes following the meeting in the Marriott Marquis, Peter asked the team leaders to introduce themselves and explain their role in the company and on the team.

Peter explained that his Planning and Control Milestone Team was responsible for the Supply Model, which combines the Planning Spine with the geography

Capable Integrated Business Management
Capable Planning and Control

- Integrated Business Management Leader: Bart Billings (ensures links)
- Product Management: Yanitza Gonzales
- Demand Management: [b]Jeff Black
- Supply Model (Planning Spine): [ab]Peter Bertrand + (Janice)
- Supply Practice: Material and Capacity Planning: [b]Janice Hackworth
- Production Operations: [b]Bill Bates
- Supplier Scheduling and Purchasing: [b]Pauline Powell
- Finance: [b]Gordon Fast
- Inventory Records: Francis Brandon
- Data Integrity—Master and Dynamic Data: Sally Kennings
- Performance Measures: Angus Martin

- Systems Analyst Support: [ab]Chris Deutsch
- Documentation Support: [a]Bob Malinkov

Figure 15.1   Process Design Teams and Leaders [[a]Full Time; [b]Core]

of plants and warehouses. "As you know, I'll also be attending the Integrated Business Management Team meetings to understand how the detailed planning processes fit with the aggregate. On the list [Figure 15.1], you'll see that Janice's name also appears next to mine. She's going to be a key player in all aspects of supply planning. Janice, I'm going to rely on your expertise a great deal. This means Janice will average about 50 percent of her time on this work; but that will vary from as much as 100 percent for a few days down to just 20 percent at other times. Janice will speak for me in my absence. I'll keep in close touch with you, Janice, so we'll always be aligned. This will also ensure that the planning model and our designs stay aligned with each other, while giving me time to deal with both intra- and inter-milestone issues.

"We've developed an Output-Gantt chart that shows all the outputs as deliverables from the tasks required to achieve team objectives. The Output-Gantt is quite simple to follow. All input tasks are excluded for simplicity. These are driven by your personal Input-Gantt charts and your commitment. As a reminder, 'Silence-is-Approval'.

"Over the next few weeks, we have some design team workshops scheduled. We start with a two-day workshop facilitated by Roxanne on the Supply Model; that's already scheduled. Core members, as indicated with the [b] against your name on the team list (and in Figure 15.1), must attend as well as the rest of you if at all possible. Most design activities can run in parallel since we all know what our deliverables are. The Output-Gantt chart shows them and their due dates. Have I said before, 'Don't miss your due dates'?" Everyone laughed at Peter's unnecessary repetition of his favorite message.

"I'm suggesting we have a abbreviated name that we use for our Capable Planning and Control Milestone work. How about the acronym, 'CPC,' standing for Cosmetics Planning and Control, but easier to say? What do you think?"

"I like the idea of an acronym," Janice said as the rest nodded approval. "I think it might be even better," she continued, "to call this the Customer Service Team (CST) conference room to keep focus on our real objective." There was unanimous approval, and the new name was adopted.

"Great; I'll have a sign made for the door. Now let's get back to the schedule. I've also scheduled the Inventory Accuracy workshop with Dan and the Data Integrity workshop with Tom. The Design Leaders, Francis and Sally, have made sure that all their design team members are available. Francis is including some shop floor team leaders and lead operators from the warehouse. Gordon Fast from Finance will be there to make sure we incorporate the needs of the Finance group. Bob and Chris, you'll be attending the Data Integrity Workshop with Sally so that you can see where we're headed from the standpoint of documentation and IT support. But don't just observe. We need your best thinking about this subject, too. I'll confirm the schedule for the other workshops next week."

Peter then handed the meeting over to Roxanne. "Thanks, Peter. I'd like to explain what we at Effective Management mean by the term 'workshop.' Workshop means that you do the work, and I facilitate. I'll bring along some slides to help you get organized and to remind you of key concepts and principles that must be built in to your designs. Please bring along your course notebooks for reference. We'll spend 20 percent or less of the time on reviewing the educational material, then get down to the design work." She explained that the main objective for the next six to eight weeks was building the design for the Planning Spine [Figure 15.2] and enablers such as inventory accuracy and data integrity processes. All process design team activities will be directed toward completing this model.

After a brief review of the Planning Spine with the promise of more coaching to come, Roxanne asked Peter to take over. He turned to the first objective of the team, building the Planning Spine.

"Let me recap. We'll be leading the process design teams' work and integrating their proposed designs into a supply model for our business. The process design teams' outputs will be put together and tested in our ERP system. As I understand it, when we get it right, we'll have the optimized 'input-process-output' elements linking customer needs right through our supply chain and into the suppliers' plans. We'll test all designs before they go into the model, and we'll be careful not to say 'no' to an idea before we think through it, try it, and provide feedback to the team. I want all the teams to know that we're listening. One exception. At no time will we violate the key principles and concepts we've learned in the detail courses and workshops. Part of my job is to keep us all true to the Class A concepts and principles. Using our own ERP test database will allow us to make sure we're integrating all the designs and allow us to test creative possibilities. We've actually set up three database sets to work with. Later I'll give you new secure sign-in details."

Gordon interrupted, "Why three database sets?"

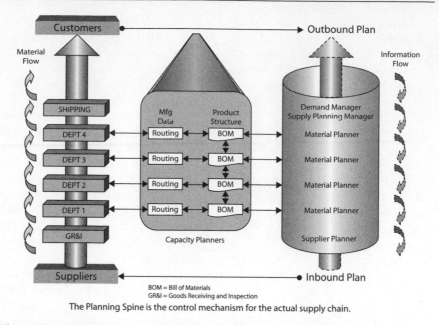

The Planning Spine is the control mechanism for the actual supply chain.

Figure 15.2 Integrating the Internal Supply Chain: The Planning Spine
Source: Oliver Wight. Copyright Oliver Wight International, Inc. Used with permission.

"Thanks, Gordon; good question. We need one to build our Planning Spine covering the internal supply chain and interfacing with the outside world. This is the real CST database. Only tried and tested stuff goes there. The second database, CST-Test, is where we'll develop and test alternatives. With David's approval we're going to learn by doing, rather than risk 'analysis-paralysis.' This is the dataset we'll use the most. The third dataset, CST-Train, will be used later to support all the training we'll need to do as we complete the design. I expect we'll also develop some CBT modules to help with the training."

David raised his hand, "Better explain CBT, Pete."

"Okay. CBT means computer-based training. It allows people to use their computer work stations independently to learn at their own pace how we'll be using the ERP system to run the business in the future. The CBT modules will provide a learning library for new people, for ongoing refresher training, and to help roll out process changes." Peter asked Roxanne if she'd like to add anything.

"Thanks, Peter. I do have a couple important points. We need to standardize our terminology during implementation so we know we're talking about the same things. First, we need a working definition of the words 'Planning,' 'Scheduling,' and 'Execution.' This is what I suggest:

"*Planning* is about the future. It defines what we require to happen to meet the Master Supply Plan at all levels from end-item to supplier requirements. It commits the supply chain to provide the resources (people, equipment, facilities, and, of course, money) to support that plan. However, it does not result directly in things being produced. The calculations are done automatically by the Enterprise Resource Planning (ERP) system utilizing user-defined rules based on inventory records and master data, such as item, routing, work location, and bill of materials masters. The master supply planner has accountability for the overall validity of these integrated plans.

"*Scheduling* is the process of sequencing specific operations at each work location, within delivery and capacity constraints. All schedules must be doable and are reviewed for validity at least daily. Scheduling starts when a Material Planner releases an order, mostly prompted by the ERP system through action messages. This work order commits the supply chain to produce a specific product and quantity at a specific time. From this point on the order is under control of the material and capacity planners, not the system. The output is a detailed Production Schedule by work location. The Material Planner owns and controls the start and due dates of all released orders. The Capacity Planner has the ability to override the operation due dates but cannot override the order due date.

"*Execution* means working to the detailed Production Schedule or Supplier Schedule to supply the ordered product. The shop floor (company's or supplier's) follows sequentially the work as shown on the detailed Schedule, updated at least daily, to transform incoming materials and components into the scheduled supply item, thereby meeting the overall plan.

"As you can see, there is a time-based flow from Planning → Scheduling → Execution."

Peter added, "I see what you mean. If you'd been talking about scheduling, I might well have been hearing planning. I like the clarity of your definitions. For the moment, team, I suggest we adopt these." Everyone agreed. "Any more useful definitions, Roxanne?"

"Sure, Peter, you'll see some of these on the Planning Spine model—the planning roles. I'm going to describe planning roles for Capable level. But the closer you move to a 'flow' supply environment, typically in Phase 2, the more you'll find that these roles become combined and managed by one individual or a small team focused on the end-to-end flow from supplier to customer. But all our Capable level reference material and coaching relates to these roles:

- *Demand Planning Manager* is a senior manager reporting to Marketing. This is an analysis and facilitation role for the demand planning processes. Sales and Marketing own the agreed Demand Plan, including the sales revenue and margin plans, but the Demand Planning Manager is responsible for managing the data. He or she is responsible for coordinating the Demand Review preparation cycle and facilitating the Demand Review portion of the Integrated Business Management process. A key aspect of the role is working closely with the Supply Planning Manager and Master Supply Planner in balancing supply and demand, and for actively participating in the Integrated Reconciliation. Put simply, the Demand Planning Manager is responsible for all requests for product from the supply chain, whether in the form of demand forecasts, distribution replenishments, interplant demand, or customer orders.

- *Supply Planning Manager* is the person who coordinates and facilitates the Supply Review and reports to the executive responsible for the supply chain plan; in your case, that is David Simpson. The key output of this coordination is the agreed-to monthly aggregate Supply Plan by product family. The Supply Planning Manager coordinates the Supply Review preparation cycle, facilitates the review, and actively participates in Integrated Reconciliation. Closely allied to and assisting with this role is the Master Supply Planner. The Supply Planning Manager is normally not involved with the near-term detailed planning. That's the responsibility of the Master Supply Planner.

- *Master Supply Planner/Scheduler* is a senior planner who manages the end-item level Master Supply Plan inside the planning time fence. This is established in part to be consistent with the cumulative lead time, and governs the actual output of the supply chain. The planner is responsible to ensure that commitments to customers are met in full, and that both inventory and efficiency of the business are optimized. The role usually includes development and analysis of the supply plan outside the planning time fence through 24 months. The Master Supply Planner ensures this long-range schedule supports the long-range Demand Plan. The resulting item-level plans must aggregate to the previously agreed aggregate Supply Plan. The Master Supply Planner is also responsible for the overall quality and effectiveness of the detailed supply, capacity, and material planning processes, and works closely with the Demand Planning Manager and Supply Planning Manager in balancing supply and demand. The key output of this individual's work is the Master Supply Plan that drives the detailed material and capacity plans through the ERP system."

Peter interrupted again. "Looking at the Planning Spine model [Figure 15.2], two questions come to mind, Roxanne. First, why are the Demand Planning Manager and Supply Planning Manager shown next to each other on the model? And second, where's the Master Production Scheduler role in all this?"

"Excellent question, Peter; I'm glad you asked, but let me answer your questions in reverse order. The Master Supply Planner might well have been called the Master Production Scheduler in the past. But the title is no longer appropriate when you consider how the responsibilities develop as a company moves from Capable Planning and Control to Advanced and then on to Excellent. The title 'Master Production Scheduler' is historically supply-side focused and brings to mind the old days when manufacturing's motto was 'you can sell what we make.' Hardly customer focused!"

Peter replied, "But that's exactly how we seem to plan today given our long production cycles. It just might help explain part of our customer service problem! I agree that today's planning model isn't very customer focused."

"And there's more, Peter. Remember our definition of scheduling? Scheduling covers the short- to medium-term planning horizon. But today, companies must create supply plans covering the next 24 months and sometimes even longer, so the old term is limiting. I still like and use the term 'Master,' as in Master Supply Plan. This takes us back to your first question. The Master Supply Plan is developed by the Master Supply Planner, as the item-level expression of the Supply Planning Manager's aggregate Supply Plan. It drives all other plans, but it is co-owned by the Demand Manager. That's a new concept for most companies beginning this journey. Many of my clients— usually the best at customer service—have the Supply Planning Manager and Demand Planning Manager co-located so that they can work closely together in developing the optimal Master Supply Plan for the business. And there needs to be a Master Supply Planner at each facility with the responsibility to support their facility's supply plan as assigned by the Supply Planning Manager. An alternative to co-location used by some companies, almost as effective, may mean using technology so they can collaborate as though they were actually sitting together. That's why there's no space between the roles in the model."

There were disgruntled looks on the faces of the plant master production schedulers, but Peter decided to reinforce Roxanne's message to head off any negative comments.

"That design will change a few things and will take time to get used to. But I can see some big advantages to that planning model. After all, manufacturing has no purpose other than to serve marketing does it?" As he studied the faces of his team members and recalled the positions taken by Tony, he suspected a paradigm shift of that magnitude would take persistence and coaching to achieve. He continued. "As we begin to fully understand and appreciate the benefits of this change, I know we can get people aligned and supportive. It's absolutely consistent with the focus and integration that David's been talking about all along." With that encouragement from Peter, Roxanne continued.

"While the Master Supply Planner establishes the Master Supply Plan and responds to the requests for short-term demand changes from the Demand Manager, the person in this role must also respond to customer orders. These changing demands often require decision-making trade-offs. As robust as your new planning processes will become, you'll always encounter the need for trade-offs between customer service, inventory, and costs; it's just a fact of life, especially in Phase 1. But you'll soon see that as your processes improve, the impact of these trade-offs will diminish noticeably. We'll talk more about this later in your implementation."

"Let's move on to the next planning level. *Material Planners* are accountable for managing the item ordering rules in the master data files for inventory and safety stock levels, and for responding to ERP system action and exception messages to synchronize the internal supply chain. This is the key day-to-day objective in maintaining material plan validity—the 'matched set of parts' term that Oliver Wight coined some years ago. Before you get the wrong impression, I had better qualify what I just said. The Master Supply

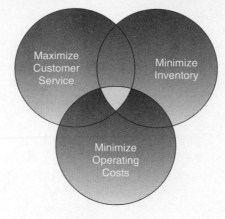

Plan automatically feeds MRP, the Materials Requirements Planning calculator within your ERP system. In a Capable Planning and Control environment the MRP software calculates a complete, valid material plan from end item to supplier requirements, all synchronized and all conforming to your optimized rules to support your Master Supply Plan [Figure 15.3]."

"We run MRP today," said Sandy Bar-Nestor, "but you make it sound a whole lot better than it is."

"There's a reason for that, Sandy. You've never really built a working Planning Spine, the sum of all the integrated business rules governing how you run your internal supply chain. You've never exploited the capabilities of your ERP system because your current business processes aren't designed for integration. They're designed for functional optimization, or even worse, functional reaction." Sandy didn't look convinced, but allowed Roxanne to continue.

"*Supplier Planners*, often called Supplier Schedulers, are the day-to-day points of contact for your suppliers. They maintain material plans in MRP by supplier and by commodity. The output is scheduled by supplier by item/part number. They maintain valid supplier schedules that summarize requirements by supplier across the entire planning horizon. They are often matrix-managed, solid line to planning excellence; dotted line to purchasing. In some companies with a low volume of call-offs from suppliers, these two roles may be filled by the same person. The Supplier Planner works within the commercial contract, negotiated by the Purchasing or Procurement organization, between the company and the supplier. If you consider the contract as the long-range plan, then you can consider this role as scheduling. It includes scheduling inbound deliveries, ensuring deliveries arrive on schedule, and monitoring supplier delivery performance on behalf of the buyer. The primary tool for communication between the Supplier Planner and the supplier is the Supplier Schedule, a direct extract from the material plan but organized by supplier, rather than by product stream. All Supplier Schedules directly extracted from the material plans are preauthorized by the agreed-to Master Supply Plan and do not require secondary authorization, approval signatures, or intervention by the buyer." Pauline Powell, a purchasing buyer, interrupted at this point.

"Hold on right there, Roxanne—it's company policy that all purchase orders valued over $5,000 must be referred to the buyer on a Purchase Requisition, so the buyer can authorize a purchase order using our skill and judgment before that money can be spent. I often change requisitions to better match the latest price breaks. I can't accept this Supplier Schedule procedure. You'll certainly support me on this, won't you, Peter?"

"One thing I'm learning rapidly with this initiative, Pauline, is that the old saying is true, 'If you always do what you've always done, you'll always get what you've always gotten.' And we sure don't want to perpetuate what we've always gotten! While I suspect Roxanne is right, I would like a little more clarification and rationale, Roxanne."

"Thanks Peter. Pauline, you've raised an appropriate and fairly common concern. The way Cosmetics Products operates today, I'm not going to argue that your current procedure is right or wrong. What I know for certain is that perpetuating your current procedures in your new design would be absolutely wrong. We'll provide a day's education on the details, and go through any concerns at that time. But let me ask you a question, Pauline. How much of your day is spent processing purchase requisitions and purchase orders, and in talking with suppliers about urgent or late deliveries?"

"I'd say about half of my time."

"Good. How quickly are you able to process requisitions?"

"Well, obviously I have other responsibilities, but I make sure I clear my inbox by the time I leave work every Friday."

"So, Pauline, it is possible that a requisition arriving at your desk late Friday could wait until the following Friday to be approved and a purchase order created and sent to the supplier?"

"Sure. That can happen, but it doesn't happen often. I usually take care of them within a couple of days."

"Do you consider carefully screening purchase requisitions and purchase orders as a valuable use of your purchasing skills and abilities?"

"Well, it is an important requirement within our procedures, but in terms of skills, it doesn't require much. I could contribute more to the business by spending more time developing our suppliers' capability to support Cosmetics Products. But that's not possible. I have to get the purchase orders moving to support production."

Roxanne now broadened her response as she turned to the group. "I need to remind all of you that I am not criticizing the way you work today. I know you are all working hard and doing your best with the procedures that exist today; we all have to accept that. But, as with many of your processes, there are much more effective ways to do things. At some point it won't be Pauline I'll be having this conversation with, it might be you. So don't think Pauline is alone here.

"Now here's the brief answer to your question, Pauline. First, the annual Business Plan is authorized by the senior executive. Then each month, the aggregate Supply Plan supporting that Business Plan is updated and authorized during the Management Business Review. In preparation for the Management Business Review, the Master Supply Plan is reviewed and approved each month during the Supply Review, and adjusted as needed weekly as part of the weekly Master Supply Planning meeting. Additionally, the Master Supply Plan is maintained daily so that it is always valid, with no 'past-dues,' and it continues to aggregate to match the authorized Supply Plan. To support the detailed material plans, you will develop authorized Cosmetics Products' business rules. These will define precisely how you want material plans to be calculated and managed. Finally, the Material Planners are responsible for following the order replenishment policies and managing inventory to the authorized levels. Providing that the replenishment order is a direct flow through MRP to the Supplier Schedule, the material release has already been authorized on several levels. There is no need to involve the buyers; there is no need for a purchase requisition; and there is no need for approval of such purchase orders. They become nonvalue-added and redundant pieces of paper. So, Pauline, this frees up your time to develop the suppliers; an activity that is much more rewarding than chasing paperwork!" Pauline nodded, though still concerned about how to get agreement to change the current purchasing policy. "If we've covered that question sufficiently for now, I'd like to continue.

"Let's move on to the role of the Capacity Planner. The *Capacity Planners* are responsible for ensuring capacity constraints are identified and managed to support the production schedule while optimizing efficiency. The cardinal rule is to meet the order due date. The planner analyzes required and available capacity with the owner of the resource. Analysis is accomplished using the ERP system's detailed capacity planning module to determine the order's *operation* start and completion dates based on the routing. Capacity Planners may override the operation schedule and select alternative routings to meet the order dates or improve efficiency. The output is a detailed Production Schedule by work location."

Peter declared a 30-minute break for lunch, to everyone's relief. Working through the details of terminology to create a common language, while essential, was proving to be tedious.

After the break, Peter addressed the group. "Now that we've been through the first education sessions, I know most of you have questions or concerns. I've set aside the next three hours to address those questions and concerns. Here's your chance to get all your issues on the table." The lively session that followed was a combination of education and team building. Between mini-lectures, Roxanne observed behaviors. She began to develop a sense of who tried to dominate, who was behaving negatively, who was not engaged, and who was silent, yet engaged. She also observed and was impressed with Peter's leadership abilities, critical to the success of the Customer Service Initiative. At appropriate times, he was assertive; at other times he drew in the quieter members; he sought alternative perspectives to negative comments; and generally kept team behaviors appropriate. He was, as Greg assured her, a good choice to lead the teams.

The meeting with the Planning and Control Milestone team enabled the design teams to begin their work. Roxanne coached them to seek help quickly when they ran into a barrier. "Try to resolve your issues using the concepts and principles you've been learning. But don't waste too much time in debating alternatives. If you have questions about the best approach, talk with Peter. He'll call me to help if necessary."

The Process Design team leaders arranged their own design team work plans, all beginning the week after the milestone meeting. Peter set a deadline of six weeks for each team to complete the design for their portion of the Planning Spine model, recognizing that implementation would begin when the design was approved by the steering committee. "Here's a simple requirement; don't be late! I'll be around to remove any roadblocks, assist in answering questions, and arrange for periodic visits so that Roxanne can address your questions and review your progress. In return, I expect you to tell me immediately of potential problems. That will allow us to shift resources around if necessary to stay on schedule. You need to know that I don't respond well to schedule surprises. Don't count the hours; just get the job done.

"By the way, thanks to each of you team leaders for getting me your output-Gantt charts. With the few adjustments we've discussed over the past week, they look good and fit the overall time line.

"Looking at the schedule, our next meeting is our regular weekly meeting on Friday at 8:00 A.M. This week we'll select four or five representative finished products and create the master data for them. Then in our meeting on the following Tuesday, we'll review what we've learned and split up into teams working in parallel to finalize bills of material (BOM) structures and item master data. We'll then enter the bills and item masters in the ERP system test database and run system reports to check how everything fits together. I can tell you I'm glad we don't have to implement a new ERP system at the same time we're doing this work. Roxanne tells me that lots of companies have to do that at a cost of many months added to their implementation schedule.

"We're also going to kickoff all the other teams next week, except for the Supplier team. We'll need to have our own act together, meaning have valid and stable supplier schedules, before we approach our suppliers." Peter fielded a few more questions and adjourned the meeting.

On Friday morning, the Capable Planning and Control Milestone team members received their secure login and security codes for the three newly created database sets. With access to ten new workstations, they selected five major SKUs that were representative of all the key types of products. They split into pairs and began collecting BOM and item master data for each SKU and component material. Each pair reviewed every ERP item data field for appropriateness, paying particular attention to validity of order quantity, order multiples, lead times, and safety stocks. It was immediately obvious to them that the master data had never before been reviewed with such a holistic approach. There was little relationship between order policies for the parent items and their components. One of the teams discovered that a body lotion was manufactured in bulk batches of 5,000 liters, but the filling and packaging lot size was set up for the equivalent of 6,000 liters. As a result, to package a batch of product, two lots of bulk product were produced with the surplus held in inventory. A good deal of that surplus routinely expired and was scrapped before the next packaging run. The same team then began to find errors in component quantities when comparing the system quantities against the product engineering design documents. The team reconvened at 5:00 P.M to finish its assigned products. Late that evening, Francis Brandon entered all the corrected master data into the ERP system. The team had finished its first task, but realized there was far more work to do than they had anticipated. And they hadn't even looked at Work Location or Routing records.

Process Design team leaders met with their teams to review and reach agreement on the approved output-Gantt chart. After some initial push-back to try to get more time and to argue about dates, they got the message. The dates were firm and would be changed only if there were a lack of resources. Greg's support of this initiative ensured that they would always find the necessary resources. Peter had to work directly with three managers who were reluctant to release their team representatives.

At the same time, the Capable Integrated Business Management teams participated in the five workshops for the Integrated Business Management process [see Figure 6.2]. Within a period of 10 days, they had designed the process and procedures for all the steps and established a calendar, ambitiously starting the very next month. They realized that all the required input data would not yet be complete at this stage, but knew that everyone would benefit by following the process and learning to work as a team. With such a short time line, they would use current data in the new format. They would find gaps in the data but would use what they learned to improve overall quality of the data. As data improved, so would the process.

The teams learned quickly and improved their procedures. Spreadsheets were created and current master data downloaded from the ERP system to facilitate review, correction, and automatic uploading back into the Test database to perform simulations. Jeff Black quickly developed representative demand plans for the 5 SKUs and sent them to Janice Hackworth, who began developing the Master Supply Plan. Janice and her Supply Planning team quickly learned that no one understood the software module well enough to create plans in the system. She used spreadsheets for now to accelerate the process design work, and began scheduling planners for necessary system retraining. Procedures were developed to allow MRP to be updated several times each day if necessary. Notes were kept by each team so that they could later formally document the new policies and procedures they were developing.

All the teams were staying on schedule and meeting due dates for Planning Spine development. The Cosmetics-Test database was being loaded and the test script was nearing completion.

It was time to start the test. The first run would represent an "ideal" state, assuming no problems. Janice assigned the work stations and the various supply planning roles. The first script covered three days; IT would provide an historical record of the test so that the same scenario could repeated later but with specific problems, such as a production batch failure, introduced.

The team was nervous but excited as they assembled for the first three-day scenario. Peter reminded them that one of their tasks was to discover and correct errors but the primary job was to make the model simulate their business. Until they achieved that objective, they could not move on. Peter and Janice would move among the workstations to observe and coach. They executed the first MRP run in 20 minutes. The date was advanced to "Day-2," and the master supply plan was "exploded" through all levels to create an end-to-end supply plan. Action message reports were divided and distributed by planner code. Each planner reviewed the messages to see what they could learn about their plan. If the master data was correct and loaded perfectly in the system, there would be no error messages. That's not what happened.

Of the 183 action messages in the report, only about 80 were expected. The team spent three hours tracking the sources of the errors, and determining the root causes for elimination and learning. Many were caused by inventory imbalances within the plan that caused reschedule in or out recommendations. These problems were corrected quickly. There were only a few BOMs, but inventory imbalances at the top level cascaded down through all planning levels causing multiple reschedule messages. After they completed the corrections, Peter ran the MRP scenario again. This time there were no messages. Now they were ready to begin planning!

Bob Malinkov and Chris Deutsh from IT set up a "lessons learned" archive in the database so that issues could be numbered and tracked until they were closed. They also set up a projector so that workstations could be projected to facilitate learning for the entire team. First they projected a demonstration of releasing orders level by level to see how the system worked. Peter was observing Richard Jones working with the bulk manufacturing simulation and motioned for Janice to join him. Richard had uploaded data from his familiar planning spreadsheet and was manually developing a manufacturing schedule. Janice asked him to project his plan and got everyone's attention. "Richard, please explain what you are doing."

"Sure, Janice. I noticed that the order dates and quantities didn't look right, so I . . ."

Janice interrupted. "When did you notice they were wrong?"

"When I was watching the first simulation, I spotted the problem and knew I could fix the problem easily in my spreadsheet. The spreadsheet is easy to use and has worked really well since I developed it 18 months ago."

Janice looked at the other team members, "Anything wrong with what Richard did?"

The other planners were quiet. Most of them would have done exactly the same thing if they hadn't been running this scenario. Bill Bates from Production Operations finally spoke up.

"If I've understood it right, we should not need any spreadsheets to support MRP. I think that's what Janice meant when she said we have to make the planning model work inside the system. So if there's anything wrong, Richard, you should have stopped the scenario so we could all learn how to find and fix the root cause."

Peter jumped in, "That's exactly what we want to do. No spreadsheets to run the scenario and the business. Find out what's wrong and get it cleaned up in the system. Roxanne told me that the planners face the toughest challenge. They have to unlearn the way they've been doing their work. Now I know what she meant! So thanks for the learning opportunity, Richard."

Richard responded. "You're welcome, Peter. I'm learning fast, but not fast enough. I know I have to get my other work done, but I need to work on this more often than in our weekly meetings. Is it possible for the team to come to the Customer Service conference room every morning from say 7:00 A.M. to 9:00 A.M. to work on the model until we've got our Planning Spine nailed down? I think that would accelerate our progress." Peter was pleased with this idea, and all the team members agreed.

As the team worked through more difficult scenarios to build more detail in the Planning Spine, they began documenting their new processes. They were developing confidence in their processes, in the system, and in their ability to get rid of the spreadsheets they had depended on to run the business.

Over the next few days, the team "lived" through 15 MRP days in the model, basing all order planning on recommendations from MRP. They started to build a Planning Manual containing the new Cosmetics Planning and Control procedures and standardized approaches to planning and problem solving. They were also developing flow diagrams to help everyone understand how the processes were integrated and to clarify inputs, outputs, and account-abilities for executing the process. There would be a copy of this manual on every planner's desk. Along with the CBT modules being developed, the manual would be required reading for all new planners.

Simulations increased in difficulty to include the kind of major problems that the planners faced on very bad days. Confidence continued to build as the team learned how the planning system could help them cope with these problems and avoid customer service failures. A few teams completed their tasks, but most came across difficult design problems. Their Effective Management coaches had seen many of the problems before and were helpful in guiding the teams in the right direction through coaching and additional detailed education.

The Demand Management process design team, led by Jeff Black, received a great deal of early management attention. The current demand planners were confident that their business was not forecastable. Education began with a two-day Managing Demand course that Roxanne tailored to the Cosmetics Products business. It would be presented by EM's fashion industry forecasting expert, Liam Lawlor, who had been a Demand Manager in both fashion and catalog companies. Peter and David attended, as did Alexandra, but only for the first day because of an important customer meeting. Liam reviewed the classic statistically based forecasting model, very close to what the demand planners used. He next showed them a slide of quotes from many companies [Figure 15.4].

Everyone laughed as they recognized that they, too, had made similar comments about forecasting, except for the last. He asked them if they thought supply could produce better forecasts than sales or marketing, and if so, why. Liam turned to Janice Hackworth, who was sitting in on the class to learn more about her interfaces with the Demand Planning Manager.

"Any ideas, Janice?"

"Frankly, we have to second-guess the forecast because the SKU forecasts we receive from Sales and Marketing are so inaccurate. The only thing that comes to mind about our forecasting process is that we don't even try to plan at SKU level in supply except for the next few days in packaging. We tend to plan at the bulk product level."

"If I can restate what Janice said, supply doesn't forecast at SKU level. Why not, Janice?"

"Because the SKU demand mix changes all the time. We have long cumulative lead times and so have to plan at a more aggregated level where historical demand is more consistent over time. The packaging lines and packaging materials have shorter lead times than the bulk materials. So, we can more readily change packaging schedules to deal with mix changes."

Liam then demonstrated that their current forecasting model was unrealistic for their needs, and indeed would never produce effective forecasts.

- No one can forecast our business.
- Forecasts are always wrong.
- Not worth doing.
- We cannot control our demand.
- Sales and Marketing only need a financial forecast.
- Salespeople should be out selling not doing paperwork.
- Supply Chain could forecast better than Sales or Marketing.

Figure 15.4   What People Say and Believe about Forecasting
Source: Oliver Wight. Copyright Oliver Wight International, Inc. Used with permission.

"I need to remind you that Supply shouldn't be forecasting at all. Their job is to create and execute plans that support the forecast. Have you considered you may be forecasting demand at the wrong level? That some of your SKUs are very forecastable, but most of your smaller SKU's might be unforecastable?"

He also suggested that they might be too focused on the numbers, and explained that effective forecasting is built on assumptions that are the foundation for the calculated numbers. Assumptions, he said, must be explicit, documented, and reviewed every month. Focusing on the assumptions rather than the resulting numbers would quickly improve understanding of markets, and produce better numbers. "I won't take you through this example yet, but I want to show you the assumption format that one of my clients uses. It is simple, but effective [Figure 15.5]. You'll see more of this in the Demand Planning course."

Liam next described unconstrained demand—a forecast unconstrained by any consideration of supply constraints. The forecasters liked this concept since they often felt schizophrenic trying to create forecasts they knew could not be supported by Supply. Out of self-defense they would alter the true forecast

Volumes resulting	Degree of Control	Now	3 mths	6 mths	9 mths	12 mths	15 mths	18 mths	21 mths
		1,000							
Market Assumption		Market Assumption Projection							
Population of users (by sector)	Some	20,000	22,000	22,000	22,000	22,000	22,000	23,000	24,000
Growth of Economy in sector	None	0.5%	0.5%	0.5%	0.25%	0%	0%	0%	0%
Rate of new product introduction	Control	4 year	2	1	1	0	0	2	2
Number of competitors	Some	20	18	16	14	10	8	8	8
Competitor activity	None	Price war	Price war	Price war	New products	Promotions	Promotions	Promotions	Promotions
Market price movement	Some	−5%PA	0	−10%		−10%		−5%	
Promotional activity	Some	High	High	High	Med	Med	Med	Med	Low
Market share	Full	25%	25%	25%	26%	30%	30%	35%	35%
Sales Assumption		Sales Assumption Projection							
Customer population — size S	None	200	200	180	150	120	120	100	100
Customer population — size L	Some	20	25	30	35	40	40	40	40
Share of customers	Full	40%	50%	50%	50%	50%	50%	50%	50%
Avg. # of products per customer	Full	5	5	5.5	6	6	6.5	7	7
Competitor activity	None								
Etc. ...									

Figure 15.5 Assumption Management: Demand
Source: Oliver Wight. Copyright Oliver Wight International, Inc. Used with permission.

to match what they thought could be produced. Liam explained that, when necessary, the forecast would be constrained to match supply, but later in the Integrated Business Management process through Integrated Reconciliation.

In response to a complaint about their statistical forecasting tool unreliability, Liam discovered that the forecasters didn't really understand the ability to modify the forecasting algorithm. "This isn't a subject for the Demand Planning course, but I want to point out that you do have a great deal of control with that tool, and with the overall forecasting process, that you don't seem to be exploiting." He explained a number of forecasting algorithms used by most tools: time series, simulation, probability, Delphic for completely new products and, ultimately, Collaborative Demand Planning involving key customers. The team was listening and visibly overwhelmed by these new concepts.

"Don't worry yet about how you will select the best algorithm. Just be aware of this important principle. Whatever algorithm or model or process you use, you must always test the forecast bottom-up versus top-down using the same set of assumptions. By that, I mean aggregate your detailed forecasts up to category and family forecasts. Then look at the family and category history and disaggregate them down applying assumptions for the future and compare the outcome of the two processes. Call it a 'sanity check' if you will. Reconcile any significant differences and modify your assumptions where necessary. I can tell you that your forecasts will begin to improve immediately. I can also tell you that your business is absolutely forecastable!" Liam now turned to Jeff Black.

"Now Jeff, let me ask you a fundamental question about forecasting. What is the greatest source of forecast error?"

Jeff offered his opinion. "Based on what you just said and our experience, I suppose it is a pretty close tie between not knowing our customers well enough and using the wrong forecasting method."

"Those are certainly contributors, Jeff, but not the biggest cause for most businesses. The main contributor to forecast error is . . . long manufacturing lead times. The longer the cumulative lead time, the greater the exposure to forecast error! I want you all to consider this [Figure 15.6].

"If your lead time for end-item sales were one week, you'd probably be in a Finish-to-Order (FTO) supply model; you would have pretty good SKU forecasts, wouldn't you?"

Janice replied, "Well, yes. But I don't see how that could work for us. Our packaging lead time alone is two weeks, not counting some long manufacturing and supplier lead times. That's why we have to have SKU forecasts at three months, and a detailed review of them at one month before we get into actual production."

"I understand, Janice. With your current process, that makes sense. But suppose you asked Sales and Marketing for forecasts at the product level, not the SKU level. That more aggregated forecast would be more reliable. The law of big numbers says that variability within a larger population is normally less than variability in a smaller population. The forecast still won't be perfect,

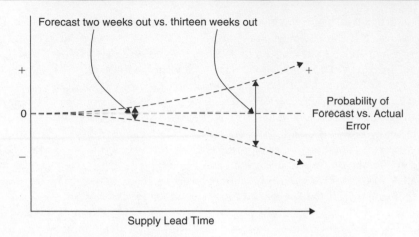

Figure 15.6 The "Horn of Probability"
Source: Oliver Wight. Copyright Oliver Wight International, Inc. Used with permission.

but you would experience less forecast error. Isn't it the variability in the small SKUs that causes you the greatest problems?"

"Liam, that makes a lot of sense, but we make to stock. We're not set up to make the products after we receive orders."

"Good point, but now is the perfect time to consider what it would take to change your supply model as you design your Planning Spine. What would it take to create your Master Supply Plan at the product level; and finish the SKUs based on customer and distribution orders? Companies in your industry who make the change achieve significant bottom-line benefits. They delay committing bulk product to final packages until the last minute and see savings through massive reductions in SKU inventory, damage, obsolescence, and warehouse costs." Janice thought for a moment before responding.

"I don't know what it will take but it sounds intriguing. We can certainly use the working capital cash that would be freed up and the reduced inventory! Peter, we had better take that as an action item for the Planning and Control Milestone team. Let's propose we develop a FTO model and see what it would take for us to get there."

Liam added a point of clarification. "Peter, the model won't have to be either/or. In all likelihood you'll end up with a combination of FTO and MTS, that's Make-to-Stock. For some of your small volume SKUs, you probably won't want to incur frequent setup changes and will simply make to a target warehouse inventory. It's a trade-off. As a first step, you might consider getting your top ten or so SKUs that you are set up to run every week or day, or so, into an FTO model. That will probably give you most of the benefits.

1. Integrated Business Management means 'One Set of Numbers.'
2. Unconstrained Demand must be understood and visible.
3. Accountability and responsibility established with Sales and Marketing.
4. Successful Demand Planning is dependent upon a formal process.
5. Management of changes to Assumptions and integration with Sales and Marketing plans.
6. Knowing your customer and your customers' customers will help reduce variability in demand.
7. Establish the optimum 'level' at which to demand plan (e.g. Family, Product, SKU/end-item).
8. A Demand Control process is an essential part of Demand Management.
9. Measurement is an essential part of understanding and improving.
10. Inaccuracy must be understood and managed for service.

Figure 15.7   The Ten Keys of Demand Planning
Source: Oliver Wight. Copyright Oliver Wight International, Inc. Used with permission.

"Finally I'd like to leave you with this summary—for both your milestones [Figure 15.7]."

Two early results were reported to Peter for the weekly Steering Committee meeting. The Inventory Accuracy Team, following the multistep methodology taught by Effective Management, had determined their baseline accuracy. They were shocked to discover that their inventory records were only 43 percent accurate. This reinforced the reasons why planners were reluctant to give up their spreadsheets and rely on ERP action messages instead. The team reported that they were moving aggressively to implement control group cycle counting to discover and eliminate the root causes of inaccuracies.

The Data Integrity Team, similarly, had completed its baseline audit of Bill of Material accuracy. They sampled more bills than they planned because accuracy was far worse than expected. To their astonishment, baseline accuracy was 18 percent. They found problems with system access security, change control, scrap, and yield factors—additional reinforcement of the underlying reluctance to use the ERP system. They recorded the results of their investigation in the *e*List. They looked forward to their scheduled tasks with trepidation, but also with excitement that the work would contribute directly to improved customer service.

Roxanne assured Peter that these inventory and data accuracy results were not unusual at the start. She also assured him that implementing best practice business processes would enable Cosmetics Products to improve use of the ERP system, planning, and as a result, customer service. Peter wasn't looking forward to reporting these dismal accuracy results to the Steering Committee.

At the end of the Steering Committee meeting, Greg asked Peter to thank the teams for their progress and reports. He, too, was a bit shocked by the accuracy baselines, but he was also encouraged. "Look," Greg said to Peter, "the accuracy is no worse than it was yesterday. The good news is that today, we know exactly where we stand. I'm encouraged that the teams now know the gaps, the root causes, and have plans in place to reach at least 95 percent."

He concluded the Steering Committee meeting by saying, "I've never been more confident that we can meet our customer service objective. Keep up the progress. The train I mentioned in the kick-off meeting is definitely moving!"

16

CUSTOMER SERVICE

Your silence meant to others that you were in agreement with the demand forecast. It's not acceptable to ride the fence or second-guess those numbers later.

We just didn't see the pattern that is so obvious to us now.

While the Capable Planning and Control Team worked on the supply model and Planning Spine, Bart Billings, the Integrated Business Management Milestone Leader, was organizing the tasks for his team. The Integrated Business Management in Practice Course that had been held in a downtown hotel had covered most of what the Leadership Team needed to know about the process. Now they had to define the Cosmetics Products' process. The milestone team, which included Peter, first needed to reach agreement on the makeup of product families and the unit of measure for each. After some study and discussion, the team agreed to start with their product categories as the product families. Roxanne supported that decision provided they remained open to change as they learned by doing; it would not be difficult to change family definitions in the early stages of their work. They selected Body Lotions as a representative family, including all SKUs except for Accessories, which they'd handle later.

The initial unit of measure selected was sales units, which wasn't satisfactory to Manufacturing since sales units ranged in size from 5ml single-use samples to 500ml units for salon sales. After considerable discussion, Sales agreed to use liters as the unit of measure for body lotions. Bart Billings, Demand Manager, offered to provide mix factors for the various packing options to enable a future view of packaging resource requirements, including bottles, pouch foil, tubes, wipes, and so on. While planning body lotion bulk manufacturing in liters was logical, mix and conversion factors would be needed in finishing operations to assess future filling and packaging equipment capacity requirements.

Alexandra and Greg approved this proposal. Peter could now ask Janice Hackworth to begin to create the item-level master supply planning model using the demand forecast in liters. Conversion of unit volume to financial units would be a simple mathematical exercise handled by the ERP system.

The next task was to define and document official sources of the aggregate numbers for demand and supply, for mix factors, and key resources to be monitored. These data sources would be placed under robust change control, meaning limited access and formally documented policies and procedures. The only person authorized to modify demand numbers would be the Demand Manager or his designated backup; supply numbers would be controlled only by the Supply Planning Manager; and through the Supply Planning Manager, access to the operational resource definitions and numbers would be limited to a carefully selected group of planners. However, all numbers would be visible to key players.

Bart's Demand team then turned to the task of redefining key performance measures according to Class A best-practices at the Capable level, which included defining the hierarchy of measures, the metrics for each measure—that is, determining the data source, timing, algorithm, calculations, and output—and how these would fit into the balanced score card they were tasked with developing. Angus Martin led the Performance Measures team and had worked with Jeff Black, Janice Hackworth, Bill Bates, Production Operations Process Design Team Leader, and Peter Bertrand to develop the initial standards for defining metrics and measures. To their relief, they discovered quickly that most of the raw data were already available. They would simply have to limit access to that raw data to the people who were tasked, under the new policy and procedures, with managing the underlying metrics and calculating the measures.

At the time of the kick-off meeting, David purchased a license for Effective Management's Enterprise Sales and Operations Planning Tool' (ESOPT) software. This tool operates outside the ERP system but through an interface pulls in any data required for calculation, analysis, and presentation of data in graphical format. ESOPT also has its own database, including assumptions and history tracking, making it a comprehensive tool for displaying a great deal of data to facilitate senior management decision making. Results can be projected on a screen during any Integrated Business Management meeting. While spreadsheets can be used, this ready-made tool can be started-up quickly, simplifies the presentation of family status and trends, and enables instantaneous analysis of "what-if" scenarios in both unit volume and financial terms. The graphics make the presentation of analysis results understandable and efficient.

Janice Hackworth, Supply Planning Manager, was eager to use the aggregate supply data in master supply planning modeling. She learned that the ERP system enabled her to hardwire aggregate and detailed supply plan numbers. Bart Billings, Demand Manager, discovered at the same time similar functionality that enabled hardwiring of aggregate and detailed demand numbers. Neither had been aware of this functionality but found it to be intuitive and easy to use. Both were relieved to use just one system instead of the multiple spreadsheets that required them to input the same data in several places and continuously reconcile the data between spreadsheets.

Bart, Peter, David, and Alexandra agreed the Integrated Business Management process was ready to test for the first cycle of meetings, at least for the Body Lotions family.

Each of the reviews was dependent on timely availability of reliable data. The team soon discovered that, for this first cycle, the previous month's sales actuals weren't going to be available until the tenth day of the current month, far too late for a monthly meeting cycle. By communicating the urgency and streamlining procedures, actual sales were reported, at least for the Body Lotions family, on the second day of April. Similarly, development of the supply organization's actual results and performance measures for the same family were accelerated and provided that same day.

For this first cycle, it was not possible to reach agreement on new product introduction information. The team agreed reluctantly to use the most recent data available to Sharon Rogers, the newly assigned Product Coordinator since, in the future, she would be accountable for gathering this information. Realization of this shortcoming had the interesting effect of energizing the current Product and Brand Managers to take more interest in the product pipeline and its potential impact on the product portfolio and customer service. The effect of this wake-up call was recognized immediately in improved product development, introduction procedures, and decision-making. Manufacturing could now prepare to meet published development volumes and dates. The milestone team began to experience what Roxanne had told them—the first step in improvement is standardization [see Figure 7.1]. By simply following robust product management procedures, Cosmetics Products was planting the seeds for improving customer service.

As the journey unfolded, Greg knew that much of his personal drive and energy was fueled by the support and encouragement of Penny and their boys. There were long days and weeks, and short breaks rather than their usual two-week vacations. His family could sense that Greg was doing what was needed. They could also sense his excitement and confidence about the progress his team was making.

Just four weeks after they started the process, Greg settled into his chair in the executive conference room for the first Management Business Review (MBR) meeting, the culmination of their first monthly Integrated Business Management cycle. The executive team was present, along with key planning managers, the Body Lotions Product Manager, and the Purchasing and Finance managers. Tom, their Effective Management coach, had been present for all the preceding Reviews. He would provide the team with feedback and coaching following this MBR to facilitate their continued learning. Tom had Greg added a self-evaluation step to the published MBR agenda. The whole process was remarkably different from what Cosmetics Products had previously called its Sales and Operations Planning meeting. Greg attended that meeting only one time when he joined the company, found it to be little more than a debate about short-term forecast numbers and never again participated.

In preparation for this MBR, Greg had already been briefed by Bart about the issues that surfaced and were resolved during each stage of the month-long process, and about a significant issue yet to be resolved. The formal Integrated Reconciliation Review resulted in just one issue to be decided during the MBR. Greg and the rest of the executive team were counting on Tom to help steer them through the agenda.

At the beginning of the MBR, Tom reviewed their progress to date as the first step on their journey. He encouraged them to keep their expectations realistic for this first MBR. "Let's look at this as a beginning," Tom said [Figure 16.1].

"As you know from your own assessment, today you're in Transition 1 (T1), Disconnected Management Processes. Your first objective is move up to

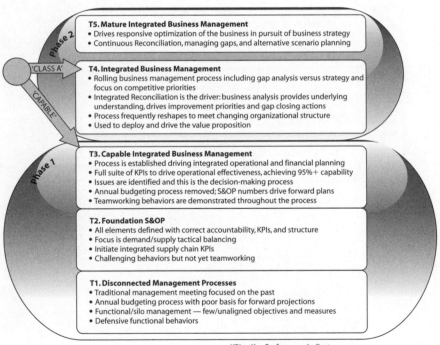

KPI = Key Perfomance Indicator
S&OP = Sales and Operations Planning

Figure 16.1   Maturity Journey: Integrated Business Management
Source: Oliver Wight. Copyright Oliver Wight International, Inc. Used with permission.

'Foundation Sales and Operations Planning' (T2) over the next few months. That progress will afford you a better balance between supply and demand. This alone will help improve customer service and set the stage for even further improvement as the validity of your supporting plans improve.

"As progress in both milestones improves the credibility of your financial numbers, you'll find the MBR focus will shift more toward a review of business performance against strategic goals and objectives. At that point, you'll have achieved Capable Integrated Business Management (T3). It is only as you move beyond Capable Integrated Business Management that you'll realize its true power. We aren't concerned with that yet; it's probably a year or more away. Now, let's look at a typical MBR agenda [Figure 16.2]."

Bart interrupted. "For the moment, we're using exactly this agenda. We may need to modify it after a couple cycles, but we're staying with it for now. Just as a reminder to the team, we decided to use the Product Categories as our families for the moment mostly to support planning for Sales and Marketing, but the structure has the agreement of all functions. These families don't exactly align with Manufacturing's views of products and capacity requirements, but the supply organization can still perform Rough-Cut Resource Planning by restructuring the SKUs into Supply Planning families. We discovered this manipulation and analysis to be pretty straightforward in the ESOPT that we've licensed. Sorry to interrupt, Tom."

1: Key performance indicators
 • Revenue/profitability
 • Customer satisfaction
 • Demand planning performance
 • New products on time
 • Supply performance
2: Business trends
3: Major changes analyzed: internal and external
4: Key issues reviewed by "family"
 • Alternatives presented
 • Opportunity/vulnerability
 • Operational and financial impact
 • Decisions taken
5: Latest view aligned to:
 • Annual business plan
 • Strategy
6: Plans agreed
7: Input to next cycle
8: Self-review of the meeting behaviors

Figure 16.2 Management Business Review Agenda
Source: Oliver Wight. Copyright Oliver Wight International, Inc. Used with permission.

"Thanks, Bart. That's a good add. I want to reinforce the point that you'll need to remain open to modifying your product families as you learn more about using those families to manage the business more effectively."

During this first cycle, there was agreement to focus on just one family comprising nearly 60 SKUs, excluding Accessories, in the Body Lotions category. Greg reminded everyone, however, that he expected all families to be reviewed in April's MBR.

Greg added, "When we've gained some experience with this new process, I want the MBR to be the first agenda item of our monthly Leadership Team meeting. I expect the MBR to be a crisp, decision-making meeting. We need to devote the right amount of time to this topic without delaying the other important agenda items. That means we all need to do our homework and come prepared for the MBR. Anything else I should add, Tom?" Greg asked.

"I think you've covered it well, Greg. I'm really glad you added those last points. Keep reminding yourselves that this is first and foremost a decision-making meeting. You'll agree on the plans for managing this family for the next 24 months. You'll need to decide on any required gap-closing actions and be prepared to resolve all open issues."

"Thanks, Tom," Greg replied. "My expectation regarding issues and decisions is that we'll review briefly any issue and its business context, have time to ask clarifying questions, and then discuss the recommended solution and alternatives. Many of you have already worked with Bart in developing today's issue and alternative recommendations. That prework is critical to the success of this process and to our business. Your effectiveness in this forum also correlates directly with the effectiveness of your subordinates in all the preparation and Review meetings leading up to the MBR. Likewise, your effectiveness will correlate directly with how well you engage in the Integrated Reconciliation process. I recognize that we're all still learning, but we need to learn quickly. Resolve any questions you might have ahead of the MBR so that you're prepared to make required decisions when you walk in the door. That completes my opening comments."

Tom had helped each Review team implement the ESOPT and coached them on the information needed for the overall process. This allowed them to import information directly from their other systems; document assumptions; conduct "what-if" scenario analysis; display graphical representations of sales, production, and inventory plans; display key resources for capacity analysis; and see gaps between current revenue and profit projections and commitments. So it was with great anticipation that Greg waited for Bart to fire up the system and to see the charts depicting the Body Lotions family.

The picture that emerged from the historical data, previous month's actual results, and future projections was not pretty. The period of heavy shipments for this family always occurred in early October when stores filled their shelves and stockrooms in anticipation of fall and winter dry skin conditions and for the buildup to the Christmas season. This shipment period was critical to category profitability for the entire year. Nevertheless, customer service performance was traditionally poor every fall when Cosmetics Products failed to ship, or undershipped orders for many SKUs while having surplus inventory of other SKUs. After last fall's heavy shipment period, customer service improved slightly, but several high-volume SKUs continued with backorders exceeding 10 percent. Backorders were often canceled when customers turned to Cosmetics Products' competitors to fill their shelves, stockrooms, and end-aisle display space. Greg's only solace was the coaching from Tom who had said that, through implementation of the Planning Spine, backorders should soon drop to less than 5 percent, trending to less than 2 percent by the time the Capable Planning and Control level was achieved. Tom's coaching helped Greg remain upbeat about the progress they were making in attacking the underlying causes of the poor results to date.

With final reminders that the MBR was for decision making, not information sharing, and for improving results, not assigning blame, Greg turned to Bart to lead the team through the agenda.

"Thanks, Greg. Since this is our first meeting, we have no outstanding action items or special issues; so we'll skip that agenda item. Why don't you take us through the performance scorecard review, Janice, and then introduce the issue and decision we need to make?"

Janice Hackworth, newly appointed Supply Planning Manager, began her portion of the agenda. "We'll get to the issue and needed decision later when we get into the family overview charts. For now, let's move to the performance review chart in your information packet.

"We're focusing only on the Body Lotions family key performance indicators (KPIs) in today's meeting. By next month, we'll be able to present performance results for the entire business. For now we just need to become familiar with the format and content. The bad news is that nearly all our newly defined Class A measures and other KPIs for which we've been able to get data are below required levels."

Janice spent a few minutes defining the key measures and summarized what work was being done by the milestone team to improve results. She explained that at the MBR in May more specific plans would be presented for each measure below the required minimum or negatively affecting customer service.

"This isn't what I was hoping to see," commented Greg after reviewing the graphical dashboard of results, "but it's pretty much what I expected." Greg shook his head and gestured for Janice to continue.

"Since this is our first MBR, I thought I'd ask Matt to bring all of us up to date on the complete Body Lotions new products pipeline. Matt would you do the honors?" Janice turned the meeting agenda over to Matt Rutherford, VP Engineering and Product Development. Matt discussed the status of each new product on the development path. He specifically highlighted one project that had slipped several months, and another whose launch could be accelerated if desired. Alexandra commented that, based on her Product Manager's perspective, the delayed product was key in getting the portfolio a "new and improved" look in the consumers' eyes since it addressed the current trends toward aromatherapy and skin detoxification. Unfortunately, the product that could be accelerated was timed to launch with related accessories that could not be accelerated.

Tom interrupted. "Matt, have you rescheduled the new product commitment date to reflect the delay?"

"We decided not to do that, Tom. We wanted to stay with the original date so we could pick up the Past Due alerts from the planning system."

"So, Matt, the demand plan we're looking at includes volume that you know can't be sold and shipped. And I'll bet that new product is replacing another product. If I'm right about that, chances are pretty good that you'll run out of the current product before the new product is available. That's what I call a 'double whammy!' Consider this an example emphasizing the need for realism from everyone, whatever the causes."

"You're right about that, Tom," commented Greg. "Bart and Jeff, I want you to take care of that demand issue ASAP. Matt, and for everyone else in this room, if you have a problem, raise it with Bart for review in Integrated Reconciliation. That's how we agree what to do about our plans when we see potential issues. I really dislike surprises like this. Remember that for next time!"

Tom added, "Here's the good news. When you've incorporated new products properly, the Integrated Business Management process will be a great help in delivering product launches on schedule."

There were no more questions or comments about new products, so Janice continued with the agenda. "Now, since we are dealing with only one family and this is our first meeting, I'm going to move right to the family review for Body Lotions. I'll be presenting this today, but we'll change that over the next few months so that the appropriate product manager, brand, or category manager accountable for each family will lead the family reviews."

Janice projected a sales chart that showed low first quarter sales. She explained that the below-forecast sales resulted from a production shortfall but was quick to add that there was also a significant forecast error. As Greg looked at the screen projection of the family's Demand Summary, he turned to Alexandra.

"So you're telling me, Alexandra, that we forecast more demand than actually materialized, but then we couldn't even produce what we expected to sell? That really concerns me, since this is one of our higher profit lines. We can't afford to fall short on this family. I'll get to the production issue in a minute, but first, why did we miss the sales forecast?"

"I'd like to answer Greg's question, Alexandra," said Carole Brown, Body Lotions Product Manager. "I haven't been in agreement with the forecast for these products for a long time." She continued in some detail before declaring, "I believe the next few months' sales forecasts are at least 20 percent too high."

There was a palpably uncomfortable silence in the room for what seemed a full minute. As Alexandra was about to respond to Greg's question and to Carole's comment, Tom interrupted. "Greg, what's your reaction?"

"I'm not sure what you're thinking, Tom. I know we just experienced a very uncomfortable silence. What's your advice to me and to all of us?"

"Perhaps I was a bit vague, Greg. Carole, I don't want you to take this personally. Just consider it coaching for the entire team. There's a cardinal rule for the meeting we call the Demand Review. Some of our clients refer to this review as their 'consensus forecast meeting' with 'consensus' being the operative word. It's essential that Sales, Marketing and Demand Management end up in absolute agreement or at least consensus about the assumptions and the unconstrained demand for SKU's and families. If that team can't reach consensus on the forecast, how can you expect your supply team to create its plans and supply alternatives? If there is no consensus, plans brought to the MBR are worthless. I watched the President of one business correctly bring an MBR to an abrupt and embarrassing end when her Marketing and Sales VPs openly disagreed about the forecast during that meeting. So, if you really were not in agreement with the forecast, Carole, you should not have agreed during the Demand Review. 'Silence is approval.' Your silence meant to others that you were in agreement with the demand forecast. It is not acceptable to ride the fence or second-guess those numbers later. In other words, based on what you're saying, there was no consensus on which the supply team could do its work, and no possible chance of having an effective meeting today."

Tom turned to Greg. "That may have sounded harsh, but that's what I was thinking, Greg." Tom's ability to give straight feedback surfaced again.

Carole responded before Greg could comment. "I know you said not to take your comments personally, Tom, but that felt pretty damned personal!"

Greg could empathize with Carole's feelings, but knew that Tom was right. Greg also knew that he needed to establish a culture that welcomes critique, even harsh critique.

"I certainly appreciate your candor and can understand your feelings, Carole; but in a spirit of learning from our mistakes, I have to agree with Tom. We all need to seek and welcome constructive criticism from Tom and from each other. Otherwise we'll never improve customer service. Quite frankly, I've also had some of those same concerns about our forecasts but didn't articulate them either; so Tom's comments are directed to me as well as to you. Looks like we all have a lot of learning to do!"

Alexandra finally regained the floor. "I was about to say, Greg, *mea culpa*. The buck stops with me, not Carole. As we reviewed the history of this family, we became aware of a strong sales plan bias. It appears that we routinely forecast high, plan for that high level of revenue and profit, and then watch as actual sales, revenue, and profit fall short of forecast, month after month. Carole brought it to my attention in the past, but I just didn't listen carefully enough or understand the implications of forecast bias. At the time, we were already planning the following month's sales and weren't paying enough attention to what happened in the previous month. It's no wonder Manufacturing has been second-guessing our forecasts! I think we've all learned a valuable lesson today."

Alexandra continued. "Greg, we're still exploring the reasons why, but obviously our current sales and marketing efforts are not building the market share, volume, or margins we need. I'm learning a big lesson from the Integrated Business Management process in this very first month. For now, we'll lower the forecast while we figure out what is causing our unfounded optimism."

Bart added, "Alexandra is right, Greg. We haven't yet determined the cause of the continuing shortfall, but there is some good news."

Greg looked skeptical. "If you can find any good news in all of this, Bart, I'm all ears."

"This isn't a new problem, Greg. We've been suffering from it for a long time. We've started to document our demand assumptions and examine the plans and results in an entirely different way. For the first time, we understand that we have a fundamental problem with this family. This month it literally jumped out of the data at us. We knew something wasn't right, of course, but in the past we've been looking at all the SKUs individually. We were in data overload and couldn't see the forest because the trees kept getting in the way. We just didn't see the pattern that is so obvious to us now. It's also obvious that this Integrated Business Management process is going to make us face and address issues proactively."

"Okay," Greg responded, "I think it's a bit of a stretch to call it 'good news,' but I agree that recognizing a performance pattern, even a bad one, is better than not recognizing that there is a pattern at all. Now, I'll ask the hard question. What are you and your demand management team doing about it, Bart?"

"For the short term, we'll reduce forecasts across the board for the SKUs that have habitually fallen short of our prediction. When the issue came up in the Reconciliation Review, we built a scenario in the ESOPT tool depicting a sales plan reduction of 20 percent. On my laptop, while we've been talking, I've added to the scenario the delay of the new product, so we can look at the impact of both on the screen.

"As you can see, the new sales plan lowers the revenue and profit forecast for the family and for the entire business, of course, but it now reflects what we really expect to happen. To offset that loss, we'll develop additional marketing and sales initiatives in other families. If we can get the product from the plants, these initiatives should make up for the predicted revenue and profit loss in the Body Lotions family. Janice and I will review the supply capability to meet the increased volumes for the other families. We'll present details about those new initiatives in next month's MBR." Those present were disappointed to see more bad news, but impressed with how quickly the new scenario could be developed and projected during the meeting.

Janice took control again, "Let's get back to the agenda. We have one issue statement and an evaluated recommendation for decision today. You've all seen it, but I'll remind you that it deals with the need for additional production capacity for the Body Lotions family. It was a complex issue for us to sort through during the Demand, Supply, and Reconciliation reviews, but I believe the recommendation is clear and the case compelling." Greg picked up his copy of the issue document.

"Now, David, it's your turn to help me understand what's going on. Let me get this straight. We have undersold this family, but despite that, we're looking simultaneously at dismal customer service performance and high inventories. What the heck's going on? This isn't making any sense to me. I was told we had plenty of capacity. We just reduced the forecast and now you're telling me we *still don't* have enough capacity! Enlighten me, please."

David responded. "We believed we had capacity, Greg. In aggregate, it appears that we do have plenty of capacity, but when you get into the details of the product mix, it's not quite that straightforward." David then went into a blow-by-blow account of how they created the shortfall through a series of events and decisions that just like dominoes, cascaded problems through the entire supply chain. He then told Greg that the situation was even worse than what he just described. I'll try to clarify what happened." Before he could continue, Tom interrupted him.

"David, at the beginning of this meeting, Greg reminded us that this is not an information-sharing session. Keep it business focused. This is not the place to air dirty laundry. The past is past; we just need to learn from it, and keep focused on planning the next 24 months.

"So, David, in one sentence tell us what will happen if you don't get the additional capacity described in the issue recommendation."

"Well, Greg, we still have to analyze our capacity in a little more detail given the 20 percent reduction in the demand plan, but I know we'll still be near the maximum of our capability, and maybe even higher. That would put us near a 100 percent loading, which is high risk and unrealistic. We've already been using most of our 10 percent capacity reserve for several months. Since Marketing plans to grow this product family, we'll need to increase our capacity before they start advertising and selling the additional volume. Given the equipment and installation lead times, it will be year-end before we see any new capacity on line—after the heavy shipping period. Jeff will need to build that constraint into his demand management plans. While we're at it, have a look at months 18 through 24. I've never been able to see that far out in our plans before, but, assuming this reduced demand plan is approximately right, we'll still need a major capacity increase by the middle of next calendar year. If we do it right and continue to manage demand, we'll avoid having this issue on the agenda again. Sorry, Tom. That was a bit more than one sentence."

Alexandra jumped in, "Greg, this product line is strategic to our growth and profitability. I'd recommend we seek immediate authorization of capital funds for the capacity increase. While we're developing the capital request and justification documents, we'll go through the forecast again and give you the demand that we believe we can achieve with various marketing programs." There was a brief period of silence before Tom offered a comment.

"This is what we call teamwork, and it's the first sign that you are making progress! Congratulations!"

"Thanks, Tom, but we still have a long way to go. David, how confident are you of the amount of money you put into the Issue Document?" Greg asked.

"It's a rough estimate, but we are confident that the $3.5 million is adequate since we've purchased similar equipment recently," David replied.

"I saw that number and was hoping I wouldn't have to carry that much bad news to Susan after our very first MBR, and only one family at that!"

"The new equipment won't be operational for nine months after we order it, but there are some additional steps we can take to help ease the capacity constraint sooner," David continued. "We'll work with the supplier of our current high speed lines to increase their output. They've been eager to make those upgrades, but we just haven't wanted to spend the money. The supplier wants to bid on any new equipment we buy in the future, so should give us a great price for the rate increase upgrades. We can be confident they'll meet their rate increase commitment to us; if they fail, they know they won't have a chance to get the contract on additional production lines. That's the second part of our recommendation, following the forecast reduction recommendation.

"The third part of the recommendation is to maintain maximum capacity on a day-to-day basis by hiring additional employees to keep the lines running around the clock. Making that move will result in a slight productivity decrease that Sara Miles estimates will cost us about one percent of margin on those products. The employees we add will also be trained on the new lines when installed, so we aren't looking at them as 'temporary help.' We estimate three months to get new people on board and trained. During that period, we'll ask the current employees to work more overtime than they would like. They're great people and will be happy to help us so long as they see we have a business need and a plan to get out of this situation. Operating at maximum capacity during this period of low seasonal demand allows us to build inventory and be better prepared late summer when shipments pick up again."

Zachary, VP of HR, spoke up. "David, your case is mathematically correct, but don't underestimate the effect on our employees. Almost everyone likes some overtime, or longer shifts, for a while. Then it either becomes an expected part of their income or they begin to resent it. They'd rather be with their families or taking care of personal business, especially in the summer months when their children are on summer break from school. Further, we know from experience that overworking people leads to lower and lower productivity, more mistakes and accidents, and threatens quality. It's a shortsighted solution which I can't support for any significant length of time."

A long silence followed before Tom intervened. "Zach, were you involved in the Integrated Reconciliation discussion?"

"No," said Zachary, "but I should have been involved."

Tom intervened again. "Look, it's early in the life of this process. A few glitches are inevitable. Let's chalk this one up to experience and learn from it. Now, about half an hour ago you had a plan that included lots of overtime. Since then we've learned that the Demand Plan will be reduced by 20 percent. We've just looked at the Demand Scenario, but I suggest you repeat Integrated Reconciliation before proceeding. Let's call it a 'do over.' Do a more thorough simulation of this family's supply and demand picture over the next 24 months with all the changes you've discussed, reassess the Rough-Cut Resource situation, and then restart this family review before we end this month's MBR. Involve all the executives and the other key representatives here and see what you learn. Greg, is there any possibility of extending this meeting to resolve this issue?" Greg thought for a moment.

"Thanks, Tom, that's a good idea. Bart, how soon do you think we can be ready to restart the family review?"

"Shouldn't take any longer than an hour, Greg," Bart replied.

Tom continued with his coaching intervention. "I want you to commit to each other that this is the first and last time you let this happen. Integrated Reconciliation requires all stakeholders affected by a decision to be involved, not just those raising the issues. Learn from this experience."

Greg called a one-hour MBR meeting recess. The Integrated Reconciliation team completed its simulation and alternative solution analysis in less than that time, and the MBR team immediately reconvened.

Bart began again. "Let's start over with the issue and Body Lotions family review. The situation is the same; we are still recommending additional capacity, but we have another option. I'll present the first option; Matt will present the second." First he described the standard engineering approach and schedule for adding the capacity. Other members of the Integrated Reconciliation team contributed to the discussion when Greg questioned elements of that proposal. Then David displayed the impact of that option on Supply Demand balance. The graphical presentation of the scenario allowed Greg to see instantly that the new capacity would miss the peak sales season. He began to make a point about the impact on customer service as well as on share and profitability when Matt interrupted him explaining that he had a second, recommended option to present.

"Greg, we also saw that this standard construction and start-up approach would miss the season and knew that was unacceptable. That discussion led to our recommended solution. There is some risk and expense involved, but I've studied the techniques at length and know of businesses that have successfully used them. I'll be talking with their Engineering Directors in the next few days to gather more information. Before I get into the details, however, let me ask you a question. Starting with a plot of land, how long does it take to build a modest one-floor house?"

"That's an easy question, since my nephew and his new wife just did it. It took them four months, but more likely it takes six to allow for weather interruptions and availability of framers, roofers, and so on."

"I agree that would be typical. But that same project could be completed in less than a week by using what is called a blitz-project approach. I've seen a film of such a house being built. In fact it took less than 24 hours to complete.

"Our second and recommended proposal is to use some of those techniques in our capacity increase project. We'll have to do much more precise project planning, and we'll incur some premium costs for labor, equipment, construction and freight, maybe as much as 10 percent over that $3.5 million we quoted earlier today. However, if we reach the decision within the next week, we can have the equipment on site within three months. I'll assign my best project manager who has a track record of delivering on time and budget. We'll have the additional equipment installed and commissioned by the first week of September, giving us about three weeks of contingency time before the real demand crunch. Zachary, you raised some very valid HR concerns an hour ago. Bring Greg up to speed on your latest thinking about those concerns."

"Greg, using a mix of our current people and new hires, we can have people ready to use the new equipment by the beginning of September. We'll begin their technical training on the new equipment while it's still in the manufacturer's facility. I called the most likely vendor's HR manager a few minutes ago to confirm that our people would be welcome in their factory to participate in the equipment shakedown and commissioning. He was delighted; said that approach will reduce the start up learning curve and make us an even more satisfied customer! Our people will be able to test run the equipment and practice some of those fast changeover and cleaning techniques in changing sizes and products before the equipment even gets into the plant. David will work with Sam Elliott at corporate to ensure we can accelerate the equipment contracts without creating any external auditor issues. Gordon will cover the financial aspects of the blitz proposal. Gordon, you're up."

Gordon Fast, senior Finance manager, began his comments. "Looking at the premium costs for the blitz approach, and comparing those with the financial impact of missing peak season sales again, it's a no-brainer. I rounded Matt's $350,000 incremental cost increase up to half a million for this comparison. Compared with the loss of $2 million in incremental profit, which doesn't even factor in the impact of continuing customer discontent, it really is a no-brainer. My recommendation is that we go with the blitz schedule."

Greg looked stunned and pleased. "I have to tell you that regardless of the decision we reach, I've dreamed of the day when you would perform as a real team. If you're all confident we can actually execute this plan, I'm in complete agreement. How long will it take to get the documents ready for me to take to Susan?"

Sara Miles looked a bit sheepish at this point and said, "Well actually Greg, we've nearly finished pulling together what you need. The documents will be ready for your signature by the first thing tomorrow. Gordon and his analysts will stay late if necessary to finalize the business case. You can meet with Susan any time after 8:00 A.M."

Greg commented aloud, more to himself than to the assembled team, "Roxanne told us we would be surprised with what we learned in the first cycle of meetings. She was right again!" He looked thoughtful as he spoke sincerely to the team, "I'm impressed! I know we've stumbled a bit in this first cycle, but we'll learn from those mistakes and not repeat them next month.

"One more thing," Greg continued. "I don't want to operate this close to capacity. Let's agree that we shouldn't be planning to use more than about 85 percent of our planned capacity for routine requirements so that can respond to changing customer and consumer demand and have capacity available for development, testing, and maintenance." Everyone nodded in agreement.

"I guess that's it for today." Nods around the room indicated agreement, but Bart spoke up.

"Hold on a minute, Greg. We can probably pass on the meeting critique today since we had quite a bit of it as we went through the meeting, but you need formally to approve the demand, production, and inventory plans for the Body Lotion family, and we need to review the decisions made. I would suggest that you ask each of your team members for their commitment to this Body Lotions Family plan. Let's just make sure there is no misunderstanding."

Greg went around the room starting with Sales and Marketing, then Operations and Supply Chain, Human Resources, Engineering, and last but not least, Finance. Each team member responded affirmatively. With that the meeting ended. Bart would publish the decisions from the meeting by the end of the day.

The next morning Greg called Susan to talk about the capital equipment funding request. After hearing the urgency in his voice and impact on the revenue, she squeezed him into her schedule. Greg began the meeting by showing Susan the demand, supply, and rough-cut charts from the ESOP tool. She came to quick agreement that they needed to act quickly. Deferring some other capital expenditures to free up the money might take some time, but she gave him the authority to buy the equipment immediately.

The blitz schedule project was underway. Greg had a real Leadership Team, no longer a dysfunctional committee.

After talking to Susan, Greg sat in his office staring at Amalgamated's well-manicured grounds, but looking at nothing in particular. He replayed the MBR meeting in his mind. He was impressed with the team's approach in analyzing and presenting the Body Lotions family, and surprised by how thoroughly and professionally the presenters made their case. He thought, "Perhaps this is what Tom meant when he told me that Integrated Business Management Process is a superb process for developing the next generation of executives. That's a major benefit that I hadn't even considered." He recognized that the learning was just beginning and wondered what they might discover in May.

He couldn't decide whether it was good to find lots of problems and get all of them on the table as opportunities, or hope for just a few problems. "That really is another 'no-brainer,'" he thought to himself. "The problems are hovering all around us just waiting to be discovered, regardless of what I hope for."

The teams developing the Planning Spine processes, business rules, and procedures were also making rapid progress. The planners on the team could at last see how their ERP system would help them maintain valid plans and monitor progress against those plans. The Data team set up and applied all the system security profiles and implemented a robust change control procedure. Monthly data integrity audits reflected rapid accuracy improvement in all data structures. The data team was confident of achieving 95 percent accuracy within the next two to three months, and at least 98 percent in the not too distant future. Interestingly, the number of data corrections and journal entries being made in Finance had fallen off significantly as a result of better data and more accurate and timely transactions on the shop floor. The Inventory Accuracy team included some shop floor people who began to understand and train others on the importance of transaction integrity and timeliness. Inventory accuracy was improving but was not yet good enough. The data team was preparing requests for more modern measuring equipment such as mass-flow meters and load-cells, and bar-coding printers and scanners. Additional training and behavior changes, the inexpensive part of their improvement plan, would get them to 95 percent quickly and yield even further improvement over the next few months.

The Inventory Accuracy team was confirming the theory that poor performance is attributable more to inadequate training, processes, equipment, and other system design issues than to the people working within that system. Those involved were energized and committed to achieving their goals. Control Group Cycle Counting accuracy results had already increased to over 96 percent. The team was nearly ready to implement routine cycle-counting procedures in all plants and warehouses.

Since the kick-off meeting in downtown Atlanta, Roxanne had been on site with the Customer Service Initiative team for several days every month along with Dan and Tom, each at first for as many as five days, but now fewer than that as the people continued to grow in their knowledge, confidence, and effectiveness. In addition, Tom and Dan visited with the headquarters and plant design teams periodically to coach them on emerging design team issues and questions. The ability of Roxanne's team to transfer its knowledge to Cosmetics Products was apparent, as evidenced by the rapidly improving results.

The Conference Room Pilot was successful, requiring only a few process and ERP system configuration modifications. The test demonstrated goodness of fit for the Planning Spine model and its rules. Several Leadership Team members dropped in from time to time to observe and provide support. The pilot team was satisfied with the results and proposed implementing the new business processes for Body Lotions. They would need to pay close attention to common ingredients and products that were also used in other product categories, but were determined to ensure that the live pilot would not disturb or be disturbed by other categories' activities. The Steering Committee agreed and targeted September 1 as the cutover date for all of Cosmetics Products, with the live pilot on Body Lotions beginning on July 1.

The live pilot required the most up-to-date forecasts and current orders. The Demand Team had been working on improving the forecasting process and resulting forecast accuracy by documenting Sales and Marketing assumptions for the Body Lotions family. Not surprisingly, the team would find themselves engaged in heated discussions about the forecast numbers until they began to develop a common understanding about demand drivers. For the first time, Sales and Marketing began an assumptions-based consensus of future volumes. They also learned that unconstrained demand did not mean inflated numbers intended to keep pressure on Manufacturing, but realistic estimates based on the market assumptions without regard to any internal supply constraints. As suggested by Dan, they focused first on developing the 24-month, month-by-month aggregate family forecast. A key assumption was that by year-end they would no longer be struggling with poor customer service and, as a result, sales would increase by 7 percent. This aggregate volume became their consensus forecast. They committed among themselves to maintain a high degree of accuracy with the aggregate forecast and found that they could use history as one element of the forecast going forward, and as a "sanity check" during the critical first three months where SKU forecasts were needed to drive the supply chain. For small volume products with volatile customer preferences, they agreed to forecast the volume for those products in aggregate by week through the first 13 weeks to ensure an adequate supply of bulk products. Then, driven preferably by point-of-sale data to determine current customer preferences, they would disaggregate the weekly aggregate forecasts into SKU forecasts. In turn, these SKU forecasts would be used to determine filling and packaging material, labor, and equipment requirements.

Manufacturing would now have to follow closely the weekly bulk product and SKU requirements driven from forecasts and orders. The new manufacturing measures would support cross-functional supply chain performance, rather than seek to optimize internal Manufacturing objectives such as utilization.

Developing the SKU mix percentage history was presenting a significant challenge since the SKU history file had not been adjusted for Cosmetics Products' own behaviors. Sales and Marketing had not kept track of backorders, promotion lifts, late shipments, and the amount of backorders more than six weeks old that were scrubbed from the files. As a result, statistical forecasts would be essentially meaningless for the next few months. Regardless of those challenges, it was becoming clear to the Demand Management and the pilot teams that long production cycles were a significant contributor to poor responsiveness and customer service.

The negative implications of utilization as a key measure and the resulting long manufacturing run operating strategy, originally established by Tony, were now clearer than ever to the Pilot Team. That team brought its concerns and recommendations about the long cycle times to the Implementation Team and later to the Steering Committee. They proposed an operating strategy change to more frequent, smaller batch runs both in bulk manufacturing and on the filling and packaging lines. Unless set-up times were reduced, however, this change would further constrain supply capability, an unacceptable trade-off for Body Lotions. Peter agreed to contact Samantha Williams, Effective Management's Agile, Lean, and Six Sigma expert to see if there might be some simple "Single Minute Exchange of Dies" (SMED) techniques that could, as quickly as possible, reduce changeover times. Bill Bates, Production Operations Team Leader agreed to host her visit to the plants. Angus Martin also agreed to put top priority on developing appropriate manufacturing performance measures to replace dependence on utilization as the key measure for Manufacturing.

During an earlier visit, Roxanne had explained the value of using Overall Equipment Effectiveness (OEE) to replace Utilization as a measure of machine-paced processes, although there could still be some value in tracking Utilization if a company chose to do so. She emphasized the point that OEE is a more holistic and meaningful measure of work location performance because it aggregates the combined effects of process availability, performance, and quality. She also advised them that the measure should not be put in place without clear definition and examples being incorporated into documented procedures and until appropriate education had been provided to the supply organization on its purpose and usefulness. She shared experiences of companies failing to properly prepare their organizations before building the measure into incentive plans, only to experience distortion of the results to the point that the measure was abandoned. In using OEE, she explained, Cosmetics Products would need to be clear that OEE should not be used as a Capacity Planning factor since 'Load Factor' is more reliable and effective for Capacity Planning, and it works for both machine-paced and labor-paced operations. During the Schedulers' education, Effective Management would explain and recommend the use of Load Factor for Capacity Planning and Overall Equipment Effectiveness to track machine-paced process performance.

Within four weeks, the demand forecast was ready for the live pilot; the planning model had simulated producing varying body lotion bulk manufacturing batch sizes and frequencies while optimizing equipment effectiveness. A new SMED task force under Samantha's and Angus's guidance had already identified some low-hanging fruit and reduced changeover times by 60 percent with very little spending. The SMED team of operators and mechanics was excited about its progress and anticipated they could eliminate 75 percent of the time wasted by ineffective set-ups, changeovers, and cleanings.

Internal cascade education and training built on a combination of Business Excellence concepts and newly documented Cosmetics Products procedures began immediately. Chris Deutsh, Systems Analyst, who had been working with the design teams since the beginning, reported that IT was ready to support the live pilot and had developed supporting plans for the full cutover on September 1. He took advantage of a break in production for major maintenance activities on the last two days of August to ensure integrity of data loading and to validate that the newly configured system would correctly support the business. This break would also allow Finance to run end-of-month reports to mark the end of the system's current configuration.

The live pilot was a complete success. During its first month, Planning produced plans that were executed flawlessly by Manufacturing and the rest of the supply chain. Customers received their body lotions orders in full as promised more than 90 percent of the time, even while other Cosmetics Products categories were still performing below 50 percent. The more customer-centric master supply plans, supported by Available-to-Promise (ATP) functionality, allowed realistic promises to be made. The Demand Management Team had difficulty implementing a Demand Control process in the ERP system to spot abnormal demands, but developed a simple procedure outside the system to be used temporarily. At order entry or using a system report for electronically processed orders, the clerks would identify orders accounting for more than 10 percent of the SKU available-to-promise quantity. Follow-up with the appropriate demand and sales representatives allowed them to catch and manage a few unexpectedly large (unforecast) orders.

At the end of the month, Customer Service representatives surveyed a number of customers and learned that the customers recognized the difference in service with this product category. The team was now confident that it could resolve the causes of the remaining missed or delayed shipments and exceed 95 percent on time and in full line fill by year-end. There were no impediments to moving forward across all products except for the needed capacity increase being addressed by the blitz schedule project.

The Steering Committee gave unanimous approval for the Planning and Control Milestone Team to roll out the planning model and the Planning Spine concepts across all Cosmetics Products categories.

After five months, all Capable Planning and Control performance measures were nearing required levels and still trending in the right directions. Finance reported that, at least for Body Lotions, ERP system generated data required little investigation or correction as a result of improved master data and transaction integrity. The benefit would also have been seen in other categories, except that master data in those categories had not yet been updated. Finance confirmed significant reduction of finished goods, work-in-process and component inventories. The monthly wall-to-wall physical counts had been replaced for all inventories, storage locations and categories by far more efficient and accurate process control cycle-counting procedures. Productivity was also increasing as a result of more effective schedules, fewer unplanned changeover events, and trust in ERP system numbers.

Less visible but equally successful was improving effectiveness of the Integrated Business Management process. The Leadership Team had become more effective with each process cycle, making better cross-functional decisions and providing more effective guidance to the business. Greg now had a mechanism to understand the business and to control Cosmetics Products top-down and bottom-up.

Success continued with the September 1 Planning and Control process cutover to all product categories. Within two months, performance measures in all categories replicated the upward trends seen in Body Lotions and were nearing 90 percent in nearly all measures by year-end. At the same time, the teams celebrated Body Lotions' measures all reaching Capable Planning and Control levels of performance (95+ percent).

The blitz project successfully commissioned the additional capacity in September, in time for the peak season. After a few trial runs for validation, the process was handed over to production, fit-for-use. The future was looking brighter for Cosmetics Products.

Greg was seeing tangible benefits in all areas as a result of the Customer Service Initiative and eagerly shared the progress with Susan during their monthly meetings. Customer service results continued inching upward even while finished product, raw material, and work-in-process inventories were being reduced across the Division. Finally, the right products were being delivered to the distribution centers and customers in full at the right time.

Every month, each milestone team conducted internal self-assessments of their progress against the Checklist. In January, Peter asked Roxanne and Tom to conduct an interim assessment to calibrate and confirm their internal assessments. The assessment conducted by Roxanne and her team confirmed that milestone teams were making good progress, but resulted in a few specific recommendations, as expected. The teams welcomed the external assessment and responded to Roxanne's and Tom's recommendations with increased focus and enthusiasm. By the end of May, just over a year after the first MBR meeting, Cosmetics Products Division had sustained Capable levels of performance for more than three months. The teams were ready for a Effective Management's final assessment.

Greg phoned Roxanne personally to check her availability. Given her frequent visits, Roxanne was aware that Cosmetics Products was complying with the milestones requirements, including the projected business benefits. She agreed to schedule herself and Dan to conduct the final assessment over three day period in the second week of July.

Greg, along with everyone else in Cosmetics Products, was confident yet tense as the assessment week finally arrived. His final message on the day before Roxanne and Dan arrived was to encourage assessment participants to be open and honest with the assessors. He reminded them that their success to date had been a result of their openness with each other and with Roxanne, and that now was not the time to change that behavior.

Assessment presentations and results reviews were well prepared and progressed smoothly over the three days. Roxanne and Dan were paying close attention to the behaviors and interactions among the people. Polished presentations could always be created to hide real issues; both Roxanne and Dan had experienced that in the past. They asked to visit several operating areas to confirm what was being presented. The visits confirmed the presented results; observed behaviors were as they'd hoped. Bottom-line financial benefits were far above what had been predicted. Roxanne and Dan conferred for an hour to compare notes and then provided a brief wrap up at the end of the final session. Roxanne announced that Cosmetics Products had successfully achieved both Capable-Level Milestones with flying colors. Greg was elated, but Dan advised them there were lots of areas for further improvement that they would highlight in the report to be provided within two weeks.

Greg started planning the official Milestone Award ceremony and the celebration. When the report arrived on July 22, Greg called his team, the Milestone Leaders, and the Design Team Leaders together for a meeting to see for themselves that they had officially and successfully passed the assessments and to thank them again for their work. He gave the report to David to follow up on the detailed assessment results and the list of improvement actions.

Greg phoned Roxanne while the team was still with him in the conference room to thank her for the formal certification and the report; and to invite her to an award ceremony and dinner, which they agreed to schedule on August 15.

Normally the Effective Management Coach presented Class A Milestone awards, but Roxanne wanted to acknowledge the strong support that Susan Barnett, CEO, provided for the work and for Greg through the period in which his business results were getting worse. In a phone call before the awards dinner, Roxanne arranged for Susan to present Greg with the awards. With the local newspapers there to record the event, Susan first presented Greg the Capable Planning and Control Award, which he in turn handed directly to David, thanking him publicly for kick-starting the Customer Service Initiative. Susan next presented Greg the Capable Integrated Business Management Award, which he hugged for a few seconds before handing it over to Alexandra. Greg then presented certificates to each member of the Milestone and Process Design Teams commemorating their significant contributions and accomplishments. Following a brief address by Greg, and a corporate acknowledgement from Susan, the dinner and celebration began.

Roxanne caught up with Greg and Susan before she left. "I just want to leave you with a few thoughts. Of course you're proud and satisfied with the justly deserved results and awards—a bit like the laurels the Greeks awarded to their top athletes—and that's appropriate. But beware of what might happen next. There's an old saying, 'If you're resting on your laurels, you're wearing them in the wrong place.' Don't let everyone become complacent; they need the next challenge, and then another one after that. I know without question that your division is now the best in Amalgamated, but remember the Total Quality Management adage, 'Being the best is the enemy of being better.' Just think about that. Meanwhile enjoy your accomplishments!"

Greg's accomplishments did not go unnoticed by either Amalgamated's Executive Team or Board of Directors. As Susan had predicted, they'd given Greg a long leash and financial support, then watched for signs of the recovery. As the recovery came, the Board realized the importance of their faith in Susan's and Greg's leadership at a time when Cosmetics Products was on a rapid slide to oblivion.

"Well, Greg, how's it feel now?" Penny said when Greg, smiling broadly, arrived home late that evening.

"Fantastic. It still hasn't sunk in—not the awards, but the progress we've made and the business results we've achieved. I've been invited to visit Blackstone to talk with Martin Bennett."

"Your old CEO, Greg? That sounds promising doesn't it?" said Penny.

Greg nodded. "They've started stocking most of our product lines again, and I'm interested in what he has in mind. You know, getting Blackstone's business back has been a personal achievement that means as much to me as any award. Guess I still admire Marty and appreciate his support. I'm really looking forward to seeing him again." He collapsed into his recliner and closed his eyes, contented.

"Greg," called Penny as she sat on the chair next to him.

"Yeah?"

"I haven't heard you say anything about what happens next. You're not bailing out now are you? I thought you'd have plans for the next round of improvements."

"Penny! Give me a break. You sound just like Roxanne."

"Well, Greg, if Roxanne told you the same thing … You know, when I was in business, I saw it happen all too often. Someone makes the big leap forward and then just rests on his laurels while others overtake him."

"Odd that you should mention the laurels while I'm sitting in my recliner."

"I don't know what you mean by that, but what I mentioned is called the 'hare and tortoise effect.' Don't believe that the world, or your Board for that matter, is going to admire this accomplishment until you retire. Why don't you do a mental SWOT analysis—headlines only. I'll pour you a glass of wine, but I'll only let you have it when you tell me your weaknesses and threats."

Greg groaned, but began mulling over what opportunities he needed to address next, with Penny as his very welcome and skilled resident coach.

17

CUSTOMER SATISFACTION

Greg, you once told me … that the status quo was the reason you were in such a mess. Sounds like you might be falling back into that 'status quo' trap.

Your job is to keep the ideas and improvements flowing and aligned with your vision.

And there's worse news. The order lead time for (the competitor's) products varies between two and four days for A-Items, compared with five to seven days for ours.

Greg arrived at work the next Monday morning with a list of ideas he'd written at 1:00 A.M. on a nightstand notepad next to his bed. He'd long since learned that until he wrote down the thoughts that woke him in the middle of the night, he couldn't get back to sleep. Now, sitting in his office and reviewing the list, he was uncertain what to do. In addition to his list, the teams had developed a long list of additional areas to address as they designed and implemented their new business processes. He knew he had to keep the momentum going while people were still engaged and willing to accept change. How to sort the critical few from the long list was the question. He picked up the phone and called Roxanne.

"Roxanne? It's Greg. Is it possible for you to give me a day of your time this week? I need to talk through my thoughts and get your advice about where we go next."

Roxanne took the call as she was leaving for the airport to visit another client "Hi, Greg, it's good to hear from you. I'm looking through my calendar . . . let me see. I'm leaving for Chicago today and will be back on Thursday evening. I could arrange to be there on Friday if that works for you."

Friday wasn't ideal: he had an 8:00 A.M. to 10:00 A.M. meeting that couldn't be rescheduled, but he could free up the rest of the day. They agreed, and Roxanne adjusted her schedule to meet Greg on Friday. She was pleased that Greg valued an ongoing relationship between Effective Management and Cosmetics Products, and even more pleased that her relationship with Greg was evolving from educator-coach to mentor-coach. Cosmetics Products would need additional education as they moved forward with additional milestones, but the ongoing work for Roxanne would be mentoring Greg and coaching those doing the work.

"Roxanne, I'm so glad you could make it on short notice." Greg greeted Roxanne as they settled down to start their discussions that Friday. "I can't begin to put into words what it's like now that we're routinely delivering to our customers 95 percent on time in full. Remember our first meeting? What a difference! And we've won back most of the customers we lost. We're doing well, but there is so much more to do that I'm concerned we'll overload our teams. I've made a list and ..." Roxanne stopped him.

"Greg, stop for a minute; you're beginning to worry me! You once told me, and I agreed, that the status quo was the reason you were in such a mess. Sounds like you might be falling back into that 'status quo trap.'" Greg was taken aback, not by Roxanne, but by his own words as Roxanne continued.

"Remember that delivering 95 percent on time in full means you're still lying to one customer in twenty. You're promising, but not delivering." Greg was shocked that he had forgotten that discussion. After a short pause, he replied.

"'Lying' is a tough word, don't you think? But I suppose that's how it must feel to each customer we let down. Come to think of it, that's exactly how I felt about Cosmetics Products when I was their customer. So, where do I go from here? That's my question for today. I have a long list of problems and possibilities."

"Before we get into that, Greg, just talk to me about the current general business situation for Cosmetics Products. Understanding your current competitive priorities will help us determine where to go next."

Greg spent the next ten minutes outlining the market situation from Cosmetics Products' perspective: where they had been in the past, where they were now, their competition's strengths and weaknesses and how their Customer Satisfaction Index (CSI) had improved from less than 20 percent two years ago to 55 percent during the most recent quarter.

It was the first time Greg had mentioned a CSI.

"Greg, you've never mentioned CSI before."

"We knew from the Checklist that we needed to track customer satisfaction, so I adapted the measure we put together when I was with Blackstone. We called it our Customer Satisfaction Index or CSI. In the past I didn't need a CSI score to tell me we had a big problem. But now with customer service over 95 percent, it can tell us a good deal. We solicit feedback using forms we send along with selected customer shipments, then we take the 10 percent or so that are returned to us and calculate a quarterly score."

"That sounds like an interesting approach, Greg. Using the same criteria, how does your index compare with your industry sector's performance? Also, what's the score for your top three competitors?" Greg was silent; Roxanne continued. "You need a better context and independent view for a useful Customer Satisfaction Index. It's one of the topics that I wanted to talk to you about today, so I'm glad you brought it up. Here's my question. What does benchmarking tell you about your performance relative to upper quartile companies in your industry?" Again Greg was silent for a time before responding.

"You know I came in really happy this morning, and now I'm rapidly getting depressed! Do you ever ask easy questions?"

"I don't necessarily enjoy doing this, but I've heard you say, 'the truth will set you free, but it hurts at first.' I am so pleased with the progress you've made to date. We had a well-deserved celebration of that progress, didn't we?" Greg nodded. "But now the best thing for me to do to help you is to get your eyes off the past success, get your eyes off the rearview mirror so to speak, and get you focused on the highway ahead. If you, as President, aren't looking ahead, you're not in control of your destiny." Greg stood up and paced slowly around his office for several minutes.

"You know, you and my wife make a great team, Roxanne. So, eyes forward from now on. Let me call Alexandra and David. They know you're here. I hope they can join us for this conversation."

Greg knew there was still much more to do, but now he wasn't as confident about the ideas on his list. His total focus over the past 15 months had been on customer service through achieving the two milestones; it had worked. Now he needed others' input.

He called his VP of Sales and Marketing. "Alexandra, I'm in my office with Roxanne; can you join us?" He then called David, his VP of Supply Chain and Manufacturing. David, like Alexandra, was anticipating Greg's call and was available. Greg was grateful that, since they'd nearly eliminated all firefighting, his executives actually had time in their days to manage the business and be available for meetings like this, rather than having to react to the latest crisis.

When they convened, Greg replayed his initial conversation with Roxanne. Their reaction was much like Greg's.

"Alexandra," said Greg, "Give us your perspective on our competitive position. How well are we doing in relation to our top three competitors in terms of customer service? And, do we have any customer satisfaction information on them?"

"Well, Greg, the stories I get back are anecdotal at best; no hard data. My people in the field tell me that we're now at least in the same ballpark as the competition, but we don't know exactly how we line up."

"Fair enough. What about our Customer Satisfaction Index [CSI]?"

"It's around 55 percent, up significantly, but I have no idea how the competition is performing on that basis."

"Thanks, Alexandra. Now, David. How does our quoted service lead time compare with that of the same top three competitors?" David held his hands palm up, meaning "no idea."

"Okay, Roxanne, over to you."

Roxanne reminded them that the *Class A Checklist*, a benchmark publication in itself, stresses that deep understanding of the marketplace and of the competition is essential for business survival. Using an internal customer satisfaction measure has been proven to be notoriously inaccurate and unhelpful since internal measures don't provide competitive context. She suggested they use an accredited external CSI organization to get a more objective and useful view of their performance.

Greg changed the subject and talked about his conversation with Penny, which had led him to conclude that Cosmetics Products Division needed to complete its journey to Class A Business Excellence.

"I browsed through all chapters and found lots of gaps, made a list of things too long to be accomplished at one time. I started to create some priorities, but quickly decided to call Roxanne for her guidance."

Roxanne jumped into the discussion. "Just as your competitive crisis of poor customer service led you to the Capable Integrated Business and Capable Planning and Control Milestones, you should now look at your competitive priorities to determine your next milestones. The path to Business Excellence is laid out in steps that address the most pressing competitive priority at the time so that you realize immediate business improvements. You took care of your customer service problem. With that problem behind you, we need to understand what now is keeping you awake at night. But first, I'm curious, David. How did the installation of that new process line go?"

"It's been a great success, Roxanne. We took into account what you advised us about planning for flexibility and agility rather than just volume. It took us some time to understand and appreciate what you meant, but the advice was very helpful. As a result of our blitz project and SMED progress, we can now make products economically in smaller quantities and more frequently. Additional capacity constraints have been identified. Some we're solving with additional capital equipment, but many others have been solved by key operating technicians taking over leadership of several SMED projects. They've converted much of the internal setup (machine idle) to external setup (machine running) with almost no expenditures. They've built those ideas into many other areas. When you sent Samantha Williams to facilitate our workshop, she encouraged us to learn about Total Productive Maintenance (TPM) and specifically introduced some basic concepts of autonomous maintenance and 5S, the basics of TPM's industrial housekeeping principles. We've actually started to learn more about those concepts. Although it's still in its early stages, we're seeing benefits from these initiatives, much of the gain coming from our employees' involvement. Exciting times on the shop floor! That, and the new process line, is how we're enjoying more capacity along with increased flexibility and agility."

"Greg, what David said is extremely important. It means you have a workforce that's not resisting ongoing change. A little fanning of the flames will keep everyone further improving the processes you designed and implemented during the Customer Service Initiative. Recall that I said, 'Job Number Two is all about improving Job Number One.' And with the encouragement and support of the Leadership Team, your staff will come up with lots of ideas they'll want to try. You're now beginning to move into a culture of true Integrated Business Management. You're seeing how everything you do is interdependent. Successful implementation of new ideas will lead to more new ideas. Your job is to keep the ideas and improvements flowing and aligned with your vision.

"I can almost guarantee that, with the education, training, and the successes you've had, the manufacturing and supply chain people will want to do more. You need to encourage and support that kind of thinking, enthusiasm, and reasonable risk taking. Start thinking of velocity ratio as the universal test for your priority setting. Now that you're in control of the business, if a project increases velocity, chances are it's the right thing to do. If it reduces velocity, it is absolutely the wrong thing to do. Of course, there may be regulatory changes imposed on you that reduce velocity, and you'll do those—just try to be smart in the way you implement them."

"Both in planning and operations, I can see this happening already," said David. "They're working together to reduce lead times and lot sizes. In fact, while you were here I wanted to mention a suggestion from Janice Hackworth, our Supply Planning Manager, that we invest in a finite scheduler to help load the lines more effectively. What do you think?"

"Good for Janice," said Roxanne. "Given the number of different products you have and the alternate routings you can use to produce them, a finite scheduler could help. If you're going to invest, however, I suggest you consider an advanced planner, optimizer, and scheduler. We call it an 'APOS' system for short." Greg spoke up at this point.

"What is it? I've heard some people use that acronym."

"As a first benefit, the advanced planner, optimizer, and scheduler can help level the load in the factory to optimize productivity while still meeting all customer requirements. That's only a small part of its overall capabilities, such as modeling, but that's where I suggest you start. As you continue on the journey to full Class A Business Excellence, you'll absolutely need such a system to sit alongside your ERP system and its data warehouse. Here's a model of what I'm talking about." She handed Greg a double-sided card from her case [Figures 17.1 and 17.2].

"You can see how far you've come already; now you're recognizing the need to add more planning support. Next, you'll need Knowledge Management

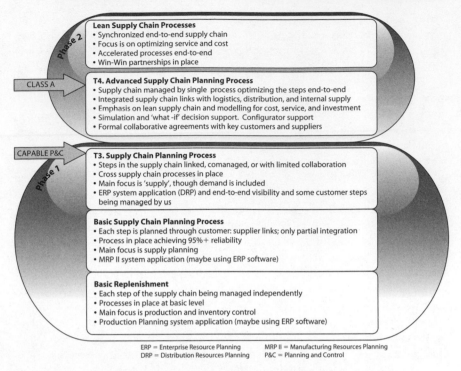

Phase 2

Lean Supply Chain Processes
- Synchronized end-to-end supply chain
- Focus is on optimizing service and cost
- Accelerated processes end-to-end
- Win-Win partnerships in place

CLASS A →

T4. Advanced Supply Chain Planning Process
- Supply chain managed by single process optimizing the steps end-to-end
- Integrated supply chain links with logistics, distribution, and internal supply
- Emphasis on lean supply chain and modelling for cost, service, and investment
- Simulation and 'what -if' decision support. Configurator support
- Formal collaborative agreements with key customers and suppliers

CAPABLE P&C

Phase 1

T3. Supply Chain Planning Process
- Steps in the supply chain linked, comanaged, or with limited collaboration
- Cross supply chain processes in place
- Main focus is 'supply', though demand is included
- ERP system application (DRP) and end-to-end visibility and some customer steps being managed by us

Basic Supply Chain Planning Process
- Each step is planned through customer: supplier links; only partial integration
- Process in place achieving 95%+ reliability
- Main focus is supply planning
- MRP II system application (maybe using ERP software)

Basic Replenishment
- Each step of the supply chain being managed independently
- Processes in place at basic level
- Main focus is production and inventory control
- Production Planning system application (maybe using ERP software)

ERP = Enterprise Resource Planning   MRP II = Manufacturing Resources Planning
DRP = Distribution Resources Planning   P&C = Planning and Control

Figure 17.1   Maturity Journey: Managing the Supply Chain
Source: Oliver Wight. Copyright Oliver Wight International, Inc. Used with permission.

Systems, most of those shown in the model, to support you on the rest of the journey. These new systems, properly implemented, support significant increases in velocity."

David replied. "I can see that Roxanne, and thanks. How do I get my supply chain business improvement team started in that direction?"

"The best way is to send them to the public course we offer on that subject. Just one caveat. Before you can fully exploit these more advanced capabilities, you'll need very high performance from your supply chain processes. That means you'll need to eliminate much of the supply chain performance variability. Now that you're at the Capable level, you can utilize your Six Sigma Black and Green Belts to help you in that effort. I suggest that you contact Samantha Williams again to help you as well. She teaches that course for us and already knows many of your people who will be involved.

"And now, a question for you, Alexandra. Tell me how your new product introductions are going and what you've done to control your portfolio. I recall that was a major problem for you when we started the Customer Service Initiative."

"New product introductions are not as bad as they were, but are still an issue. With David's new flexible process line, we're less reliant on SKU forecasts, and

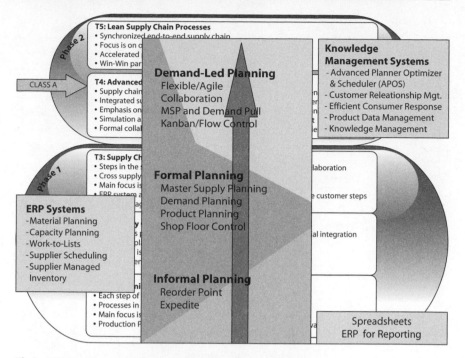

T5: Lean Supply Chain Processes
- Synchronized end-to-end supply chain
- Focus is on
- Accelerated
- Win-Win par

Phase 2

CLASS A

T4: Advanced
- Supply chain
- Integrated s
- Emphasis on
- Simulation a
- Formal colla

Demand-Led Planning
Flexible/Agile
Collaboration
MSP and Demand Pull
Kanban/Flow Control

Knowledge Management Systems
- Advanced Planner Optimizer & Scheduler (APOS)
- Customer Releationship Mgt.
- Efficient Consumer Response
- Product Data Management
- Knowledge Management

T3: Supply Ch
- Steps in the
- Cross supply
- Main focus is
- ERP system a

Phase 1

Formal Planning
Master Supply Planning
Demand Planning
Product Planning
Shop Floor Control

laboration

customer steps

al integration

ERP Systems
- Material Planning
- Capacity Planning
- Work-to-Lists
- Supplier Scheduling
- Supplier Managed Inventory

Informal Planning
Reorder Point
Expedite

- Each step of
- Processes in
- Main focus is
- Production

Spreadsheets
ERP for Reporting

Figure 17.2   Maturity Journey: Planning System Support
Source: Oliver Wight. Copyright Oliver Wight International, Inc. Used with permission.

we've gotten much better forecasting bulk requirements. We're disaggregating the bulk forecasts as required using the latest SKU mix factors. While manufacturing has really improved their responsiveness and reliability, the development process is still out of control. We missed the best launch window for two out of the last three product introductions. It wasn't a total disaster, but we missed sales opportunities. With one of the products, instead of beating the competition we came in after their launch, which means a fairly significant profit loss over the life-cycle of that product.

"As for the portfolio, we track the number of products we market and sell, but don't have any overt program to rationalize products. Field Sales tell us that every SKU is important to their ability to sell an entire line of products and represents a source of revenue. They simply won't tolerate deleting anything from the portfolio. Manufacturing would certainly like for us to trim the portfolio's size, but we don't have a good way of determining what to cut, beyond a profitability estimate. But that's where we get back into the argument that certain low-profit products help Field Sales get their foot in the customers' doors. That's about it. By the way, we've also been thinking about more system support, starting with a Customer Relationship Management system."

Roxanne responded: "Thanks, David and Alexandra. You're right to keep things moving. Remember to keep the Leadership Team involved so that your efforts remain strategic. There are all kinds of exciting opportunities available to you, but much of it may be strategically irrelevant or too advanced for Cosmetics Products at your stage of development. Now back to today's agenda. The situation is as I suspected. The weak area seems to be Product Management. Please understand I'm not pointing fingers. It is what it is. Greg, we had this conversation, was it eighteen months ago? At that time, we recognized that Product Management was not understood and that the development people were not even using their own development processes effectively.

"Alexandra, do you have any sense of how often your top three competitors miss their introductions?"

"That's a difficult one. As you know, I visited with Marty at Blackstone last week about our companies' relationship. Although he didn't say this directly, there was an underlying message that our competitors rarely miss a launch date and that he was expecting that same performance from us."

"OK, take that as a benchmark. Greg, you talked about shredding that drawer full of vision, mission, and strategy statements. How much time have you and your executive team spent redefining your vision, mission, and strategic plan given where you are today?"

"That one's from left field, Roxanne. As you know, we've been totally focused on the two milestones. We did a quick review and update to provide general direction for the Customer Service Initiative, but we didn't give the vision, mission, and strategic plan the full attention they deserve. But wait a minute; I see where this is leading. What I'm thinking, and I need input from David and Alexandra, is that our next competitive priorities should be Managing Products and Services, and Managing the Strategic Planning Process, if I've remembered the chapter titles properly."

Alexandra spoke first. "Every day I come in I look at a poster I framed. It says, 'If you don't know where you're going, any road will do.' We're not quite that bad, but I do understand that having a clearly defined strategic direction supported by appropriate tactics would improve our performance. And I certainly agree that improving our product management processes and skills would significantly increase credibility with our customers and increase sales."

David added, "I have to agree with what Alexandra said, and would add that we'd see about a 5 percent capacity increase if we could get more reliable product development dates."

Greg nodded his head. "Exactly my view also. So, Roxanne, we'll check with the other Leadership Team members, but I believe we'll be agreed on strategic planning and product management as our next areas of competitive priority. And I'll get the team together to begin a serious review and revitalization of our vision and mission statements. Glad you reminded me of that."

"Thanks for your perspective, Greg" said Roxanne. "You've confirmed for me what I thought were your next competitive priorities. Let me help you with defining more realistically what I see as your next steps. Please understand that you and your team must make the decision on the next milestones. I'm just providing some coaching.

"But I want to recommend a pairing of milestones, rather than a chapter focus. The first is obvious, Capable Product Management, as you said. That will give you the processes and control you need to improve your portfolio management, including adding and removing products. Focusing only on Chapter 5, Managing Products and Services, as you suggested initially, Greg, wouldn't be effective since that would leave out important dependencies and requirements from the other Checklist chapters.

"The second milestone I'm recommending is Foundation Enabling for Sustainable Improvement [see Figure 6.7]."

Greg interrupted. "Sorry, Roxanne. How does that relate to my strategic planning concerns?"

"Greg, it all comes back to integration and sustainability. Working only on the strategic planning chapter in isolation would miss important dependencies and supporting requirements, just as I pointed out with the Capable Product Management milestone. Foundation Enabling for Sustainable Improvement includes those elements of strategic planning that you need today, and also covers critical dependencies such as the people culture. These two milestones, in my judgment, will raise your customer satisfaction significantly."

That comment resonated with Greg. "This should be our Customer Satisfaction Initiative—I like that!"

David interrupted, "Are we talking about another fifteen months, Roxanne, with all those resources we needed for the Customer Service Initiative? I don't know if we can handle that workload given the increased production volumes we're seeing."

"I've considered that as well. Let's take a look at the scope of the Foundation Enabling Milestone." She handed out printed reports from the *e*List software. As you can see, Foundation Enabling pulls together primarily elements from Chapters 1, 2, and 3; that's Managing the Strategic Planning Process, Managing and Leading People, and Driving Business Improvement, and includes important linkages to the other chapters. The good news is that you've already covered about 25 percent of what's required when you completed the previous milestones. All milestones build incrementally. You don't start from scratch. This Foundation Enabling Milestone mostly involves your Leadership Team, along with Human Resources and your business improvement people, who didn't have a great deal of involvement with the earlier milestones. Foundation Enabling will provide them the opportunity to build a foundation for future company initiatives. That's why we call it a foundation milestone. As it happens, the work on this milestone also provides a substantial contribution, about 50 percent, to the Capable Product Management Milestone. With a couple of cross-team members, the Product Management Team will find it can focus on developing those product management processes and skills Alexandra referred to. Together, these two milestones and ongoing improvement of what you've already accomplished will also take you three-quarters of the way to completing the Advanced Integrated Business Management Milestone. That's the incremental nature of these milestones. In terms of time to complete these two milestones, I would estimate twelve months. Now a final reminder, everything you work on is integrated, so make sure you have strong cross-functional linkages within and across the teams.

"And don't forget to study your competition and your industry to learn how they stack up on these processes and measures. You need to get serious about competitor analysis and benchmarking, and target consistently to be in the upper quartile of competitors in your industry.

As the meeting drew to a close, Greg knew he needed to involve the rest of his Leadership Team. In particular, he wanted to look at the milestones in more detail with Zachary and Gabriella.

At home that evening, Greg reviewed his day with Penny. By listening and asking a few pointed questions, she helped him develop his thoughts into a firm plan of action.

Greg arranged the next Leadership Team meeting to be extended by two hours to introduce his ideas and proposed action plans for moving forward. Greg needed his team's input to reach a decision. After considerable discussion, they concluded that they needed to get on with the Customer Satisfaction Initiative with its Capable Product Management and Foundation Enabling milestones, as Roxanne had suggested. Their objective was to maintain their improvement momentum toward upper quartile performance and prevent their competitors from setting the Cosmetics Products agenda.

Sara Miles, VP Finance, told them that although it sounded financially justifiable to her, she needed a little time to examine the financial justification. David took joint responsibility with Sara for developing the business case. He was confident, because of the foundation already established, that the investment would be much less than with the Customer Service Initiative. Greg agreed to put the topic on their Leadership Team staff meeting agenda in three weeks and offered his team Roxanne's coaching and mentoring services in the meantime. He knew that they had to return to the Proven Path that served them well during their first initiative [see Figure 10.3]. His team took advantage of the offer and spent several days with Roxanne developing the Proven Path Leadership phase elements and critiquing their ideas and plans for moving ahead. Day by day, support for the Customer Satisfaction Initiative was growing throughout Cosmetics Products, and also with Susan, Amalgamated's CEO, through Greg's frequent progress reports.

With great anticipation Greg joined his Leadership Team three weeks later for his scheduled staff meeting. Alexandra had requested to lead the first agenda item, although vague about the topic. She brought Sharon with her for the presentation.

"Sorry for being so demanding about being first, but Sharon and I have some important and relevant news. These are preliminary findings; we'll need another month to confirm what we are learning. Nevertheless, we've managed to find out a bit more about our competitors' customer service performance. First, we've learned that customer service provided by two of our key competitors rarely falls below 98 percent as measured by percent of order-line items delivered On-Time-in-Full to first promise [OTIF-P]. And we believe that for the past several weeks running, they've been very near 100 percent."

"That's not so far from 95 percent, is it?" asked Greg.

"I wish," replied Alexandra. "The scaling between customer service 50 percent and customer service 100 percent is exponential, not linear. They must be doing some things better than us."

The executive team was stunned by the news. They had convinced themselves that their 95 percent performance to first promise was a benchmark for their industry.

"And there's worse news. The order lead time for their products varies between two and four days for A-Items, compared with five to seven days for ours. In combination, that's not a pretty picture. But cap that news off with the news that those competitors rarely miss a promised new product launch date."

"Now I'm confused. If that's the case, why have our sales been increasing?" asked Sara.

"First, we have our products on the shelves much more often than in the past so that consumers can find them. On top of that, our customers tell us that their customers—the consumers—like our products, and our approach to promotions and trade support. They also tell us that our brand name and reputation for good value are keeping us in the game." There was a depressing silence before Greg broke in.

"I'm glad you gave us this information, Alexandra. We could have basked in our recent successes, but you've provided even more incentive to get us moving again."

As David expected, the business case for the new initiative was solid and had Sara's complete support. With that news, the Leadership Team made two decisions: they would launch the Customer Satisfaction Initiative, and they also committed to complete the entire journey to Class A Business Excellence with its required upper quartile performance. Greg would once again be the Initiative Champion and Peter Bernard, the Initiative Coordinator. Sharon Rogers, Director of Marketing and Product Coordinator, was assigned to the role of Capable Product Management Milestone leader, with Alexandra as the Milestone Champion. Gabriella Jemison, VP of Quality and Regulatory, Heath, Safety, and the Environment would be Champion for the Foundation Enabling for Sustainable Improvement Milestone, with Peter Bernard again doing double duty as the Milestone Leader.

Over the next four weeks, milestone and process design teams were commissioned, and initiative and design team plans were developed and approved. The Leadership Team completed the Leadership Phase and officially launched the Customer Satisfaction Initiative. Launching this initiative was less of a challenge than the first because of the extensive education and learning that occurred during the Customer Service Initiative. The Cosmetics Products organization now had a common language and level of Business Excellence understanding that was accelerating their progress.

True to his word, while the two new milestones proceeded in parallel, Greg arranged for a full week off-site strategy workshop for his team. Greg asked Peter Bertrand to attend this important event, which would be facilitated by Roxanne and Tom. Greg's objective was to develop the clearest and most relevant Cosmetics Products vision, mission, and strategy statements in the history of their business. Objectives for the week would also include developing at least a rough draft of their customer-focused strategic business objectives and a 10-year strategic plan.

Roxanne suggested some simple definitions to help their communications and get the team started:

A Vision Statement should define the desires of the CEO of that business. It must be attractive, credible, and challenging for the organization. It must be brief, inspiring and memorable. The desirability of this future state as described by the Vision needs to engage hearts and minds at all levels. It provides a sense of purpose to the organization, poses a significant yet attainable challenge, and draws everyone and every activity into the pursuit of that challenge. By definition, a vision statement is somewhat imprecise. It is a living statement that can be enhanced but should not require alteration often. An organization is directionless without a vision to guide its management and workforce in day-to-day decision making.

It is a guiding light against which an organization can test its strategies and build its future.

A Mission Statement outlines how the organization intends to progress from the current state to the future state defined by the Vision; it embraces every part of the company, individually and collectively, within an achievable time frame. More actionable and precise than the vision statement, it provides the framework for formulating the business strategy, which in turn leads to broad, actionable, and synergistic multiyear action programs and initiatives in all functional areas.

In essence, the mission statement provides top management the opportunity to reflect seriously on the current state of the business, and to reach consensus on the desired changes to lead the business into the desired future.

"Don't confuse vision and mission. That's a common mistake," Roxanne added. "Vision is a conceptually created picture of the future; Mission relates to today and how you begin moving toward that stated future."

Company Values establish the foundation for behaviors and ethics with respect to all stakeholders (society, shareholders, customers, and employees). Values and strategy must be aligned and supportive, and stated values must be authentic, meaning that they can be espoused by the people in the organization. They must be lived by all functions and all levels of the organization. All people must know them, understand them, and know there are consequences for failing to live them.

Company Strategy determines and reveals more specific direction in terms of long-term objectives, action programs, and resource allocation priorities. It is a long-term plan to achieve sustainable advantage by addressing appropriately the opportunities and threats of the company's environment. It is an actionable expression of the strategic intent of the company to carry out its mission and achieve its vision.

Guiding Principles are enabling statements that encourage behaviors necessary to foster the positive culture and environment required for high performance, self-directed teams, and individual empowerment at all levels of the organization. Some companies combine Company Values and Guiding Principles.

Strategic Business Objectives, typically four to six key business objectives, driven by competitive priorities, are designed to execute the business strategy while meeting or exceeding shareholder and customer needs. These strategic objectives are most often financial or market focused. They are defined by the Leadership Team, and then formalized, documented, and communicated broadly throughout the organization. Each strategic business objective is assigned an executive sponsor accountable for ensuring the objective is achieved within the stated time frame.

Critical Success Factors are broad, time-phased, measurable factors that, if achieved, guarantee the successful achievement of the strategic business objective to which they are related. Typically, three to four critical success factors per strategic business objective are assigned to specific individuals.

The Business Plan is a two- to three-year plan derived from and designed to support the company's five- to ten-year strategic plan. From the business plan, the company creates its annual budgets, which define at what pace the company will achieve its strategic plan.

The Annual Budget/Operating Plan is the traditional twelve-month plan representing the company's expectations for its fiscal year. Typically developed through a budgeting process prior to the beginning of the fiscal year, the budget is a fixed view used to establish company and component business unit financial performance objectives. The budget normally represents the first twelve months of the two- to three-year business plan. The budgeting process is greatly simplified, streamlined, and accelerated in companies that benefit from a mature Integrated Business Management process.

A Key Performance Indicator (KPI) is a measure accepted to be of extreme importance to the company in achieving its critical success factors, strategic objectives, budgets, and business plans. If not correctly implemented, measured, tracked, and managed, performance will fall short and likely result in a decrease in customer satisfaction, employee morale, and profitability.

"You know," exclaimed Greg. "I've been in executive teams for years and used many of these terms without really examining their meanings."

"It really is helpful to see this list. Having alignment on the meaning of these terms could have saved me lots of arguments in the past." David added. "Specifically, I've been confusing Vision and Mission. We should rewrite these descriptions using familiar Cosmetics Products terminology, but this gives us a great start." They agreed to devote a portion of their ongoing team meetings to further develop the definitions.

Roxanne was glad she started the session with those definitions. Building on the them, she began to lead the team through the strategic planning workshop, a key element of accomplishing the enabling milestone. Over the next few months, the Leadership Team, as a milestone subteam, would focus on addressing, designing, and documenting milestone elements from the strategic planning chapter. Other subteams would ensure all the other enabling milestone elements across the Checklist chapters were covered. Peter would ensure integration and cross-fertilization of ideas and alignment on decisions that affected both teams.

The Leadership Team made significant progress during the workshop and agreed to meet two afternoons each week over the next few months to refine the definitions, to complete their first ten-year strategic plan, and to finalize the more detailed and time-structured three-year business plan. The strategic plan predicted and supported significant growth. Building on early signs of rapid growth, Cosmetics Products strategy had them becoming market leader in their chosen markets. Their aggregate strategic plans were built into their Enterprise Sales and Operations Planning Tool as product family plans (product category plans in the case of Cosmetics Products) so that through the monthly Integrated Business Management process, they could keep the business "on strategy."

Zachary led a subteam to develop the Managing and Leading People chapter requirements of the Foundation Enabling Milestone while Gabriella led a subteam focused on the Driving Business Improvement requirements of the milestone. For both Zachary and Gabriella, this was the first time they had really come out of their technical specialist roles to make broader contributions to improving entire business. They found the opportunity energizing, a change noticed by many others. Peter remained in close touch with all the teams to ensure seamless integration of the developing business processes.

The Product Management Milestone team requested refresher education on the role and importance of product management in driving business success. Sharon Rogers, Marketing Director and Product Coordinator, attended the education session and all workshops to demonstrate her leadership and support of the needed changes. Prior to the Customer Service Initiative, Product Management had meant managing new product development and introductions. Alexandra and Sharon recognized the limited scope of that definition and the need for creative capabilities suited to a more contemporary definition of product management [Figure 17.3].

- Product Management is founded on:
  - Meeting Marketing Strategic Business Objectives through:
    - A deep understanding of the marketplace
    - Creating and sustaining a winning portfolio
    - Determining the right product/service to offer
    - Creating, maintaining, and implementing product plans that describe how products will be created, changed, controlled, and supported
    - Ensuring it all happens
  - Winning in the marketplace

Business and Marketing Strategy Drive Product Management

Figure 17.3   Product Management
Source: Oliver Wight. Copyright Oliver Wight International, Inc. Used with permission.

Alexandra and Sharon also saw advantage to them of changing the organization relationships [Figure 17.4], and completed the necessary product management organization and process changes within a few months. They now had in place an executive business filter that had already improved the new product proposal selection and prioritization process. This led to their developing a New Product Master Plan, a single list of approved projects that were budgeted and resourced.

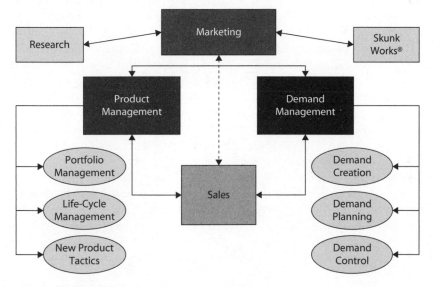

Figure 17.4   Typical Organizational Structure
Source: Oliver Wight. Copyright Oliver Wight International, Inc. Used with permission.

Product development processes also needed attention in support of the new Initiative. Using his extensive project management experience and skills, Peter contributed to process improvements and helped streamline, standardize and strengthen product development and launch processes. Cosmetics Products had developed and documented a product development and launch Stage and Gate process, based on Bob Cooper's work, long ago. However, the launch process, although complete and well developed, was never fully implemented. Peter observed that Gates were defined but were, in effect, always open instead of locked. There were no documented Gate criteria templates, and the wrong people were making Gate decisions. He also observed that Stages were not supported by stage planning templates; each project leader was creating a unique input-Gantt for each project. There was no consistency between projects, and the input-Gantt charts were not managed. Not surprisingly, it was impossible to manage resource allocation properly, which had adverse consequences on the entire supply chain. Emergency requests for test batch production were frequent and resulted in either product launch delays or customer service issues caused by unplanned changeovers to accommodate the requests. The team concluded that poor project and resource planning accounted for most of the delayed introductions.

With occasional coaching from Tom, Peter introduced Cosmetics Products to the rigors of a formally implemented Stage and Gate process. He reminded everyone that, without standardization, there could be no control; and without control, there could be no improvement [see Figure 7.1]. There was the usual pushback from those who saw a formal process as creativity limiting. The team realized that the current procedures unnecessarily required all new products to follow the same path. They developed appropriate multiple paths based on development complexity of the new product. Most development personnel supported this launch model improvement. Those who still objected to the "stifling of their creativity," as they put it, were told privately that Cosmetics Products could no longer afford the negative consequences of their unbridled creativity.

The team introduced a new measure, called "Milestone Adherence," to track the percentage of planned milestones actually achieved each month. More than anything else, this new measure would drive the success of the new launch model.

The appointed product managers attended education, training, and workshops to understand their new roles and to develop the formal processes to be followed. Most were appreciative of the trust and responsibility they were being given to help design the future of the brands and markets they managed.

In parallel with this activity, Sharon and Charlie were developing new working relationships with Sales and reinforcing the links to Managing Demand.

It was then time to provide necessary education on portfolio and product life-cycle management concepts as well as to develop a formal promotions management process. To develop the supporting business processes, the team leaned heavily on Tom for coaching. It was during this period that the new relationships between Product Management and Sales were most severely tested. On several occasions, Alexandra was called in to referee heated discussions between the groups, but through Sharon's determination to balance business needs with perceived, but not proven, customer needs for old, low-volume and low-margin products, the factions came to agreement. Within nine months the number of SKUs had been reduced by 40 percent, with no significant impact on customer satisfaction.

Manufacturing costs improved as the number of items decreased, and margins were further increased as lower margin products were deleted from the catalog. Tom observed that this was usually the case, although there are a few occasions when a low-margin product is actually justified to complete a product line for a key customer, or to meet the needs of a key customer request for a unique product or packaging presentation. Alexandra didn't want to close the door on this opportunity but knew that Cosmetics Products couldn't maintain an inventory or routinely manufacture these one-off items. They referred to these products as "specials"—special products, special packs, or special presentations. Specials were quoted with longer lead times and higher prices to offset the higher costs and still meet targeted profit margins. With the improved levels of customer service, Cosmetics Products customers were happy with the flexibility and responsiveness offered.

Alexandra's initiative to launch a quarterly Customer Satisfaction Survey process with a recognized Customer Satisfaction Index authority was paying dividends. She received the first report, which showed that, for their industry, a CSI Index of 75 percent to 85 percent was normal. Cosmetics Products, however, received a low score of 58 percent. There was continuing good news, however, in that consumers continued to rate the quality and value of their products higher, at nearly 75 percent satisfaction. Their customer service, still not competitive enough, drove their overall poor showing. Copies of the detailed report were distributed to all product managers to help them appreciate the challenges ahead.

In March, after 10 months of effort on the Customer Satisfaction Initiative, David asked Roxanne for a preassessment to check progress and identify any remaining gaps. Roxanne arranged for Tom to help her with the preassessment, confident of Cosmetics Products readiness because of her team's ongoing coaching involvement. She reminded David that she would be looking hard for signs of improved customer satisfaction, the focus of this second initiative, and expected to hear good news on that front.

She was not disappointed. Cosmetics Products had demonstrated only two consecutive months of performance at the required level for a few measures, but the trends were all positive; and March month-to-date results were all above minimum requirements. Preassessment gaps identified by Roxanne and Tom were assigned to the teams, and the Steering Committee agreed to a late April final assessment date for the Consumer Satisfaction Initiative milestones. Roxanne would assess all aspects of all four milestones to date to confirm that improvement activities were delivering continuous improvement to the bottom line. She anticipated that scores for the Customer Service Initiative elements would have climbed from 3.0 and 3.5 to as high as 4.0 in many cases.

Following the assessment, Roxanne and her Effective Management assessment team complimented Cosmetics Products on one of the best assessments they had conducted. The milestone teams had been well organized, open, and honest, and had produced excellent documentation, evidence, and business results. David acknowledged that some of the high scores were the result of the initiative, creativity, and persistence of the people on the business process teams. Roxanne had seen for herself that the team members were obviously proud of the work they shared during the assessment and were beginning to demonstrate characteristics of self-directed, high-performance teams. They understood the vision, mission, values, and strategic objectives and didn't need to wait for managers to tell them what and how to improve. The bottom line benefits were significant. Customer satisfaction as measured by the outside agency was now up to 75 percent; market share had grown six points, and profit margins had improved beyond their expectations.

Roxanne cornered Greg during the award celebration held in the headquarters auditorium two weeks after the assessment.

"So what's next, Greg?"

"Roxanne, I've learned my lesson about not sitting on my laurels! First item on our Leadership Team agenda in two weeks is determining our latest competitive priority, and our next initiative and milestones. Actually, that agenda item will follow a review of any safety and people issues, which now always headline our meetings. Recognizing the strategic importance of our people is one of the key values we established recently."

At home that evening, Penny listened as Greg recounted the events leading up to certification of two more milestones and his thinking about what was next. This time the celebration continued; Penny had made a reservation for a quiet celebration over dinner in their favorite local restaurant.

Work was again fun for Greg, but he knew there was much more to do. After all, his Customer Satisfaction Index left another 25 percent as room for improvement!

18

COMPETITIVE
PRESSURE

We have some good news and some bad news.

They aren't going to roll over just because we're getting better, are they?

So that there was no question about the Customer Satisfaction Initiative being the end of their quest for excellence, Greg and his Leadership Team used the company newsletter, bulletin boards, and every team meeting to communicate their expectations that continued process and performance improvement was essential for sustaining their recent success.

Financial performance continued to improve, making the Cosmetics Products division the best performing division on a volume-adjusted basis. Susan, the CEO, and several of her Executive Team members, including Andrew Jones, the CFO, visited with Greg's Leadership Team and toured both factories to satisfy themselves that the improved results were real and sustainable. Feedback from these visits was positive and resulted in Cosmetics Products being named Amalgamated's 'Business of the Year'. Accompanying the award was a cash bonus shared among all Cosmetics Products employees. Susan, through the Board of Directors, gave Greg a significant salary increase and stock option grant. Susan viewed Greg as Amalgamated's most valuable player for the future; she didn't want to lose him to another company. She planned to expand the work done in Cosmetics Products to the other divisions, with Greg's help.

Greg asked Sara Miles, VP of Finance, and Alexandra Templeton, VP of Sales and Marketing, to analyze the current and projected market situation, including credible worst-case scenarios. Over the following month, they utilized all publicly available information and the latest information from their benchmarking service to explore what was happening with their customers and competitors.

Alexandra presented their findings and conclusions to Greg's Leadership Team. "We have some good news and some bad news. The good news is that our market share is still growing, but the growth is slowing. Our benchmarking service spoke about potentially big changes coming from one of our leading competitors, Quintessential Beauty Care (QBC). It's obvious that they've made progress similar to ours over the past few years. That's to be expected from a strong competitor; they aren't going to roll over just because we're getting better, are they? They've recently launched several new product lines targeted at the eighteen- to twenty-five-year age group, and those products are selling well. Our detailed analysis of the data we gathered from customers and focus groups and from independent market research tell us that QBC is rapidly eroding our competitive advantage with this age group. Another key competitor, Classic Cosmetics, is pricing its products aggressively, ostensibly to erode our market share. They have the deep pockets of their holding company and present a real threat. We can't expect to go head-to-head with them in a price war. Our customers are loyal and our products are rated superior to theirs in blind tests, but marginally so. As a result, we could soon find them snapping at our heels. Worst-case scenario is a 4 percent market share loss in twelve months; more than that if we don't counter somehow."

"Did you say 4 percent, Alexandra?" asked Greg. She nodded and Greg continued. "We have to respond, and respond quickly. I need to know more about what Classic is up to. Any thoughts, Alexandra?"

"Did I mention that QBC is also beginning a business improvement program? From what I hear, I don't believe they've approached it as aggressively as we have. It seems they made great progress for a while, and then slipped a little. Our processes seem to be in better control than theirs, but if we do nothing, they just might catch up. Your other question concerning Classic I can answer, thanks to a conversation I had with Sam Elliott just before he retired. He was having lunch with one of our major transportation suppliers. There was an offhand comment made about difficult transportation issues they were having in arranging routes for Classic's products that were going to come out of the Far East. Sam didn't want to get into sensitive competitive information, so he let the subject drop. Nevertheless, that passing comment tells me Classic is outsourcing some intermediates or even finished products to a low-cost manufacturer. This is disturbing and may explain why Classic thinks they can price their products more aggressively without affecting their margins too much. We're lucky Sam overheard that comment, but we'll have to see what other information we can dig up in the public record."

Greg wasn't finished. "Alexandra, what are we going to do about QBC's new product line? We can't let them steal our customers. Those eighteen- to twenty-five-year-olds will be someone's loyal customers for the next 50 years. We need to make sure they are our loyal customers!"

"I've had a look at what they're doing, Greg, and have to admit their new packaging has a real impact on the shelf. Their television advertising is actually quite memorable and appealing. And I hate to admit it, but I'm way past my twenty-fifth birthday! Last week I formed a team including Matt and our most creative Product Development Manager—Mary Brewer, New Product Development Director, two of our Product Managers, the creative director of our ad agency, and a couple of representatives from our most advanced packaging suppliers. They will give me some proposals in the next two weeks to counter this threat. When we come up with the right response, I want to follow that blitz approach we used in installing the new production lines to launch the new products, and begin developing the next set of products to put QBC on the defensive. Just for additional input, I've also included a couple of younger women from our staff, and also one of Zachary's people, to ensure we have the perspective of a few more young people to challenge the thinking of our older folks—like me." Alexandra's sense of humor was appreciated by Greg's team, although Greg didn't smile.

"Thanks, Alexandra. Now, David, have you had any thoughts about the outsourcing issue?"

"As you'd expect, Greg, Alexandra didn't wait for this meeting to tell me, so I've had a couple of days to explore some options. I also got Dan from Effective Management to come in to give me his perspective on the outsourcing issue in general. We've always taken pride in being able to produce all our products in our two plants. But beyond that aspect of our culture, I've concluded, with Dan's coaching, that our procurement processes are not yet mature enough to take advantage of outsourcing. He reminded me that we have a number of issues with no good solutions. Some product lines would require a reformulation since they have short shelf-life components that would be prohibitively expensive to transport from so far away. I believe we'll need a procurement initiative to improve and modify our understanding, culture, and processes to be ready for outsourcing." Sara interrupted at this point.

"Actually, Greg, our current financial processes and measures, according to Dan, could lead us to make a poor outsourcing decision. As you know, we've configured our Enterprise Resource Planning (ERP) system to report in terms of standard costing in keeping with common accounting practices. We also pay close attention to unit prices. Our main monitor of procurement effectiveness is purchase price variance. We had only a couple of hours with Dan, but he convinced me that we should consider our procurement financials differently. He suggested we focus less on the purchase price and more on the total landed cost in our factories. Greg, that approach would reduce the apparent differential between outsourced components and those locally sourced. He also talked at length about 'total cost of ownership,' including disposal costs, of all our incoming materials. We've all heard stories about the unintended consequences of outsourcing, such as the toy manufacturer that found the advantages of outsourcing to low-cost labor rate factories were more than offset by high-cost litigation and loss of goodwill caused by product recalls and injuries caused by contamination. No company can tolerate that kind of damage to their company or brand image. There were similar problems with a toothpaste produced using outsourced components. Although both companies reduced their manufacturing costs significantly, their total cost of ownership made outsourcing components and labor to a low-cost country a poor decision in those cases.

"These sorts of things can happen here at home, too. But with less inventory in the pipeline and shorter lead times we can find and respond to quality or regulatory issues much faster. The benefits of having a shorter and more contained supply chain are also factors to balance in reaching the decision to outsource."

"Good summary. I think I've heard enough for now. I'll have Roxanne or Dan come in for a day to meet with us and Peter. Peter will coordinate our next Class A initiative, to help us figure out what this new market information means to our next steps."

Ten days later, the team met with Roxanne who listened to the summary of events since the last celebration. She summarized their key points on a presentation slide she was projecting so all could see it, then facilitated a discussion of their potential responses to the market challenges of competing products and aggressive pricing. Greg, as usual, was eager to get things moving.

"What I'm hearing, to be blunt, is that the competition is catching up or in some cases, staying ahead of us. Our procurement procedures are weak, and we need to put some rocket fuel in our supply chain to give it higher velocity and make it more agile and responsive, to use Roxanne's words."

"Let me build on that thought, Greg," replied Roxanne. "What the facts tell me is that you need a tailored initiative to head off the challenges and restore your growth. You need to establish and sustain a competitive advantage. In fact that could be a good name for a tailored initiative, the 'Competitive Advantage Initiative.' I want to remind you that what you do next will build on the four Class A Milestones you've achieved in the Customer Service and Customer Satisfaction Initiatives. After you outlined the situation for me during our phone conversation, I developed a spreadsheet showing the complete Checklist. It shows what you've accomplished already and the scores attained for each chapter and definition. To me, the most obvious next step to address the competitive needs you've identified is the Capable External Sourcing Milestone. You already meet many of the elements outside the External Sourcing chapter, and now you need to incorporate other specific External Sourcing chapter requirements. This means you'd need a procurement team working on improving their processes to be consistent with all your existing processes, and the future improvements." There were nods of agreement around the table.

"Now, hold on to your seats, because I'm going to suggest you add four more milestones to this Competitive Advantage Initiative." Her statement resulted in a uniform expression of disbelief.

"Hang on, Roxanne," exclaimed Peter. "We found two milestones about all we could handle. How could we possibly manage five at the same time?"

"I thought you'd ask that! It *is* possible because of what you've already achieved and the business processes you've already improved and continue to improve. Let me explain how it could work. I'm suggesting the Initiative include the following milestones:

Capable External Sourcing. This one is almost stand-alone and will bring your procurement thinking and processes up to what you'll need to achieve Class A. But it isn't totally stand-alone. Peter, it will require careful integration with the others. I see it as about a nine-month effort.

Advanced Internal Supply will build on David's work with Lean and Six Sigma. It will give you advanced 'demand-led planning' processes; leverage your new advanced planner, optimizer and scheduler software; and enable you to improve process velocity and repeatability significantly. By 'repeatability,' I mean you will essentially eliminate process variability and process failures. This milestone typically takes eighteen months to complete, but it could be less if we're clever in building on the work you've already accomplished.

Capable Management of Demand will enhance your demand planning and control capabilities and enable you to leverage these capabilities with the advanced internal supply processes. These demand and supply milestones go hand-in-hand. The Demand Milestone also involves your product managers in developing more tactical segmentation and market planning. Given your solid starting point, I'd predict about nine months to complete this milestone. By then, you'll be able to take advantage of some of the new advanced internal supply capabilities, but will need much more internal supply progress to get to a true demand-pull model.

Capable Distribution and Logistics is replete with improvement possibilities many companies ignore; you can't afford to ignore them any longer given your competitive market. The focus of this milestone is on completely integrating enhanced distribution and logistics processes to create a highly responsive delivery engine. I would estimate six to twelve months for this one depending on whether there is a need for capital investment, such as for Radio Frequency IDentification (RFID) and/or sortation capability. Let's assume nine months for now.

About nine months into these four, you'll be ready to begin the fifth, which is the *Capable Supply Chain* Milestone. This milestone will build on the progress you've made with the previous three. You'll redesign your entire supply chain, internal and external, into the most effective model for you, and to prepare for Collaborative Supply Planning. I would estimate you'd complete this in nine months, meaning the whole Competitive Advantage Initiative would take eighteen months. But you'll see incremental business improvements month by month. You won't have to wait till the end.

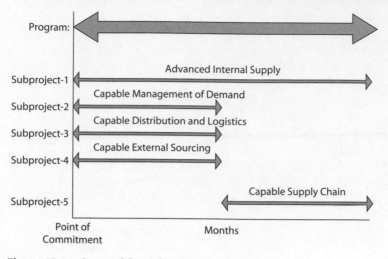

Figure 18.1 Competitive Advantage Initiative
Source: Oliver Wight. Copyright Oliver Wight International, Inc. Used with permission.

"Now to make it clearer, let me draw this out for you" [Figure 18.1].

David responded, "This doesn't look like a tailored initiative. You've just plugged in standard milestones."

"Yes, it does look like that, David. Milestone templates describe associated business processes and operating performance levels related to your position on the journey to Class A. You won't be undertaking any of these templates in their entirety. We'll identify where you have gaps and tailor the template requirements so that your work plan will be tailored versions of what appears in the template. Within about 18 months, you'll have completed this Initiative and meet the requirements for certification in all five milestones. In fact, due to the overlap of the nine milestones, by completing this Initiative, you'll also meet all requirements for certification in the Foundation Business Improvement Capability Milestone. So you'll actually be addressing a total of six milestones."

Following some intense discussion about scope and resources needed, Greg announced his decision to create what they would call the 'Competitive Advantage Initiative' encompassing the six milestones that Roxanne had described. The Leadership Team launched the Initiative. Greg chartered a subteam of David, Alexandra, Matt, Sara, and Peter to complete the Leadership Phase of the Proven Path and financially justify the work.

Two weeks later, the subteam presented its proposal for moving ahead with the Competitive Advantage Initiative. With only minor adjustments, Greg had the package he needed for Susan's approval. Sara's financial analysis reflected another significant return on investment, far above Amalgamated's financial hurdle rate. By this time, Cosmetics Products financial projections had proven so reliable, Susan's Executive Leadership team no longer questioned the validity of their estimates. Within two weeks of Susan's approval, and with some help from Dan, Peter had converted the Initiative content into a program management format with a committed calendar of events. Resources were assigned from operating departments and from a core business improvement "Center of Expertise" comprised of a few Class A knowledgeable and experienced people freed up as a result of earlier milestone productivity improvements. This unique, self-funding team of internal Class A experts was tasked with helping process owners ensure all business processes and related results would continuously improve.

Greg's Steering Committee soon learned that the External Sourcing Milestone portion of the Competitive Advantage Initiative would integrate sourcing activities more completely with operations and product management. Key objectives of the milestone:

- Improve understanding and utilization of suppliers' technologies to build Cosmetics Products' competitive advantage; and build trading partner relationships so that Cosmetics Products would be their key suppliers' "Customer of Choice".

- Develop external sourcing competencies such as e-procurement, Total Cost of Ownership analytical expertise, and the ability to recognize supply channel opportunities better.

- Create logical material groupings and optimize sourcing strategies for each grouping.

- Develop a transparent process to create better understanding between Cosmetics Products and its key suppliers of each others' operations. Then use this knowledge to improve material quality, fitness for use, cost, and deliverability, and to drive waste out of the supply chain.

- Collaborate with a smaller number of suppliers and create longer-term relationships, aligning suppliers' success with Cosmetics Products' success.

- Share all relevant information and future plans with key suppliers to help supply chain partners become better suppliers, and to help Cosmetics Products become a better customer.

- Support the ability of product managers to utilize suppliers' expertise and to involve them in the early phases of new product development projects.

- Upgrade all supplier relationships to emphasize ethical, moral, and legal behaviors at all times.

Roxanne had cautioned David and Peter that some of their biggest challenges would come in upgrading internal supply processes. Beyond improvements required by other milestone templates, the velocity focus in Advanced

Internal Supply required considerably more than token application of Lean principles ("eliminating waste in all its forms"), beginning with a basic understanding of what is considered waste. The milestone also requires elimination of variability, which requires thorough understanding at all levels of process and performance statistics. The goal is "failure free" processes through application of the Six Sigma methodology. People doing the work would learn to solve their process and performance problems, meaning that managers, supervisors, and technical experts would become coaches and resources—sometimes an impossible transition for experienced managers who were taught early in their career that controlling information was the way to increase their power and importance.

"Everyone becomes part of the team within the scope of the Advanced Internal Supply Milestone; the operative word is 'teamwork.' The supporting continuous improvement framework which W. Edwards Deming called the Shewart Cycle, or PDCA (Plan, Do, Check, Act), and its associated robust change management procedures ensure that all changes are institutionalized by being built into documented processes; informal changes to operating procedures can no longer be tolerated. Managers must become serious practitioners of empowerment, a change that often affects reporting structures.

"You'll be improving the synchronization of material flow through the supply chain as you prepare for a transition to a Demand-Pull model, where everything is driven by an objective of meeting customers' requests directly from the process line, or from a token buffer stock that is refreshed frequently, and perhaps even daily given your finishing lead times." That comment caused David to hold his head and audibly exhale.

"I believe my head is about to explode! I've read about that model as an interesting and unattainable theory; I never thought I'd ever be asked to implement it! Our Planning and Manufacturing groups have improved light-years in their agility and flexibility, but Demand-Pull will be a huge challenge. Guess it qualifies as another 'breakthrough goal' because I have no idea how we're going to pull it off!"

Greg responded, "I heard you say something like that before the Customer Satisfaction Initiative, too, David. We accomplished that one; we'll accomplish this one also. Please continue, Roxanne."

"These improvements will provide the foundation for achieving the 99.5 percent performance level required for full Class A certification. With all master data moving to at least 99.5 percent accuracy, your planners will begin to rely on the advanced planner, optimizer, and scheduler (APOS) software to take over some scheduling basics. The system is faster and effectively error-free, providing, of course, your master data and transaction integrity match the required precision and that the 'knowledge' you've built in the supply chain model in the APOS system is realistic and consistent with your operating strategy.

"I know you utilize Kanban replenishment in a few areas, but most Kanban is 'push' whenever you replenish—even more so with a seasonal demand product line. We'll introduce you to far more effective methods to reduce

Kanban stock levels by utilizing improved demand synchronization techniques that rely on enhanced demand management and control. You may even find an area where you could implement demand-led 'flow-manufacturing,' but that will probably have to wait for your next initiative.

"You'll need to minimize asset outages and unplanned downtime significantly, which means that your Total Productive Maintenance program will transition to be more of a Total Predictive Maintenance program. I realize that package of work must sound overwhelming, but as you truly empower your people and create high-performance, self-directed work teams, you'll be amazed at how quickly the improvements fall into place. As with the very first Initiative, however, the rate of progress will directly correlate with the Leadership Team's focus and commitment to excellence!"

Roxanne's enthusiasm was infectious. She continued, outlining improvements required by the Capable Management of Demand Milestone. The changes included:

- Even more aggressive improvement of forecast accuracy and a greater sense of urgency to close business plan gaps.
- More tightly forged links with Product and Supply Management to create a demand-led supply chain.
- Enhanced category management and market segmentation.
- New market exploitation tactics, leveraging the more responsive supply capability.
- Enhanced channel strategies and understanding.
- Taking the first steps, at the appropriate time, in true customer demand collaboration enabled by investment in key customer relationship-building and technology.
- Further definition and refinement of the Demand Plan, leading eventually to short-term, accurate daily predictions of product needs from the supply chain.
- New flexible time fences, reflecting the capability to be more responsive to customer requirements.
- Enhanced customer and market understanding building on the new customer relationships and utilizing the enhanced supply capability.
- Significantly enhanced supply chain flexibility and agility reflecting the passion to serve customers, but always cost-effectively.

This time it was Alexandra's turn hold her head and groan. "Daily forecasts? I know, Greg. We were successful before and we'll be successful again. Sorry for the interruption, Roxanne."

Roxanne explained that improved processes developed with the Capable Distribution and Logistics Milestone would accelerate product delivery to customers. Having safe, error-free distribution and logistics capabilities, and an enhanced ability to service more orders with smaller quantities more effectively, would be essential to their future success. "The possibility of using third-party logistics (3PL) to minimize shipping costs is an option for you, providing Cosmetics Products has adequate expertise and feedback controls to manage the providers. There is no point in degrading supply chain velocity because of an unreliable logistics provider. Treat your logistics suppliers the same as any material supplier in terms of building trading partner relationships and performance expectations.

"There's a reason I've delayed the Capable Supply Chain Milestone by nine months on this diagram [Figure 18.1]. This milestone requires capabilities established as part of the earlier milestones. It becomes rather like the final piece in this Initiative jigsaw puzzle."

Greg's Leadership Team, along with Peter, chartered the Competitive Advantage Initiative team, which included the individual milestone champions and leaders. Samantha Williams from Effective Management, supported by Cosmetics Products' Six Sigma black belts, provided further education and coaching on Agile, Lean, and Six Sigma to all design teams. Roxanne and Zachary teamed to provide education to help managers and supervisors make the transition to internal coaches and to begin building high-performance, self-directed work teams. Although a small number of shop floor managers and supervisors left the company because they could not make that transition from directing to coaching, others proved to be excellent students. Newly empowered operators, technicians, and clerical staff reveled in their ability to improve the workplace, manufacturing methods, and results. The resulting flood of improvements kept Gabriella Jemison and her organization busy validating process revisions and updating product structures to enable postponement of uniqueness during the manufacturing process. With most products, they could now postpone final product identity until the last processing step and determination of the packaging presentation as triggered by customer orders received the previous day. In one case, a manufacturing operator's suggestion led to application of the final additives through injection into a common bulk product as the materials moved from bulk storage through in-line mass-flow metered mixers on the way to the filling and packaging line. Product changeover time for that particular product line was reduced from over 70 minutes to less than 1 minute. That product and all its packaging variations became finish-to-order, reducing inventory and lead time, and reducing exposure to forecast variability during a much shortened customer order lead time. The overall impact of this and many similar improvements were being tracked on charts showing increasing velocity, declining inventories, and improving customer service.

Product introductions were now being well managed with their rigorous Stage and Gate procedures. Introductions were causing minimum production disruptions. David's planners acknowledged a capacity increase of 11 percent, which enabled Cosmetics Products to avoid, or at least delay, a significant capital investment and disruption that would have been caused by construction.

Perhaps the most challenging and exciting work was eliminating process variability and creating failure-free processes. Nearly everyone was skeptical about delivering failure-free products, especially given the natural variability of some incoming materials. Nevertheless, rigorous application of root-cause analysis and statistical analysis of process records yielded surprising improvements. In one processing operation, variable drying caused slight, but measurable variation in the surface finish of a product. A high-gloss finish presented less surface area exposure to the air than a lower-gloss or matte finish. The matte finish presented a greater surface area exposed to the air, and resulted in a shorter product life due to oxidation. Product shelf life printed on the consumer unit was determined by the worst case shelf life conditions. Creative root-cause analysis determined the variation was caused by power fluctuations during processing. The source of the variation proved to be a faulty power supply stabilizer located in the factory's electrical power system. By replacing and routinely monitoring a new unit the plant began producing uniformly high gloss product, allowing a six-month shelf-life extension. The quantity of expired product returned by retail customers plummeted.

Every department submitted reports documenting improvements in waste and variability both in production and administrative processes. One notable example was from a remote customer service office still using manual customer order processing procedures. The order entry clerk had decided to enter in the ERP system all West Coast orders on Tuesdays, East Coast on Thursdays, Canada on Fridays, and export orders on Mondays and Wednesdays. That sequence had saved her time, but added costly delays in fulfilling customer requirements. As she learned more about the capabilities of the ERP system she began processing orders within an hour of their being placed by customers. On average, she reduced customer lead time by five days.

The Capable Management of Demand team struggled at the outset of its work until Bart Billings provided strong leadership. He insisted on achievable, but breakthrough, change. He attended Effective Management's Advanced Supply Planning course and was intrigued with the possibility of merging supply and demand planning processes in advance of the supply chain becoming truly demand-led, an even greater challenge for the future. The Steering Committee approved the team's recommendation to create a Demand Control Manager role. Controlling near-term customer demand, given ever decreasing inventories and lead times, required more attention to detail than the Demand Planning Manager and an assistant could provide. Told by Samantha during a private coaching session that point-of-use buffer stocks would be determined using this near-term information, David thought he knew what she meant. But when she started discussing linearity and Heijunka as requirements for Advanced Demand Control, he realized he had once again entered deep water and would need more education quickly—before those topics became Greg's next "bright idea"!

The Capable Management of Demand team completed its work in 10 months, delayed one month due to illness of one of its key members. Nevertheless the benefits delivered exceeded expectation.

The Capable Distribution and Logistics team advanced the work of the former Capable Planning and Control team. Master data accuracy provided a major challenge, given the large number of records. Customer masters, critical for accurate invoicing, proved to be only 65 percent accurate. Although some of the errors, such as a transposed numbers in a zip code, were minor, others (inaccurate ship-to addresses, names, and telephone contact details) were more serious and caused administrative waste. Worse yet was the number of records with incorrect, and sometimes overstated, discount information. Incorrect billing statements resulted in frequent and serious customer complaints until the team corrected the records and eliminated all related billing errors. The team developed formal and rigorous change control procedures and took advantage of ERP system capabilities to cross-check data such as zip, area, and postal codes against geographic areas to eliminate this type of data entry error.

Retraining on the way the Distribution Requirements Planning (DRP) system was to be used improved both the quality of the system's recommendations and the data flow. They had found the distribution and logistics course helpful in thinking differently about their issues and potential process improvements.

The distribution and logistics group proposed changing material flow in the Atlanta warehouse to increase material handling, picking, and packing efficiency. After David verified that the team had received the recommendations from Atlanta's self-directed warehouse team, walked through the facility with the warehouse team members to review the proposed changes, and reviewed their basis for the predicted efficiency and cost improvements, he approved all changes. The team also presented a proposal for relatively minor upgrades to their bar code label printers and readers that David agreed to fund from his capital budget.

The Capable Distribution and Logistics Milestone team piqued David's interest with information from a materials handling conference one of its members had attended. They weren't ready to make a proposal yet, but showed David some sketches and literature from suppliers of automated sorting and picking (sortation) equipment. The Dallas warehouse manager and a subteam from his warehouse recently visited other companies to see the equipment in action. They reported that finished cases of product were fed into the system and magazines were loaded with individual consumer units by warehouse operators. From that point to the point where both full and mixed containers of products were assembled into unit loads for large customers, and mixed quantities of consumer units were placed into individual shipping cartons for small customers, all activity was controlled by the customer order number bar code. Little manual work was required, and the error rate was being measured in parts per million. The Atlanta and Dallas Plant managers agreed to lead a task force jointly to develop the proposal and bring it to the Leadership Team. With this continuous improvement opportunity now in development, the team successfully completed its Capable Distribution and Logistics Milestone in just nine months and began offering support to the other teams still working on their portions of the Competitive Advantage Initiative.

The Competitive Advantage Initiative Team continued its active support of the milestone teams by tracking progress of their deliverables, synchronizing activities, breaking barriers with the help of the Steering Committee, and acknowledging success. Peter coordinated milestone teams associated with the five milestones (the sixth milestone being inherent within the other five) and reported progress, problems, and plans during each Steering Committee meeting. As predicted, the Advanced Internal Supply Team was generating excitement throughout the company and delivering stunning improvements. All key performance indicators (KPIs) were now routinely at 99 percent with some of them periodically hitting 99.5 percent. Greg, David, and others recalled the time not too long ago when they had considered achieving that level of performance to be impossible.

The Capable External Sourcing team faced a cultural challenge, although formal job description responsibilities had already been changed by Zachary's Human Resources organization. Through extensive education and training, they had progressed from being buyers and expeditors, to adding value to the business as professional purchasing agents. Their most carefully managed KPI in the past, purchase price variance, was still being tracked, but it was no longer a driver of rewards and, therefore, occasional dysfunctional behavior. David, who also headed up procurement activities, learned that the term "procurement" was more than a new organizational buzz word for "purchasing." The strategic nature of the modified roles gave confidence to those involved in sourcing and contracting that they would be critical players in developing extended supply chain partners and in collaborative efforts to build winning supply chains. This paradigm shift, difficult at first, resulted in a group significantly more motivated and effective in delivering bottom-line business benefits.

One of the team's most important contributions was implementing "Total Cost of Ownership." They first categorized numerous elements of Total Cost of Ownership besides the price—as the elements included price—such as supplier performance, installation, inventory, disposal, operability of the material, participation in waste reduction activities, and environmental impact.

Their thought was to rate each purchased material or service to reach a score or rating for each potential supplier. Dan Evans, their Effective Management coach, cautioned them that making a sourcing decision based only on the rating would be unwise. The rating was useful input to the decision, but it would take a cross-functional team of knowledgeable individuals to determine which supplier would be most effective and reliable. Following Dan's counsel, they developed a charter for a Strategic Sourcing Committee that would develop recommended suppliers for new or changed materials and services, including sub-contracting. Their recommendations would be reviewed and approved by the Cosmetics Products Leadership Team. Progress was rapid, as were the resulting benefits of their work in selecting new suppliers and materials based on Total Cost of Ownership. Sam Elliott, Amalgamated's Senior Vice President Supply Chain, reviewed the policy, procedures, and results and announced to all Division Presidents and Supply Chain VPs that he wanted the new processes implemented across all divisions. The Capable External Sourcing team completed its milestone in nine months. Members of the team volunteered to help other Divisions implement Total Cost of Ownership as an aid to decision making.

The Capable Supply Chain team began its work nine months after the other teams started, and included appropriate members from other design teams as supply chain experts. Armed with what they had learned in the Managing the Extended Supply Chain course, they attacked their remaining best practice gaps in several supply chain redesign workshops that David also attended. They were grateful for the delay since they could take advantage of work accomplished by the other milestone teams. The external supply chain work was new and challenging even at the Capable Milestone level. Technically, they were responsible for fewer than five topics, but the need to integrate their process design with procurement, suppliers, all internal supply points, distribution and logistics, and a third-party distributor for one channel, made the work complex. They were building a foundation for the future Advanced External Supply Chain Milestone. Peter's integrating role and skills proved invaluable in facilitating the integration aspects of their work.

In the early days of the Class A work, Roxanne advised Greg and his leadership team that one way to beat the competition would be to out-innovate them—keeping them off balance with a pipeline of products making obsolete their own products so frequently that the competition couldn't keep up. If a competitor had a lengthy supply chain with elements in remote regions of the world, it might never recover, and so remain at a permanent disadvantage. The new products wouldn't require breakthrough innovations; they just had to be perceived as different, of good value, attractively packaged and creatively advertised. Those truly new products offering unique and attractive features, could also command premium prices. The image of an innovator, higher market share, bigger margins, and competitors put back on their heels was a winning and hard-to-overcome combination. At the time Roxanne provided that advice, however, Cosmetics Products was in no condition to achieve such a desirable state of affairs.

Despite the concerns of some, Roxanne assured them that a formal and disciplined product development and launch process wouldn't constrain people's creativity. Companies who enter into a Class A journey develop a burning passion for improvement and innovation, and an intolerance of the status quo.

Cosmetics Products' new product development and launch process was now in place, but the Product Management and Product Development organizations found software support for creating new formulations and package designs meeting all regulatory requirements problematic. Design errors and misdirected activities were common and time-consuming because the archive of past development activity was difficult to mine for information, user-unfriendly, and populated with often inaccurate data. Product managers, supported by Alexandra and Samantha, requested a marketing-led expansion of the Knowledge Management Systems [see Figure 17.2] infrastructure to include a Product Data Management (PDM) module as part the Competitive Advantage Initiative. The requested PDM functionality would be used to control formulations during development; facilitate learning from past experiences; structure regulatory requirements into development templates, automatically provide feedback of potential breaches before any actual trial, and generally accelerate the overall development process. The PDM module would be hardwired to the ERP system as the official source for authorized formulations, including Bills of Materials and Routings. This expansion of the Knowledge Management System would cause some additional learning time. Data accuracy auditing and change control software would have to be extended to the PDM system to ensure the resident formulations reflected the latest product engineering standards.

Following funding approval, IT resources, product managers and product engineers input on the PDM module functionality, the end-users—the product and design engineers—spent six months configuring, populating, and learning to use this "experience" (knowledge) database, to encode regulatory and quality requirements and to overcome several post start-up issues, including requests for nice but unnecessary functionality. Three months after implementation the flow of product introductions had increased significantly while typical lead time from concept to launch for an average complexity product plummeted from more than 100 days to a consistent 65 to 70 days. Further leverage of the functionality in the software, improvements to the Stage and Gate process, and refinement of the associated deliverables templates nearly eliminated formulation, packaging design, and regulatory compliance errors. Time for most projects from concept to launch decreased to, on average, 40 days. Cosmetics Products was launching products and new end-aisle product displays flawlessly at the rate of over 50 per month with excellent customer service.

Cosmetics Products was becoming known within its consumer and customer base as a dynamic, modern and innovative company by frequently introducing "new and improved" products across all their product lines and categories. They could now supply reasonably low volumes with a high replenishment frequency economically. Their new agility, responsiveness, and creativity resulted in a consumer expectation that their competitors in the region could not match. Growth rate reached double digits, and the Amalgamated Board of Directors finally and thankfully could see the future they had envisioned when approving entry into the Cosmetics business. For the first time, there were questions raised in the Board meeting about the viability of expanding the business into other regions of the world. The Board agreed to table that discussion until there was further evidence that the gains made so far were sustainable.

After a 20-month effort, Cosmetics Products achieved its Competitive Advantage Initiative. With great pride, Greg received, on behalf of everyone in Cosmetics Products, six additional Milestone Awards. For the occasion, Roxanne was accompanied by Effective Management's Region President, Walt Jones. Coverage of the award by the *Atlanta Business Chronicle* and *Atlanta Journal and Constitution Business Press* further enhanced both Cosmetics Products' and Amalgamated's rapidly improving stature.

Shortly after the award presentation, their new Knowledge Management Systems and more agile development processes paid big dividends when oil prices doubled and a key ingredient increased in price by over 25 percent. The company had run several contingency scenarios in the event the oil market destabilized and was ready to move some of their product lines to new and more environmentally friendly seed-based ingredients developed recently by one of its trading partners. Advertising copy, packaging designs, and approved artwork were ready in concert with the new formulations. Cosmetics Products was the first company to introduce and advertise the benefits of these new eco-friendly formulations. News of their innovation accompanied by packages with high shelf impact and innovative advertising, and their ability to avoid punishing price increases resulted in yet another significant market share increase for Cosmetics Products. While other companies suffered losses as a result of the economic pressure, Cosmetics Products took over market leadership in the specialty cosmetics products category.

Responding to business reporters, Greg attributed their success to an intense focus on the customer and an empowered dedicated, workforce. When talking to Penny later that evening, he said "Risking your wrath about the 'laurels' thing, we've come so far that I really don't believe there's much left to do."

He was wrong. It wasn't over yet.

19

CLASS A LEADERSHIP

The training they had been doing just for the sake of training was providing no return on investment and no competitive advantage.

Treat all your people as if they were volunteers; that'll improve your behaviors and build win-win relationships.

To enable responsiveness, it becomes necessary to move the responsibility for loading orders into the constrained manufacturing environment from the supply organization to the demand organization.

While Amalgamated's Cosmetics Products Division (CPD) had been busy improving its processes, the other divisions had not been idle. When Cosmetics Products received its first two Class A Milestone awards accompanied by improved customer service results, eyebrows were raised at the Board. Some Board members asked if what CPD was doing could be replicated in other divisions. Those who were also on Boards of other companies asked the same question of those companies. Initially, Susan viewed the achievements simply as Cosmetics Products finally getting its act together. Even Greg used that description of his first initiative, but had later expressed confidence that they were committed to making even greater progress. Roger Winchester, President Home Products, who had encouraged Greg to attend Effective Management's seminar, considered beginning a similar journey, but his Home Products business results at the time were exceeding all commitments. There was little enthusiasm among Rogers's leadership team to undertake what appeared to be a major new improvement program. Given the healthy state of the other divisions, Susan suggested to the Board that they wait and see if Cosmetics

Products could sustain their improving results. At the same time, she had instructed her staff to watch closely what CPD was accomplishing and to consider when it might be best to roll out the Class A work across the rest of Amalgamated.

As improvements from the Customer Satisfaction Initiative began hitting the bottom line, it became obvious that something special was happening. The Board of Directors requested a presentation explaining how the results were being delivered. Susan tasked Sam Elliott, Senior VP Supply Chain, to pull together the summary, and a formal proposal for applying improvement methodologies to the other divisions. Andrew Jones, CFO, predicted Amalgamated's stock rating would increase at least one level if the other divisions improved as much as Cosmetics Products. Bill Crawford, Senior VP Marketing, noted that Cosmetics Products' improvement percentages were calculated against a very low baseline, but that didn't change Andrew's prediction.

After six weeks of meetings, data collection and analysis, and discussions with Roxanne and CPD executives, Sam was prepared to report to Susan and the Board.

"Susan and members of the Board, never in my career have I observed a transformation similar to what is happening in Cosmetics Products. What those folks are doing is mind-boggling, at least for an old-timer like me. I've asked Greg to review for us in detail how he and his team are now conducting strategic planning as an example of the changes delivering the impressive results. I can tell you, from what I saw, it makes the strategic planning process in the other Divisions look elementary by comparison. Over to you, Greg."

"Thanks, Sam, for that very kind introduction. I want to reinforce what I told you last week. What you saw was true team effort touching all fundamental business processes, not just strategic planning. What we've done with strategic planning is nothing compared with how we've changed our approach to managing and leading people." Greg continued his description of the changes made and the outcomes of those changes, providing detail in response to questions from Board members, who listened intently to Greg's presentation. Bill Crawford, Senior VP Sales and Marketing, offered unsolicited support.

"I've been hearing great things from Alexandra, Greg's Sales and Marketing VP, about what's going on. She often overwhelmed me with her enthusiasm, to the point that I'm afraid I tuned her out from time to time. Now I wish I'd paid more attention. Believe me; I have a long list of questions for her at our next one-to-one meeting."

After more discussion, the Board asked Susan to have all divisions begin a Class A journey following the Proven Path and using Effective Management's expertise and coaching. Greg agreed to let Peter Bertrand, his highly regarded Program Manager, and David, his Supply Chain VP, spend a few days with each division's Leadership Team explaining what they had learned about governance of the Class A work and how each division might organize for its first initiative.

Following the board meeting, Susan's Executive Team began discussing in detail how it would support rollout of the work into other divisions. The President of Food Products, Ian MacGregor, said that the Customer Service Initiative was unnecessary since Food Products regularly hit 95 percent. Susan immediately stopped that conversation.

"I now know enough about the other divisions to know, Ian, that your act is not together! Greg credits that initiative for building the foundation for later progress."

Roger added, "I agree. I'm also running at 95 percent customer service in Home Products more months of the year than not, but I can assure you we're not achieving those results as cost effectively or sustainably as Cosmetics Products. I'm looking for a lot more than simply on-time delivery."

Susan acknowledged Roger's enthusiasm and designated the Home Products division to be the first to follow Cosmetics Products. She added that, based on what she knew of each division, the others would need to invest more time to understand what was required before launching the work. Over the next hour, Susan's Executive Team debated the order of implementation. She repeatedly emphasized that time is money as she observed division presidents jockeying to start the work later. The dance being performed was disappointing; she wondered whether she should change some of the players on her Executive Team. Eventually they agreed on the sequence and timing for beginning the work in each division. Susan closed the meeting by approving the plan for all divisions to follow in the footsteps of Cosmetics Products. They all understood they would have to develop and present their business case and organization plan for the work, but there was no doubt of the outcome.

Susan was intrigued by Greg's approach to strategic planning and asked for a more detailed presentation of his methodology. After thinking for a few seconds, Greg suggested Roxanne make the presentation with him since her input was so important to the transformational changes in Cosmetics Products.

Two weeks later, Greg and Roxanne presented the new Strategic Planning approach to Susan's Executive Team. They titled the presentation, "From Vision to Value." The context of the new process was total integration of the business. They used a simple two-foot long balloon to make a point. When one of the Senior VPs was asked to squeeze the balloon in one place, it popped out in another, demonstrating the integration inside. When six of them put their hands around the balloon and squeezed all at the same time, the balloon became dangerously thinner in the spaces between the hands and, under such pressure, burst. Greg pointed out that this was an analogy of what happens to a business when its leaders don't align their thinking and planning. People may be working as hard as they can, but to change the results, the leaders have to change the processes, (start with a different balloon). At that point, Greg introduced the Executive Team to the Integrated Business Model and Integrated Business Management. Roxanne picked up the presentation smoothly. It was impossible to ignore this duo. Roxanne had provided the Executive Team an introduction to Business Excellence just after Cosmetics Products held the kick-off of its first Initiative. But they were paying much closer attention this time.

The Executive Team began its journey by implementing the Integrated Business Model [see Figure 6.1] and the Integrated Business Management process [see Figure 6.2] under Roxanne's tutelage, with occasional coaching from Greg. They found the Integrated Business Management process to be the most effective and logical mechanism for managing the business that anyone on the team had ever encountered. As happened with the Cosmetics Products Leadership Team, Susan's Executive Team transformed from a functional committee with turf protection interests to a true Executive Team with a primary focus on the success of its customers. Building on Greg's experience with strategic planning, and with Roxanne and Greg's guidance, they redesigned Amalgamated's strategic planning process. Their revised vision, mission, and strategic objectives served the corporation well as each division implemented the Integrated Business Management process.

Greg arranged for Dan to provide education and engage the Executive Team in Managing and Leading People best practices. Keely Horton, Senior VP of Human Resources, was ecstatic that the team was finally receptive to many of the Human Resource and organization development innovations that had fallen on deaf ears despite her best efforts. Now Dan was getting their attention, understanding, and commitment. Keely didn't care how the message finally got through, but acknowledged that her mistake in the past was a failure to link the concepts to bottom-line benefits, and an inability to convince her peers that their people were their only strategic advantage in the future. Products, manufacturing processes, and marketing techniques can be duplicated in short order, but the innovative capability of a high-performance, self-directed workforce applying Class A concepts and principles cannot be duplicated. Developing that culture is worth significant, focused investment in education and training. The training they had been doing just for the sake of training was providing little return on investment and no competitive advantage.

Greg still felt heady from Cosmetics Products achievements and from the affirmation of both the Operating Committee and the Board. But he no longer was tempted to become complacent. He'd already tasked Alexandra, David, Zachary, Gabriella, and Peter to brief him on the gaps that needed to be closed to achieve a full Class A Business Excellence award, the first that would be awarded in their industry.

Alexandra met with Roxanne and determined that the team appointed by Greg should schedule a two-day workshop to design the next steps. Roxanne was not available in the time frame Alexandra wanted since she had just engaged a new client, but agreed to have Dan lead the workshop. She knew the approaches and messages of all her colleagues were consistent. Following the workshop, Alexandra and the other executives presented their proposal to Greg.

Alexandra began. "Greg, Dan reminded us that the first step was to know exactly where we are today and determine what is missing—the gap. We created a pretty extensive chart that covered the wall of the conference room showing all the excellence definitions across the top and, below each, what we've already achieved through each milestone. We used a color code to indicate the current score of each, based on the process owners' latest quarterly self-assessment scores. It was rewarding to see the continued progress toward our objective of 100 percent performance on every measure." Anticipating a comment from Greg, she quickly added, "I know that required minimum performance levels are 99.5 percent, Greg, but our goal has to be 100 percent, knowing things happen and we'll miss now and then. We've become intolerant of preventable failures. Take Inventory Record Accuracy, as just one example. We brought accuracy up to 95 percent sustained performance as part of the Capable Milestone. Today, given further improvements in ownership, process, technology, and transactions, we're up to 99.6 percent over the past 3 months. We want to understand what's causing that 0.4 percent accuracy loss, and then eliminate the causes. We're using the same continuous improvement approach for all the measures.

"When we examined progress through the Customer Service and Customer Satisfaction Initiatives and added in the improvements since then, we concluded we're not that far away from Class A. A few scores are at 3.5, but most at 4.0, and a significant number are already at 4.5. To be certain about that, we reviewed some of those scores with Dan and found that we're pretty well calibrated. Nevertheless, as Dan pointed out, looking at what's required for the final surge to Class A, we still have some remaining definitions that will take a good deal of work.

"We studied the pattern of checklist definitions that hadn't been addressed to see if there might be a common denominator. In an inspired moment, Zachary spoke up." And at this point, Alexandra projected a slide that contained only one word. "He said 'Leadership'. As far as we've come already, it's pretty obvious to me that our next Initiative should be called the 'Leadership Initiative'."

Zachary explained his rationale for his statement, which was very compelling. "At the end of the meeting, with Dan's help, we agreed on two tailored milestones that would meet Effective Management's standards for the Business Excellence Class A award. The first milestone is actually a combination of 'Advanced Managing and Leading People' and 'Advanced Strategic Planning'; we're simply calling it the 'Strategy and People Milestone,' which can be structured to cover all the remaining gaps, providing we continue to drive the scores upward on all other elements (the definitions and descriptions) of the milestones already completed."

Greg interrupted, "Okay, I want a list right now of everyone who says I need to improve my leadership!" he said with a smile and acknowledged Zachary. "Thanks for the insight, Zach. Give me some additional details."

Alexandra began outlining the details of the new Initiative. "The 'Strategy and People Milestone' involves closing all the remaining gaps in Chapters One and Two: Managing the Strategic Planning Process and Managing and

Leading People. This milestone includes some elements that have already evolved naturally: for example, formal strategy deployment based on business priorities, and expressed as specific goals throughout the organization; formal evaluation and control techniques, such as diagnostics and reflection days; and feedback mechanisms. We've been doing these regularly. We've also enhanced our risk assessment processes, based on the Checklist best practices. With these improved Chapter One (Managing the Strategic Planning Process) procedures in place, the remaining work is driving it all to completion and excellence. The main emphasis of this tailored milestone, then, will be the gaps in Chapter Two (Managing and Leading People). Once again, some of the elements of that chapter, such as 'Leadership' and 'People in Teams' have already come a long way toward meeting the Checklist requirements. Empowerment is already the norm in Cosmetics Products.

"During the work we did on Managing Products and Services, we became aware of our weaknesses in understanding and managing core competencies and the related people implications. We've made a ton of progress in this area, but we still have more to do. We recognized very early the benefits of open two-way communications, but we still have some people who are reluctant to challenge managers and supervisors when their behaviors don't reflect our values. We're getting used to making organization changes in support of the maturity journey; there's plenty of evidence of that, but we need to ensure we maintain our agility here. The Checklist, Zach tells me, has been helpful to him in seeing the gaps in Human Resources processes and culture, and in determining how to close them. We're also well on the way to excellence with our Knowledge Management System [see Figure 17.2] and competency, again pushed by the Managing Product and Services work. The Knowledge Management System went live eight months ago and is already showing benefits in faster and more predictable product design and development; we plan to expand that technology into marketing and sales, and every other appropriate area, which means just about everywhere.

"A specific area that needs attention is our responsibilities to our community, society, and the world we live in. I'm proud of some of the things we've sponsored locally, but it's been an informal effort with no specific strategy, resources or budget. I recently talked to the Chief Sustainability Officer of a major global company headquartered in Rochester, New York. She's an executive with a strong personal interest in ensuring her company's actions consider the perspective of disadvantaged groups and of the environment. We have no intention of recommending that position or organizational structure as yet, but we're still studying and learning. We've become a learning organization, with growing pains at times, but being truly excellent means learning is a journey, not a day trip. So we may well be recommending a similar direction for us in the future."

Alexandra suggested that she and Zachary be Co-Champions of the Strategy and People Milestone, with Glenn Miller, the Finance Director, as leader of the Strategic Planning Process. Greg agreed, and Alexandra continued the presentation.

"Integrated Business Management holds this milestone, and the second milestone which we'll refer to later, together; it also ensures integration with the entire business. We need to continue bringing all parts of Integrated Business Management up to a minimum score of 4.5. We've covered every definition of Integrated Business Management (Chapter Four) already. About a third are at 4.5 or better. The rest are at 4.0. This process is the glue that holds everything together and integrates all the rest of our work. Now I'll turn it over to David."

David began, "The second tailored milestone is the Supply Chain Milestone. This involves closing all the gaps in Chapter 3, Driving Business Improvement, and all the rest of the chapters: Managing Products and Services (Chapter 5), Managing Demand (Chapter 6), Managing the Supply Chain (Chapter 7), Managing Internal Supply (Chapter 8) and Managing External Sourcing (Chapter 9). As you can imagine just from the list of chapters included, this is the more resource-intensive milestone of the two, and the reason for our projected two-year time requirement. We are recommending that I be the Champion and Charlie Beck be the Leader. Of course, Peter will again fill the role of Initiative or Integration Leader." Greg quickly agreed. David continued.

"We suggested you bring your Checklist books with you. It's good to see they are pretty well worn by now. The Supply Chain Milestone includes the missing and underperforming definitions from the chapters I just mentioned. I'll briefly go through the gaps, but with little detail. We'll stay high level with the 'Tactics' and 'Action' for now. Those of us on the Leadership Team will be involved as coaches and mentors, but not as subject experts, just as with the other milestones, except when we were involved with actually leading the Integrated Business Management work. Here are the gaps presented, for convenience, chapter by chapter.

"In Chapter 3, Driving Business Improvement, we have significant gaps in about a third of the twenty-four definitions. We need to become even more responsive to customers through increasing flexibility and agility with shorter and shorter lead times, and with flexible lot quantities. Today, the customers want what they want, when they want it. We used to joke that was unreasonable; now we know it's a reasonable expectation and that we need to meet it, but in a way that is economically sound. We have to get closer to a 'now' response which will affect all our physical logistics processes, especially in maintaining and reducing shipping costs. We'll need to embrace supply chain integration techniques in redesigning our extended supply chain. And we'll have to develop collaboration skills along all nodes in the supply chain network from one end to the other to capture the benefits of advanced supply chain planning. Our investment in the advanced planner, optimizer, and scheduler software is an essential enabler of this extended supply chain paradigm and improved responsiveness. The word 'supply' in advanced supply chain means the end-to-end network of supply points that enable delivery from the first node of the supply chain to the customer. We'll need to involve more than just our own supply points. Demand and supply at this level are complementary aspects of the same objective—delivering to customer request as often as possible.

"We'll need to embrace collaborative supply planning in which companies work together to make each other successful through leveraging supply chain capabilities from the supplier's supplier all the way to the consumer. To be successful, integration and communication between companies in the supply chain must be absolute and as close to real time as possible. Information, transactions, and event data must be exchanged and processed at ultra high speed; so fast, in fact, that there's no time for anyone to validate the data. It must be right first time, all the time. Further, this means that supporting systems must be flexible as data speeds through the software of every company along the supply chain, often on different platforms, with differing supply chain capabilities and flexibility. This is where our Advanced Planner Optimizer and Scheduler (APOS) software comes into play again. Fortunately we've kept it up to date with the latest releases. You also need to understand that when we speak of 'supply chain network,' we mean an end-to-end, demand-led model, not just manufacturing. In fact, it's risky for the business to separate demand and supply, as you'll see later.

We'll begin at first with rapid, faster-than-a-planner, order committing and constraint management techniques along the supply chain. The APOS software includes integrated simulator, modeler, and optimizer functions to enable decision making in seconds. We'll need to reconfigure our processes and organization routinely to enable us to adapt to any necessary change in marketplace requirements, or in adapting to changes prescribed by the company or the Board in their strategic objectives.

"We've already made significant progress in achieving failure-free processes in manufacturing; Six Sigma techniques have helped considerably. But now I'm talking about making similar progress in all processes and functional areas. As Alexandra mentioned, Knowledge Management is growing even more essential to our future. I'll give you an example. To use our advanced planner, optimizer, and scheduler software effectively, we've coded planners' and operators' process expertise and knowledge into the system. That's the only way we could ever have enabled 'real time' simulations, modeling, and constraint-based scheduling.

"The final gap concerns further developing our culture to promote and sustain innovation. Again we've learned from the work we did with the Capable Products and Services Milestone. We need to encourage and nurture innovation for products, for processes, for quality, and for improvements in everything we do. Even improvements in our culture and leadership are lucrative targets of opportunity for improvement.

"There are only seven remaining definitions we need to focus on, but they are major! Fortunately, we're the team that can close those gaps!" They thanked David for his confidence in them, but could sense another heavy workload coming their way.

David continued, "Let's turn to Chapter 5, Managing Products and Services. The only topic that hasn't been assessed to date is Program Management. The good news about this one is that, as you all know through Peter Bertrand's leadership in program management, we've become pretty darned good at it and can point to all our completed initiatives as evidence. Program Management will become useful in supporting phased-release product planning, further reducing our time to market I believe we have to formalize and document what we've learned about the topic and drive all the elements of the chapter to a minimum of 4.5.

"Chapter 6, Managing Demand, and Chapter 7, Managing the Supply Chain, are next. Building on our Advanced Internal Supply processes, this will look more like the familiar milestone format as we further integrate and upgrade supply and demand processes. You may remember that some years ago, we learned about Input/Output/Queue Control as a way to control work flow in the manufacturing process. We learned that typically the person doing that job required a good deal of shop floor experience. Now we'll load all our process knowledge into the appropriate Knowledge Management System, in this case in our advanced planner, optimizer, and scheduler. We also said that we need to be extremely responsive in meeting customer orders. To that end, it becomes necessary to move responsibility for loading orders into the constrained manufacturing environment from the supply organization to the demand organization. With Lean and Quick Response/Continuous Replenishment manufacturing, there will be very little inventory remaining with which to buffer demand fluctuations and mismatches with supply. The tracking mechanism is called 'Linearity.' The CEO of a major electronics corporation said he considered Linearity to be the most important measure after the financials. To support increased responsiveness, it'll be possible to work with new, flexible time fences, flexible lead times, and flexible manufacturing and shipping order quantities. On the demand side, we'll no longer refer to 'abnormal demand', but to 'opportunity demand'. We will have the capability to run simulations to see how we can meet, not turn away such unforecast business economically using our new agility and flexibility.

"There will be new protocols and processes for win-win collaboration and data sharing up and down the extended supply chain, embedded in new, more appropriate trading partner Service Level Agreements. There will be more emphasis on the demand at any given supply point to govern the short-term, and to prepare line-side damper stocks to take out the inevitable ripples in demand-supply balance. Notice I said 'ripples,' not unmanaged swings.

"All this will be supported by driving internal supply and external sourcing best practices, as referenced in Chapters 8 and 9, up to scores of 4.5 at a minimum. And that's about the extent of the additional improvement required." David sat down to a stunned silence. Greg, swallowing hard at what he just heard, responded.

"Well, you just added several additional pages to the list of things I now know I don't know! I didn't even understand some of the things you just said." Greg cleared his throat. "How long do you predict before we accomplish all this? It sounds at least as big as the mountain we just climbed."

Peter responded. "Greg, we've done what we believe is a realistic evaluation, did some risk analysis, and put some contingency in the plan for unforeseen events. I believe David mentioned earlier that this work would take about two years. David and I both believe we can complete all the necessary work in something close to that since we have a solid foundation for the required improvements."

After further discussion, Greg called for a summary of views around the table. All supported moving ahead. Greg declared that the only award he wanted now was the Class A Award to confirm that Cosmetics Products had achieved Business Excellence, all milestones, all chapters. For Greg, this was the next meaningful step. No more Class A Milestone awards.

Greg advised Susan of Cosmetics Products' intent and received her full support. Greg's Leadership Team initiated its communication network so that everyone in Cosmetics Products knew of the decision: the 'why,' the 'what,' and the 'how' of the Leadership Initiative.

Roxanne was advised of the decision to take the next step, and that the step was full Class A certification. She committed her organization to support this important decision. As usual, Greg requested Effective Management's intense coaching in the beginning to challenge their thinking and get them going in the right direction. After that period, the support would again taper off to periodic visits for dealing with problems and conducting interim assessments.

And so their 'change for the better' culture based on people, learning, knowledge, and improvement, once again accelerated the pace of change.

As the Strategy and People Milestone of the Leadership Initiative got underway, Greg integrated formal progress reviews into the monthly Leadership Initiative Steering Committee meeting. Gabriella and Zachary formalized and expanded their quarterly industry benchmarking survey of Product and Regulatory business practices and results, while Alexandra and David provided quarterly survey results for the more detailed business processes and market performance.

Greg and Zachary wanted to see best practices in place for people processes and culture. Roxanne arranged for Greg and Zachary to make a return visit to Tender Care Pet Products in Kansas City, Missouri [see Chapter 7]. Shannon Stillwell was now CEO, and George Parker, Senior VP Human Resources. Roxanne informed Greg and Zach that Tender Care had achieved Class A standards on the management processes (generally Checklist Chapters 1–4), but were not as advanced as Cosmetics Products on product, demand, and supply processes. Their competitive priorities, and resulting sequence of milestones, had been very different from Cosmetics Products. But in the areas of business management and people, Tender Care was setting a standard worth examining.

Shannon began with a review of Tender Care's culture and approach to strategic planning and business management. Seeing Tender Care's strategic planning process in action allowed Greg to begin internalizing ideas for moving ahead.

He and Zachary were most interested in the discussion regarding people, and the management of health, safety, environment, and community relations. Tender Care was well ahead of them with a carefully and strategically structured approach. Sharon openly shared their many successes and also their failures that she valued as learning opportunities. Tender Care's view of leadership was thought provoking and better developed than what Greg and Zach had developed for Cosmetics Products. Tender Care had some simple principles, such as "Treat all your people as if they were volunteers; that'll improve your behaviors and build win-win relationships." George displayed a chart showing Tender Care employee and management retention rates as best in class. Their Lost Time and Recordable Injury Rates showed a five-year decline and a period of five years, four months with no lost time injuries. They explained that safety was everyone's responsibility and the number one priority. Greg had thought his 20-month stretch without lost time injury was impressive. He now recognized that the procedures he had to review and sign as he entered Tender Care's headquarters were not just formalities. Greg had entered the lobby with a briefcase in one hand and his laptop in the other. After signing in, he was given a safety requirements card to review and sign. He tucked it into his coat pocket without a second thought. As he started walking toward the stairs to the second-floor meeting room, he was taken aback by a Tender Care employee insisting on carrying one of his bags and pointing at the handrail, saying "Please hold on to it as you go up the stairs."

He mentioned the incident to Shannon and George. George responded that Tender Care people know that 70 percent of all staircase accidents are avoidable when people use handrails at home and at work. The employee, he explained, was doing what any Tender Care employee would have done seeing the potential for an accident. Greg realized that Cosmetics Products had more to do to make safety an integral part of its culture and in peoples' lives at home and at work.

George then described Tender Care's weekly housekeeping and safety audits in which managers and line operators toured all plant and office locations ensuring housekeeping and safety issues were identified and corrected immediately. He also referred to the "Friday Penance," an insider's term referring to a one-hour visit to the shop floor by each member of the plant leadership team every Friday afternoon to help operators clean up all work locations. It meant getting in touch with their real business by putting on protective gear and working alongside the shop floor personnel. During that hour, team leaders, not the executives, were in charge. George went on to explain the responsibilities of the team leaders, all experienced hourly employees. They owned their production processes, including quality, performance, and production results. They were responsible for meeting the schedule and for determining with the detail planning tool what, if any, overtime would be worked. George explained how team leaders evaluated team and individual performance using "360° Reviews," including feedback from peers and those at both higher and lower hierarchical levels of the organization. Team leaders developed their teams, participated in interviewing and hiring managers new to the organization, and took corrective action when team or individual performance fell short of expectation. The role of the manager changed markedly to coach, mentor, and provider of resources. Zach knew that Cosmetics Products had started to move in that direction, and appreciated the culture change yet required to catch up with Tender Care.

Environmental concerns had driven many of Tender Care's policies, procedures, and investment over the years. As Shannon said, "You must be extremely careful with animal scraps and process liquids." Almost every by-product was sold or recycled. Water taken into the factory to support manufacturing processes was returned to the environment cleaner than when it entered. Liquid, solid, and gaseous emissions met or bettered all environmental standards. "Meat processing is, shall we say, aromatically unpleasant. Since we value good relationships with our neighbors, we use the latest technology to negate that aroma, and we survey our neighbors regularly to make sure they know that we care about them and the neighborhood. They tell us we're doing a good job with emissions control." Greg couldn't keep himself from sniffing, and agreed that the air was clean. A later review of all emission records verified that Tender Care Pet Products beat all regulatory requirements by a fair margin.

As a corporate value, Tender Care held local management responsible for maintaining good community relations. Tender Care intended to be viewed as a good corporate citizen and encouraged its managers and employees to participate in community organizations, charities, and governance. Tender Care's Voice of the Community executive coordinated civic and government activities and helped identify volunteer opportunities. Shannon coordinated Tender Care's charitable contribution strategy herself. The examples continued until Greg and Zach had to run to catch the last flight back to Atlanta. Greg and Zach ended their day much wiser about the standards they would be expected to achieve. They thanked Shannon and George for their time and information. Shannon smiled, saying, "I hope you realize that this wasn't a gift. Roxanne tells us you're considerably ahead of us in other areas, particularly in your supply chain processes. Here's the deal. I would like to send two of our supply chain experts to Atlanta to learn what you've accomplished in the areas of advanced planning and supply chain integration. Are you willing to host their visit?" Greg was delighted to return the favor, and suggested they contact David Simpson, VP Supply Chain, to make the arrangements.

Greg and Zach returned to Atlanta and began to synthesize what they learned into a presentation for the Leadership Team. The visit to Tender Care and subsequent education session kick-started the Leadership Initiative and brought Cosmetics Products to Class A standards in just 20 months, with one exception.

They had not yet achieved upper quartile performance in their industry sector, the final piece of the picture required for full Class A Business Excellence.

Peter integrated all existing improvement opportunities into the Supply Chain Milestone template and identified the gaps that had to be closed. The milestone included several parallel elements managed by design teams and, as with previous milestones, integrated by the Initiative team.

The Supply, Demand, and Logistics team created to drive the division to full Class A required education on operating in an advanced extended supply chain environment. Tom tailored a two-day "Managing the Extended Supply Chain" course, building on the Advanced Supply Planning course. This was followed by a two-day workshop to optimize Cosmetics Products' supply chain network nodes and identify required process and organization changes.

The team found that the Extended Supply Chain course completed the picture of the future by using advanced demand and supply operations and planning as a springboard for extended collaborative supply planning. The course was exhaustive and stretched the thinking of the participants. They began to use the term "Service Management," recognizing that the entire company would have to become even more customer-centric [Figures 19.1 and 19.2].

To be totally customer-centric, supply chain network predictability would have to become an implicit characteristic. That meant implementing across the supply chain the characteristics of predictability. Tom listed them:

- Knowledge-based and data-based
- Performance measurement
- Customer-centric thinking and behaviors
- Alignment to common business plan

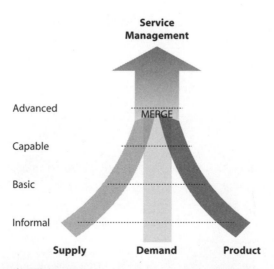

Figure 19.1   Service Management
Source: Oliver Wight. Copyright Oliver Wight International, Inc. Used with permission.

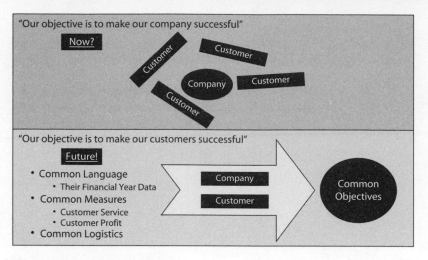

Figure 19.2   Customer-Centric
Source: Oliver Wight. Copyright Oliver Wight International, Inc. Used with permission.

- Understanding each business—Strengths, Weaknesses, Opportunities, and Threats
- Hitting the schedule (every schedule) 99.5 percent +
- Understanding and improving process reliability, including forecast accuracy
- Solving problems using root cause analysis
- Achieving right-first-time, every time quality
- Empowered teamwork

It also meant solving many extended supply chain issues [Figure 19.3].

"One of the issues to be resolved," said Tom, "is how to plan the supply chain network as a whole, allowing for constraints, synchronizing all supply points along the supply chain, and meeting promises to customers, fast and cost effectively. Experience shows that collaboration and visibility along the extended supply chain is required, in a shared business plan model.

"You have to remember that the supply chain needs to be all things to all customers. By that, I mean the supply chain must meet the specific needs of each customer if it is to be truly customer-centric.

"The model and related supply option is determined by where and how you meet the customer. You have several basic choices:

- *Make-to-stock (MTS):* End items are put into inventory in anticipation of demand.
- *Assemble-to-order (ATO):* Components are placed on order or put in inventory in anticipation of demand and then assembled as specific orders are received.

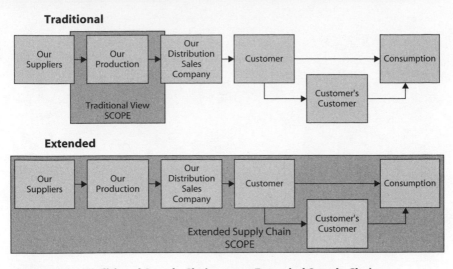

Figure 19.3   Traditional Supply Chain versus Extended Supply Chain
Source: Oliver Wight. Copyright Oliver Wight International, Inc. Used with permission.

- *Finish-to-order (FTO):* Materials are brought to varying degrees of completion, and completed to customer specifications when an order is received.
- *Make-to-order (MTO):* Material is ordered and labor invested only after a customer order is received; if the product must be designed to meet unique customer. specifications when an order is received, the supply option is called *design-to-order* or *engineer-to-order*.

"The choice, or choices, will depend mostly on how long the customer will wait for product, which is often determined by the responsiveness of your competitors. If customers expect your product in an amount of time (called 'wait time') less than your make or finish lead time, you will be forced into make-to-stock. Of course, if your value proposition is attractive enough, it is possible to change the customer's expectations. Many will then wait for some useful lead time, so you can finish-to-order, and at the same time increase the number of options for the customer. This capability can also lead to implementing a Configurator at order entry in conversation with the customer, or through web-based interactions. By the way, your APOS system has this functionality too! But typically, it is the fastest credible competitor who influences the customer's perception of acceptable wait time. Some companies employ multiple models to meet varying customer needs; to do so, the company must have a complete understanding of the customer's needs, the products' characteristics, and its own capabilities.

"Which leads us to the concept of supply option reality on the customer's terms [Figure 19.4].

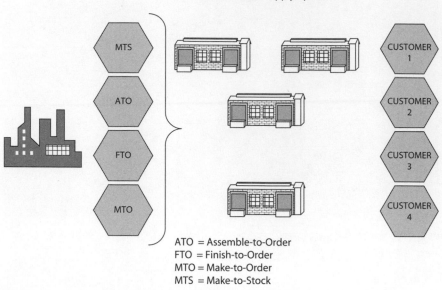

The supply chain needs to support all the differentiated supply options

ATO = Assemble-to-Order
FTO = Finish-to-Order
MTO = Make-to-Order
MTS = Make-to-Stock

Figure 19.4   Business Styles: Reality
Source: Oliver Wight. Copyright Oliver Wight International, Inc. Used with permission.

"The entire supply chain must be organized to support the selected supply options. This in turn," Tom reminded them, "leads to supply chain segmentation as a means of offering differentiated service and supply, depending on the customer group [Figure 19.5]."

Tom continued, "It's worth remembering that this is extremely important for Cosmetics Products because of the volatile nature of consumer demand for fashion products. When Tender Care Pet Products reaches this decision point, their more stable portfolio and more predictable demand will allow them simpler and different choices than you'll have to deal with. That means their demand control mechanisms will be less complex than yours."

Tom added, "On top of all this, you need to apply Lean thinking." He listed these points:

- *Leading Ideas:* Make your customers and their customers more successful.
- *Key Insight:* Process discipline and teaming enable performance.
- *Key Invention:* Projects produce the cash to pay for the programs.
- *Major Concept:* Customer anticipation coupled with compressed time enables agility.
- *Fundamental Concept:* Resource deployment, process design, and how work gets done must be driven by competitive priorities.

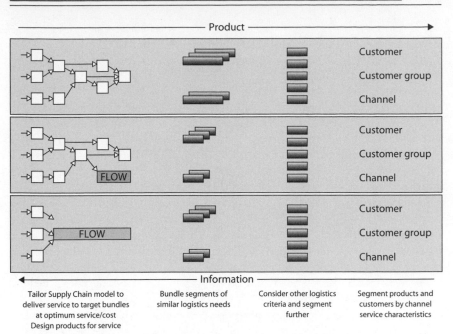

Figure 19.5 Differentiated Supply and Service through Segmentation
Source: Oliver Wight. Copyright Oliver Wight International, Inc. Used with permission.

Tom continued, "Providing Quick Response/Continuous Replenishment means anticipating customer demand to prepare the supply chain for response. This means:

- Interactive and dynamic demand management processes with the customer, including customer-managed forecasts
- Customer ePOS (real-time point of sale) data for fast-moving consumer goods
- Supplier-Managed Inventory (SMI) based on the customer's own data about current sales, promotions, and demand plans resulting in less inventory in the supply chain (it is not SMI when the customer just pushes inventory back onto the supplier's books)
- Responsive supply chain capability
- Realistic, honored time fences in the customer's ordering system
- Partnerships

"And, by the way, you'll need to educate your customers, just like you educated your suppliers during the Customer Service Initiative, to enable them to participate.

"The supply chain model must optimize the logistics footprint as an element of eliminating all forms of waste and reducing cash tied up in inventory. The control given by having your own logistics operations needs to be balanced by the opportunities and cost advantages offered by third-party logistics (3PL), or even alliance logistics (4PL)."

"More decisions to be made; my head is going to explode again! Is there any good news?" muttered David to himself.

Answering David's unasked question, Tom continued. "The good news is that your advanced planner, optimizer, and scheduler, with a bit of upscaling, will provide more than adequate support for all these needs, including direct interface with supplier and customer data systems, and collaboration.

"On the demand side, forecast modeling by account manager, linked to the latest customer and consumer ordering and shipment patterns, help predict near-term customer activity. By 'the latest,' I mean based on the previous 5 or 10 days for your fashion-sensitive products. A similar modeling process would be used to evaluate and respond to the impact of promotions. Promotions management is an acquired expertise based on the types of promotions used, the frequency, and the extent and dynamic nature of the promotions portfolio. The role of the Demand Control Manager must be expanded to include the prediction of mix, volumes, and geographies, as well as order-promising based on linearity constraints. All of this knowledge should be incorporated into the Knowledge Management System to enable the Demand Control Manager to truly manage opportunity demand with the objective of accepting as much demand as possible, but intelligently, and always within the supply chain network's capabilities. Let me give you an example of some leading edge capabilities.

"Today, some software applications are capable of processing billions of point of sale transactions, through retailer planning systems, linked directly to the distribution resource planning, master supply planning, and scheduling systems of manufacturing companies. Forecasts are developed by item and by store across an 18- to 24-month horizon and updated daily. In this process, which is an advanced form of supplier managed inventory, but across multiple nodes through the distribution network, the supplier or manufacturer is the recipient of improved forecasts and real-time inventory data, updated in real time, in all distribution nodes from the manufacturer to the customers' shelves. As a result, supply chains are reducing working capital by millions of dollars while reducing out-of-stocks and increasing availability of consumer units on store shelves. The result: increased velocity, increased sales, and reduced cost of goods sold. That combination is a winner for any supply chain.

"The Lean Supply Chain is continuously reducing inventories as it increases velocity and becomes more cost effective, but that leaves it with very little ability to respond to uncontrolled demand. That's why it is becoming critically important to merge demand and supply planning and activities."

Workshop participants had been given plenty to think about. However, their success with earlier initiatives enabled them to see the work ahead as just another series of healthy challenges.

During the Leadership Initiative, several unexpected events delayed completion. First, it became obvious that Cosmetics Products needed to create a full-time Packaging Engineering department to more effectively meet the challenges of continued expansion of its portfolio of products and promotion materials and an increasing demand for unique customer packaging formats and presentations. The Amalgamated Packaging Engineering group could no longer meet the needs of all Divisions. Greg's Leadership Team agreed with the direction but still wanted a close linkage with the corporate group to avoid unnecessary duplication of technology.

The rate of packaging changes had caused Procurement to begin to seek and develop packaging suppliers who used lean and agile manufacturing techniques. Their research based on a total-cost-of-ownership (TCO) model led them to Blingco Products Inc. in Cumming, near Atlanta. Blingco was a green-field start-up organization that had invested in good people and technology. Additionally, their parent company insisted that all education, processes, and technology be built on Class A concepts and principles. This became Cosmetics Products' first truly collaborative trading partner model, the first of what would become many for the Division.

Greg and his team had to resolve other emerging issues.

The Accessories Category had always been the problem child. Not strictly a core competency, it was a business difficult to control, but essential to many promotions. Customers and consumers loved special promotions containing a free accessory with the purchase of a product. Included in the options the executives considered was moving the business to a collaborative supplier-partner, but they couldn't find a supplier willing to handle the many different accessory types of accessory: leather, plastic, metal, glass and even electronics. Another option considered was outsourcing to a design and manufacturing agency in the Far East. The cost model suggested that the typical accessory cost at the final promotion assembly stage would be one-third that of the U.S. manufactured item, even with a TCO-based analysis. Attractive, but with one caveat. With a total lead time from idea to packaging of 16 weeks, Procurement was certain this option would not pass risk-assessment criteria. But Marketing was attracted by the increased margin potential. The end result was segmentation of accessories into "standard accessories" with the highest volume and fairly stable demand being outsourced to the Far East; and "tailored accessories," which were unique designs for a specific customer or promotion being manufactured by a much smaller Accessories division.

These decisions and risk assessments were facilitated by the division's move to activity-based costing (ABC). Andrew Jones, Amalgamated's CFO, had long ago stated that a move to ABC would occur "over his dead body," but later agreed to a pilot of the approach in Cosmetics Products, which began in the logistics organization. The resulting increase in knowledge of the nature and control of cost drivers, and the way ABC brought clarity to cost implications and decision-making processes impressed Andrew. The expansion of ABC to the rest of Cosmetics Products followed rapidly. It was now clear that many SKUs previously believed to be profitable were actually being subsidized by other products. This knowledge led to further portfolio rationalization and margin increase. As other divisions followed Cosmetics Products lead in Class A Initiatives, they, too, would move on to activity-based costing.

This major Supply Chain Leadership Initiative achieved sustained performance, including Upper Quartile performance in the U.S. Cosmetics Products industry, in 26 months, only two months behind schedule.

The course of life is never predictable: events outside their control contributed to the delay. David experienced a family crisis that required him to be out of the country for four weeks. Since formal succession planning was part of the new culture, Janice Hackworth, Supply Planning Manager, filled the role admirably during his absence. Six months after David's return, Sam Elliott, Senior VP Supply Chain, announced his retirement. Susan, in agreement with her Executive Committee, took Greg's recommendation and promoted David into Sam's role. Greg later confirmed Janice's promotion as a permanent replacement for David. Janice and Greg agreed to promote her backup into the role of Supply Planning Manager, and succession planning continued.

But the biggest change, about nine months into the Leadership Initiative, was Susan's announcement that she would be leaving Amalgamated in two months to accept the position of CEO of a global pharmaceutical company. Everyone was happy for Susan, but recognized that her loss would result a major leadership gap. Andrew Jones and James Richards, Chairman Emeritus, were named by the Board of Directors to lead the executive search. But during a meeting of Susan's Executive Team, Sam Elliott, whose retirement was now imminent, proposed Greg be promoted to CEO to maintain momentum and take advantage of all that he had learned. Greg was stunned but elated that his peers recognized his accomplishments and had enough confidence in his abilities to even entertain the notion. He excused himself from the meeting so that the others could openly discuss the proposal. Susan chaired the discussion but excused herself from the vote. After 30 minutes, Greg was called back into the conference room. Susan announced to Greg that her Executive Team was in unanimous agreement with Sam's recommendation. She and Andrew would speak with James Richards and carry the recommendation to the Board of Directors.

Two weeks later, the move was official. Greg was named CEO and Alexandra was promoted to the position of President, Cosmetics Products Division. Susan's vision of a viable Cosmetics Products business and her trust in Greg's ability to right the ship were rewarded.

Just three months after Greg's promotion, three Effective Management coaches conducted a four-day assessment. Following a compilation and analysis of the results through the eList and on-site assessments, Cosmetics Products was awarded Class A status in Business Excellence. As before, Greg and Alexandra organized a special celebration. They invited the entire Cosmetics Products organization, Amalgamated's Executive Team, the Board of Directors, Susan, local dignitaries, the local business press, and, of course, Roxanne, Dan, and Tom to the same Atlanta hotel where the initial kick-off event had been held. Sentimental, yes; but a memorable event.

This time, Alexandra called the meeting to order, acknowledged Greg and introduced Roxanne. "Greg, Susan, Alexandra, Board Members, and ladies and gentlemen. We completed the assessment of Cosmetics Products' processes and business results against the *Class A Checklist for Business Excellence*. I am extremely pleased to present Cosmetics Products its Class A Certification in Business Excellence. Your progress and results have been nothing short of remarkable!"

Roxanne continued her brief presentation making note of some of the impressive achievements. At the end of her remarks, Tom and Dan joined Roxanne uncovering the highly valued Class A Business Excellence Award. Roxanne called Greg and Alexandra forward and presented them with the Award to the flashes of the press photographers' cameras, and applause from the assembly.

Martin Bennett, President and CEO, Blackstone Pharmacies, next presented his company's "Supplier of the Year" Award to Cosmetics Products, noting his delight with the improvements made. He also announced that, based on seeing the turnaround at Amalgamated, he had just reached agreement with Effective Management to conduct a diagnostic assessment of Blackstone.

James Richards, Chairman Emeritus and grandson of Amalgamated Consumer Products Corporation's founder, expressed his thanks for the work done, benefits delivered and the rewards achieved. He said the accomplishments of Cosmetics Products were completely in the spirit of his grandfather, who would have been delighted with the stewardship of his company had he been present this day.

With that, Alexandra allowed Greg to hold the Award himself. She stepped back, publicly acknowledging his leadership in the achievement. Greg held the plaque for a time, and then raised it for all to see. He passed the Award back to Alexandra, who showed it to the other Leadership Team members and then set it on a stand and invited everyone to take a closer look. Greg then ended the official meeting and opened the doors for the celebratory dinner in the main ballroom.

Roxanne was interviewed by the local business press later and was asked to comment on what she considered the major contributors to winning the award. She replied without hesitation, "Commitment, persistence, and determination—led from the top. First, Greg had a personal commitment to excellence. He was the champion and never wavered in his commitment to success. Second, the company had an excellent succession plan in place. Alexandra picked up the reins when Greg was promoted and never missed a beat. Greg created one of the strongest leadership teams it has been my privilege to work with, and now he seems to be doing the same thing with Amalgamated's Executive Team. Watch this space for future announcements; Amalgamated's just beginning!"

At home, Penny remained the conscience that wouldn't let Greg give up his quest for excellence beyond excellence. Greg reminded Penny that his next challenge was a big one in getting all of Amalgamated to Class A. "That can't be nearly as difficult as it was the first time through!" she chided Greg. "After all you already know the road and location of all the potholes. You know, when you look closely at those maturity maps you've been studying, the company is already about half way to Class A, isn't it? The rest should be easier."

Greg tried to point out that the higher you move in the Transition chart, the harder it is to make it to the next level. "Well," she said as she smiled, "you know where I am if you need some help and guidance!" Penny was ever effective in keeping Greg's hat size from increasing. Both knew that Greg counted on Penny's encouragement, support, understanding, and straight feedback in good times as well as in the midst of seemingly unmanageable challenges.

20

SUSTAINABILITY AND MORE . . .

After all, the art is synchronization with a matched set of parts. Pushing and shoving is dysfunctional and results in gross mismatches.

I can foresee a day when they'll be left with niche markets only, and we'll be in the same league as the really big players, at least in the U.S. market.

Conscious incompetence is far better than unconscious incompetence.

It had taken enormous commitment, years of constant focus, and a division manager retiring early, but all divisions of Amalgamated Consumer Products Corporation had achieved the Class A Business Excellence Award. Greg knew now that the biggest danger was the possibility of regressing into complacency, even though the organization's culture had changed dramatically from when he joined the company. Penny reminded him, "When you're at the top, you have a long way to fall. Where's your safety harness, Greg?" The wise advice struck home. Several years ago, when Cosmetics Products completed its Customer Satisfaction Initiative, he had come close to easing up and basking in the glow of success. That possibility was short-lived when, once again, both Penny and Roxanne sounded the alarm and urged him and the Cosmetics Products team back into action. In his new role, he needed to keep his Executive Team and Division Presidents energized and committed to continuous improvement.

He continued to rely on Roxanne as his confidante, meeting with her about every two months. He brought up the subject of complacency during one of those meetings. After explaining what he was trying to accomplish, he asked her opinion about how to continue the progress.

Roxanne thought for a minute. "I'd like to start, Greg, by asking what you personally will do to sustain the gains, *and* to realize even more and bigger gains?"

"I've thought a lot about that, Roxanne. I'll be visiting every plant and office at least twice a year. I've asked Cynthia (who had followed with him when he was promoted CEO) to arrange and publish a visit schedule covering the next 12 months. In fact, I leave for the Dallas Plant to see Savannah Richmond and her team next Tuesday. I've told all division Presidents to inform the plant and office leaders that I don't want fancy presentations. I want to tour the facilities, talk to people at all levels, be available for group meetings to answer their questions about the business, and to find out from them what's new and what's troubling them. Those visits will also give me a better perspective on the talent we have coming along in the organization. I've also included a one-to-one meeting with the HR Directors who know I want the truth, and only the truth, about the health of the organization."

"That's a great start, Greg. What will you be doing to fan the flames of 'change for better,' the sort of stuff that energized everyone in Cosmetics Products in the past?"

"Good question. I've been working with two of my senior VPs, Alice Boyer, Engineering and Product Development, and Keely Horton, Human Resources. We've learned through the Product Management Milestones the importance of keeping a visible pipeline of ideas. We decided to use the same approach in each division to track how ideas, innovations, and improvements are moving along. As you know, we understand 'our second job' here; this approach gives us a formal repository for all ideas. We have all ideas and projects from every organization on a shared server and promote idea sharing between sites. We promote a learn-by-doing approach with carefully controlled pilots. The person who came up with the idea is provided necessary support and empowered to see if the idea works. If it works as intended or can be modified to work as intended, we roll out the improvement broadly. By the way, it's not a suggestion scheme with rewards. All ideas get a thank-you from the line manager, usually the person's team leader, and a note is placed in the personnel file so that the person is recognized again during his or her next performance review. Accepted ideas, and they're running at a remarkable 40 percent, result in a thank-you note from the division President. I personally meet with people who are responsible for breakthrough improvements. People whose ideas are accepted are also noted on our 'Second Job' intranet page with a photo and description of them and their ideas. We've been tracking ideas per employee, our measure of Total Employee Involvement, and the numbers have soared to the high end of the upper quartile of companies that track a similar measure. Or at least they had soared. We're seeing a recent decline in the number of ideas entering the pipeline and we haven't been able to determine an obvious reason."

"Any less obvious reasons, then? Tell me what was going on when the ideas were really flowing into the pipeline."

"Well, Amalgamated was in the last stages of getting our Class A awards. People were trying to close the final gaps, and drive results to the required high performance levels."

"And what did that feel like, to you?"

"No question about it, Roxanne, it was an exciting time." Greg recounted some of the challenges, successes, and disappointments he experienced at that time. Then he stopped. "I think I know what's missing now. At that time, we had a tough, seemingly impossible, challenge in front of us; we were all engaged in meeting the challenge while we continued to run the business; we worked side by side regardless of our functions or official jobs to help each other; we overcame barriers and celebrated successes, big and small. The organization was vibrant, and it was probably the most fun I've had at any time in my career.

"So I simply need to replicate what was going on then. I need to come up with a new, engaging challenge, and empower people to work on it. The question now is how to define that challenge. Why didn't I see that before?" Roxanne was a practitioner, as are all good consultants, of the teaching methods of Socrates. Socrates asked questions that led his students to discover their own answers. Roxanne mostly asked questions, providing guidance and teaching only when necessary.

"You've got it, Greg. Next, two more questions. What are Amalgamated's competitive priorities today? My second question is whether your vision and mission are still relevant, given the progress you've made?"

"I see where you're headed, Roxanne. I suppose in the past few months we've all relaxed a bit. I now need to engage my Executive Team in a discussion about our competitive priorities for each division. It's also time to schedule another session to review Amalgamated's vision and mission statements and our strategic objectives. With our enhanced Integrated Business Management process and tools in place and working extraordinarily well, this should be a far easier task than in the past. As you suggested some time ago, we've upgraded our process to enhance modeling at both detail and aggregate levels, and we implemented a Corporate Performance Management system. It gives us an overview picture of Corporate and Division-by-Division performance, as well as a view of strategy deployment, financial reality and opportunities, business intelligence, and other key pointers to potential threats or opportunities.

"It is important for us to get a fresh look at the competition, threats, and opportunities. We've obviously been talking about these regularly, or we wouldn't be Class A, but we've not been thinking about them in the context of 'the impossible dream' to really energize us and take the business to another level."

"When did you last look at the maturity maps and Transitions, Greg? You and your team could begin there."

"Good point. In fact, I'll look at them myself to see if they get my creative juices flowing."

"One more thing to think about again is succession planning," Roxanne continued. "You did this well in Cosmetics Products, but I'm not so sure about where you are with Amalgamated's senior management. People constitute the greatest strength of companies, and often present the greatest potential weakness. Like a race engine that outperforms its rivals, Amalgamated is a finely tuned organization now. You wouldn't allow just any mechanic to tune a high performance engine; the risk would be too high. Yet I'm always surprised by companies that make that very mistake.

"For example, I know two young managers, let's call them Bill and Doug, who, coincidentally, met each other during one of our Supply Planning in Practice courses. They'd just been hired as Supply Planning Managers in two different automobile companies. Bill was in a Class A Japanese Company; Doug in an American company, not yet Class A, but getting there. Coincidentally, they met again five months later on one of Effective Management's Proven Path Club seminars. They talked about their experiences over coffee. Bill asked Doug how it was going. Doug replied that after his initial training and orientation, he started working with the existing Supply Planning Manager and within six weeks was doing the job on his own. In response to Doug's question about Bill's experience with the Japanese auto company, he said that after five months he was still learning what happens on the production line, how the people, processes, and tools worked together, the quality culture, and the high-performance team culture. If he continued to make good progress, he would begin working in the Supply Planning office in another six weeks. Which company was doing a better job of protecting its performance and culture; and which was putting itself at greater risk?" Greg agreed that without question Bill would be better prepared and "fit-for-purpose" to be a contributing team member.

"And if I'm going to protect my 'finely tuned engine' here, we need to do a more thorough job of preparing new people coming into our organization. Is that your message, Roxanne?"

"Yes, but let me expand that message and be more specific. This is a true story about a Class A company. Some time ago, the company's COO developed a heart condition and was advised by his doctor to move to a less stressful position, which he did. Within six weeks, the Board of Directors appointed to the COO position 'a high profile achiever' from outside the company. For three months, the financials improved as he cut what he called excessive overhead. But then the company started a downhill slide, soon undoing six years of progress. The new COO stated frequently, 'All this people stuff is nonsense.' He instructed those who wanted to stay on his staff to 'forget the soft stuff' and to push their people relentlessly until they exceeded all performance objectives. He insisted on overloading production lines by 20 percent stating, 'What these guys need is a challenge to make them work harder.'

Morale and productivity declined, inventories overflowed the warehouse and were even being stored in rented truck trailers lined up in parking lots. Customer service suffered since the product in the warehouse and trailers was too often the wrong product. After all, the key to success is synchronization of customer requirements with a flow of matched sets of parts and end-items. Dysfunctional pushing and shoving of the supply chain results in gross mismatches and poor customer service. The company's total sales of finished product fell by nearly 30 percent. All performance measures declined to below 95 percent and customer service plummeted to 65 percent during the seasonal peak, resulting in nearly $100 million in lost sales. Sadly, direct confrontation by his direct reports did no good in changing his behaviors. Making matters worse, no one was willing to risk going to members of the Board of Directors to express their concerns. It was only when the end of quarter results were reported that the Board saw how badly results had deteriorated in what had been the company's best division. They reacted swiftly by sending in a consultant with Class A credentials to determine what had happened. It didn't take long to discover the source of the problem: the new COO. Within the month, the Board bought out the COO's contract and replaced him with someone from inside the company. It took three months to restore performance to the Capable level, and a further two years to restore their Class A status. Poor execution of succession planning, and lack of 'fit-for-job' requirements at all levels were the root causes of the decline."

She paused and waited for Greg to respond. "We spend a good deal of time at the lower levels planning for succession, and I believe we did a pretty good job with the executives in Cosmetics Products, but I get your point. We have work to do here with the corporate executives. I need to start grooming the successors for the people on my staff and, at some time soon, for my own role if we intend to sustain our gains and deliver even further gains." Roxanne just smiled.

With this in mind, Greg talked with Roxanne about the people on his staff and potential retirements in the next two years. He tried to balance in his mind the value of bringing in fresh thinking and the value of continuity gained by promoting people who had been through the years of improvements and knew how processes should work.

They discussed other issues, including Greg's desire to promote Peter Bertrand as a well-deserved reward for his key role in coordinating all the Class A Initiatives so successfully. Peter had matured into a very capable manager and had developed an enormous understanding of all aspects of the business as a result of his involvement with all the teams. He was a team player, and he got the job done. Roxanne suggested that Peter could be invaluable in reenergizing the company's move to the next level, and recommended that Greg figure out a way to make him a member of Amalgamated's Executive Team. Greg understood the advantage for him and for Peter and agreed to consider the recommendation.

Back in his office, Greg had Cynthia photocopy all the Maturity Transition charts. Out of the formidable stack, he decided he would first concentrate on eight supply chain related charts. He would compare Transition 4, their current status, with Transition 5, the next level of maturity. First he looked at Demand Planning and Demand Control charts [Figure 20.1].

Greg was looking for the characteristics that differentiated companies in Transition 5 from those in Transition 4. He knew the descriptions in the charts weren't extremely detailed, but contained enough detail to be useful for senior executives. It appeared to Greg that current Demand improvement activities were supportive of Transition 5 characteristics, although it would take too long to actually get there at the current rate of improvement.

He looked next at the Internal Supply charts [Figure 20.2].

He saw in Supply Planning reference to artificial intelligence (AI) systems and Upper Decile performance. In Transition 5 of the Supply Execution chart he saw near 100 percent performance expectation. He wanted to review this with David, but it appeared there was more they needed to accomplish in the physical world of manufacturing. He could envision no way of achieving this level of performance without additional automation and intelligent control systems. "Right-first-time" suddenly took on a new dimension.

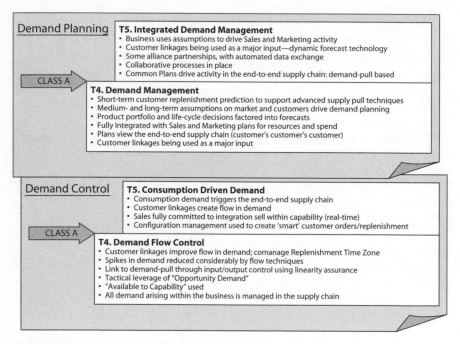

Figure 20.1   Demand Maturity Transitions 4 and 5
Source: Oliver Wight. Copyright Oliver Wight International, Inc. Used with permission.

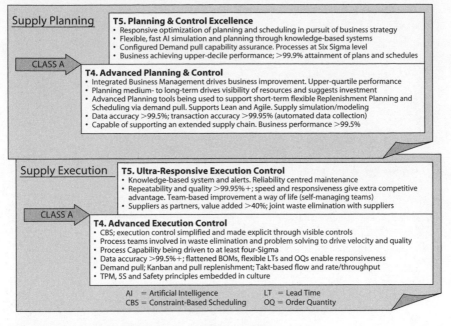

Figure 20.2   Supply Maturity Transitions 4 and 5
Source: Oliver Wight. Copyright Oliver Wight International, Inc. Used with permission.

He turned to the Product and Knowledge Management charts [Figure 20.3].

The traffic light suddenly turned red for Greg. He realized he needed to look at these maps as an integrated package. Until this point, he had been viewing them as Cynthia printed them, chart by chart. But now he moved to the conference room and laid them out on the long table, side by side, and read across from chart to chart. Now they made much more sense! He realized that Knowledge Management was a key requirement everywhere and was relieved that they had already invested in a system. He would need to determine if it would fully support Transition 5. He saw the term "parametric design," and hoped Matt would know what that meant since he had only the vaguest idea. He saw requirements for additional automation in planning and office activities as well as in manufacturing and decision support, with something called "alerts," with "auto-responses." That also was new to him. And he needed to learn more about what was called "auto-sales" and "auto-marketing," terms equally unfamiliar.

Greg could now view Supply Chain and Distribution Transitions [Figure 20.4] in the context of the others on the table; what was needed began to fall into place for him.

He next added all the other Transition charts to the side-by-side display on the conference room table. He began making notes about his discoveries and

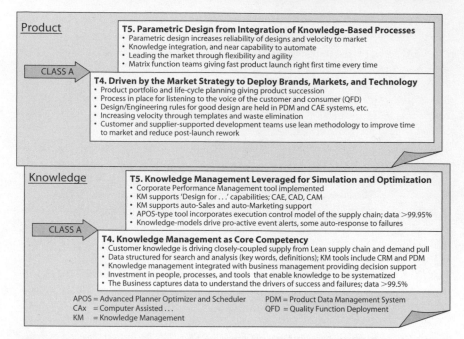

Product

T5. Parametric Design from Integration of Knowledge-Based Processes
- Parametric design increases reliability of designs and velocity to market
- Knowledge integration, and near capability to automate
- Leading the market through flexibility and agility
- Matrix function teams giving fast product launch right first time every time

CLASS A

T4. Driven by the Market Strategy to Deploy Brands, Markets, and Technology
- Product portfolio and life-cycle planning giving product succession
- Process in place for listening to the voice of the customer and consumer (QFD)
- Design/Engineering rules for good design are held in PDM and CAE systems, etc.
- Increasing velocity through templates and waste elimination
- Customer and supplier-supported development teams use lean methodology to improve time to market and reduce post-launch rework

Knowledge

T5. Knowledge Management Leveraged for Simulation and Optimization
- Corporate Performance Management tool implemented
- KM supports 'Design for . . .' capabilities; CAE, CAD, CAM
- KM supports auto-Sales and auto-Marketing support
- APOS-type tool incorporates execution control model of the supply chain; data >99.95%
- Knowledge-models drive pro-active event alerts, some auto-response to failures

CLASS A

T4. Knowledge Management as Core Competency
- Customer knowledge is driving closely-coupled supply from Lean supply chain and demand pull
- Data structured for search and analysis (key words, definitions); KM tools include CRM and PDM
- Knowledge management integrated with business management providing decision support
- Investment in people, processes, and tools that enable knowledge to be systematized
- The Business captures data to understand the drivers of success and failures; data >99.5%

APOS = Advanced Planner Optimizer and Scheduler
CAx = Computer Assisted . . .
KM = Knowledge Management
PDM = Product Data Management System
QFD = Quality Function Deployment

Figure 20.3   Product and Knowledge Maturity Transitions 4 and 5
Source: Oliver Wight. Copyright Oliver Wight International, Inc. Used with permission.

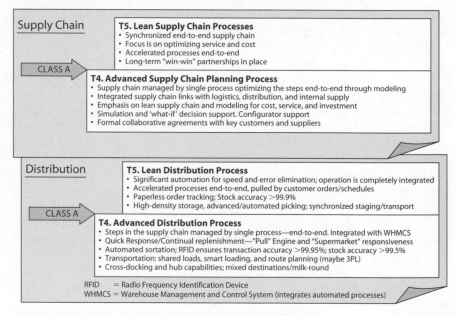

Supply Chain

T5. Lean Supply Chain Processes
- Synchronized end-to-end supply chain
- Focus is on optimizing service and cost
- Accelerated processes end-to-end
- Long-term "win-win" partnerships in place

CLASS A

T4. Advanced Supply Chain Planning Process
- Supply chain managed by single process optimizing the steps end-to-end through modeling
- Integrated supply chain links with logistics, distribution, and internal supply
- Emphasis on lean supply chain and modeling for cost, service, and investment
- Simulation and 'what-if' decision support. Configurator support
- Formal collaborative agreements with key customers and suppliers

Distribution

T5. Lean Distribution Process
- Significant automation for speed and error elimination; operation is completely integrated
- Accelerated processes end-to-end, pulled by customer orders/schedules
- Paperless order tracking; Stock accuracy >99.9%
- High-density storage, advanced/automated picking; synchronized staging/transport

CLASS A

T4. Advanced Distribution Process
- Steps in the supply chain managed by single process—end-to-end. Integrated with WHMCS
- Quick Response/Continual replenishment—"Pull" Engine and "Supermarket" responsiveness
- Automated sortation; RFID ensures transaction accuracy >99.95%; stock accuracy >99.5%
- Transportation: shared loads, smart loading, and route planning (maybe 3PL)
- Cross-docking and hub capabilities; mixed destinations/milk-round

RFID = Radio Frequency Identification Device
WHMCS = Warehouse Management and Control System (integrates automated processes)

Figure 20.4   Supply Chain Maturity Transitions 4 and 5
Source: Oliver Wight. Copyright Oliver Wight International, Inc. Used with permission.

listing questions prompted by the review. At last he was developing a vision of the future, albeit still a bit fuzzy, and a sense of what he now knew he didn't know. He recalled someone telling him early in his career that conscious incompetence is far better than unconscious incompetence. The last hour's study moved him solidly into conscious incompetence. He now knew what he had to learn next. But he couldn't go there by himself; he needed to get the rest of his team to the same level of understanding.

Greg later discovered that David, too, had been trying to understand the characteristics of Transition 5. He could answer many of Greg's technical questions about the new terms relating to supply and planning, but was having difficulty seeing how the work to reach Transition 5 would come together, especially to deliver nearly 100 percent reliable performance.

Finally, Greg asked Cynthia to schedule a full day off-site meeting for his Executive Team and Peter Bertrand, with Roxanne, to plan for sustainability and future improvements. Roxanne suggested to Cynthia that Les Johnson, one of Effective Management's Transition 5 experts, would bring a broader perspective and experience for that session. She explained that Les had experience actually working in the rarefied atmosphere of Transition 5 companies. Les led that effort for his company, before joining Effective Management, and became the first company in that industry to be certified at that level. Amalgamated would be joining a very small and elite group if and when they became one of the few Upper Decile performers in a mature industry sector.

When the team assembled, Greg first introduced Les, then explained his conversations with Roxanne on sustainability and succession planning. Les provided some insights from Transition 5 and 6 companies. This led to an energetic debate before they agreed in principle to move toward the new succession and development philosophy, and charged Keely Horton, Senior VP Human Resources, to prepare a structured proposal and related costs, if any. Greg reminded his team that two Senior VPs would be retiring within six months. He wanted a succession pilot program created to learn how to be more effective in bringing senior managers into the company, or into more senior roles in the case of promotion. Again he turned to Keely to shepherd this effort. Keely reminded Greg that she would be one of the two retirees, along with Andrew Jones, CFO. "Who knows better what onboarding activities, education, and training will make your replacement effective?" chided Greg. Keely agreed to begin developing the plan immediately and would personalize the plan based on the chosen successor.

They also agreed with little hesitation to create and fill an executive position reporting to Keely with responsibility for managing the social responsibilities of the company, both internally and in the public forum. Keely would flesh out the specific responsibilities and compensation plan after speaking with her counterparts in other socially responsible companies.

Then Greg invited everyone to stand along one side of the long table. He arranged all the Transition charts side by side, just as he had done for himself.

Les took over at this point, asking people to read Transition 5 characteristics on the sheet directly in front of each individual. When finished with that chart, he asked them to move one position to the right, as in a loop, and repeat the process until they arrived back at their starting point. Sequence didn't matter, he explained, since all the processes were integrated. Depending on the individual's background and knowledge, each saw the whole picture from a slightly different perspective that enriched the team's understanding of the whole picture of Transition 5.

They perceived a significant challenge, and felt they'd been thrown into the deep end of the pool. Les answered direct questions from the team for the next hour. As the questions waned, David asked Greg a question.

"That was a very interesting exercise, Greg, but what was your purpose? I know you must have one."

"I'm going to answer that question with one of my own directed to all of you. What do you think of the opportunity Transition 5 provides? I know I normally ask you to make decisions based on hard numbers and facts, but I want to talk about feelings for a moment. What are you feeling having just read the characteristics of Transition 5 companies?"

Alexandra, now President of Cosmetics Products, was first to reply. "I was confused at first by the information overload and the new terminology, but as Les answered our questions and explained some of those terms, I began to see some real possibilities. As you all know, I go through in detail the quarterly benchmark data and monthly competitor marketing activity reports. Over the past five years, each of our divisions has hurt their competitors, especially our Cosmetics Products and Home Products competitors. Several smaller competitors have gone out of business or had to sell some of their brands, many of which are now, happily, in our portfolios. Over the past twelve months, however, we've started to see some aggressive responses from the bigger competitors in those two sectors. First we noticed significantly improved advertising using very creative humor to get consumers' attention. More recently we're seeing improving customer service to the wholesalers and major retail accounts to the point that their lower prices are eroding a little of our market share. Typically we're seeing from them good package design and a 5 percent margin increase for the customers—the retail outlets; we suspect it must be cutting into their profits, but we need to respond. We need to keep clear blue water between them and us. If we can do that sustainably, I foresee a day when they'll be left with niche markets only, and we'll be in the same league as the really big players, at least in the domestic market. You know, I feel really excited about the possibilities of Transition 5. I needed that boost!"

"Anyone else?" asked Greg.

Over the next 45 minutes, each offered an opinion and recommendation, varying from cautiously positive to enthusiastic, for pursuing Transition 5, which they began calling "Ultraresponsive." And that became the name of the new initiative, the "Ultraresponsive Service Initiative."

"And that's why I took us through this exercise," Greg said. We were becoming complacent, at least I was. We had lost the excitement of the challenge. Competitors were taking advantage of that and beginning to catch up. As I read the characteristics of Transition 5, the excitement of the challenge began returning. Seems it has for the rest of you as well."

As before, this new challenge excited and motivated the people, and once again there was a buzz of anticipation in the air. Les Johnson felt he'd helped the team align, but that it would be better if he let the group develop its own proposals. With Greg's agreement, he left and invited them to call him at any time.

Organizing the new Initiative proceeded with Greg and his staff completing the Leadership Phase of the Proven Path, including a sound business case for the Initiative. Greg presented his plan to the Board and received enthusiastic support to launch the Ultraresponsive Service Initiative. The announcement throughout Amalgamated energized the organization and rekindled the sense of exploration, creativity, and fun. The challenge presented to this true learning organization improved morale, even though everyone recognized the breakthrough nature and difficulty of accomplishing the stated objectives. The growth objectives, for example, caused concern among some that they would begin competing directly with some of the industry giants in the Americas. Most welcomed the excitement of that challenge and still found it hard to believe Amalgamated had grown so large over the past few years.

Les came in regularly to coach, to encourage, and to conduct focused assessments to ensure processes remained integrated and on track. David perceived a conflict in one important area between what they had learned, and what they were actually experiencing. During one of Les's visits, David set aside some time to discuss it a fairly technical but important concern.

David recognized a conflict between what he had understood about the three "Value Disciplines," Product Leadership; Customer Intimate; Price Competitive, and what they were now experiencing with their current speed and agility, differentiated process lines, and segmentation [Figure 19.5]. They no longer saw the necessity of "focusing on one discipline" within the organization, as they'd been taught in the early days of Cosmetics Products' first initiative. This seemed to be even truer in the case of the Ultraresponsive Service Initiative. David was concerned that he was missing something. To his surprise, however, Les agreed with his statement, adding, "When you were still getting your act together, back in the days of your Customer Service Initiative, what you heard about focusing on one Value Discipline was absolutely necessary. Since then, you've shifted paradigms several times, to the extent that in most cases the need to focus no longer applies, especially as you move into Transition 5. That need began to change when you approached Class A and you were facing a completely different situation. However, you must never let go of your focus on the customer in your Value Proposition, which defines the holistic benefits you want your customers to experience when doing business with your company. That must always include a desired external perception that distinguishes your company, such as a Product Leader for products under specific brands. But within the organization the supply chain must be responsive to all three of the disciplines in any mix. Your Value Proposition should also include the ease of placing orders; the courtesy experienced in phone calls; error-free communications and product; and all the other attributes you would like your customers to experience." After a few more minutes of discussion, David understood and was satisfied that when they were at the Capable level, they had needed to focus on one Value Discipline, but with the enablers created in reaching Class A, they were no longer constrained.

While Amalgamated implemented the new Initiative, Greg and his Executive Team made several other key decisions affecting all the other work. He was now glad he'd not reduced staff in response to the resulting productivity gains. Some of those individuals would be invaluable in helping Amalgamated move to Transition 5. Amalgamated formed a company-wide Business Excellence team to support Initiative teams in all Division and to develop a charter and program to maintain the culture of continuous improvement even beyond Transition 5.

Both Cosmetics Products' and Home Products' eco-friendly product lines continued growing at double digit rates. Amalgamated could now provide consumer-responsive products at acceptable prices and margins. Consumer Products was becoming reliant on the capabilities of a highly competent Texas supplier of unique component materials. A risk assessment highlighting this crucial dependency led Greg to a decision to vertically integrate the company into Amalgamated. The long-term positive relationship between the companies enabled the friendly merger to be completed within six months. During the negotiations, Amalgamated demonstrated its interest and sensitivity to the views of the employees and the community in which the factory was located. They volunteered their manufacturing, logistics, and human resource values and plans with the county and local planners, and flew a contingent of plant personnel to Atlanta to visit with their peers in Cosmetics Products. The integration of the new company into Amalgamated included plans to bring their Planning and Control and Integrated Business Management processes to the Capable level within nine months. Meanwhile, the Texas management team was immersed in learning Amalgamated's culture using the succession planning model, values, and principles of doing business. Amalgamated also benefited from areas where the Texas company excelled. After working through a few difficult acquisition problems, the company was absorbed into the Amalgamated culture and contributed to Amalgamated's growth strategy.

After lengthy discussions with his Executive Team, and consideration of the Board of Directors, Greg was nearing a decision on another strategic move for Amalgamated. For some time he had been convinced the time was right to enter the European Union (EU) market, somewhat bigger than the U.S. market and essential to meeting the corporation's long-term growth objectives. Greg decided to begin the expansion in Spain. Amalgamated had a number of Hispanics at all levels of the organization; language would not be a barrier for them, and market research confirmed a potentially significant market for Amalgamated's products. Rosetta Ruiz, who had replaced Andrew Jones as CFO, was delighted with this news and modified her employees' personal objectives to incorporate this new strategic objective. She followed the advice of professional financial advisors, and discovered available grants if their factory were built in a "development" area. An expansion team, called Team Spain, ensured there was suitable infrastructure for component delivery and outbound shipping. Team Spain proposed first opening a Distribution Center in Barcelona since logistics support in that very large market area was superb. Packaging changes were planned to add necessary language copy, incorporate Spanish market advertising aesthetics, and comply with EU regulations. The need for a few minor formulation adjustments would present minimum challenges and not affect formulation costs.

Expansion of their products into Spain was successful, meeting all volume and profit objectives. A green field site was acquired in eastern Spain, and the first buildings were erected within a year. The first construction priority was a mixing and finishing line to minimize shipping costs for intermediates and finished products. High-quality packaging and container suppliers were identified and brought into the supply chain as partners rather than as adversaries. The strong working alliance with its suppliers increased the company's flexibility in adding product sizes, creating short lead-time promotions, and creating new and innovative packaging.

The management staff selected for construction and start-up was composed primarily of managers transferred from Atlanta and Dallas, either already Spanish-speaking or provided intense language skills courses to minimize language problems. Local management talent was identified by a management recruiter in Barcelona. Amalgamated invested heavily in the new Spanish managers who spent two months in Atlanta and Dallas learning about the company, its products and, importantly, about the concepts and principles of Class A. The new plant and distribution center were designed and operated from the beginning with Class A policies and procedures, and used Amalgamated's global ERP system with advanced planning, optimizing, and scheduling capabilities. The Business Excellence team visited the new site frequently during the first year and reported the site was in compliance with Class A standards based on a detailed internal assessment. Amalgamated was now considering expansion into Germany. The even stricter environmental regulations there would provide a useful validation of their eco-friendly product model, including packaging and product disposal.

Back in Atlanta, Alexandra, now promoted to Senior VP Marketing and Sales, and Henry Stinson, Senior VP Quality and Regulatory Affairs, teamed up to drive quality and Sales and Marketing performance measures within the Ultraresponsive Service Initiative to 100 percent. When Greg mentioned that Transition 5 performance measurement requirement was 99.95 percent,

Alexandra translated that performance to 500 ppm failures. Now that Amalgamated shipped more than a million units every day, 500 ppm meant approximately 3,000 failures each week, a clearly unacceptable level of failures for Amalgamated's Executive Team. A strong desire to achieve Transition 5 and its expectation of nearly failure-free performance led to further interest in robotics and other forms of automation to eliminate the potential for human error. In turn, using robotics necessitates nearly 100 percent data integrity since robotics lines cannot produce error-free product without error-free input data. Similarly, transactions would have to be at least 99.9995 percent right first time with real-time automated input. The decision whether to move to a broad scale deployment of robotics in fully integrated automation was still in the future for the Executive Team, but the Initiative to take Amalgamated to Transition 5 had reenergized all of Amalgamated, resulted in positive press coverage, and proved again that success breeds success.

Alice Boyer, Senior VP Engineering and Product Development, suggested that Amalgamated invest in a "Skunk Works"® to expand the boundaries of current thinking and to prepare for technology beyond today's limits. She stressed the importance of keeping such a group isolated from the highly controlled business environment, company regulations, and free from all but health, safety and legal constraints. The Skunk Works, she explained, should be co-led by a person who was a true entrepreneur and a second person who was a sound business manager from the Atlanta headquarters office. The new group's mission would be to transform, or even create, customer and consumer desires into breakthrough products and services. Given the combined capabilities of their people, processes and tools, ideas could pass through product design, development and launch at high speed. Increasing use of and reliance on the integrated knowledge management systems would be critical to success at meeting product specifications and dates right-first-time, with manufacturable products. Their mission would be to make Amalgamated the most innovative consumer goods company on the planet! Greg asked for information about how other leading-edge companies managed similar innovation teams. Alice was ready for the question and summarized the procedures of several other companies in different industries.

Greg later shared his thinking and recommendation with his Board of Directors. The Skunk Works was created and staffed. Within nine months of its formation, it had created two totally new-to-the-world Home Products innovations. One of these was based on nanotechnology, meaning Amalgamated was making yet another capital investment in its future.

Amalgamated achieved its Ultraresponsive Service Initiative, reaching upper decile performance and Transition 5, within two years. Their rapid growth continued at the planned rate domestically and globally. Several of their competitors retrenched to become producers of niche products, selling off some of their products to other companies, including Amalgamated. The work begun in

Cosmetics Products had transformed the entire company and far exceeded the expectations of the Board of Directors and shareholders.

The question about robotics resurfaced. Amalgamated's Executive Team was ready to consider the significant investment required to overcome barriers to further continuous improvement. The benefits were now obvious to the team: near elimination of human error, significantly increased agility, reduction of quality defects to nearly zero ppm through further reduction of process variation were all necessary to further distance themselves from their competitors. The only question to be addressed was one of return on investment. The team would make its decision following a three-month opportunity and feasibility study.

With its corporate culture of continuous improvement, abhorrence of the status quo, recognition of the strategic value of its human assets, ability to conceive and launch products well inside competitors' lead times, and commitment to sustainability, Amalgamated Consumer Products Corporation would continue to transform challenges into business opportunities with its high-performing, self-directed team approach. Amalgamated's people would continue to be its greatest strength in its continuing journey to be a leading global company.

No less important, the quality of life at work and at home improved noticeably as employees at all levels regained control of their business. Now that routine things happened routinely, people from the executive ranks to the shop floor spent their time improving processes, products, and results for all stakeholders. They also spent more time with their families.

Greg and Penny watched their boys grow into responsible adults, the younger of the two now completing a premed program with a goal of becoming a neurosurgeon; the older about to complete his second Masters degree, an MBA to go along with his Masters in engineering. As they finished dinner and strolled back to their private villa overlooking the island's lagoon, they also rediscovered that two-week vacations were as relaxing and romantic as they had been ten years earlier.

The end . . . of the beginning.

Epilogue

In dysfunctional companies, those considered the better players
are the ones who actually cause the most disruption to the supply chain.

The customer isn't always right, but is always the
customer, and don't you forget it!

Most companies, like Cosmetics Products, are dysfunctional to varying degrees. Both the best and the worst companies are typically led by strong individuals or family members who want to succeed. Only those who truly understand the integrated nature of a company and the need for education, leadership, and customer focus, however, win in the marketplace. Those who don't, create dysfunctional organizations that act a bit like elephants, wandering around gathering their food by almost superstitiously following the same tracks for the same food day after day, year after year. That's their paradigm. The only time elephants alter their direction is when they smell smoke and fear a fire. The elephants may make it to safety if they can change their paradigm and move fast enough, but many of them don't succeed. Much like the elephants, dysfunctional companies sooner or later are faced with their own "burning platforms."

Consider this real-life situation. The chief financial officer (CFO) of a major corporation, concerned about an unacceptable balance sheet, issued an edict through the chief operating officer (COO) to reduce all inventories by 7.5 percent. This, he had calculated, would restore the balance sheet to health. Had he understood the integrated nature of the supply chain, he would have predicted the consequences of his edict. Inventory of all types was reduced across the board by 7.5 percent as ordered. Shortly thereafter, customer service declined, as did market share and revenue. At the end of the quarter, the CFO was faced with a balance sheet that now looked even worse! He learned that you can't steer a business from the balance sheet, as many businesses attempt. The balance sheet simply accumulates the results of hundreds of processes, thousands of decisions and hundreds of thousands of transactions.

In that regard, a business is like a race car. When finely tuned, its engine performs incredibly well. But it doesn't take much change to reduce its performance. Push it too hard trying to overcome declining performance, and it will explode.

As with the engine, seemingly insignificant changes in one area of a business produce consequences of varying magnitude in almost all other areas. Federal, state and local governments, too, often overlook complex interdependencies and experience serious unintended decision-making consequences. The art of decision-making is to understand and avoid the unintended consequences through fully integrating processes and aligning plans. As Greg was reminded frequently in our story, everything is interdependent. Consider the traditional children's game of "pick-up sticks." Every executive team should have this game on its conference room table as a reminder of what happens when it attempts to tweak one part of the business in isolation.

In dysfunctional companies, those considered the better players are the ones who actually cause the most disruption to the supply chain, such as untamed expeditors, salespeople who over-sell, manufacturing people who give unrealistic promises and then force product through the supply chain. With excellent companies, the better players are those who understand the integrated nature of the supply chain, who leverage its capabilities, and who embrace and lead continuous improvement efforts.

Greg was a natural leader who was limited by his lack of understanding of the complex system of people, processes, and tools that surrounded him. But throughout the course of his Class A journey he actively learned and developed the required level of understanding. Greg made the effort required to understand integration and learned from his mistakes—those extremely dysfunctional decisions he made early in the story.

Greg's success can be repeated by all leaders who follow his path, but less than 1 percent will. Those who don't, often haven't developed a customer-centric vision and mission and haven't demonstrated that they value their people. Interestingly, we often ask the question, "Do you value your employees?" The usual response is "Yes." We follow with the question, "How would *they* know that?" Too often, the response is silence.

In this book, we also explain that companies have a debt to all stakeholders, including society in general. Their debt to society begins to accrue when parents bring their children, your future employees, into the world and nurture them; it continues to accrue as a result of the contribution of local child support services including health care organizations and educators from kindergarten through college, and from all the infrastructure and utilities we take for granted. Without this enabling infrastructure, no company could survive. While the objective, and requirement, of all business is to make a profit, that profit cannot be at the expense of the company's employees, the community, or society in general. If you break this unwritten contract, your debt will be called in soon, and your company will fail.

Sadly, most managers seem to have forgotten that their objective is to make a profit not just today, but also in the future. Too many managers don't even have an effective mechanism in place for either predicting or managing the future. You observed Greg learning how to do both by implementing Integrated Business Management. From the very beginning, Greg was a champion of the customer; after all, for several years he had been a disgruntled Cosmetics Products customer himself. But Greg had neither the processes nor the profound knowledge required to translate into reality that desire for excellent customer service which was required to produce the profit he needed. Through the processes created under the tutelage of Effective Management, he learned to see his customers and his business in a new light. The adage, "The customer isn't always right, but is always the customer, and don't you forget it!" became his mantra.

When you put customers first, you would never put untrained people on production lines, in laboratories, or on customer contact phone lines. The best companies ensure that new people are fully "fit-for-purpose" before being permitted to influence service to customers. Yet many companies are quick to do just that with executives and managers. They believe they can parachute new people into these roles without making them fit-for-purpose. In this story, we included examples of how it should be done at both the operating and management levels. How closely does your company follow these practices?

Of course, there is no Effective Management company or Effective Management Class A Checklist. But there is *The Oliver Wight Class A Checklist for Business Excellence* and Proven Path that represent a continuously increasing benchmark standard of achievement and a proven methodology for attaining Oliver Wight Class A status. Don't be discouraged when you read through the Checklist for the first time. It appears daunting and is, unless you approach it as Greg did, following a proven milestone path. Remember, too, that it took Cosmetics Products about eight years to achieve Class A status. For many companies, it will take even longer. The more committed the senior executive and senior management team, the faster will be the progress. Greg was hesitant at first, but his declining business results, his willingness to learn from others, and the strong support from Susan, gave him a foundation for success and the drive to succeed.

Our founder and inspiration was the late Oliver (Ollie) Wight. Ollie recognized the problems faced by manufacturing companies; understood the synergistic power of People, Processes, and Tools; and had a deep commitment to help business leaders "transform the face of industry." He helped his clients simplify and solve seemingly intractable business issues and achieve results previously thought unachievable. He was often heard to say, "Computers are not the key to success, people are!" This deep-seated belief in people as the only competitive advantage remains a core belief of all Oliver Wight consultants and employees around the globe.

Whatever your industry, we recommend, at the very least, beginning a Business Excellence journey with the Capable Integrated Business Management and Capable Planning and Control Milestones. Completing these first milestones will make a remarkable difference in your organization and your bottom line. Then move ahead with milestones tailored to your most pressing competitive challenges. Almost certainly, when you begin to see the holistic transformation of your company, you'll continue along the journey to Class A.

To achieve the benefits of Class A, you'll need active commitment from the very top of the organization, the involvement of nearly everyone in the business, and persistence. Above all, as business leaders, you must lead with a passion for excellence and success. Will you?

Reader's Reference Guide

This book is for executives, senior and upper-middle managers. It depicts one Company's journey to 'Class A Business Excellence'. It is based on a representative, but fictional, mid-size company with multiple operating divisions. Many people and business processes are touched by a journey of such magnitude. This Reader's Reference Guide lists the people and positions they hold as you meet them in the story—the players'.

In the story, the company and players embark on carefully structured 'Business Excellence Improvement Initiatives', which are described in related chapters of the story. The breakdown of each Initiative is included in this guide, showing the Company's journey, driven by their competitive priorities. Your company's journey could well be different, but still needs to be carefully structured, depending on your competitive priorities. The meaning and objective of each Initiative is described in detail in the story.

THE COMPANY AND PLAYERS

The Company

Cosmetics Products Division of Amalgamated Consumer Products Corporation, Inc.

The Players

Amalgamated Consumer Products Corporation, Inc.

Susan	Barnett	Chief Executive Officer (CEO)
Alice	Boyer	Senior Vice President, Engineering and Product Development
Bill	Crawford	Senior Vice President, Sales and Marketing
Sam	Elliott	Senior Vice President, Supply Chain

Keely	Horton	Senior Vice President, Human Resources
Andrew	Jones	Chief Financial Officer (CFO)
James R.	Richards, Sr.	Founder
James R.	Richards III	Chairman Emeritus
Henry	Stinson	Senior Vice President, Quality and Regulatory Affairs

Cosmetics Products Division

Sandy	Bar-Nestor	Internal Supply Team Leader
Bill	Bates	Production Operations Team Leader
Charlie	Beck	Sales Director
Peter	Bertrand	Business Excellence Initiatives Coordinator
Bart	Billings	Demand Manager; Integrated Business Management Process Leader,
Jeff	Black	Northeast Regional Sales Manager; Managing Demand Team Leader
Mary Ellen	Brewer	New Product Development Director;
Tony	Caruso	Vice President, Manufacturing
Kari	Crawford	Vice President, Sales and Marketing
Carole	Brown	Body Lotions Product Manager
Chris	Deutsh	IT Specialist
Janice	Hackworth	Supply Planning Manager
Carlos	Hernandez	Finance Director
Gabriella	Jemison	Vice President, Quality and Regulatory Affairs
Mary	Jenkins	Dallas Plant Production Planner,-later Division Supply Manager
Bob	Malinkov	IT Specialist
Angus	Martin	Performance Measures Specialist
Sara	Miles	Vice President, Finance
Glenn	Miller	Finance Director
Savannah	Richmond	General Manager, Dallas Plant
Cynthia	Roberts	Executive Assistant to the President
Sharon	Rogers	Marketing Director, Product Review Coordinator
Matt	Rutherford	Vice President, Engineering, Product Development, and Information Systems
Greg	Sanders	President, Cosmetics Products Division–later, Amalgamated CEO
David	Simpson	Vice President, Supply Chain—later, and Manufacturing
Brion	Smith	General Manager, Atlanta Plant
Alexandra	Templeton	Vice President, Sales and Marketing
K. Stuart	Tillman	Division President before Greg Sanders
Zachary	Zellers	Vice President, Human Resources

Other Amalgamated Divisions

| Ian | McGregor | President, Food Products |
| Roger | Winchester | President, Home Products |

Effective Management, Inc.

Roxanne	Barnes	Class A Coach and Cosmetics Products Account Manager
Jim	Clark	Class A Coach for Capital Equipment
Dan	Evans	Class A Coach
Les	Johnson	Transition 5 Coach
Liam	Lawlor	Private Class Instructor
Mary	Medford	Public Class Instructor
Stan	Stevens	Public Class Instructor
Samantha	Williams	Agile, Lean and Six Sigma Coach
Tom	Wilson	Class A Coach

Others

Martin	Bennett	President and CEO, Blackstone Pharmacies
Allen	Burke	Operations Vice President, Tender Care Pet Products
Bob	Radcliff	President and CEO, Capital Equipment
Dan	Rogers	Vice President Supply Chain, Capital Equipment
Shannon	Stillwell	President and COO, Tender Care Pet Products

Cosmetics Products Division's Initiative and Milestone Journey

Initiatives Champion – Greg Sanders
Initiatives Coordinator – Peter Bertrand

1. **Customer Service**
    a. Capable Integrated Business Management
        i.   Milestone Leader – Bart Billings (Demand Manager)
        ii. Milestone Champion – Alexandra Templeton
    b. Capable Planning and Control
        i.   Milestone Leader – Peter Bertrand
        ii. Milestone Champion – David Simpson

2. Customer Satisfaction (External/Internal)

   a. Capable Product Management
      i. Milestone Leader – Sharon Rogers
      ii. Milestone Champion – Alexandra Templeton
   b. Foundation Enabling for Sustainable Improvement
      i. Milestone Leader – Peter Bertrand
      ii. Milestone Champion – Gabriella Jemison

3. Competitive Advantage

   a. Advanced Internal Supply
   b. Capable Management of Demand
   c. Capable Distribution and Logistics
   d. Capable External Sourcing Processess
   e. Capable Supply Chain
   f. Foundation Business Improvement Capability

4. Leadership

   a. Strategy and People (Advanced Strategic Planning + Managing and Leading People)
      i. Milestone Leader – Glenn Miller
      ii. Milestone Champions – Alexandra Templeton and Zachary Zellers
   b. Advanced Supply Chain Management
      i. Milestone Leader – Charlie Beck
      ii. Milestone Champion – David Simpson

5. Ultra-Responsive Service

Index